● Sixth Edition

Qualitative Research Methods for the Social Sciences

Bruce L. Berg

California State University, Long Beach

PEARSON

Boston • New York • San Francisco
Mexico City • Montreal • Toronto • London • Madrid • Munich • Paris
Hong Kong • Singapore • Tokyo • Cape Town • Sydney

Senior Series Editor: Jeff Lasser
Editorial Assistant: Erikka Adams
Senior Marketing Manager: Kelly May
Production Editor: Roberta Sherman
Editorial Production Service: Progressive Publishing Alternatives
Composition Buyer: Linda Cox
Manufacturing Buyer: JoAnne Sweeney
Composition: Progressive Information Technologies
Interior Design: Denise Hoffman
Cover Administrator: Kristina Mose-Libon

For related titles and support materials, visit our online catalog at
www.ablongman.com.

Between the time website information is gathered and then published, it is not
unusual for some sites to have closed. Also, the transcription of URLs can result in
typographical errors. The publisher would appreciate notification where these errors
occur so that they may be corrected in subsequent editions.

Library of Congress Cataloging-in-Publication Data

Berg, Bruce L. (Bruce Lawrence)
   Qualitative research methods for the social sciences / Bruce L. Berg.—6th ed.
      p.   cm.
   Includes bibliographical references and index.
   ISBN 0-205-48263-5
   1. Social sciences—Research—Methodology.   I. Title.

   H61.B4715 2006
   300.72—dc22

                                                              2005058685

Printed in the United States of America

10   9   8   7   6   5   4   3   2   1   CMA   10   09   08   07   06

Contents

Chapter 3

Ethical Issues   53

Chapter 4

A Dramaturgical Look at Interviewing   89

Chapter **5**

Focus Group Interviewing   144

Chapter 6

Ethnographic Field Strategies   171

Chapter 7

Action Research   222

Chapter 8

Unobtrusive Measures in Research   239

Chapter 9

Historiography and Oral Traditions   264

Chapter 10

Case Studies   283

Chapter 11

An Introduction to Content Analysis   303

Chapter 12

Writing Research Papers: Sorting the Noodles from the Soup   340

Preface

I T HAS BEEN 18 YEARS since I sat down to draft the first edition of *Qualitative Research Methods for the Social Sciences*. Back then, as today, my goal is to offer a handbook for anyone interested in but unfamiliar with qualitative research methods. Throughout the years and six editions of this book, I have sought to create a guide both simple enough to follow and comprehensive enough to provide a wide array of fairly mainstream data-collection, organization, and analysis strategies. Beginning in the fifth edition, I also sought to bring fledgling qualitative researchers into the cyber age and began increasing the book's focus to include discussions of various Web sources, Web sites, and ways to incorporate the Internet into qualitative research other than by merely seeking literature. Throughout the years, I have envisioned my book being studied along with more general quantitative texts used in traditional research methods classes taught in various social science disciplines. As a supplement to other methods books, this book offers a way to better round the course to include a clear and concise qualitative orientation. I am gratified to learn that many programs have adopted my book as the main text (along with a supplemental book of readings) or as a standalone book in qualitative research methods classes.

Following the path I began to blaze in the fifth edition, the sixth edition intentionally focuses greater attention on using the Internet as both a resource and a means for accessing qualitative data. This new frontier of the Internet remains at present a nearly unharvested field of qualitative potential. The research style presented in this edition remains chiefly sociological; the application of data-gathering and data-analytic strategies, however, is not designed exclusively for students of sociology or for sociologists alone. In fact, an increasing number of my readers have come from the disciplines of English, nursing, education, social work, and business, as well as from the more traditional social sciences such as psychology, anthropology, criminology, and criminal justice.

The book's central purpose remains a desire to instruct inexperienced researchers in ways to effectively collect, organize, and make sense of qualitative data. This edition also seeks to demystify the research process. I believe that what makes the research process frightening for many is a fear of the unknown. When novice researchers learn how a process or technique works, it becomes comfortable, relaxed, and—dare I say it?—easy!

In keeping with my general pedagogical style, this edition of the book moves readers beyond the point of collecting data without knowing what to do with it. The goal is to get fledgling researchers to design, collect, and analyze data and then to present results to the scientific community. This sixth edition continues to focus on current issues in the world of researchers, which include a serious concern about ethical behavior and protocols in research and a more reflexive and sensitive role for the researcher. Many research texts place ethics in the last chapter, or at least toward the conclusion of the book, creating the subliminal image of ethics being less important than other elements in research. In contrast to this style, I have placed the discussion of ethics in the third chapter; my intention in doing so is to impress on new researchers the importance of ethical concerns before they actually begin the research collection, organization, and analytic process. The discussion on ethics follows the chapter on design in hopes that these ethical concerns become a natural inclusion in the researcher's design process.

As in previous editions of this book, I emphasize a more reflexive researcher role and recognize the benefits of this orientation. In several places throughout the text, researcher reflexivity and research voice are explained and discussed. In fact, the use of the first person (*I, my*, etc.), which I began using in the second edition of this book, is a small example of my more reflexive researcher's role and voice. The orientation offered in this text does not fully embrace all elements of reflexivity but discusses several of the basic elements associated with this position. This is particularly true in Chapter 7, "Action Research," which discusses how the researcher may collaborate with shareholding subjects in the research, as well as in the section on photovoice, which describes a technique for allowing the participatory subject to offer his or her reflexive voice through photographs and narratives of these photographs.

As somewhat of a traditionalist, I continue to believe that researchers learn their craft through a combination of trial and error and "getting their hands dirty" with data. I also believe this process works best when guided by a more experienced researcher—a mentor. Yet even this approach works more effectively when the apprentice has a firm understanding of the basic elements of the research process. This book is designed especially for accomplishing this purpose.

As has been true in each of the previous editions of this book, my personal bias as a symbolic interactionist guides the choices I make and explanations I offer throughout this text. Once again, I admit that the techniques presented are grounded in that theoretical approach. However, I continue to believe that the various techniques and strategies offered in this book can be equally effective when grounded in other theoretical perspectives. Inexperienced researchers should therefore take my presentation as suggestions and recommendations toward establishing a research foundation and not as the only methodological orientation available to them.

Finally, it is my deepest hope that after reading this book, students will think about research in a positive and even playful manner. Research can be extremely enjoyable when undertaken in the proper frame of mind. Even a trip to Disneyland can be ruined if you focus too much on the costs, the congested traffic, or the long lines. Many people go to Disneyland and never even notice these inconveniences. Research can be like a trip to Disneyland: it can be exciting, interesting, and rewarding, or it can be tedious, expensive, and frustrating. Trips to Disneyland, like undertaking research projects, are in large part a matter of how you think about them. But first you have to be able to think about research in a positive fashion. I hope that my book allows you to open your mind and your heart to the research process—enjoy the trip.

Acknowledgments

As in previous editions of this book, my first thanks go to my family: my beautiful wife of 30 years, Jill, and our two children, Kate and Alex. Their support for me during the original writing of this book and through each successive revision has been unflinching. They have provided me with loving sustenance that has allowed me to survive a heart attack, followed a few years later by quadruple bypass surgery—a scary time for all of us. I also continue to owe a debt of gratitude to my students, who provide regular feedback on material in this book and keep me grounded. I thank them again for their honesty, their patience, and their helpful suggestions.

I offer a special thanks to Karen Hansen, my editor for eighteen years. Even when others took a more hand's-on role in the actual editing of my book, and did an excellent job, Karen has always been *my editor.*

I am also very grateful to David Burlingame, Grand Valley State University; Phyllis Kuehn, California State University, Fresno; Tommie Nelms, Texas Womens' University; and Suzanne Renee Smith, Washington State University, Vancouver, readers and users of this book who provided constructive criticism as I set about revising this sixth edition. I am also indebted to Peter Adler, University of Denver; Robert Benford, University of Nebraska; Thomas G. Bloomberg,

Florida State University; Kristen Esterberg, University of Massachusetts at Lowell; Daniel J. Klenow, North Dakota State University; James A. Pearsol, Ohio State University; Stephen Sweet, Cornell University; Jean Thoresen, Eastern Connecticut State University; Joseph A. Kotarba, University of Houston; and Kevin M. Thompson, who reviewed earlier editions of this book for Allyn and Bacon.

Chapter 1

Introduction

I N 1989, WHEN I FIRST PUBLISHED *Qualitative Research Methods for the Social Sciences,* there were few books that concentrated on how to do qualitative research and how to conduct relevant qualitative analysis. In earlier editions of this book I have noted that by the 1980s many of the classic works in qualitative research had been permitted to go out of print. Books such as Becker's *Sociological Work: Methods and Substance* (1970), Denzin's *The Research Act* (1978), Filstead's *Qualitative Methodology* (1970), Glaser and Strauss's *The Discovery of Grounded Theory* (1967), and, of course, Webb and his associates' *Unobtrusive Measures: Nonreactive Research in the Social Sciences* (1966, 1981) ceased in large part to be on the required reading lists of most students of the social sciences. Thanks, in part, to Sage Publishing, qualitative materials experienced a revival of sorts throughout the late 1980s and 1990s, with Sage's development of a string of short works called *Sage University Papers Series on Qualitative Research Methods.* In addition, in 1989, Sage began publishing a series of lengthier works on qualitative methods in its *Applied Social Research Methods Series.* This series continues today to offer a variety of solid reference books on an assortment of qualitative methodological areas.

Today I am quite pleased to see a continued increase in the number of texts that examine various aspects of qualitative research—even books once nearly exclusively associated with quantitative research, such as Earl Babbie's *The Practice of Social Research* (2004), which began in 1998 to contain whole chapters on qualitative interviewing, field research, and unobtrusive measures. Others, such as W. Lawrence Neuman's *Social Research Methods* (2006) and Frank Hagan's *Research Methods in Criminal Justice and Criminology* (2006), offer a taste of both quantitative and qualitative research strategies. I am also quite gratified when I find an increasing number of books that seem to imitate my lead and offer fledgling students of qualitative research an opportunity to learn how to actually undertake various qualitative technologies and analytic strategies. It is all the more flattering when authors such as Kristin Esterberg (2002) adopt certain conceptual terms, such as the phrase "becoming invisible," during fieldwork. I adapted this concept from Stoddart (1986), but it did not until recently seem to be catching on (see Esterberg, 2002, p. 71).

I now offer a sixth edition of my book, once again focusing on innovative ways to collect and analyze qualitative data gathered in natural settings. Once again I address largely those data-collection strategies that may be characterized as mainstream strategies, even though various dynamic—perhaps even radical—qualitative innovations have emerged during the past several decades. But rather than offering glossy definitions for these strategies or confusing novice researchers with simplified versions and descriptions, this text concentrates on basic procedures. There are two major divergences that should be highlighted. First, with the framework of certain traditional data-collecting strategies, I do offer some contemporary variants that I find interesting, innovative, and effective. An example of this is *Photovoice* as an extension to more traditional aspects of *Unobtrusive Measures* (Chapter 8). Second, and in keeping with a new tradition I began in the fourth edition, I offer an increased focus on the use of computers and the Internet in qualitative research.

Quantitative Versus Qualitative Schools of Thought

As Dabbs (1982, p. 32) remarks, "Qualitative and quantitative are not distinct." Yet in many social sciences, quantitative orientations are often given more respect. This may reflect the tendency of the general public to regard science as relating to numbers and implying precision. It is not the purpose of this text to argue against quantitative procedures; the purpose, instead, is to demonstrate the fruitfulness and often greater depth of understanding we can derive from qualitative procedures. Thus, the orientation of this book does not entirely either embrace or reject Kaplan's (1964, p. 206) statement that "if you can measure it, that ain't it!"

Certainly, qualitative methodologies have not predominated in the social sciences. After all, qualitative research takes much longer, requires greater clarity of goals during design stages, and cannot be analyzed by running computer programs. Qualitative research methods and analytic strategies are not associated with high-tech society in the ways quantitative techniques may be. Nonetheless, as Bogdan (1972) makes clear, qualitative research has left its mark conceptually and theoretically on the social sciences. The lasting contributions to social understanding from qualitative research, as well as the sheer number of contributing social thinkers, are significant.

Even though the virtue of qualitative research is seldom questioned in the abstract, its practice is sometimes criticized for being nonscientific and thus invalid. However, these critics tended to lose sight of the probability factor inherent in quantitative practices and replaced it with an assumption of certainty. Of course, some qualitative research projects have been just as poorly conducted as some quantitative studies, but one need not dismiss the entire qualitative school of thought just because some studies inadequately applied the paradigm and methods.

In his attempt to differentiate between quantitative and qualitative approaches, Dabbs (1982, p. 32) indicates that the notion of *quality* is essential to the nature of things. On the other hand, *quantity* is elementally an amount of something. Quality refers to the what, how, when, and where of a thing—its essence and ambience. Qualitative research thus refers to the meanings, concepts, definitions, characteristics, metaphors, symbols, and descriptions of things. In contrast, quantitative research refers to counts and measures of things. This distinction is illustrated in Jackson's (1968) description of classroom odors in an elementary school:

> [The] odors of the classroom are fairly standardized. Schools may use different brands of wax and cleaning fluid, but they all seem to contain similar ingredients, a sort of universal smell which creates an aromatic background that permeates the entire building. Added to this, in each classroom, is the slightly acrid scent of chalk dust and the faint hint of fresh wood pencil shavings. In some rooms, especially at lunch time, there is the familiar odor of orange peels and peanut butter sandwiches, a blend that mingles in the late afternoon (following recess) with the delicate pungency of children's perspiration.

It would be impossible to capture the odors that Jackson alludes to with any type of count or measure. Clearly, certain experiences cannot be meaningfully expressed by numbers. Furthermore, such things as smells can trigger memories long obscured by the continuing demands of life. Qualitative research strategies provide perspectives that can prompt recall of these common or half-forgotten sights, sounds, and smells.

More recently Miles and Huberman (1994, p. 40) quote a quantitative researcher Fred Kerlinger as saying, "There is no such thing as qualitative data. Everything is either 1 or 0." Countering this argument, D. T. Campbell has stated, "All research ultimately has a qualitative grounding" (Miles & Huberman, 1994, p. 40). Yet this sort of back-and-forth arguing would seem rather unproductive, and it seems more useful to consider the merits of both quantitative and qualitative research strategies. Unfortunately, because qualitative research tends to assess the quality of things using words, images, and descriptions whereas most of quantitative research relies chiefly on numbers, many people erroneously regard quantitative strategies as more scientific than those employed in qualitative research.

Some authors associate qualitative research with the single technique of participant observation. Other writers extend their understanding of qualitative research to include interviewing as well. However, popular qualitative research additionally includes such methods as observation of experimental natural settings, photographic techniques (including videotaping), historical analysis (historiography), document and textual analysis, sociometry, sociodrama and similar ethnomethodological experimentation, ethnographic research, and a number of unobtrusive techniques.

American colleges have become pragmatic places where students train to get jobs rather than to obtain educations. As a consequence, students and graduates of social science programs increasingly use the research of others and conduct research themselves. Thus, students must confront the myriad problems associated with understanding empirical results as well as the process of research itself. This book provides much-needed assistance for all researchers, including the inexperienced, through a discussion of various qualitative research strategies, design development, data organization and presentation, and analysis procedures.

Like other texts on qualitative methods, this one emphasizes methodological strategies. However, methodology cannot be examined in a vacuum. Instead, the core substance of qualitative sociological practice, including methods, theory, and substantive interests, must be explored (Bogdan & Taylor, 1975; Denzin, 1978; Denzin and Lincoln, 2005; Leninger, 1998; Lofland & Lofland, 1984; Lofland, Snow, Anderson, & Lofland, 2006; Miles & Huberman, 1994). In this text, data-gathering techniques are intentionally coupled with theoretical perspectives, linking method to theory. Data-gathering, therefore, is not distinct from theoretical orientations. Rather, data are intricately associated with the motivation for choosing a given subject, the conduct of the study, and ultimately the analysis.

Advocates of such particular methodological styles of research as participant observation are frequently more concerned with asserting or defending their techniques than with indicating alternative ways of approaching the study subject. In contrast, this book describes in detail seven primary ways to collect qualitative data: interviewing, focus groups, ethnography, sociometry, unobtrusive measures, historiography, and case studies. In addition, this book examines a framework for undertaking participatory research studies, sometimes called action research. These methods include an examination of basic theoretical assumptions of each technique and advice on how to start each procedure and how to resolve problems that may arise. In addition, the technique of analysis is related to grounded theory and the use of narrative ethnographies. Also, as an essential element or consideration in any research study, this book explores the ethical dimensions of conducting research on humans.

This sixth edition of *Qualitative Research Methods for the Social Sciences* begins with the assumption that readers know little or nothing about the research process. Chapter 2, therefore, offers a basic description of how to design a research project.

Use of Triangulation in Research Methodology

Most researchers have at least one methodological technique they feel most comfortable using, which often becomes their favorite or only approach to research. This might be why many previous qualitative research texts presented only a single research technology (participant observation, interviewing, or unobtrusive measures). Furthermore, many researchers perceive their research method as an atheoretical tool (Denzin, 1978). Because of this, they fail to recognize that methods impose certain perspectives on reality. For example, when researchers canvass a neighborhood and arrange interviews with residents to discuss their views of some social problem, a theoretical assumption has already been made—specifically, that reality is fairly constant and stable. Similarly, when they make direct observations of events, researchers assume reality is deeply affected by the actions of all participants, including themselves. Each method, thus, reveals slightly different facets of the same symbolic reality. Every method is a different line of sight directed toward the same point, observing social and symbolic reality. By combining several lines of sight, researchers obtain a better, more substantive picture of reality; a richer, more complete array of symbols and theoretical concepts; and a means of verifying many of these elements. The use of multiple lines of sight is frequently called *triangulation.*

Triangulation is a term originally more common in surveying activities, map making, navigation, and military practices. In each case, three known points or objects are used to draw sighting lines toward an unknown point or object. Usually, these three sighting lines will intersect, forming a small triangle called the *triangle of error.* The best estimate of the true location of the new point or object is the center of the triangle, assuming that the three lines are about equal in error. Although sightings could be done with two sighting lines intersecting at one point, the third line permits a more accurate estimate of the unknown point or object (Berg & Berg, 1993).

Triangulation was first used in the social sciences as a metaphor describing a form of *multiple operationalism* or *convergent validation* (Campbell, 1956; Campbell & Fiske, 1959). In these cases, triangulation was used largely to describe multiple data-collection technologies designed to measure a single concept or construct (data triangulation). However Denzin (1978, p. 292) introduced an additional metaphor, *lines of action*, which characterizes the use of multiple data-collection technologies, multiple theories, multiple researchers, and multiple lines of action. Figure 1.1 illustrates the various lines of action possible in a triangulated research study.

For many researchers, triangulation is restricted to the use of multiple data-gathering techniques (usually three) to investigate the same phenomenon. This is interpreted as a means of mutual confirmation of measures and validation of findings (Jick, 1983; Knafl & Breitmayer, 1989; Leedy, 2001; Mitchell, 1986; Sohier, 1988; Webb et al., 1981). Fielding and Fielding (1986, p. 31) specifically address this aspect of triangulation. They suggest that the important feature of triangulation is not the simple combination of

Figure 1.1 Multiple Lines of Action in Triangulation

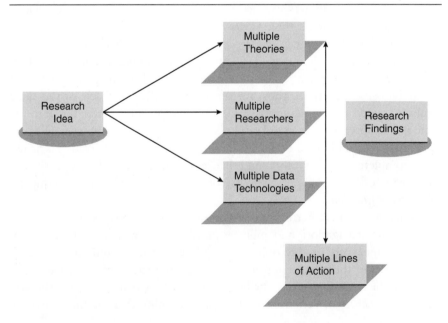

different kinds of data but the attempt to relate them so as to counteract the threats to validity identified in each.

Denzin (1978) insists that the multiple-methods approach is the generic form of this approach. But triangulation actually represents varieties of data, investigators, theories, and methods. Denzin (1978, p. 295) outlines these four categories as follows:

> (1) Data triangulation has three subtypes: (a) time, (b) space, and (c) person. Person analysis, in turn, has three levels: (a) aggregate, (b) interactive, and (c) collectivity. (2) Investigator triangulation consists of using multiple rather than single observers of the same object. (3) Theory triangulation consists of using multiple rather than simple perspectives in relation to the same set of objects. (4) Methodological triangulation can entail within-method triangulation and between-method triangulation.

The research literature continues to support Denzin's (1970, 1978) recommendation to triangulate during research. For example, Goetz and LeCompte (1984) describe its use as a means of refining, broadening, and strengthening conceptual linkages. Borman, LeCompte, and Goetz (1986) and LeCompte and Preissle (1993) similarly stress that triangulation allows researchers to offer varied perspectives other than their own. Chava Frankfort-Nachmias and David Nachmias (1996, p. 206) suggest that researchers can "minimize the degree of specificity of certain methods to particular bodies of knowledge" by using "two or more methods of data collection to test hypotheses and measure variables; this is the essence of triangulation" (see also Frankfort-Nachmias and Nachmias, 2000). Mills (2006) recommends the integration of triangulation into *action research* designs (action research is discussed in Chapter 7). Wolfram and Hassard (2005) argue that a shift to a more reflexive consideration of *researchers stance* through triangulation can lead to a better understanding of organizational theory. Unfortunately, the practice of triangulation often does not move much beyond a single theoretical explanation or an alternative hypothesis (Fielding & Fielding, 1986; Hammersley, 1984; Wolfram and Hassard 2005). Hence, this cursory use of a triangulation strategy fails to capture the essence of what Denzin (1978, p. 28) describes as the "logic of triangulation":

> I conclude that no single method will ever meet the requirements of interaction theory. While participant observation permits the careful recording of situations and selves, it does not offer direct data on the wider spheres of influence acting on those observed. Because each method reveals different aspects of empirical reality, multiple methods of observations must be employed. This is termed triangulation.

In a manner similar to that of Denzin (1978) and Webb and colleagues (1981), this book stresses several discrete yet intertwined strategies and techniques involved in each of the seven primary research schemes. In fact, the decision to discuss field research strategies under the broad umbrella of *ethnography* ensures the inclusion of a wide combination of elements, such as direct observation, various types of interviewing (informal, formal, semiformal), listening, document analysis (e.g., letters or newspaper clippings), and ethnomethodological experimentation. Spradely (1979) calls this creating "an ethnographic record." Novice researchers are thus instructed in the use of research strategies composed of multiple methods in a single investigation. Denzin (1978, p. 101) also suggests that triangulation includes multiple data-collection procedures, multiple theoretical perspectives, and multiple analysis techniques. The use of multiple research design strategies and theories increases the depth of understanding an investigation can yield (see also Dittmann, 2005; Janesick, 1994; Miles & Huberman, 1983).

Qualitative Strategies: Defining an Orientation

A simplistic explanation of qualitative techniques might lead researchers to believe in the adequacy of any procedure resulting in nominal rather than numerical sorts of data. Such an assessment, however, fails to appreciate both the theoretical implications of qualitative research and the basic purpose of scientific research in general. We do not conduct research only to amass data. The purpose of research is to discover answers to questions through the application of systematic procedures.

Qualitative research properly seeks answers to questions by examining various social settings and the individuals who inhabit these settings. Qualitative researchers, then, are most interested in how humans arrange themselves and their settings and how inhabitants of these settings make sense of their surroundings through symbols, rituals, social structures, social roles, and so forth.

Research methods on human beings affect how these persons will be viewed (Bogdan & Taylor, 1975). If humans are studied in a symbolically reduced, statistically aggregated fashion, there is a danger that conclusions—although arithmetically precise—may fail to fit reality (Mills, 1959). Qualitative procedures provide a means of accessing unquantifiable facts about the actual people researchers observe and talk to or people represented by their personal traces (such as letters, photographs, newspaper accounts, diaries, and so on). As a result, qualitative techniques allow researchers to share in the understandings and perceptions of others and to explore how people structure and give meaning to their daily lives. Researchers using qualitative techniques examine how people learn about and make sense of themselves and others.

As Douglas (1976, p. 12) suggests, the methods used by social scientists fall along a continuum from totally uncontrolled (and perhaps uncontrollable) techniques arising in natural settings to totally controlled techniques of observation. It remains, then, for researchers to choose their procedures keeping in mind the problems that may arise in specific research settings among certain research groups and in unique research circumstances. The analysis of qualitative data allows researchers to discuss in detail the various social contours and processes human beings use to create and maintain their social realities.

This is not to suggest that qualitative methods are without methodological rigor. In fact, good qualitative research can be very rigorous. As will be demonstrated in the chapters that follow, qualitative methods can (and should) be extremely systematic and have the ability to be reproduced by subsequent researchers. Replication and reproducibility, after all, are central to the creation and testing of theories and their acceptance by scientific communities.

In some methodological situations, this may include the use of various descriptive or nonparametric statistics (frequency distributions, proportions, ratios, chi-square, etc.). On the other hand, the orientation presented in this text should not be understood as intentionally promoting stark positivism. Rather, the intention is to offer an introductory level of information developing and conducting high-quality qualitative research. From my perspective, this means research that can stand the test of subsequent researchers examining the same phenomenon through similar or different methods.

Theoretically, this explanation of the general purpose of qualitative research derives from a symbolic interactionist perspective that is central to the concept of qualitative methodology presented here. *Symbolic interaction* is an umbrella concept under which a variety of related theoretical orientations may be placed. The theme that unites the diverse elements of symbolic interaction is the focus on subjective understandings and the perceptions of and about people, symbols, and objects.

From a Symbolic Interactionist Perspective

Symbolic interactionism is one of several theoretical schools of thought in the social sciences. It involves a set of related propositions that describes and explains certain aspects of human behavior. Human beings are unique animals.

What humans say and do are the results of how they interpret their social world. In other words, human behavior depends on learning rather than biological instinct. Human beings communicate what they learn through symbols, the most common system of symbols being language. Linguistic symbols amount to arbitrary sounds or physical gestures to which people, by mutual agreement over time, have attached significance or meaning. The core task of symbolic interactionists as researchers, then, is to capture the essence of this process for interpreting or attaching meaning to various symbols.

The substantive basis for symbolic interaction as a theory is frequently attributed to the social behavioral work of Dewey (1930), Cooley (1902), Parks (1915), Mead (1934, 1938), and several other early theorists, but Blumer is considered the founder of *symbolic interactionism*. In fact, he coined the term symbolic interaction. In articulating his view of what symbolic interaction is, Blumer (1969) first establishes that human beings account for *meaning* in two basic ways. First, meaning may be seen as intrinsically attached to an object, event, phenomenon, and so on. Second, meaning may be understood as a "psychical accretion" imposed on objects, events, and the like by people. Blumer (1969, p. 5) next explains:

> Symbolic interactionism . . . does not regard meaning as emanating from the intrinsic makeup of the thing, nor does it see meaning as arising through psychological elements between people. The meaning of a thing for a person grows out of the ways in which other persons act toward the person with regard to the thing. Their actions operate to define the thing for the person; thus, symbolic interactionism sees meanings as social products formed through activities of people interacting.

Blumer thereby suggests that meanings derive from the social process of people or groups of people interacting. Meanings allow people to produce various realities that constitute the sensory world (the so-called real world), but because these realities are related to how people create meanings, reality becomes an interpretation of various definitional options. Consequently, as Thomas states, "It is not important whether or not the interpretation is correct—if men define situations as real, they are real in their consequences" (Thomas & Swaine, 1928, p. 572).

For instance, the first day of each semester, students walk into their classroom and see someone who appears to be the professor. This supposed professor begins to lecture, distribute syllabi, discuss course requirements, and conduct various other traditional first-day activities. Few, if any, students ask to see their professor's credentials. Yet the students, within certain limits, perform their roles as students so long as this professor continues to perform the role of instructor. Suppose that several weeks into the semester, however, the class is notified that the person they assumed to be a professor is really a local dog catcher who has no academic credentials. The question then becomes whether the reality of the classroom experience during the previous weeks is void merely because the dog catcher was incorrectly interpreted as a professor. It would, of course, remain to be seen whether any information conveyed by the dog catcher was accurate, and certainly the classroom remained a classroom and the students continued to perform their expected roles. From Thomas's perspective, these youths had defined the reality of the class, and it became real for them.

Historically, the symbolic interactionist orientation that originated with Dewey (1930), Cooley (1902), Parks (1915), and Mead (1934, 1938), and later Blumer (1962, 1990) among others, is called the Chicago School orientation because it arose as the Department of Sociology at the University of Chicago and evolved along with the development of the city of Chicago, which served as a kind of natural research laboratory for these researchers. After World War II, another segment of the symbolic interaction paradigm began to arise in the Department of Sociology at the University of Iowa, under the leadership of Manford Kuhn (Holstein and Gubrium, 2000), and later under Carl Couch (1988).

The Iowa School became distinctive for operationalizing concepts in symbolic interaction, including concepts such as the self and reference group in standardized ways so that hypotheses testing could be accomplished. Among the more prominent contributions to symbolic interaction from the Iowa School is the development of a research instrument called the *twenty statements test* (TST). The TST can be used to identify self-designations that result from social roles an individual plays rather than from his or her personal self-concepts. The TST is a rather simple tool that asks the subject the question "Who am I?" The subject then fills out 20 blank spaces in answer to this question. The responses are scored as representing either an external or internal self-concept. Figure 1.2 offers an example of the TST.

The twenty-question test can be used for a rough assessment of an individual's sense of self or identity. The test has the virtues of being straightforward and simple and providing a relatively direct measure of the subject's self-concept. In contrast to this systematic orientation, the Chicago School's orientation relied more heavily on participant observational research. Thus, the Chicago School was somewhat more anthropological and sought to understand the meanings of individuals and groups without an emphasis on revealing generalizable patterns of human behavior.

Symbolic interactionists tend to differ slightly among themselves regarding the relative significance of various aspects of an interactionist perspective. Several basic elements, however, tend to bind together even the most diverse

Figure 1.2 The Twenty Statements Test

Please write twenty answers to the question "Who am I?"

I am . . .

1. _____   11. _____

2. _____   12. _____

3. _____   13. _____

4. _____   14. _____

5. _____   15. _____

6. _____   16. _____

7. _____   17. _____

8. _____   18. _____

9. _____   19. _____

10. _____   20. _____

Scoring Instructions: Categorize each of the twenty statements in terms of each giving a description of the subject as **external** or **internal.**

External: This phrase locates the individual in society by describing some social role he or she plays or enacts. For example, the names of social roles one holds are all *external*: mother, father, son, daughter, student, salesman, police officer, store clerk, baseball fan, etc.

Internal: This phrase locates the individual inside his or her self by describing an internal or interior quality or trait one possesses. For example, names of personal intrinsic qualities or characteristics one possesses are all *internal*: shy, ambitious, insecure, happy, sad, ambiguous, curious, depressed, hard working, industrious, etc.

Place an E for external or an I for internal beside each of the twenty statements; then, total up the number of statements representing each category.

Total Number of External Descriptors: _____

Total Number of Internal Descriptors: _____

symbolic interactionists. First, all interactionists agree that human interactions form the central source of data. Second, there is a general consensus that participants' perspectives and their ability to take the roles of others (empathy) are key issues in any formulation of a theory of symbolic interaction. Third, interactionists agree with Thomas (Thomas & Swaine, 1928) concerning "definitions of a situation": how inhabitants of a setting define their situation determines the nature and meaning of their actions as well as the setting itself.

Objects, people, situations, and events do not in themselves possess meaning. Meaning is conferred on these elements by and through human interaction. For example, the videocassette recorder (VCR) in a college classroom may be defined by the professor as a teaching device to be used for showing educational videos. For the student using a VCR in his or her dormitory to view rented movies, this instrument may be seen as a source of entertainment and pleasure, and for the inmate held in a maximum security prison who watches home movies sent from his or her family, it may be considered a window to the outside world. The meanings that people attach to their experiences and the objects and events that make up these experiences are not accidental or unconnected. Both the experiences and the events surrounding them are essential to the construction of meanings. To understand behavior, one must first understand the definitions and meanings and the processes by which they have been created. Human behavior does not occur on the basis of predetermined lockstep responses to preset events or situations. Rather, human behavior is an ongoing and negotiated interpretation of objects, events, and situations (Bogdan & Biklen, 1992). For researchers to understand the meanings that emerge from these interactions, they either must enter into the defining process or develop a sufficient appreciation for the process so that understandings can become clear.

Although social roles, institutional structures, rules, norms, goals, and the like may provide the raw material with which individuals create their definitions, these elements do not by themselves determine what the definitions will be or how individuals will act. In essence, symbolic interactionism emphasizes social interactions (action with symbolic meaning), negotiation of definitions, and emphatic role-taking between humans (Gecas, 1981; Turner, 1978).

Why Use Qualitative Methods?

Many researchers believe that the social sciences have depended too much on sterile survey techniques, regardless of whether the technology is appropriate for the problem. For instance, nurses, when encouraged to do research at all, are strongly urged to use scientific strategies of quantification over more sociologically or anthropologically oriented ones considered less scientific. Unfortunately, clinical settings in which nurses are likely to conduct their research fail to meet most quantitative requirements for representativeness and sufficiency of sample size to allow statistically meaningful results.

For instance, let us say the average number of beds in a critical care unit varies between 8 and 12. Even when there are multiple units (such as in a medical intensive care unit or a cardiac intensive care unit), typically fewer than 40 cases are available at any given time. With regard to research strategy, such a situation should preclude most quantitative investigations. On the other hand, 40 cases would prove ample for a number of qualitative strategies. In fact, as Chapter 8 describes, a setting such as a hospital would provide researchers with numerous opportunities to implement unobtrusive measures.

It is also important to examine the reasons for the charge that qualitative methods are nonscientific. As Schwartz and Jacobs (1979, p. 4) point out, "There are many, in both qualitative and quantitative sociology, who advocate and bask in the value of science." Further, Borman, LeCompte, and Goetz (1986, p. 51) have argued that criticism of qualitative approaches arises out of an "erroneous equation of the term 'empirical' with quantification, rather than with any real defect in the qualitative paradigm itself." Although various technologies may be used by different researchers, it turns out that everyone is doing science, provided that *science* is defined as a specific and systematic way of discovering and understanding how social realities arise, operate, and impact on individuals and organizations of individuals.

Scientific researchers may, thus, emphasize a more positivist view or may be primarily interested in individuals and their so-called life-worlds. In the case of the former, positivists utilize empirical methodologies borrowed from the natural sciences to investigate phenomena. Quantitative strategies serve this positive-science ideal by providing rigorous, reliable, and verifiably large aggregates of data and the statistical testing of empirical hypotheses.

In the case of life-worlds, researchers focus on naturally emerging languages and the meanings individuals assign to experience. Life-worlds include emotions, motivations, symbols and their meanings, empathy, and other subjective aspects associated with naturally evolving lives of individuals and groups. These elements may also represent their behavioral routines, experiences, and various conditions affecting these usual routines or natural settings. As Schwartz and Jacobs (1979) suggest, many of these elements are directly observable and as such may be viewed as objective. Nonetheless, certain elements of symbolism, meaning, or understanding usually require consideration of the individual's own perceptions and subjective apprehensions.

A Plan of Presentation

Having briefly outlined the basic assumptions and qualitative orientations of symbolic interaction, it is now possible to weave in various methodological strategies. Chapter 2 provides the basic information necessary for understanding the research enterprise. This chapter discusses the research process and proposes a spiraling model to follow when developing a research agenda. Chapter 2 also offers advice to the novice researcher about how to organize and conduct a literature review.

Chapter 3 considers a number of ethical concerns that are important for new investigators to understand before actually conducting research. Among the salient issues considered are covert versus overt research concerns, privacy rights, human subject institutional review boards, and informed consent in human subject research.

In addition to providing a general discussion of various forms and styles of traditional interviewing techniques, Chapter 4 uses a kind of symbolic interaction known as *dramaturgy* and suggests an effective research strategy for conducting in-depth interviews.

Chapter 5 also addresses the area of interviewing but moves toward a specialized style, namely, group interviews or focus groups. This chapter examines the early origins of focus group interviews, their development during the past several decades, and their growing use in the social sciences.

Chapter 6 builds on the foundation constructed by Chapters 1 through 4 and extends the research process into the natural setting by examining ethnography. Along with interviewing, Chapter 6 discusses watching and listening, field notes, and a number of other field research concerns. This chapter examines ethnography both as a means of collecting data (what some call the *new ethnography*) and as an end in itself (narrative ethnographic accounts).

Chapter 7 considers a recent dynamic mode of research, namely, action research. Action research has a substantial history in educational and nursing research and is moving rapidly into broader scientific endeavors as well.

While Chapters 4, 5, and 6 separately address the concept of interviewer reactivity, Chapter 8 offers several strategies that avoid reactivity entirely: It explores the use of unobtrusive measures.

As foreshadowed slightly in Chapter 8, the use of certain unobtrusive data has grown quite specialized. Chapter 9 examines a specialized and systematic use of certain kinds of running records, namely, historiography. In addition to the use of records, Chapter 9 considers oral histories and life histories as variations in historiography.

Chapter 10 examines a technique used to study individuals in their unique settings or situations. This technique is commonly called the *case study method*.

This chapter also discusses how case studies may be undertaken on communities and organizations.

Chapter 11 dovetails with each of the preceding chapters on research technique. Included in this chapter are recommendations for how novice researchers may organize their data and begin to make sense of what may be volumes of notes, transcripts, and trace documents and artifacts. Chapter 11 also briefly considers the use of computers to assist in this data management scheme.

Chapter 12, the final chapter, offers recommendations for how novice qualitative researchers can disseminate their research findings.

Trying It Out, a section at the conclusion of each of the data-collection technique chapters, offers suggestions for practicing each of the seven strategies.

REFERENCES

Babbie, E. (2004). *The Practice of Social Research* (10th ed.). Belmont, CA: Wadsworth.

Becker, H. S. (1970). *Sociological Work: Method and Substance*. Chicago: Aldine.

Berg, B. L., & Berg, J. (1993). A reexamination of triangulation and objectivity in qualitative nursing research. *Free Inquiry in Creative Sociology 21*(1), 65–72.

Blumer H. (1962). "Society as Symbolic Interaction." In A. Rose (Ed.), *Human Behavior and Social Processes* (pp. 181–184). Boston: Houghton Mifflin.

Blumer, H. (1969). *Symbolic Interactionism: Perspective and Method*. Englewood Cliffs, NJ: Prentice-Hall.

Blumer, H. (1990). *Symbolic Interactionism: Perspective and Method*. Los Angeles: University of California Press.

Bogdan, R. (1972). *Participant Observation in Organizational Settings*. Syracuse, NY: Syracuse University Press.

Bogdan, R., & Biklen, S. K. (1992). *Qualitative Research for Education* (2nd ed.). Boston: Allyn and Bacon.

Bogdan, R., & Kopp-Bilken, S. (2003). *Qualitative Research for Education* (4th edition). Boston, MA: Allyn and Bacon, Inc.

Bogdan, R., & Taylor, S. J. (1975). *Introduction to Qualitative Research Methods*. New York: Wiley.

Borman, K. M., LeCompte, M. D., & Goetz, J. P. (1986). Ethnographic and qualitative research design and why it doesn't work. *American Behavioral Scientist 30*(1), 42–57.

Campbell, D. T. (1956). *Leadership and Its Effects Upon the Group*. Columbus: Ohio State University Press.

Campbell, T. T., & Fiske, D. W. (1959). Convergent and discriminant validation by the multivariate-multimethod matrix. *Psychological Bulletin 56*, 81–105.

Cooley, C. H. (1902). *Human Nature and the Social Order*. New York: Scribner.

Couch, C. (1988). *Social Process and Relationships*. New York: Rowman and Littlefield.

Dabbs, J. M., Jr. (1982). Making things visible. In J. Van Maanen (Ed.), *Varieties of Qualitative Research*. Beverly Hills, CA: Sage.

Denzin, N. K. (1970). *Sociological Methods: A Sourcebook*. Chicago: Aldine.

Denzin, N. K. (1978). *The Research Act*. New York: McGraw-Hill.

Denzin, N., & Lincoln, Y. S. (2005). *The Sage Handbook of Qualitative Research* (3rd ed.). Thousand Oaks, CA: Sage.

Dewey, J. (1930). *Human Nature and Conduct*. New York: Modern Library.

Dittmann, M. (2005). Psychologists tout multiple methodologies in education research. *Monitor on Psychology. 36*(2), 20.

Douglas, J. D. (1976). *Investigative Social Research*. Beverly Hills, CA: Sage.

Esterberg, K. G. (2002). *Qualitative Methods in Social Research*. Boston: McGraw-Hill.

Fielding, N. G., & Fielding, J. L. (1986). *Linking Data*. Newbury Park, CA: Sage.

Filstead, W. (1970). *Qualitative Methodology: Firsthand Involvement and the Social World*. Chicago: Markham.

Frankfort-Nachmias, C., & Nachmias, D. (1996). *Research Methods in the Social Sciences* (5th ed.). New York: St. Martin's Press.

Frankfort-Nachmias, C. & Nachmais, D. (2000). *Research Methods in Social Science* (6th ed.). New York: W. H. Freeman.

Gecas, V. (1981). Contexts of socialization. In M. Rosenberg & R. H. Turner (Eds.), *Social Psychology: Sociological Perspectives* (pp. 165–199). New York: Basic Books.

Glaser, B., & Strauss, A. L. (1967). *The Discovery of Grounded Theory: Strategies for Qualitative Research*. Chicago: Aldine.

Goetz, J. P., & LeCompte, M. D. (1984). *Ethnography and Qualitative Design in Educational Research*. New York: Academic Press.

Hagan, F. E. (2006). *Research Methods in Criminal Justice and Criminology* (7th ed.). Boston: Allyn and Bacon.

Hammersley, M. (1984). The researcher exposed. In R. Burgess (Ed.), *The Research Process in Educational Settings: Ten Case Studies*. New York: Taylor & Francis, Palmer Press.

Holstein, J., & Gubrium, J. (2000). *The Self We Live By: Narrative Identity in a Postmodern World*. New York: Oxford University Press.

Jackson, P. W. (1968). *Life in Classrooms*. New York: Holt, Rinehart, & Winston.

Janesick, V. J. (1994). The dance of qualitative research design. In N. Denzin & Y. S. Lincoln (Eds.), *Handbook of Qualitative Research*. Thousand Oaks, CA: Sage.

Jick, T. D. (1983). Mixing qualitative and quantitative methods: Triangulation in action. In J. Van Maanen (Ed.), *Qualitative Methodology* (pp. 135–148). Beverly Hills, CA: Sage.

Kaplan, A. (1964). *The Conduct of Inquiry*. Scranton, PA: Chandler Publishing.

Knafl, K. A., & Breitmayer, B. J. (1989). Triangulation in qualitative research: Issues of conception, clarity, and purpose. In J. M. Morse (Ed.), *Qualitative Nursing Research: A Contemporary Dialogue*. Rockville, MD: Aspen.

Kuhn, Manford, and McPartland, T. S. (1951). An empirical investigation of self-attitudes. *American Sociological Review*, 19, 68–76.

LeCompte, M. D., & Preissle, J. (1993). *Ethnography and Qualitative Design in Educational Research* (2nd ed.). San Diego: Academic Press.

Leedy, P. D. (2001). *Practical Research: Planning and Design* (7th ed.). Upper Saddle River, NJ: Prentice Hall.

Leninger, M. M. (1998). *Qualitative Research Methods in Nursing* (2nd ed.). Columbus, Ohio: Greyden Press.

Lofland, J., & Lofland, L. H. (1984). *Analyzing Social Settings* (2nd ed.). Belmont, CA: Wadsworth.

Lofland, J. & Lofland, L. H. (1995). *Analyzing Social Settings* (3rd ed.). Belmont, CA: Wadsworth.

Lofland, D., Snow D. A., Anderson, L., & Lofland, L. H. (2006). *Analyzing Social Settings: A Guide to Qualitative Observation and Analysis* (4th ed.). Belmont, CA: Wadsworth.

Mead, G. H. (1934). *Mind, Self, and Society.* Chicago: University of Chicago Press.

Mead, G. H. (1938). *The Philosophy of the Act.* Chicago: University of Chicago Press.

Miles, M. B., & Huberman, M. A. (1983). *Qualitative Data Analysis.* Beverly Hills, CA: Sage.

Miles, M. B., & Huberman, M. A. (1994). *Qualitative Analysis: An Expanded Sourcebook* (2nd ed.). Thousand Oaks, CA: Sage.

Mills, C. W. (1959). *The Sociological Imagination.* New York: Oxford University Press.

Mills, G. E. (2006). *Action Research: A Guide for the Teacher Researcher* (3rd ed.). Upper Saddle River, NJ: Prentice Hall.

Mitchell, E. S. (1986). Multiple triangulation: A methodology for nursing science. *Advances in Nursing Science 8*(3), 18–25.

Neuman, W. I. (2006). *Social Research Methods: Qualitative and Quantitative Approaches.* 6th ed. Boston: Allyn and Bacon.

Parks, R. (1915). *Principles of Human Behavior.* Chicago: Zalaz.

Patton, M. Q. (2001). *Qualitative Research and Evaluation Methods* (3rd ed.). Thousand Oaks, CA: Sage.

Schwartz, H., & Jacobs, J. (1979). *Qualitative Sociology: A Method to the Madness.* New York: Free Press.

Sohier, R. (1988). Multiple triangulation and contemporary nursing research. *Western Journal of Nursing Research 10*(6), 732–742.

Spradley, J. P. (1979). *The Ethnographic Interview.* New York: Holt, Rinehart, & Winston.

Stoddart, K. (1986). The presentation of everyday life. *Urban Life 15*(1), 103–121.

Thomas, W. I., & Swaine, D. (1928). *The Child in America.* New York: Knopf.

Thurmond, Veronica A. (2001, September 22). The point of triangulation. *Journal of Nursing Scholarship.*

Turner, V. (1978). Foreword. In B. Myerhoff, *Number Our Days.* New York: Simon and Schuster.

Webb, E., Campbell, D. T., Schwartz, R. D., & Sechrest, L. (1966). *Unobtrusive Measures: Nonreactive Research in the Social Sciences.* Chicago: Rand McNally.

Webb, E. J., Campbell, D. T., Schwartz, R. D., Sechrest, L., & Grove, J. B. (1981). *Nonreactive Measures in the Social Sciences.* Boston: Houghton Mifflin.

Wolfram, J. C. & Hassard, J. (2005) Triangulation in organizational research: A re-presentation. *Organization 12*(1), 109–133.

Chapter 2

Designing Qualitative Research

THIS CHAPTER CONSIDERS VARIOUS ways of thinking about and designing research. It includes discussion of the relationships among ideas, theory, and concepts, and of what I have long believed is the most difficult facet of research: *operationalization.* This chapter further offers a strategy for conducting literature reviews and explains the importance of carefully designing and planning research in advance. Let's begin with some thoughts about ideas, concepts, and theory.

Theory and Concepts

In the natural sciences, certain patterns of relationships occur with such regularity that they are deemed *laws:* occurrences of universal certainty. No such laws are found in the social sciences. This does not, however, mean that social life operates in a totally chaotic or completely irrational manner. Rather, social life operates within fairly regular patterns, and when carefully examined, these patterns make considerable sense. One primary purpose of social scientific research is to make sense from these various patterns. This is accomplished by creating, examining, testing, and refining theory. What then is theory? *Theory* can be defined as a general and more or less comprehensive set of statements or propositions that describe different aspects of some phenomenon (Babbie, 2003; Hagan 2006; Senese, 1997). In an applied context, theories can be understood as interrelated ideas about various patterns, concepts, processes, relationships, or events. In a formal sense, social scientists usually define theory as a system of logical statements or propositions that explain the relationship between two or more objects, concepts, phenomena, or characteristics of humans—what are sometimes called variables (Babbie, 2003; Denzin, 1978; Polit, Beck, & Hungler, 2003). Theory might also represent attempts to develop explanations about reality or ways to classify and organize events, describe events, or even predict future events (Hagan, 2006).

In order to construct theories, one needs some smaller components or what Jonathan Turner (1989, p. 5) calls the "basic building blocks of theory," namely, concepts. *Concepts*, then, are symbolic or abstract elements representing objects, properties, or features of objects, processes, or phenomenon. Concepts may communicate ideas or introduce particular perspectives, or they may be a means for casting a broad generalization. In terms of ideas, concepts are important because they are the foundation of communication and thought. Concepts provide a means for people to let others know what they are thinking and allow information to be shared. Thus, instead of describing a youth who is involved with drugs, crime, or truancy, or has problems with parents and other adults, I might simply use the concept of *delinquent* to communicate these same elements (ideas).

Concepts can be found everywhere, and people use them all of the time without actually thinking about them as *concepts*. For example, age is a concept that is so commonly used that few people stop to think about what it means. Even though people often think they understand the meaning of the concept, they may hesitate when asked to offer a specific definition. Age actually represents an abstract idea about the number of cumulative years that an individual has been alive. Although this may seem to make the term stiff, it also ensures that there is a common understanding for the meaning of this concept. Concepts used in social scientific research similarly may seem obvious at first, but they must always be clearly defined.

Typically concepts have two distinct parts: a *symbolic* element (a word, symbol, term, etc.) and an associated *definitional* element. People learn definitions for certain concepts in a variety of ways. For example, children may learn the concept of *honesty* explicitly when a parent or teacher specifically instructs them on its meaning. Or it may be learned implicitly through a more diffuse, nonverbal process of observed instances in which either dishonest behavior is corrected or honest behavior is rewarded (either through comments or actions). In either case, eventually each of us comes to apprehend the meaning of honesty. Yet, if asked to define it, people may offer slightly different shades of understanding. One person might say, "Honesty is not lying to people." Another might offer, "Honesty is not taking property that belongs to other people," and a third individual might claim that "honesty is being able to be trusted to do what you promise to do." Obviously, these responses suggest that even a fairly common concept may have multiple meanings. In the social sciences vague or unclear definitions create enormous problems. Specificity is critical when conducting research. Therefore, an important part of developing social scientific theory is first to define relevant concepts that will be used in a given research process or project. Indistinct, unclear, or vague definitions of concepts create obstacles to the advancement of knowledge and science. After noting that there were many different definitions in the literature for the concept *gang*, Richard Ball and G. David Curry (1995, p. 239) explain:

> Few if any gang researchers and theorists have been sufficiently conscious of their own definition strategies, with the result that their definitions carry too many latent connotations, treated correlations or consequences as properties or causes, or contributed to similar errors of logic.

The need for this sort of specific definition of concepts will be made clearer later in the discussion on operationalization.

Concepts rarely occur in isolation. Rather, they occur in what Neuman (2000, p. 43) refers to as *concept clusters* or what others may call *propositions*. One can connect different concepts or conceptual thoughts to each other through propositions. *Propositions*, then, are statements about relationships between concepts (Maxfield & Babbie, 2001). Taylor and Bogdan (1998) suggest that although a concept may not fit (may not convey the intended meaning), propositions may be either right or wrong statements of fact, although the research may not be able to prove them. Propositions, as discussed later, are the statements that make up theories.

Ideas and Theory

Every research project has to start somewhere; typically, the starting point is an idea. The big question, however, is how to go about finding an idea that will serve as a good launching point to a research project. For some students this genuinely is the most difficult part of the research process. Actually, many people arrive at their research ideas simply by taking stock of themselves and looking around. For example, a nurse might observe a coworker coming to work under the influence of alcohol and begin to think about how alcohol would influence nursing care. From this initial thought, the idea for researching impaired nurses might arise. A counselor at a delinquency detention center might notice that many of her clients have been battered or abused prior to their run-in with the law. From her observation, she might wonder how abuse might be linked with delinquency and how she could investigate this linkage.

Consider Phil Brown (1998, 2002) who grew up in the Catskill Mountains and watched as this once thriving, largely Jewish resort area in upstate New York lost its luster and faded into near oblivion. As an adult, Brown has written extensively—and largely autobiographically—about this once culturally rich and influential area.

Another example of an individual who looked around herself to identify an idea for research is Shelly Peterson (1998, 2001). As an elementary school teacher, Peterson was interested in learning more about the existence of gender characteristics in her students' writing. She surveyed approximately 100 teachers and found that the characteristics in girls' narrative writing demonstrated more emotion and more prosocial behaviors (helping, sharing, empathizing) than did characteristics in boys' narratives, which tended to be more aggressive and described more high-intensity, dangerous actions. Thus, for many researchers, it is simply enough to look around their environment and identify an idea worthy of research.

In some situations, ideas move from information you hear but may not actually experience yourself. For instance, you're sitting at home listening to the news, and you hear a report about three youths from wealthy families who have been caught burglarizing houses. You wonder: Why on earth did they do something like that? What motivates people who don't need money to steal from others? Or you read in the newspaper that a man living around the corner from you has been arrested for growing marijuana in his garage. You think back to the times you passed this man's house and smiled a greeting at him. And you wonder: Why didn't I realize what he was up to? Who was he going to sell the marijuana to anyhow? From these broad curiosities, you might begin to think about how these questions could be explored or answered and how you might research these phenomena.

The preceding examples serve two important purposes. First, they point out how ideas promote potential research endeavors. Second, and perhaps more important, they suggest a central research orientation that permeates this book. This orientation is the attitude that the world is a research laboratory and that you merely need to open your eyes and ears to the sensory reality that surrounds all of us to find numerous ideas for research. In fact, once you become familiar with this orientation, the biggest problem will be to filter out all the many possible researchable ideas and actually investigate one!

Most experienced qualitative researchers will agree that if you drop a qualitative investigator into any neighborhood, he or she will manage to identify a research idea, develop a research plan, and project potential research findings. This notion is likely to contrast dramatically with the inexperienced researcher's fear that he or she cannot even think of anything worthwhile to research. There may be considerable truth to the optimistic view of experienced researchers.

This does not mean, however, that all research ideas will be equally easy or interesting to research.

Some ideas will be more difficult to investigate than others. This is because those who control access to a given location—what the literature calls gatekeepers—or the subjects themselves may be reluctant to cooperate. Gatekeepers are discussed in greater detail in Chapter 6. Also, some ideas may initially seem extremely interesting but become rather plain or uninspiring on further investigation.

So, you begin with an idea. But how is this related to theory? There are some who argue that ideas and theory must come before empirical research. This has been called the *theory-before-research* model (Nachmias & Nachmias, 1992, p. 46). This orientation has been nicely described by Karl Popper (1968), who suggests that one begins with ideas (conjectures) and then attempts to disprove or refute them through tests of empirical research (refutation).

In contrast to the theory-before-research proponents, there are some who argue that research must occur before theory can be developed. This *research-before-theory* orientation can be illustrated by a statement from Robert Merton (1968, p. 103):

> It is my central thesis that empirical research goes far beyond the passive role of verifying and testing theory; it does more than confirm or refute hypotheses. Research plays an active role: it performs at least four major functions, which help shape the development of theory. It initiates, it reformulates, it deflects, and it clarifies theory.

In other words, research may suggest new problems for theory, require theoretical innovation, refine existing theories, or serve to vary past theoretical assumptions.

The approach offered in this book views theory-before-research and research-before-theory perspectives as highly compatible. Often methods texts and courses describe the research enterprise as a linear progression. In this progression, you begin with an idea, gather theoretical information, design a research plan, identify a means for data collection, analyze the data, and report findings. This may be diagrammed as follows:

Idea → Theory → Design → Data Collection → Analysis → Findings

For the most part, this orientation resembles the theory-before-research model. But it could also be drawn as the research-before-theory model:

Idea → Design → Data Collection → Theory → Analysis → Findings

Figure 2.1   The Spiraling Research Approach

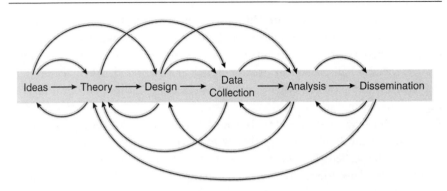

In either case, you have the feeling that each of these components is a distinct and separate successive stage, that you first derive an idea and then move on to either theory or design and so forth. In essence, it seems that you complete various necessary tasks of each stage and then move forward, leaving the completed state behind.

In this chapter, I argue for a different model for the research enterprise, a model that encompasses both the research-before-theory and theory-before-research models. This is possible because the proposed approach is conceived as spiraling rather than linear in its progression. In the proposed approach, you begin with an idea, gather theoretical information, reconsider and refine your idea, begin to examine possible designs, reexamine theoretical assumptions, and refine these theoretical assumptions and perhaps even your original or refined idea. Thus, with every two steps forward, you take a step or two backward before proceeding any further. What results is no longer a linear progression in a single, forward direction. Rather, you are spiraling forward, never actually leaving any stage behind completely. This spiraling approach is drawn in Figure 2.1.

To simplify understanding of the individual elements of this model as I discuss them, let's redefine the stages slightly, as follows:

Ideas → Literature Review → Design → Data Collection and Organization → Analysis and Findings → Dissemination

As illustrated, you begin with some sort of rough *idea* for a research study. The next stage in the process is to begin thinking and reading about the topical idea. As you begin reading related and relevant literature on the topic you should also start turning this idea into a *research question* or even a set of researchable foci. As suggested by the fluidity of the spiraling approach offered in this chapter, your research idea should flow into a potential research question that may continue to shift, change, and take form as the research process unfolds. Even though your research question(s) may change as you proceed through the research process, it is important to establish a focus for your research question or a series of research aims.

Reviewing the Literature

After developing a rough idea for the study, you will need to begin examining how others have already thought about and researched the topic. Let's say an idea for some research begins with an interest in alcohol use by male college students. You might formulate a rough question for research such as: What is the relationship between college and drinking among American males? This rough idea already shows elements of refinement. It has been limited to consideration of only American males. The next step is to visit the library to get started on a literature review. Because every library is different, you will need to familiarize yourself with the sorts of periodicals and books that are readily available to you. Some libraries have subscriptions to many journals, but not all of these may be useful for social science research, let alone a specific topic such as alcohol drinking by American male college students. Different libraries also provide different methods for accessing materials. Some libraries have online search services such as Infotrac or Research Navigator's ContentSelect, which will search for and deliver full articles directly to you online. Others have large selections of in-print periodicals maintained both in current stacks and in bound versions in back stacks or in the open library.

Many libraries also offer the convenience of various indexes of periodicals and books in print with thousands of journal and monograph references indexed by both author's name and subject topic. In some cases, you will find these as bound texts in the reference section of the library. In other cases, these indexes have been placed in CD-ROM format. If you have never used one of these indexes or are unfamiliar with the use of computers, you might want to consult the reference librarian.

The next task is to begin thinking creatively about cryptic subject topics related to your rough research idea or question and to search for these topics in the indexes. For the preceding example, you might make a list that includes "alcohol use," "collegiate alcohol use," "alcohol on campus," "drinking," "males and alcohol," "Americans and alcohol," "social drinking," "substance abuse in college," "campus problems," and so forth. It is important to develop a number of different subject areas to search. Some will be more fruitful than others, and perhaps some will yield little information. This is because both the print versions and computer-based versions of indexes are created by humans.

Because of this, indexes unavoidably suffer from the problem of terminological classification bias. In other words, even though these indexes are cross-referenced, if you do not use the same term or phrase used by the original indexer, you may not locate entries he or she has referenced.

For instance, several years ago, I became interested in the idea of doing research about women in policing. More directly, I was interested in the effect of policing on female officers. I asked my graduate student to see if she could locate some material about female police officers. When she returned the next day, she reported that there was virtually nothing in any of the index databases on the topic "female police officers." I asked if she had tried "women in policing," or "women police officers," or even "minorities in policing." Sheepishly, she explained she had not thought to do that and returned to the library. The next time she returned to my office, she carried a list of literally dozens of references for me to consider. The lesson to be learned from this is that you must not be too restrictive in your topics when searching for reference materials in indexes. In fact, most CD-ROM–based indexes provide users with a thesaurus to assist them in locating subject terms used to index material on the CD-ROM.

One important recommendation is that you avoid becoming too computer dependent during your literature search. Again, because computer listings are sometimes limited by the way they are indexed, not all the relevant information for a study may be recognized in a computer-based search. During one revision of this book, I asked one of my graduate students, a bright, first-year doctoral student, to locate some recent materials on "active informed consent." This ethical concern is discussed in Chapter 3. My graduate assistant was very well versed in computers and adept at surfing the Internet. Naturally, he sought an answer to my request by diving right into the Internet.

I waited several days before asking him if he had located any recent articles or chapters on active informed consent. He said there were none. I asked if he had gone to the library and looked up "informed consent," "passive consent," "active consent," or any similar topics. With a note of anger in his tone, he informed me that he had done better: he had checked with various Internet information sources and search engines. I then asked if he had gone to the library and physically looked through the last several years of such journals as *Journal of Ethics* or *Social Problems,* or through any educational, nursing, or medical journals. With even more anger, because I was questioning his work, he admitted he had not. He also naively insisted that if he couldn't find it through the Internet, it didn't exist.

I suggested we take a trip to the library, and together we scoured the literature. Within 15 minutes we had located four potentially usable items. My graduate assistant sheepishly admitted that these items had not shown up in any of his computer searches.

The moral of this story is simple. Search engines and the vast information available via the Internet are wonderful tools and places to begin searching for literature. They can provide enormous amounts of information. Frequently, however, there is no substitute for physically thumbing through journal indexes. It is also important when using the Internet to be careful about the legitimacy of materials taken from the Web. You should carefully consider the source of all Internet material before too heavily depending on it as evidence or support of your position or claims.

Evaluating Web Sites

In the 14 years since the first edition of *Qualitative Research Methods for the Social Sciences* was published, much has changed in the world of computers and the Internet. Back then the Internet was a new source of entertainment and offered the potential of becoming a very fast communications and information-delivery source. Today it is an indispensible tool for many businesses and home users. I myself have grown comfortable with the immediacy of seeking and obtaining information on a variety of topics through a quick Google search. In fact, as I was revising this sixth edition of the book, sitting in the office of my Southern California home, I suddenly realized that my entire house was shaking: I was in the middle of a fairly large earthquake (5.1 on the Richter scale). I almost automatically left my word processor program and jumped to my browser, where I clicked my way to the Southern California Earthquake Data Center (www.data.scec.org). Once there, I was able to see on a map exactly from where the quake had emanated and its magnitude—pretty neat stuff. But many people today, especially inexperienced researchers, take the Internet for granted; and such complacency with this technology can be dangerous for a researcher. Yes, the Internet is enormously fast, and yes, it has evolved in less than two decades to provide access to literally millions of documents. However, the quality and integrity of all the available documents are not equal. The Internet epitomizes the concept of *Caveat lector: Let the reader beware.*

The Internet allows you to access information from a variety of governmental and private sources as well as from online electronic journals, books, commentaries, archives, and even newspapers. Most governmental agencies have Web sites that offer the public copies of recent (and often backlogged) reports, pamphlets, news releases, and other forms of information. There are also Web sites, however, that offer inaccurate, erroneous, or fabricated information. During the past several years, the number of bogus Web sites, phony banking alerts—so-called *phishing scams*—adware and spyware abuses, and other intrusive problems on the Internet have been staggering. The problem is so bad that there are actually browser program extensions designed to detect fake URLs (e.g., *SpoofStick*, 2005). Whether you surf the Web simply as a consumer of fun information or in order to research some topic, it is critical that you carefully evaluate documents before relying on them in your reports. Here are a few questions you might want to consider before accepting information from a Web site as valid:

1. *Whose Web site is it, and what's in the URL (Uniform Resource Locator)?* Before you even start to consider the veracity of the text on a particular Web site, look at the URL to get a sense of the authenticity of the material on that site. Some of the things to look for are as follow: Is this somebody's personal Web page? Check to see if the site is listed under a personal name (e.g., bberg or berg) preceded or followed by a tilde (~), a percent sign (%), or even the words *users, members,* or *people.* Personal pages are not necessarily inaccurate, but you should nonetheless consider the authority and expertise of the author very carefully. Today, just about anyone with a computer and a telephone or DSL line can launch and maintain his or her own Web site. Some people have sites to allow them to show off their vacations, poetry, or special mementos. Other sites are intended as commercial ventures, selling everything from sex to Bible lessons. Many professors and professional researchers disseminate their research by simply making their reports and published articles (sometimes even entire books) available on their Web sites. When you consider using information taken from an individual's personal Web site, you still should be cautious and consider the credibility of the individual who is operating and maintaining the site.

2. *What is the nature of the domain?* The *domain* represents a kind of hierarchical scheme for indicating the logical and sometimes geographical venue of a Web page. In the United States, common domains are .edu (education), .gov (government agency), .net (network related), .com (commercial), and .org (nonprofit and research organizations). Outside the United States, domains indicate country: ca (Canada), cn (China), uk (United Kingdom), au (Australia), jp (Japan), fr (France), and so forth. Is this an official government Web site or that of a well-known and reputable organization? Is it operated and maintained by a private group that has a special purpose or motive for having the site and offering the materials you are considering? For example, there are a number of Web sites sponsored by hate groups. The information offered on such sites may sound like the reports of scientific studies, and the reports and documents may even look official. Yet, much of the information on these sites is likely biased and designed to be self-effacing and positive in order to sway readers to think favorably about the group's viewpoints—no matter how vile those viewpoints may be.

As an example of the importance of a domain name, suppose you were looking for information on the President of the United States. One source would be the official Web site of the White House in Washington, D.C. You type in http://www.whitehouse.org, thinking this will bring you to the site, but the actual domain is .gov, not. org. What you get is a site with the banner heading The White House, with both a picture of the actual White House in the upper left-hand corner and what—at a glance—looks like the presidential seal in the upper right-hand corner. But this is not the official Web site of the nation's President; it is an ultraconservative, somewhat leftist (with religious overtones) Web site, with articles largely antagonistic to the U.S. government and the President. A closer look at that presidential seal, by the way, reveals not an eagle but a vulture at its center.

3. *Is the material current or dated?*   You should check to see how frequently the Web site is updated. If the materials have not been updated recently, you may want to question how reliable a source it is. Consider also whether links are active or have expired or moved. You might also consider how current even the working links are (do these sites seem to be updated on a regular basis?). Naturally, just because a site is well maintained and information is regularly updated doesn't mean it is necessarily a good site in itself, and some material may not require constant updates. However, issues of currency are important when conducting research and should be considered when evaluating information taken from a Web site.

4. *Can the information be corroborated?*   Sometimes the material you find on a Web site seems odd or unusual, and further investigation suggests that it may not be truthful. When this happens, do not use it! Often when you undertake a search using an Internet search engine, you get many *hits*. Do not use only the first one you find. Carefully check a number of comparable sites to ensure the information is comparable. If you find that there are glaring contradictions or discrepancies, you should be very cautious about using this information.

Although there are no absolutely certain ways to guard against inaccurate information on the Web getting into your research (unless you exclude any Web-based information), these suggestions will at least help in filtering out most of the false documentation from too easily sifting in.

By now, you should have begun to amass a large quantity of documents to include in your review of the literature. Naturally you will need to begin taking some form of notes on the various pieces of literature you have obtained. There are a number of ways you can keep such records and notes. What follows is one way I call the *two-card method*. This procedure is a long-standing albeit very time-consuming strategy. Inexperienced writers and researchers may want to try using this method fairly precisely. More experienced investigators may decide to make variations on it. In either case, it provides a means for developing systematic literature and permits one to write very effective papers.

The Two-Card Method

As indicated by the name, this strategy requires you to create two types of 4 × 6-inch index cards. The first is the *author card*. Annotate each with the reference information for every article of literary material you locate and examine. Whenever possible, you should also include the library call numbers. Several of my students in recent years have preferred to use electronic index cards, as provided in some computer software packages. Although any entry format on the card or electronic card can be used, I recommend that you use a consistent entry style (see Figure 2.2).

Author cards should be kept in alphabetical order to ensure that you will always have complete information for citations and the ability to locate the document at a later time. Even fairly experienced writers have misplaced a document or returned it to the library, only to find they need it or the citation material later. Often, even with considerable effort, these writers are unable to locate the necessary information. Author cards provide a kind of insurance against not having the correct information when you need to write up references or check up on information. Also, should you continue researching in this area, you will have a head start on future literature reviews.

Figure 2.2 Author Card

[Author's Name]

Berg, Bruce L.,

    [Date]   [Title of document and publication
    1992   information]

               Law Enforcement: An Introduction to Police in
               Society. Boston, Mass.: Allyn and Bacon

[Library Call #]

Figure 2.3 Topic Card

[Topic Label] Police Detective

[Author's Name]

Berg, Bruce (1992:p83)

   [Verbatim Quote]

Detective, as a noun, makes its first appearance in lay parlance in the 1840s in order to identify the police organizational position of an investigator (Klockars, 1985; Kuykendal, 1986, 175). The central function of early detective work in police organizations was apprehension.

The second type of card is called the *topic card.* Topic cards also should follow a consistent pattern and include the author's name, the date of the publication, a brief topical label, and a short verbatim excerpt (see Figure 2.3). Because the author cards contain the title and publication information, duplicating those details on the topic cards is not necessary.

Many students have either been taught or have developed similar note-taking strategies. In some cases, these other strategies call for the use of legal-length note pads. This technique, however, inhibits your ability to sort through or organize the excerpts, short of cutting sheets into pieces. Additionally, these other strategies usually ask you to paraphrase the material you take down as notes. Certainly, paraphrasing is somewhat less tedious to accomplish than the verbatim annotation of excerpts, as promoted in my plan. However, there are several critical reasons why I recommend the use of verbatim quotes on these topic cards.

First, it reduces the physical amount of material you will ultimately use when you get down to writing reports about the research. Anyone who has undertaken a large writing project, even a term paper, should relate to the problem of having stacks of photocopies and piles of books cluttering the room. Trying to find some specific piece of information under such circumstances is quite burdensome.

Second, you can very quickly sort the topic cards into their categories (e.g., placing all the cards about police detectives together). In this manner, you can assemble the piles into an organized sequence that will reflect how you plan to write the report or paper. This allows you to read through the relevant materials for each section rather than repeatedly read through all of the material in order to write a single section.

Third, topic cards allow you to assess whether multiple authors actually have made similar statements about issues or situations. In turn, you are able to make strong synthesized statements regarding the work or arguments of others. For example, you might write, "According to Babbie (2003), Frankfort-Nachmias and Nachmias (2000), and Leedy & Ormrod (2004), the design stage is a critically important element in the development of a research project." Making such a synthesized statement, which collapses the arguments of three individuals into one, can be easily accomplished because you would have a topic card for each author conveying this sort of general sentiment.

If you, as an investigator, paraphrase material on the topic cards, it is possible that you might slant or alter meanings. Without intending to, you might have misread, misinterpreted, or poorly paraphrased material. When you go through the topic cards looking for agreement among authors, you might find paraphrased statements that *seem* to represent similar ideas but that actually do not accurately represent the sentiments of the original authors. Using verbatim excerpts ensures that this will not occur. Either the authors did say similar things or they did not.

The obvious question at this juncture is: How much should you annotate on the topic cards? While there are no hard and fast rules, I recommend only about two to four paragraphs. The purpose of these cards is to reduce the amount of material ultimately necessary for the writer-investigator. To completely transcribe works tends to defeat this purpose. Bear in mind that you might find three or four different topics in a short article, or you might find six or seven. Likewise, you might find 10 or 12 topics to excerpt from a book, or you might find only a single topic worthy of excerpting.

Usually the excerpt will fit on a single card (front and back). However, on occasion, you might find it necessary to use a second or even a third card. It is important to number or letter subsequent cards in order to keep them in correct sequence. In the event that you find an enormous cache of simply wonderful material, you can make a note of this on the card. This is a better strategy than copying 10 or 11 cards. Simply excerpt the usual three or four paragraphs and then write something like "more great material!" In this case, you will want to have the source nearby when you write the paper.

Excerpting on topic cards can be fairly tedious. You should not plan on spending many hours at a time writing topic cards. Instead, plan to spend only an hour or so at each topic card writing session. Even small amounts of time, such as 10- or 15-minute intervals, can be successfully used for this purpose. Remember, what this strategy loses in excitement, it gains tenfold in organization and effective writing later.

This strategy also is very portable. You can slip index cards into your pocket, bag, briefcase, or backpack along with a book or photocopy of some article. While waiting for a doctor's or dentist's appointment, you can easily be reading and excerpting material. Or you might do topic cards while riding a train or bus. The important thing to remember is that as you are reading and creating topic cards, you also should be thinking about the material.

As mentioned previously, the two-card method is especially effective for the inexperienced researcher. For those more experienced—at least at library-based literature review endeavors—various alternatives are certainly available. Some of these involve *abstracting*, or *excerpting*, material or various paraphrasing techniques. However, even fairly systematic paraphrasing strategies move one further away from the verbatim excerpting of material. This, in turn, runs the serious risk of misinterpretation, misuse, or misapplication of the original author's intended meaning. I would encourage students to experiment with the two-card method and to make various modifications, such as, perhaps, placing the material on a computer (creating electronic cards). Alternatively, you might create a systematic listing or a kind of index of the topics and abbreviated versions of the topic card contents.

The basic idea of the two-card method is to cut down on the physical volume of material necessary for writing a comprehensive or exhaustive literature review. In addition, while undertaking the review of literary materials, your thoughts should begin to turn toward refinement of the original research idea or question. What are some specific research questions that need to be considered in the eventual research? How have others theorized about the topic? How have others researched the topic? What have others found in previous research? Is there an interesting angle or approach that would set your research apart from that of others or refine findings offered by past research? You also should begin to consider exactly how you will frame your research questions or problems.

Theory, Reality, and the Social World

Larry Reynolds and Nancy Herman-Kinney (2003, p. 1045) suggest that "interactionists have often been described, and sometimes describe themselves, as fundamentally 'unscientific,' doubtful of the possibility of an objective truth." In some ways, this is a true statement, but at the same time, it misses the very nature of the perspective: its flexibility and diversity. That orientation also ignores the fact that many interactionists who question quantitative purist approaches see themselves as very *scientific* because they adopt various systematic processes and employ rigorous standards when gathering information (data). Norman Denzin (1992, p. 2) states that symbolic interactionists have been "haunted by a double-edged specter." While many argue for a subjective and interpretive approach to human behavior, other interactionists strive to build a science of human conduct that is much more a social realist approach built on natural science criteria. This tension is frequently apparent in qualitative writings and raises the question: "How can one be objective while still being subjective?" To be certain, I cannot fully answer this question in this methods book. However, as may already be becoming clear, I too walk that slender tightrope between objectivity and subjectivity in terms of how one goes about designing his or her research study. One good way to begin is to clearly understand the distinctions between objective and subjective reality, or what can be described as the distinction between *cognitive reality* and *physical* or *sensory reality*, and their relationship with theory.

In cognitive reality—the thoughts that you can conjure in your mind—anything is possible; however, in sensory reality very clear limitations exist. For example, if you close your eyes, you should have little trouble imagining yourself standing on a railroad track with a train engine speeding toward you. Now, in your mind, you can raise your hands in front of your chest and imagine that as the train is about to strike, you can hold it at bay, as if you were a super being. Yet, in the sensory world, you would be unwise to attempt a similar feat. Sensory reality is the world around you. It is the world filled with smells, tactile surfaces, loud sounds, beautiful or unpleasant sights, and the tastes of sweets, sours, tarts, and spices.

Social scientists tend to move smoothly from one reality to the other during the early phases of a research study. After all, when you conceive an idea for your research, you are operating in the cognitive realm. When you turn to a review of the literature, you slide into the sensory world, but just long enough to formulate concepts and work with theory to develop a doable research question or series of research aims—then back to sensory reality, where you will need to frame your newly created research question or problem.

Framing Research Problems

Research problems direct or drive the research enterprise. How you will eventually conduct a research study depends largely on what your research questions are. It is important, therefore, to frame or formulate a clear research problem statement. Remember, the research process begins with an idea and only a rough notion of what is to be researched. As you have been reading through and collecting information from the literature, these rough questions have become clearer and theoretically more refined.

Let us return to the original research idea: What is the relationship between college and drinking among American males? After reading through some of the literature, you might begin to refine and frame this idea as a problem statement with researchable questions:

> *Problem Statement.* This research proposes to examine alcohol drinking behaviors in social settings among college-age American males.
>
> *Research Questions.* A number of questions are addressed in this research including (although not limited to) the following:
>
> 1. What are some normative drinking behaviors of young adult American males during social gatherings where alcohol is present?
> 2. How do some young adult American males manage to abstain from drinking (e.g., avoidance rituals) while in social situations where alcohol is present?
> 3. How do young adult American males define appropriate drinking practices?
> 4. How do young adult American males define alcoholism?

These questions did not just happen spontaneously. They were influenced by the literature about drinking practices among Americans. They resulted after the investigator began thinking about what issues were important and how those issues might be measured. This required the researcher to consider various concepts and definitions and perhaps to develop operationalized definitions.

Operationalization and Conceptualization

When someone says, "That kid's a delinquent," most of us quickly draw some mental picture of what that is, and we are able to understand the meaning of the term *delinquent*. If, however, someone were to ask, "How would you define a delinquent?" we would probably find that some people think about this term differently from others. For some, it may involve a youth under the legal age of adult jurisdiction (usually between 16 and 18 years of age) who commits law violations (Bynum & Thompson, 1992). For others, a delinquent may be simply defined as a youthful law violator (Thornton & Voigt, 1992). Still others may require in their definition some notion of a youth who not only breaks a law but who is also convicted in court of this law violation (Siegel & Senna, 1988). In other words, there are a number of possible definitions for the concept *delinquent*.

If you, as a researcher, are interested in studying the behavior of delinquent girls, you will first need to clearly define *delinquent*. Because humans cannot telepathically communicate their mental images of terms, there is no way to directly communicate which possible meaning of delinquent you have in mind. To ensure that everyone is working with the same definition and mental image, you will need to *conceptualize* and *operationalize* the term. This process is called *operationally defining* a concept.

Operational definitions concretize the intended meaning of a concept in relation to a particular study and provide some criteria for measuring the empirical existence of that concept (Frankfort-Nachmias & Nachmias, 2000; Leedy & Ormrod 2004).

In operatively defining a term or concept, you, as a researcher, begin by declaring the term to mean whatever you want it to mean throughout the research. Although it is important for your readers to understand what you mean when, for example, you use the concept *delinquent,* they need not necessarily agree with that definition. As long as they understand what you mean by certain concepts, they can understand and appraise how effectively the concept works in your study.

Once defined, the concept needs some way to be measured during the research process. In quantitative research, this means creating some index, scale, or similar measurement indicator intended to calculate how much of or to what degree the concept exists. Qualitative investigators also need agreement over what a concept means in a given study and how that concept is to be identified and examined. How will the researcher gather empirical information of data that will inform him or her about that concept?

Consider, for example, the concept *weight.* As a researcher, you might define the concept *weight* as the amount of mass an object possesses in terms of pounds and ounces. Now everyone holds the same concrete meaning and mental image for the concept *weight.* How shall this concept be measured? Operationally, weight can be determined by placing an object on a scale and rounding to the nearest ounce. This operational definition clearly tells others what the concept is designated to mean and how it will be measured.

Unfortunately, not all concepts are as easy to define as weight or as easy to measure. Polit and Hungler (1993), for example, suggest that many concepts relevant to research in nursing are not operationalized simply. For instance, in nursing research, the quality of life for chronically ill patients may be defined in terms of physiological, social, and psychological attributes. If the nurse researcher emphasizes the physiological aspects of quality of life for chronically ill patients in his or her definition, the operationalized component may involve measuring white blood cell counts or oxygen output, assessing invasive surgical procedures or ventilation procedures, measuring blood pressure, and so forth.

If, on the other hand, quality of life for chronically ill patients is defined socially, the operationalized elements of the definition would need to measure family or social support, living arrangements, self-management skills, independence, and similar social attributes. Likewise, if the nurse researcher uses a more psychological conceptualization, the operationalized measures would be directed along the lines of the patients' emotional acceptance of chronic illness.

Let's try another illustration of defining and operationalizing. Say you are interested in studying to what degree or extent people are religious. To begin, you must define the concept *religious*. For this example, *religious* will be defined as how actively one is involved with his or her religion. Next, you must decide what kinds of information inform others about someone's active involvement in religion. After consulting the literature, you decide that you know how religious someone is by knowing whether that person believes in a divine being, attends organized religious services on some regular basis, prays at home, reads religious materials, celebrates certain religious holidays, readily declares membership in a particular religion, participates in religious social organizations, and contributes to religious charities.

In effect, you, the researcher, are saying, "I can't immediately apprehend a person's religiousness, but I can think about what elements seem to go into making up or representing observable behaviors that I understand and associate with meaning *religious*." By obtaining information regarding the subset of observable attributes delineated earlier to represent religious, you can study religiousness. As you think about the observable attributes of religious—or of any other concept—you should again peruse the literature. By spiraling back into the literature stage, you can seek ways in which others have examined the concept. You may borrow some of these previous attributes, or you may create others.

In some forms of qualitative research, the investigator is not as rigorously concerned with defining concepts in operational terms as outlined here. This is because some forms of interpretative and phenomenological research seek to discover naturally arising meanings among members of study populations. However, in many cases of qualitative research, failure to define and operationalize concepts will spell disaster. If, as a researcher, you have not made clear what your concepts mean, your results may be meaningless in terms of explanatory power or applicability. If you have not thought about how data will be collected to represent attributes of the concept, it will be very difficult for you to determine answers to research questions. And if you have not worked with the literature in developing relevant meanings and measurable attributes, it will be impossible for you to see how eventual results fit into this extant body of knowledge.

Your next problem, then, is to determine exactly how information about various attributes will be obtained. As you reach this point, you move one foot forward toward the design stage of the research enterprise. Naturally, your other foot will remain in the literature stage.

Designing Projects

The design for a research project is literally the plan for how the study will be conducted. It is a matter of thinking about, imagining, and visualizing how the research study will be undertaken (Leedy & Ormrod 2004; McTavish & Loether, 2002). Or as Valerie Janesick (1994) metaphorically describes it, design is the *choreography* that establishes the *research dance*.

My daughter Kate recently planned a trip to Vienna to study for a month and to tour various countries in Europe for several weeks. As part of her planning, she arranged her lodgings in each country, the purchase of a Euro-pass, and tickets to several plays and operas all in advance and via the Internet. She even determined she could travel from Spain to France on a night train and thereby save on the cost of a hotel room. Her meal expenses were worked out to the last penny, and she even carried a list of things people had indicated they would like her to bring back for them as souvenirs. My son, on the other hand, recently took a trip to Palm Desert with a friend. I asked him the name of the hotel where he was staying, and he said he had no idea, but his friend did. I asked if he knew which city in Palm Desert he would be in, and again, he told me, "I have no clue." I asked if he was bringing any cash, and he said, "That would probably be a good idea, huh? Thanks for reminding me. I'll stop at the bank on my way out of town." This example illustrates that when you have two different people, you often have two different styles of planning. My daughter is meticulous about planning every minute of her trips. My son is a bit looser about details. Designing a research project can similarly run the gamut of being very well planned and organized or more loosely designed. Some researchers, such as Robert Bogdan and Sari Knopp Biklen (2002, p. 49) recommend that you "hang loose." I, on the other hand, support a more intentional and planned approach—or at least an approach that falls some-where between a detailed plan and no plan at all.

In either case, the design stage of research involves a series of important decisions about the research idea or question(s). What types of information will be gathered and through what forms of data-collection technologies? Where will the research be undertaken, and among what group or groups of people (questions of site, setting, and sample)? When conducting research, you must decide whether to use a single data-collection strategy or to combine several strategies (data triangulation). Will you undertake the study alone or with the assistance of others (multiple investigator triangulation)? You must consider whether the study will be framed by a single overarching theory or by several related theories (theoretical triangulation). How much will the project cost in terms of time and money, and how much can you actually afford? Are the data-collection strategies appropriate for the research questions being addressed? What will the data (physically) look like once they have been collected? How will the data be organized and analyzed?

In effect, during the design stage, you, the investigator, sketch out the entire research project in an effort to foresee any possible glitches that might arise. If you locate a problem now, while the project is still on the drafting board, there is no harm done. After the project has begun, if you find that concepts have been poorly conceived, that the wrong research questions have been asked, or that the data collected are inappropriate or from the wrong group of people, the project may be ruined.

In addition, the researcher must consider what Morse and Richards (2002) call the pacing of the project. By *pacing*, Morse and Richards (p. 66) mean planning the sequence of various components of the study and the movement between data gathering and data analysis. This planning requires considerable decision making during the design stage and the flexibility to make additional changes during the course of the research: once you select a data-collection strategy, say field observations, when do you start? Once you have begun, when do you stop? Should you include interviews along with your field observations, even though you did not originally plan to do so? All of these decisions affect both the pace, duration, and design of your research.

Researchers in the social sciences typically conduct research on human subjects. The design stage is a time when you, the researcher, must consider whether ethical standards and safeguards for subjects' protection are adequate. You must make certain that subjects will be protected from any harm. Chapter 3 discusses issues of research ethics in detail. For now, regard the design stage as the time when ethical proprieties such as honesty; openness of intent; respect for subjects; issues of privacy, anonymity, and confidentiality; the intent of the research; and the willingness of subjects to participate voluntarily in the study are appraised.

Setting and Population Appropriateness

During the research phase of a project, the investigator must consider a rationale for identifying and using a particular setting as a data-collection site (Marshall & Rossman, 1999). Decisions must also be made regarding who will serve as the researcher and who will comprise the research study population. While choices may be numerous, some advice is in order. First, it is best to be practical. Select a site or setting that is reasonable in size and complexity so the study can be completed within the time and budget you have available. It is also wise to consider your own level of skill, which as a novice researcher is likely to be limited and your confidence somewhat uncertain. The study site or setting should be a location where:

1. Entry or access is possible.
2. The appropriate people (target population) are likely to be available.
3. There is a high probability that the study's focuses, processes, people, programs, interactions, and structures that are part of the research question(s) will be available to the investigator.
4. The research can be conducted effectively by an individual or individuals during the data-collection phase of the study (e.g., an African American researcher should not undertake research among members of the Ku Klux Klan).

The research question is generally regarded as the primary guide to the appropriate site or setting selection (Flick, 1998; Leedy & Ormrod, 2004; Marshall & Rossman, 1999; Silverman, 1999). For example, if the research question has to do with why some battered women remain with their battering spouses, the data-collection site must be a safe place related to battered women, such as a shelter for battered women and children. If the research question has to do with the formation of informal cliques in high schools (e.g., jocks, nerds, druggies), then a different data-collection location is necessary, one where high school youths are likely to gather and may actually involve several locations (e.g., a local park, skating rink, public pool, restaurant, mall).

In many cases, the decision to use a particular research site is tied closely to obtaining access to an appropriate population of potential subjects. Poor study site selection and poor sample decisions may weaken or ruin eventual findings. You must be careful to identify an *appropriate* population, not merely an easily accessible one. For instance, let's say you wanted to conduct a study investigating the opinions or practices of Native Americans. One easy way of locating a site and population might be to turn to college students. After all, college students are easy to locate on college campuses. They are likely to be willing to take part in an interview—either out of curiosity or to help out another student. But you must ask the question: What pertinent information will the average non–Native American college student have regarding how Native Americans think, perceive their social world, or practice their particular life styles? In other words, if you want to know about Native Americans, then you need to locate a setting where Native Americans can be accessed.

Sometimes researchers identify what they believe to be an appropriate study population, but they cannot immediately see where an appropriate setting might be for data collection. For example, several years ago, I had a student interested in conducting a study about fear of crime among the blind.

On the surface, this sounds like a good research topic. The problem arose when I asked him how (and where) he planned to access such a population of potential subjects. He thought for a while and made a trip to the library before returning to announce that he wanted to conduct interviews. I agreed that that might be an acceptable way to collect data on peoples' perceptions of their fear of crime. I next asked the student: Where are you going to locate subjects? This question created a new problem for the student, who was so proud that he had determined a means for data collection that he had not thought about where he would locate subjects to interview.

Several days later the student returned with a plan and a story of his own. The student told me that he had discussed his need to access blind people to conduct a study of their perceptions of fear of crime with another faculty member. The faculty member—who was obviously not terribly versed in methods—suggested that the student simply go to one of the large introductory classes and divide the class in half. Then he suggested that the student have half the class place blindfolds over their eyes and spend a period of time walking around campus (ushered by one of the other nonblindfolded students). Following this experience, the students could switch off, so both groups experienced *blindness*. Next, the class could be administered a pencil-and-paper survey about their fear of crime, having now experienced the precariousness of not being able to see. The student immediately recognized that this would not be an appropriate setting or sample for his study. Wisely, however, he did not argue with the faculty member but rather thanked him and explained that he wanted to conduct a more qualitative study.

The student then explained his actual plan to me. He indicated that he intended to attend a summer camp for the blind sponsored by several nonprofit agencies. He had learned that the population of the camp came from the entire state and that no one who wanted to attend was ever turned away (those who could not afford to pay were awarded camp scholarships). Thus, the camp contained a population from various socioeconomic strata, races, ages, and both men and women. The student spent the summer and was able both to conduct nearly 60 interviews and some limited participant observation (Rounds, 1993).

Sampling Strategies

The logic of using a sample of subjects is to make inferences about some larger population from a smaller one—the sample. In quantitative research, the investigator is keenly concerned with *probability sampling*. The concept of probability sampling is based on the notion that a sample can be selected that will mathematically represent subgroups of some larger population (Senese, 1997). The parameters required for creating these probability samples are quite restrictive but allow the investigator to make various inferential hypothesis tests (using various statistical techniques). The most commonly discussed probability sample is the *simple random* sample. The simple random sample most closely approximates the ideals in probability sampling. To accomplish a simple random sample, each element in the full population must have an equal and independent chance of inclusion in the eventual sample to be studied. Simple random sampling typically begins with a full listing of every element in the full population to be investigated. Once this list of all of the elements has been constructed, the size of the sample must be determined. Once this has been accomplished, a random numbers table, computer, or other procedure for randomly selecting elements from the list will be applied (see Figure 2.4).

Figure 2.4 Probability Sampling Strategies

Simple Random Sampling. Typically, this procedure is intended to produce a representative sample. The process draws subjects from an identified population in such a manner that every unit in that population has precisely the same chance (probability) of being included in the sample.

Systematic Random Sampling. The use of a systematic sample provides a convenient way to draw a sample from a large identified population when a printed list of that population is available. In systematic sampling, every *n*th name is selected from the list. Usually the interval between names on the list is determined by dividing the number of persons desired in the sample into the full population. For example, if a final sample of 80 was desired and the population list contained 2,560 names, the researchers would divide 2,560 by 80. The resulting 32 becomes the interval between names on the list. It is important, however, to begin the list at some random starting place. Frequently, researchers select a number between 1 and 20 (usually taken from a random numbers table) and begin at that location on the list and then stop at every *n*th name—in our example, at every thirty-second name on the list.

Stratified Random Sampling. A stratified sample is used whenever researchers need to ensure that a certain sample of the identified population under examination is represented in the sample. The population is divided into subgroups (strata), and independent samples of each stratum are selected. Within each stratum, a particular sampling fraction is applied in order to ensure representativeness of proportions in the full population. Thus, sampling fractions in some strata may differ from those of others in the same sample. Stratified samples can be used only when information is available to divide the population into strata.

The social sciences often examine research situations in which one cannot select the kinds of probability samples used in large-scale surveys and which conform to the restricted needs of a probability sample. In these situations, investigators rely on *nonprobability samples.*

In nonprobability sampling, the investigator does not base his or her sample selection on probability theory. Rather, efforts are undertaken (1) to create a kind of quasi-random sample and (2) to have a clear idea about what larger group or groups the sample may reflect. Nonprobability samples offer the benefits of not requiring a list of all possible elements in a full population and the ability to access otherwise highly sensitive or difficult-to-research study populations. For example, it would be very difficult to undertake a study of active prostitutes, because it would be virtually impossible to create a list of all of the prostitutes in a given area. At best, one might create a listing of all the *known* prostitutes. Thus, frequently in the social sciences, a researcher is presented with interesting and potentially important research questions that cannot be answered by a probability sampling technique. From the perspective of qualitative research, nonprobability sampling tends to be the norm. The following sections describe the four most common types of nonprobability samples.

Convenience Samples   The convenience sample is sometimes referred to as an *accidental* or *availability* sample (Babbie, 1998; Mutchnick & Berg, 1996). This category of sample relies on available subjects—those who are close at hand or easily accessible. For example, it is fairly common for college and university professors to use their students as subjects in their research projects. This technique is used all too frequently and has some serious risks associated with it. Specifically, often a researcher is interested in studying characteristics or processes that college students simply are not equipped to offer information about. Consider again, for example, the suggested use of blindfolded students to study fear of crime among the blind.

Under certain circumstances this strategy is an excellent means of obtaining preliminary information about some research question quickly and inexpensively. For example, if an investigator were interested in examining how college students perceive drinking and drunkenness, he or she could easily make use of a convenience sample of college students. If, on the other hand, the researcher was interested in studying self-images among blue-collar workers, he or she could not use this convenience sample of college students and simply ask them to pretend that they are blue-collar workers when answering the researcher's questions. In other words, convenience samples must be evaluated for appropriateness of fit for a given study.

Purposive Samples   This category of sampling is sometimes called *judgmental sampling* (Hagan, 2006). When developing a purposive sample, researchers use their special knowledge or expertise about some group to select subjects who represent this population. In some instances, purposive samples are selected after field investigations on some group in order to ensure that certain types of individuals or persons displaying certain attributes are included in the study. Despite some serious limitations (for instance, the lack of wide generalizability), purposive samples are occasionally used by researchers. Teo (1998), for example, used a purposive sample to identify only technology-related firms as a target group to include in his study of management. Teo (1998) additionally wanted to include only firms with 100 employees or more because he believed that firms with fewer than 100 employees did not always have a human relations manager to study.

Snowball Samples   Another nonprobability sampling strategy, which some may see as similar to convenience sampling, is known as snowball sampling, chain referral sampling (Biernacki & Waldorf, 1981; Owens, 2005; Penrod, Preston, Cain, & Stark, 2003) or respondent-driven sampling (Heckathorn & Jeffri, 2003). Snowballing is sometimes the best way to locate subjects with certain attributes or characteristics necessary in the study. Snowball samples are particularly popular among researchers interested in studying various classes of deviance, sensitive topics, or difficult-to-reach populations (Lee, 1993).

The basic strategy of snowballing involves first identifying several people with relevant characteristics and interviewing them or having them answer a questionnaire. These subjects are then asked for the names (referrals) of other people who possess the same attributes they do—in effect, a *chain* of subjects driven by the referral of one respondent of another.

If you wanted to learn more about, say, drug use or theft by nurses, the use of some sort of probability sample would seem out of the question. But, through use of a few informants, field investigations, or other strategies, the researcher might identify a small number of nurses with these characteristics. By asking these first subjects for referrals of additional nurses, the sample eventually "snowballs" from a few subjects to many subjects (e.g., Dabney & Berg, 1994; Wright, Decker, Redfern, & Smith, 2006).

Quota Samples   A quota sample begins with a kind of matrix or table that creates cells or stratum. The quota sampling strategy then uses a nonprobability method to fill these cells. The researcher may wish to use gender, age, education, or any other attributes to create and label each stratum or cell in the table. Which attributes are selected will have to do with the research question and study focuses. Next, the researcher needs to determine the proportion of each attribute in the full study population. For instance, let's say a researcher wants to study perceptions of violence among people in the United States, with a special interest in people over the age 65. Census data would provide the researcher with reasonable estimates of people over the age 65, as well as various categories under the age 65. The research could create various age cohorts—people over 65, 45–65, 25–44, and under 25. Next, the researcher could determine the proportion of people in each of these age groups. Following this, the investigator could select a region of the country and sample people in that area, identifying the same proportion of people for each age cohort as identified in the census data.

Data Collection and Organization

As you begin visualizing how the research project will "unfold, cascade, roll, and emerge" (Lincoln & Guba, 1985, p. 210), you also must imagine what the data will look like. Will raw data be audiotape cassettes that result from long interviews? Will data comprise dozens of spiral notebooks filled with field notes? Will the data include photographs or video recordings? Will they entail systematic observational checklists or copies of files containing medical or criminal histories? Could data actually be the smudges left on a polished counter or glass display case? Just what will the research data look like?

The next question to be answered is, What do you do with the data to organize them and make them ready for analysis? As Morse and Richards (2002, p. 100) point out, "the volume of data that qualitative researchers must manage is enormous. Researchers tell stories of 'drowning in data,' of stacking piles of data in their basements, or of not being able to use their dining room table for several months while the process of analysis is ongoing." It is frequently at this point in the research enterprise that many students fall flat on their faces and find themselves hopelessly lost, even after having taken several research courses. While most research courses and textbooks are excellent at describing the basic structures of research, few move the student into the areas of data organization and analysis. Typically, the results are that students come up with excellent ideas for research, conduct solid literature reviews, produce what sounds like viable research designs, and may even collect massive amounts of data. The problem arises, however, at this juncture: What do you do with all that collected data?

If you were doing quantitative research, there might be an easy answer to the question of organization and analysis. You would reduce the data to computerizable form and enter them into a database. Then, using a packaged statistical program for the social sciences, you would endeavor to analyze the data. Lamentably, qualitative data are not as quickly or easily handled. A common mistake made by many inexperienced or uninformed researchers is to reduce qualitative data to symbolic numeric representations and quantitatively computer-analyze them. As Berg and Berg (1993) state, this ceases at once to be qualitative research and amounts to little more than a variation of quantitative data collection and analysis.

How qualitative data are organized depends in part on what the data look like. If they are in textual form, such as field notes, or can be made into textual form, such as by transcribing a tape-recorded interview, they may be organized in one manner. If they are video, photographic, or drawn material, they will require a different form of organization and analysis. But regardless of the data form, you must consider this issue during the design stage of the process. Again, this points to the spiraling effect of research activities. If you wait until data have actually been collected to consider how they are to be organized for analysis, serious problems may arise. For example, you may not have planned for adequate time or financial resources. Or you might collect data in such a way that they should be systematically organized, coded, or indexed as they were collected and not after the fact. In any event, you must direct thought toward how data will be organized and analyzed long before you begin the data-collection process.

Typically, the immediately collected raw data are not *immediately* available for analysis. Rather, the raw data require some sort of organizing and processing before they can actually be analyzed. Field notes, for example, may fill hundreds of pages of notebooks or take up thousands of megabytes of space on a computer disk. These notes need to be edited, corrected, and made more readable, even before they can be organized, indexed, or entered into a computer-generated text analysis program file. Recorded interviews must be transcribed (transformed into written text), corrected, and edited also before being somehow indexed or entered into a text-based computer analysis program. The volume of pages of qualitative raw data can sometimes be quite daunting to the inexperienced researcher. Thus, understanding how data can be organized and managed is very important. This directs our attention to notions of data storage and retrieval.

Data Storage, Retrieval, and Analysis

As Huberman and Miles (1994) suggest, "How data are stored and retrieved is the heart of data management. . . ." A clear and working storage and retrieval system is critical if one expects to keep track of the reams of data that have been collected; to flexibly access and use the data; and to assure systematic analysis and documentation of the data. In this way the study can, in principle, be verified through replication.

Levine (1985), Wolfe (1992), and Huberman and Miles (1994) all argue that data management and data analysis are integrally related. There are, in fact, no rigid boundaries between them. The main concerns are as follows:

1. A system that ensures high-quality accessibility to the data.
2. Documentation of any analysis that is carried out.
3. Retention and protection of data and related analysis of documents after the study has been completed.

From the perspective of this book, and in keeping with the preceding three issues, data analysis can be defined as consisting of three concurrent flows of action: data reduction, data display, and conclusions and verification (see also Huberman & Miles, 1994, pp. 10–12).

Data Reduction   In qualitative research, data reduction does not necessarily refer to quantifying nominal data. Qualitative data need to be reduced and transformed in order to make them more readily accessible, understandable, and to draw out various themes and patterns. Data reduction acknowledges the voluminous nature of qualitative data in the raw. It directs attention to the need for focusing, simplifying, and transforming raw data into a more manageable form. Frequently, data reduction occurs throughout the research project's life. For example, as in-depth interviews are completed and hours of audiotapes are created, the interviews are also transcribed into print by word-processing programs and/or computer-based textual analysis formats. As the project continues, further elements of data reduction will occur (written summaries, coding, development of grounded themes, identification of analytic themes, consideration of relevant theoretical explanations, etc.). This data-reduction and transformation process occurs throughout the span of the research.

Data Display   The notion of data display is intended to convey the idea that data are presented as an organized, compressed assembly of information that permits conclusions to be analytically drawn. Displays may involve tables of data; tally sheets of themes; summaries or proportions of various statements, phrases, or terms; and similarly *reduced* and *transformed* groupings of data. These displays assist the researcher in understanding and observing certain patterns in the data or determining what additional analysis or actions must be taken. As with the activity of data reduction, the development of displays is not really a separate step but rather a component of the analysis process.

Conclusions and Verification   The last analysis activity I will discuss is conclusion drawing and verification. Throughout the research process, the investigator has been making various informed evaluations and decisions about the study and the data. Sometimes these have been made on the basis of material found in existing literature (as the researcher spirals back and forth to the literature). Sometimes these evaluations and decisions have arisen as a result of data as they are collected (based on observations in the field, statements made during interviews, observations of patterns in various documents, etc.). Yet, experienced researchers do not make definitive conclusions during these preliminary periods in the research process. Rather, they hold an open and perhaps even a skeptical point of view. In fact, some of the tentative outcomes have aided in data-reduction and data-display activities. Eventually, after the data have been collected, reduced, and displayed, analytic conclusions may begin to emerge and define themselves more clearly and definitively.

Verification is actually a twofold consideration. First, conclusions drawn from the patterns apparent in the data must be confirmed (verified) to assure that they are real and not merely wishful thinking on the part of the researcher. This may be accomplished by the researcher carefully checking the path to his or her conclusion (i.e., retracing the various analytic steps that led to the conclusion). Or it may involve having another researcher independently examine the displays and data to see if he or she will draw comparable conclusions, a kind of intercoder reliability check.

Second, verification involves assuring that all of the procedures used to arrive at the eventual conclusions have been clearly articulated. In this manner, another researcher could potentially replicate the study and the analysis procedures and draw comparable conclusions. The implication of this second verification strand implies that qualitative analysis needs to be very well documented as a process. In addition to its availability to other researchers, it permits evaluation of your analysis strategies, self-reflection, and refinement of methods and procedures.

Dissemination

Once the research project has been completed, it is not really over. That is, doing research for the sake of doing it offers no benefit to the scientific community or to the existing body of knowledge it might inform. Research, then, is not complete until it has been disseminated. This may be accomplished through reports submitted to appropriate public agencies or to funding sources. It may include informal presentations to colleagues at brown-bag lunches or formal presentations at professional association meetings. It may involve publishing reports in one of a variety of academic or professional journals. Regardless of how the information is spread, it must be disseminated if it is to be considered both worthwhile and complete. Chapter 12 explains how you may go about disseminating your research results. For the purposes of designing research projects, it is important to bear in mind that this stage of the research process is integral to the whole.

TRYING IT OUT

There are a number of ways you can practice aspects related to the planning of research. A few suggestions follow that should provide an opportunity to gain some experience. Although these are useful experiential activities, they should not be confused with actually conducting research.

Suggestion 1 Using your favorite search engine on the Web, look up "Knights of the Ku Klux Klan" (if you do not know of any search engine, go to www.google.com). Now take a look at several of the hits that the search has found. Consider the merits of the documents on each of these sites. Does the material seem biased? Does the material sound reasonable? How heavily would you rely on this information in a report or research?

Suggestion 2 Locate the Index to the Social Sciences in a college or university library. Use the index to find 10 sources of reference material for a potential study on homelessness. Now go to the Web and using your favorite search engine (or go to www.google.com) enter the search term "homelessness" and locate 10 additional reference items.

Suggestion 3 Identify six concepts and operationally define each. Be sure to consult relevant literature before terms are defined. Do not make up definitions. When operatively defining how each concept will be measured, be certain these operations conform to both relevant literature and the qualitative paradigm.

REFERENCES

Babbie, E. (1998). *The Practice of Social Research* (8th ed.). Belmont, CA: Wadsworth.
Babbie, E. (2003). *The Practice of Social Research* (10th ed.). Belmont, CA: Wadsworth.
Ball, R. A., & Curry, G. D. (1995). The logic of definition in criminology: Purposes and methods for defining 'gang.' *Criminology 33*, 225–245.

Berg, B. L., & Berg, J. (1993). A reexamination of triangulation and objectivity in qualitative nursing research. *Free Inquiry in Creative Sociology 21*(1), 65–72.

Biemacki, P. & Waldorf, D. (1981). Snowball sampling: Probems and techniques of chain referral sampling. *Sociological Methods & Research 10*, 141–63.

Bogdan, R., & Knopp Bilken, S. (2002). *Qualitative Research for Education* (4th ed.). Boston: MA. Allyn and Bacon.

Brown, P. (1998). *Catskill Culture: A Mountain Rat's Memories of the Grand Jewish Resort Area.* Philadelphia: Temple University Press.

Brown, P. (2002). *In the Catskills. A Century of Jewish Experience in the Mountains.* New York: Columbia University Press.

Bynum, J. E., & Thompson, W. E. (1992). *Juvenile Delinquency: A Sociological Approach.* Boston: Allyn and Bacon.

Dabney, D. A., & Berg, B. L. (1994). Perceptions of drug and supply diversion among nurses. *Free Inquiry in Creative Sociology 22*(1), 13–22.

Denzin, N. K. (1978). *Sociological Methods: A Source Book* (2nd ed.). New York: McGraw-Hill.

Denzin, N. (1992). *Cultural Studies and Symbolic Interactionism: The Politics of Interpretation.* London: Blackwell.

Denzin, N., & Lincoin, Y. S. (2005). *The Sage Handbook of Qualitative Research* (3rd ed.). Thousand Oaks, CA: Sage.

Denzin, N., & Lincoin, Y. S. (2003). *Strategies of Qualitative Inquiry* (3rd ed.). Thousand Oaks, CA: Sage.

Flick, U. (1998). *An Introduction to Qualitative Research.* Newbury Park, CA: Sage.

Frankfort-Nachmias, C., & Nachmias, D. (1996). *Research Methods in the Social Sciences* (5th ed.). New York: St. Martin's Press.

Frankfort-Nachmias, C., & Nachmais D. (2000). *Research Methods in the Social Sciences* (6th ed.). New York: W. H. Freeman.

Hagan, F. E. (2006). *Research Methods in Criminal Justice and Criminology* (7th ed.). Boston: MA. Allyn and Bacon.

Heckathorn, D. D. & Jeffri, J. (2003). Social movements of jazz musicians. In *Changing the Beat: A Study of the Work Life of Jazz Musicians, Volume III: Respondent-Driven Sampling: Survey Results by the Research Center for Arts and Culture.* Research Division Report 43, pages 48–61. National Endowment for the Arts, Washington, D.C.

Huberman, M. A., & Miles, M. B. (1994). Data management and analysis methods. In N. Denzin & Y. S. Lincoln (Eds.), *Handbook of Qualitative Research.* Thousand Oaks, CA: Sage.

Janesick, V. J. (1994). The dance of qualitative research design. In N. Denzin and Y. S. Lincoln (Eds.), *Handbook of Qualitative Research.* Thousand Oaks, CA: Sage.

Lee, R. M. (1993). *Doing Research on Sensitive Topics.* Newbury Park, CA: Sage.

Leedy, P. D. (2001). *Practical Research: Planning and Design* (7th ed.). Upper Saddle River, NJ: Prentice Hall.

Leedy, P., & Ormrod, J. E. (2004). *Practical Research: Planning and Design* (8th ed.). Upper Saddle River, NJ: Prentice Hall.

Levine, H. G. (1985). Principles of data storage and retrieval for use in qualitative evaluation. *Educational Evaluation and Policy Analysis 7*(2), 169–186.

Lincoln, Y. S., & Guba, E. G. (1985). *Naturalistic Inquiry.* Beverly Hills, CA: Sage.

Marshall, C., & Rossman, G. B. (1999). *Designing Qualitative Research* (3rd ed.). Newbury Park, CA: Sage.

Maxfield, M. G., & Babbie, E. (2001). *Research Methods for Criminal Justice and Criminology.* Belmont, CA: Wadsworth.

McTavish, D. G., & Loether, H. J. (2002). *Social Research: An Evolving Process* (2nd ed.). Boston: Allyn and Bacon.

Merton, R. K. (1968). *Social Theory and Social Structure* (Rev. and Enlarged ed.). New York: Free Press.

Morse, J. M., & Richards, L. (2002). *Read Me First: For a User's Guide to Qualitative Methods.* Thousand Oaks, CA: Sage.

Mutchnick, R. J., & Berg, B. L. (1996). *Research Methods for the Social Sciences: Practice and Applications.* Boston: Allyn and Bacon.

Nachmias, C. F., & Nachmias, D. (1992). *Research Methods in the Social Sciences* (4th ed.). New York: St. Martin's Press.

Neuman, W. L. (2000) *Social Research Methods: Qualitative and Quantitative Approaches.* Boston: Allyn & Bacon.

Owen, B. (2005). Personal Communication at the Western Society of Criminology Meeting, Oahu, Hawaii, February, 2005.

Penrod, J., Preston, D. B., Cain, R. E., & Stark, M. T. (2003). A discussion of chain referral as a method of sampling hard-to-reach populations. *Journal of Transcultural Nursing 14*(2), 100–107.

Peterson, S. (1998). The influence of teachers' perceptions of gender on the evaluation of grade three, six, and nine students' narrative writing. *Alberta English 36*(1), 42–56.

Peterson, S. (2001). Gender identities and self-expression in classroom narrative writing. *Language Arts 78*(5), 451–457.

Polit, D., Beck, C. T., & Hungler, B. P. (2003). *Nursing Research: Principles and Practice* (7th ed.). Philadelphia: Lippincott Williams & Wilkins.

Polit, D. F., & Hungler, B. P. (1993). *Essentials of Nursing Research.* Philadelphia: J. B. Lippincott.

Popper, K. R. (1968). *Conjectures and Refutations: The Growth of Scientific Knowledge.* New York: Harper and Row.

Reynolds. L. T., & Herman-Kinney, N. J. (2003). *Handbook of Social Interactionism.* New York: Rowman & Littlefield.

Rounds, D. (1993). Perceptions of crime and victimization among individuals with legal blindness and severe visual impairment: An exploratory study. Doctoral dissertation. Department of Criminology, Indiana University of Pennsylvania, Indiana, PA.

SCEDC. (2005). Southern California Earthquake Data Center. Available online at: http://www.data.scec.org/index.html.

Senese, J. D. (1997). *Applied Research Methods in Criminal Justice.* Chicago: Nelson-Hall.

Siegel, L. J., & Senna, J. J. (1988). *Juvenile Delinquency: Theory, Practice, and Law* (3rd ed.). St. Paul: West Publishing.

Silverman, D. (1999). *Qualitative Research: A Practical Handbook.* Newbury Park, CA: Sage.

SpoofStick (2005). "Browse Freely but carry a SpoofStick." CoreStreet. Available online at: http://www.corestreet.com/spoofstick.

Taylor, S. J., & Bogdan, R. (1998). *Qualitative Research Methods* (3rd ed.). New York: Wiley and Sons, Inc.

Teo, P. K. (1998). *Investment patterns in the electronics industry.* Unpublished Bachelor's Honors thesis, National University of Singapore.

Thornton, W. E., Jr., & Voigt, L. (1992). *Delinquency and Justice* (3rd ed.). New York: McGraw-Hill.

Turner, J. H. (1989). *Theory Building in Sociology: Assessing Theoretical Cumulation.* Newbury Park, CA: Sage.

Wolfe, R. (1992). Data management. In M. C. Alkin (Ed.), *Encyclopedia of Educational Research Vol. 1* (6th ed.), 293–299. New York: Macmillan.

Wright, R., Decker, S. H., Redfern, A. K., & Smith, D. L. (2006). A snowball's chance in hell: Doing fieldwork with active residential burglars. In J. Mitchell Miller & Richard Tewksbury (Eds.), *Research Methods: A Qualitative Reader.* Upper Saddle River, NJ: Pearson/Prentice Hall.

Chapter 3

Ethical Issues

S OCIAL SCIENTISTS, PERHAPS TO a greater extent than the average citizen, have an ethical obligation to their colleagues, their study population, and the larger society. The reason for this is that social scientists delve into the social lives of other human beings. From such excursions into private social lives, various policies, practices, and even laws may result. Thus, researchers must ensure the rights, privacy, and welfare of the people and communities that form the focus of their studies.

During the past several decades, methods of data collection, organization, and analysis have become more sophisticated and penetrating. As a consequence, the extent or scope of research has become greatly expanded. With this expansion has come increased awareness and concern over the ethics of research and researchers.

To a large extent concerns about research ethics revolve around various issues of harm, consent, privacy, and the confidentiality of data (Punch, 1994). This chapter considers these important ethical concerns as associated with research in general and with qualitative research in particular.

As Babbie (1983) accurately points out, "All of us consider ourselves ethical; not perfect perhaps, but more ethical than most of humanity." Unfortunately, one problem in social science is that ethical considerations are subjective. Researchers eager to gain access to some population that might otherwise be difficult to reach may really not see that their plans are unethical. Some overly zealous researchers, while realizing that certain of their practices may be unethical, nonetheless plunge forward, justifying their actions under the excuse that it isn't illegal!

Many experienced researchers can tell with regret war stories about having violated some tenet of ethics in their less experienced years. The transgression may have involved allowing some gatekeeper to manipulate subjects to take part in a study (under veiled threat of some loss of privilege), or it may have involved some covert investigation that resulted in subtle invasions of privacy. In any case, these now experienced researchers are still likely to feel somewhat embarrassed when they think about these instances—at least one hopes they do.

Often, glaring violations of ethical standards are recognized nearly as soon as the researchers have conceived them. Frequently, during planning stages, particularly when conducting research together with a colleague, ethical problems are identified and worked through. This is not to say that practices that might appear unethical to others outside the study are always eliminated. Rather, the process, like much of qualitative research, is a negotiation, a trade-off for the amount of access to subjects the researchers are willing to accept in exchange for the amount of ethical risk they are willing to take.

It is not difficult to understand that injecting unknowing subjects with live HIV or AIDS virus is unethical. It may not be quite as easy to see that studying drug dealers and then turning over their addresses and field notes as evidence to the police is also unethical. This latter example is somewhat more difficult to see because a law-abiding attitude is probably so well ingrained in most researchers that the logical response seems obvious—namely, if citizens can assist the police, they have a moral obligation to do so. However, precisely because such tensions between logic and ethics exist, careful consideration of ethical issues is critical to the success or failure of any high-quality research involving humans.

The first portion of this chapter examines some of the historical background of research ethics, including some of the major events that influenced current ethical research practices. Ethical elements commonly considered important when researchers involve human subjects in their research are then addressed.

Research Ethics in Historical Perspective

There are almost as many historical explanations for the current interest in research ethics as there are research books on college library shelves. Some authors point to the civil rights movement during the late 1950s and 1960s as having raised researchers' awareness of ethical issues (Barber, 1973). Other writers suggest that current concerns result from attempts to control federally funded research as available funds grew in quantum leaps following World War II (Smith, 1967; Sykes, 1967). Still others point to particular studies with especially questionable ethics as "controversial," or "provocative," creating concerns over the rights and welfare of human subjects (Babbie, 2004; Hagan, 2006) or the general need to protect human subjects (Bachman & Schutt, 2003; Champion, 2006; LoBiondo-Wood & Harber, 2002). Rosemarie Tong (2003) has directed attention toward feminist ethics, suggesting feminist ethics are an attempt to revise, reformulate, or rethink those aspects of traditional Western ethics that depreciate women's moral experience.

Regardless of one's orientation or thoughts on specific elements of ethical behavior and practice in research, there is general agreement in the literature that current concerns about research ethics grew out of biomedical research, particularly the ghoulish torture and dismemberment perpetrated under the guise of medical research by Nazi physicians and scientists during World War II. For instance, in the name of science, physicians exposed subjects to freezing temperatures, live viruses, poisons, malaria, and an assortment of untested drugs and experimental operations (Berger, 1990; Burns & Grove, 2000; Hagan, 2006; Trochim, 2001). This wartime medical research led in 1949 to the Nuremberg Code, which established principles for research on human subjects, most notably that subjects must *voluntarily consent* to participate in a research study (Wexler, 1990, p. 81).

This ethical canon became the foundation of the Declaration of Helsinki, adopted by the World Health Organization in 1964 and revised in 1975 (Levine, 1986). It was also the basis for the "Ethical Guidelines for Clinical Investigation" adopted by the American Medical Association in 1966 (Bower & de Gasparis, 1978). Yet, as Katz (1972) indicates, years later and thousands of miles away from the bloodstained walls of Nazi operating rooms, extremely risky—sometimes fatal—research was being carried out on unknowing patients here in the United States. Consider, for example, the case of two research physicians at the Brooklyn Jewish Chronic Disease Hospital, who during the mid-1960s injected a suspension containing live cancer cells into 22 unsuspecting elderly patients (Levine, 1986). Although media and public pressure brought an end to the experiment, neither physician was ever prosecuted on any sort of criminal charge (Hershey & Miller, 1976).

Interestingly, before the 1960s, few laws regulated the research process. As Bower and de Gasparis (1978) suggest, with the exception of medical malpractice laws, virtually no federal or state statutes regulated research. Consequently, no legal redress was available to subjects, even if they believed they had been wronged by a behavioral scientist. Highly questionable practices in research throughout the late 1950s and 1960s repeatedly demonstrated the need for regulation and control of studies involving human subjects.

For instance, the U.S. Public Health Service once conducted a study that is regarded by many as the most glaring violation of ethical practices. This project has come to be called the Tuskegee Syphilis Study (Brandt, 1978; Gray, 2002; Hagan, 2006; Jones, 1993; Roverby, 2000). This project, which spanned more than 40 years, was a longitudinal study whose purpose was to identify a population of syphilitic black men and to observe in these subjects, over a period of time, the consequences of untreated syphilis. One of the study's original creators is attributed as having made the following prophetic statements about the project: "It will cover us with mud or glory when completed" (Jones, 1993, p. 112). Today many would likely agree that the project did indeed cover the researchers and the U.S. Public Health Service with mud.

Although the researchers on the study did not themselves infect the subjects, once the study had begun, the investigative team actively interfered with the lives and health of the subjects without their consent (Jones, 1993). The study began in 1932 when no cure for syphilis existed. After a cure (penicillin) was identified in the 1950s, the research team actively sought to keep the existence of the treatment from their subjects. This included offering free so-called treatment and health services to the sample of men, as well as contacting local African American physicians and instructing them not to treat (for syphilis) any of the 400 men involved in the study.

To ensure that an autopsy could be done on any subject who died during the experiment, the team offered free burial services. Surviving family members typically were unaware that free burial was conditional on allowing an autopsy. The study ended in 1972 after it was exposed by the news media and public pressure forced officials to terminate the study. Estimates of the number of men who died directly from advanced syphilis range from 28 to 100 subjects (Brandt, 1978). Shortly after termination of the study, the Department of Health, Education, and Welfare (the parent agency of the U.S. Public Health Service) appointed a panel that concluded that the research had been "ethically unjustified."

On May 16, 1997, 65 years after it had begun—and 23 years after it had ended—President Clinton publicly apologized to the families of the subjects, and the eight surviving subjects in the Tuskegee Syphilis Study (Clinton, 1997). In his remarks, President Clinton stated:

> The eight men who are survivors of the syphilis study at Tuskegee are a living link to a time not so very long ago that many Americans would prefer not to remember, but we dare not forget. It was a time when our nation failed to live up to its ideals, when our nation broke the trust with people that is the very foundation of our democracy. It is not only in remembering that shameful past that we can make amends and repair our nation, but it is in remembering that past that we can build a better present and better future. And without remembering it, we cannot make amends and we cannot go forward.
>
> So, today America does remember the hundreds of men used in research without their knowledge and consent. We remember them and their family members. Men who were poor and African American, without resources and

with few alternatives, they believed they had found hope when they were offered free medical care by the United States Public Health Service. They were betrayed.

The United States government did something wrong—deeply, profoundly, morally wrong. It was an outrage to our commitment to integrity and equality for all our citizens.

To the survivors, to the wives and family members, the children and grandchildren, I say what you know: no power on Earth can give you back the lives lost, the pain suffered, the years of internal torment and anguish. What was done cannot be undone. But we can end the silence. We can stop turning our heads away. We can look at you in the eye and finally say on behalf of the American people, what the United States government did was shameful, and I am sorry.

Although the president's remarks were a good beginning to restoring confidence in poor ethnic communities, the "negative legacy" of the Tuskegee study continues to impede researchers' efforts to conduct an assortment of research projects, particularly those involving minorities (Shalala, 1997).

Many other biomedical experiments conducted during the sixties were also "ethically unjustified" (Hershey & Miller, 1976), and during this same period, many behavioral scientists were involved in potentially ethically unjustified research as well—for example, Stanley Milgram's experiment on following orders and control. Milgram (1963) was interested in learning about human tendencies to obey authority figures. To observe this phenomenon, he told voluntary subjects that they were to teach another person, supposedly another volunteer subject, a simple word-association task. The other volunteer, however, was actually another investigator on the study.

The subject/teacher was instructed by Milgram to administer an electric shock to the learner (the confederate in an adjacent room) whenever the learner made a mistake. The subject/teacher was told that this electric shock was intended to facilitate learning and should be increased in intensity progressively with each error. Many of the subjects obediently (in fact, gleefully) advanced the shock levels to potentially lethal levels.

In reality, the supposed learner received no shocks at all. Rather, each time the subject/teacher administered a shock, a signal indicated that the learner should react as if shocked. Nonetheless, the deception aroused considerable emotional anguish and guilt in the subjects.

In another study, regarded by many social scientists to be as controversial as the Milgram study, Philip Zimbardo (1972) sought to examine the interaction patterns of inmates and guards. His experiment involved a simulated prison where groups of paid volunteer students at Stanford University were designated as either inmates or guards. For this study, Zimbardo constructed a model jail facility in the basement of one of the university buildings.

The design of the study called for those students who were assigned to the inmate role to be arrested by campus police and brought to the jail facility. There they were instructed to change into prison jumpsuits and were placed in cells. The guards were other students who were garbed in uniforms and were issued night sticks. The study was intended to run for a 2-week period, during which time Zimbardo expected to watch the students act out their various roles as inmates and guards. However, within the first 24 hours, as guards became increasingly abusive and inmates grew more hostile toward their keepers, verbal altercations began to break out between several of the inmates and guards, escalating to a physical altercation between one of the guards and inmates. Within 48 hours, the inmates had begun planning and executing their first escape. In just under 72 hours, Zimbardo realized that the students had overplayed their expected roles, and the experiment was called off.

Dean Champion (2006, pp. 518–519) recounts another research study of questionable ethics. This study, commonly known as the CIA's ARTICHOKE program, was undertaken by the Central Intelligence Agency of the United States government. The study sought to uncover ways to control peoples' behavior. According to Champion (2006, p. 519):

> A CIA memo dated January 25, 1952, indicated that a program, ARTICHOKE was underway and that its primary objectives were the evaluation and development of any methods by which we can get information from a person against his will and without his knowledge.

Another component of the study was to control peoples' behavior through use of drugs and chemicals that could create psychological and physiological changes. These included the use of electroshock, LSD, hypnosis, and various drugs thought to induce memory loss and amnesia. Apparently, these drugs and activities were administered to unwitting citizens and members of the armed forces.

In 1963, the CIA was forced to deal with the public disclosure of its efforts after several news agencies carried stories about this study. Naturally, the study was brought to a close. However, professional organizations such as the American Psychological Association and the American Sociological Association sought explanations for how ARTICHOKE could have been carried on for so long without the public being informed about its existence (Champion, 2006). Many social scientists continue today to question how the CIA could have enlisted so many psychologists and other social scientists to assist them in this rather blatantly unethical course of action in the ARTICHOKE study.

Another example of research with questionable ethical tactics is Humphreys's (1970) study of casual homosexual encounters called *Tearoom Trade*. Humphreys was interested in gaining understanding not only about practicing homosexuals but also about heterosexuals who briefly engaged in homosexual encounters. In addition to observing encounters in public restrooms in parks (tearooms), Humphreys developed a way to gain access to detailed information about the subjects he covertly observed.

While serving as a watch queen (a voyeuristic lookout), Humphreys was able to observe the encounters and to catch a glimpse of the participants' car license plates. Once Humphreys had their license plate numbers, he was able to locate their home addresses through the local department of motor vehicles. Next, he disguised himself and deceived these men into believing that he was conducting a survey in their neighborhood. The result was that Humphreys managed to collect considerable amounts of information about each of the subjects he had observed in the tearooms.

Shortly after the publication of Humphreys's work in 1970, there was a considerable outcry against the invasion of privacy, misrepresentation of researcher identities, and deception commonly being practiced during the course of research. Many of the controversies that revolve around Humphreys's research remain key ethical issues today. Paramount among these issues are the justifications that the subject matter was of critical importance to the scientific community and that it simply could not have been investigated in any other manner.

Naturally, this begs the question of considering the potential benefit of a research project weighed against the potential harm. This utilitarian argument essentially sets up a kind of scale in which risk and harm are placed on one side and benefits are placed on the other side (see Figure 3.1). If the determination is that the amount of benefit outweighs the amount of

Figure 3.1 The Research Risk/Benefit Scale

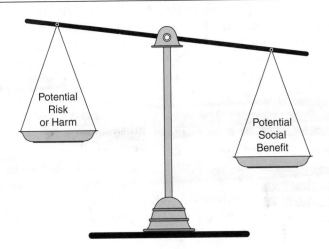

potential risk or harm, then the research may be seen from an ethical point of view as permissible (Taylor, 1994). This notion, of course, assumes that there is no potential serious risk of harm, injury, or death possible for any research subject.

In the case of Humphreys's study, there are many researchers who maintain that the social, legal, and psychological policy changes that have resulted far outweigh any minor invasions of privacy. This is not to suggest that there are not other researchers who argue that the research was unethical no matter how great the benefits have been.

From Guidelines to Law: Regulations on the Research Process

Early attempts to devise rigorous biomedical experimentation guidelines failed. One major reason was the inability to develop a single code of ethics that, as Bower and de Gasparis (1978, p. 5) put it, "could cover with equal adequacy and flexibility the entire range of biomedical experimentation." However, in 1966, the surgeon general issued what may have been the first official rules concerning all Public Health Service research. This statement specified that any research financially supported by the Public Health Service was contingent on a review by an institutional committee. The committee was charged with the responsibility of ensuring that study procedures would not harm human subjects and that subjects were informed of any potential risks (and benefits) from their participation.

Several revisions of this general policy occurred from 1967 to 1969. Finally, in 1971, the Department of Health, Education, and Welfare (DHEW) published a booklet entitled "The Institutional Guide to DHEW Policy on Protection of Human Subjects," which extended the requirement of an institutional review committee to all DHEW grant and contract activities involving human subjects. In addition, this booklet required researchers to obtain *informed consent* from subjects before including them in the research.

In 1974, the National Research Act was passed by Congress, and the National Commission on Protection of Human Subjects of Biomedical and Behavioral Research was created by Title II of this law. The National Research Act directed all institutions that sponsored research to establish institutional review committees, today more commonly called *institutional review boards* (IRBs). Locally based in-house IRBs were now charged with the responsibility of carefully reviewing any proposed research that involved human subjects.

Among several other issues, IRBs were expected to ensure that research investigators had considered both potential risks and benefits to subjects, that important scientific knowledge could be derived from the project, that legally informed consent would be obtained from each subject, and that the rights and interests of subjects were protected (Liemohn, 1979).

Another important piece of research-related legislation is the education amendments of 1974. These laws, better known as the Buckley Amendments, were intended to protect the privacy of parents and students (Holden, 1975). In essence, these laws limited access to official records concerning (and identifying) an individual, and they prohibited release of such personal information (with some exceptions) to anyone else without written consent of the student (and the parent in the case of minors).

Finally, the Privacy Acts of 1974 offered additional legal assurances against invasive research on human subjects. This legislation was primarily designed to protect citizens from large private corporations and federal institutions and from the release of potentially erroneous information and records. In addition, however, it provided individuals with judicial machinery for redressing indiscriminate sharing of personal information and records without prior written consent—including when obtained by deceptive researchers. A fair number of these regulations are informally overseen by institutional review boards. Let us consider IRBs in greater detail.

Institutional Review Boards (IRBs)

Whenever someone brings up the topic of institutional review boards, he or she runs the risk of evoking strong feelings among social science researchers. Some researchers see IRBs as handcuffs impeding their search for scientific answers to social problems. Some researchers simply believe that contemporary IRBs have grown too big for their breeches and that they tend to overstep their perceived purpose and limits. Other researchers say IRBs are staffed with clinicians unable to understand the nuances of certain social scientific styles of research. Indeed, there are many who view IRBs as villains rather than as necessary—let alone virtuous—institutions. Ideally, IRBs should be seen as a group of individuals who selflessly give their time and expertise to ensure that human subjects are neither physically nor emotionally injured by researchers. Ironically, while few researchers today really believe that IRBs are not necessary, these same individuals are likely to view IRBs in less than positive terms.

In the academic community of the new millennium, research continues to uphold its position as a critically important element. Fundamentally, and somewhat altruistically, research still holds the promise of important revelations for collective thinking and changes for the better in society. At a more prag-matic level, social science research, especially federally funded studies, offer the academician opportunities for publication that, in turn, form the rungs in aca-demic promotion and tenure ladders. Furthermore, the new millennium has brought with it a wave of new ethical challenges with the advent of Internet-based research. With these new challenges many researchers are vividly reminded of the problems that are today apparent in the research studies of the recent past that exploited human subjects in deplorable ways. The question that remains unanswered, however, is: Exactly what are the institutional review boards' duties in the new millennium?

IRBs and Their Duties

Among the important elements considered by IRB panels is the assurance of informed consent. Usually, this involves requirements for obtaining written informed consent from potential subjects. This requirement has drawn heavy critical fire from social scientists (Fields, 1978; Gray, 1977; Meyer, 1977). Qualitative researchers, especially those involved in ethnographic research, have been particularly vocal. Their concerns often pertain to the way that formal requirements for institutional review and written informed consent damage their special field-worker/informant relationships (Berg et al., 1992; Cassell, 1978; Taylor & Bogdan, 1998; Wax, 1977).

The National Commission for the Protection of Human Subjects, created by the National Research Act of 1974, has reviewed its own guidelines (Depart-ment of Health, Education, and Welfare, 1978a) and offered revisions (*Federal Register*, 1978). These revisions are more specific about the role the IRB should play than previous documents were. For example, the *Federal Register* states that board members may be liable for legal action if they exceed their authority and interfere with the investigator's right to conduct research. These revised guidelines also recommend that the requirement for written informed consent could be waived for certain types of low-risk styles of research.

Because their research procedures are more formalized and require con-tacts with subjects, the more limited and predictable characteristics of quanti-tative methodologies are generally simpler to define. As a result, the specific exemptions for styles of research that can be expedited through IRBs largely are quantitative survey types, observation in public places, research involving educational tests (diagnostic, aptitude, or achievement), and archival research (Department of Health, Education, and Welfare, 1978b).

The temporary (usually single visit) and formal nature of most quantita-tive data-gathering strategies makes them easier to fit into federal regulations. In quantitative research, confidentiality is also rather easy to ensure. Written consent slips can be separated out from surveys and secured in innovative ways. It becomes a simple task to ensure that names or other identifiers will not be connected in any way with the survey response sheets.

Qualitative research, especially ethnographic strategies, present greater challenges to IRBs. To be sure, most qualitative researchers will make every effort to comply with federal regulations for the protection of human subjects. However, compliance is not always easy. In order to ensure consistency, lists of names are sometimes maintained even when pseudonyms are used in field notes. Furthermore, the very nature of ethnographic research makes it ideal for studying secret, deviant, or difficult-to-study populations. Consider, for example, drug smugglers (Adler, 1985) or crack dealers (Jacobs, 1998). It would be almost impossible to locate sufficient numbers of drug smugglers or crack dealers to create a probability sampling or to administer a meaningful number of survey questionnaires. Imagine, now, that you also needed to secure written informed-consent slips. It is not likely that anyone could manage these restrictions. In fact, the researcher's personal safety might be jeopardized even by announcing his or her presence (overt observation). It is similarly unlikely that you would have much success trying to locate a suffi- cient number of patrons of pornographic bookstores to administer question- naires. Yet observational and ethnographic techniques might work very well (see, e.g., Tewksbury, 1990).

Many qualitative researchers have arrived at the same conclusion about the relationship between researcher and subjects in qualitative research— namely, that the qualitative relationship is so different from quantitative approaches that most conventional procedures for informed consent and pro- tection of human subjects amount to little more than ritual (Bogdan & Biklen, 1992, 2003). For example, Tewksbury (1995) located voluntary participants for a study of sex and danger in men's same-sex, in-public encounters by post- ing notices on social service agency bulletin boards, college campuses, and through personal contacts (a variation of snowballing, discussed in Chapter 2). Berg and colleagues (2004) located a population of Latino men who have sex with men (MSMs) in an HIV outreach support group and worked with out- reach workers who already had rapport with these MSMs to invite them to take part in an interview study. In effect, the qualitative research typically has a substantially different relationship with his or her subjects and one markedly distinct from the more abstract and sterile relationship most quantitative researchers have with theirs.

In the kind of research for which these guidelines are written, subjects have very circumscribed relationships. The researcher presents some survey or questionnaire to the subjects who in turn fill it out. Or the researcher describes the requirements of participation in some experiment, and the subject participates. In these quantitative modes of research, it is a fairly easy task to predict and describe to the subject the content of the study and the possible risks from participation. As Janice Morse suggests, at some institutions, the IRB requires distribution of a "Bill of Rights" whenever a subject is included in an experiment (Morse, 1994, p. 338).

With qualitative research, on the other hand, the relationship between researcher and subject is frequently an ongoing and evolving one. Doing qualitative research with subjects is more like being permitted to observe or take part in the lives of these subjects. At best, it may be seen as a social contract. But, as in all contracts, both parties have some say about the contents of the agreement and in regulating the relationship. Although it is not difficult to predict possible risks in quantitative survey studies, this task can be quite a problem in some qualitative research projects.

Consider, for example, a study in which a researcher seeks to observe the gambling behavior of people while drinking alcohol at taverns (McSkimming, 1996). Can the researcher actually determine whether people who are drinking alcohol and gambling as part of their social worlds will be at risk because the researcher is present in the same tavern watching them? Certainly, any time people consume alcohol and engage in something as volatile as gambling there is the potential for violence. From the standpoint of the IRB, a declaration from the researcher that there is no greater risk to subjects because the researcher is present observing their behaviors is likely to be sufficient; in short, the research project itself does not increase or cause risk. Of course, this does nothing to diminish the usual risk of these behaviors.

Consider also a study similar to McSkimming's. In the Nguyen (2003) study, the researcher sought to examine illegal gambling in a Vietnamese café. Nguyen visited a café known to be a location where local Vietnamese residents went to play illegal poker machines. While he had the permission of the café owner to be there, none of the players were aware of his intention to observe their gambling for a research study. Again, in itself, Nguyen's presence in the café did not alter the risks to these gamblers' (or the café owner's) of being apprehended by police should there be a raid. But the IRB to which Nguyen submitted took considerable convincing that this project would not in some way harm subjects.

Some researchers, confronted with such daunting tasks to convince IRBs of the risk-free nature of their research, have simply thrown in the towel and, in order to avoid confrontations, simply never researched certain controversial topics. That is, these researchers may have taken the moral position that not all topics are appropriate for academic study. This, however, could lead to a serious problem.

Clarifying the Role of IRBs

Initially, IRBs were charged with the responsibility to review the adequacy of consent procedures for the protection of human subjects in research funded by the U.S. DHEW. This mandate was soon broadened to include a review of all research conducted in an institution receiving any funds from DHEW—even when the study itself did not (Burstein, 1987; Department of Health, Education, and Welfare, 1989).

Part of the IRBs' duties was to ensure that subjects in research studies were advised of both the potential risks from participation and the possible benefits. This task seems to have evolved among some IRBs to become an assessment of risk-to-benefit ratios of proposed studies. In some cases, this is based on the IRB's impression of the worth of the study. In other cases, this may be based on the IRB's presumed greater knowledge of the subject and methodological strategies than potential subjects are likely to possess (Bailey, 1996; Burstein, 1987). Thus, in many cases, IRBs, and not subjects, determine whether the subject will even have the option of participating or declining to participate in a study.

According to the *Code of Federal Regulations* (CFR, 1993, Article 45, Part 46, 101–110), there are a number of research situations that do not require a full-blown institutional review. These projects are subject to what may be termed an *expedited review*. Expedited reviews may involve a read-through and determination by the chair or a designated IRB committee member rather than review by the full committee. Usually, studies entitled to an expedited review are evaluations of educational institutions that examine normal educational practices, organizational effectiveness, instructional techniques, curricula, or classroom management strategies.

Other types of research subject areas may receive an expedited review or no review, depending on the specific institutional rules of a given university or research organization. These areas include certain survey procedures, interview procedures, or observations of public behavior. The CFR provisions that exclude research areas from review state:

1. The information obtained is recorded in such a manner that the participants cannot be identified.
2. Any disclosure of the participants' response outside the research cannot reasonably identify the subject.
3. The study and its results do not place the participant at risk of criminal or civil liability, nor will it be damaging to the participant's financial standing, employability, or reputation (for example, an observational study in which subjects are not identified).

4. The research will be conducted on preexisting data, documents, records, pathological specimens, or diagnostic specimens, provided these items are publicly available or if the information is recorded by the investigator in such a manner that subjects cannot be identified.

In effect, the governmental regulations as established by the CFR allow certain types of research to be undertaken without any review by an IRB and rather depend on the professional codes or ethics of the researcher or on the various more restrictive rules of a particular university or research organization.

Today, many IRBs have further extended their reach to include evaluation of methodological strategies, not, as one might expect, as these methods pertain to human subject risks but in terms of the project's methodological adequacy. The justification for this, apparently, is that even when minimum risks exist, if a study is designed poorly, it will not yield any scientific benefit (Berg et al., 1992).

During the past several years IRBs seem to have begun to moralize rather than assess the potential harm to subjects. As an example, consider the following situation that arose recently during an IRB review of a proposal at a mid-sized university on the East Coast. The project was designed to examine ethnographically the initiation of cigarette smoking and alcohol consumption among middle school and high school youths. The design called for identified field researchers to spend time in public places observing youths. The idea was to observe how smoking and alcohol fit into the social worlds of these youths.

Several IRB committee members were extremely concerned that ethnographers would be watching children smoking and drinking without notifying their parents of these behaviors. During a review of this proposal with the investigator, these committee members argued that it was unthinkable that no intervention would be taken on the part of the field-workers. They recommended that the researchers tell the youths' parents that they were engaging in these serious behaviors. The investigator explained that this would actually be a breach of confidentiality and potentially expose the subjects to serious risk of corporal punishment.

One committee member asked, What if the youth was observed smoking crack; wouldn't the field-worker tell his or her parents then? The investigator reminded the committee that these observations were to be in public places. The field-workers did not have a responsibility to report to the parents what their children were doing—no matter how potentially unhealthy it may be. The investigator further explained that there was no legal requirement to inform on these subjects, and, in fact, to do so would make the research virtually impossible to conduct. The committee member agreed that there may be no legal requirement but went on to argue that there certainly was a moral one!

Eventually, a compromise was struck. The researcher agreed to include a statement in the proposal indicating that if the field-workers observed what they believed were children engaging in behavior that would likely result in immediate and serious personal injury or imminent death, they would intervene. Of course, such a statement seemed unnecessary for the researcher, because it was already agreed on by the research team. It did, however, appease the committee members who continued to grumble that the parents should be informed about their children's behavior.

Active Versus Passive Consent

Another type of moralizing has arisen over the controversy surrounding active versus passive informed consent by parents of children involved in research and, more recently, surrounding research conducted on the Internet. Active consent may be defined as the "formal written permission by an informed parent or legal guardian that allows a child to participate in a research project" (Deschenes & Vogel, 1995). Passive consent is usually based on the assumption that parental permission is granted if parents do not return a refusal form after being informed about the study's purpose (Deschenes & Vogel, 1995; Eaton, Lowry, Brener, Grunbaum, & Kahn, 2004; Ellickson & Hawes, 1989).

Even the federal government has gotten into the picture. In 1995, it began considering a bill that would require active consent for research involving children. If this legislation had passed, it would have put a considerable damper on the research undertaken by many educational researchers.

In the past, researchers who have employed an active consent style have reported that it yields unacceptably low response rates. This translates into the underrepresentation of relevant study subjects, often the very ones involved in or at risk from the study behaviors (Kearney et al., 1983; Severson & Ary, 1983; Thompson, 1984).

To avoid excluding relevant study subjects, many researchers have turned to the passive consent method (Ellickson & Hawes, 1989). The moral question here rests on the argument that passive procedures do not fully inform parents about the research or give them sufficient opportunities to refuse participation. Some researchers question whether parents have actually intentionally decided to allow their child to participate and have consciously not sent in the refusal notice. In this case, one might interpret nonresponse as more of an indicator of sloppy or lackadaisical parental attitudes—but not necessarily consent.

Active consent requires informed consent rigor that may be too stringent for many qualitative research endeavors. This is especially true because most qualitative projects implement a series of diligent data safeguards, such as removal of identifiers, to ensure confidentiality. Carefully designed passive consent procedures can avoid various negative consequences of active consent, while still ensuring parents are being informed.

The use of active consent begs the question of how extensive it must be and how it should be implemented in qualitative research. For example, if an investigator is interested in observing the interactions between children at play and during their studies, how extensive would the active consent need to be? Certainly, if observations are being made in a classroom, all of the parents would need to be notified, but would all have to actively agree before the researcher could enter the room? If one parent said no, would that mean that the child could not be included in the researcher's notes or that the research could not be undertaken? If the researcher wanted to observe this class of children on the playground, would he or she need the active consent of the parents of every child in the school?

Recently, the issue of active and passive consent made headlines, when New Jersey passed a law stating that all research undertaken in New Jersey schools requires the active consent of parents. Put quite simply, if parents do not say yes, their child cannot take part in the research (Wetzstein, 2002). The controversy originated for New Jersey students and parents in 1999 when a survey containing over 156 questions was administered to more than 2,000 public middle school and high school students in Ridgewood, New Jersey. The survey asked teens about their sexual activity, birth control use, drug and alcohol use, cigarette smoking habits, binge eating, depression, suicide, stealing, physical violence, and relationships with family members and friends (Viadero, 2002).

The problem with such active consent requirements, as previously indicated, is that 20 to 30 percent of parents typically fail to return the consent forms. This can result in serious problems with study samples, causing researchers to drop certain schools from their studies because of low response rates from potential subjects' parents.

Again, these concerns do seem to direct themselves more to quantitative than to qualitative research studies. To a certain extent, a qualitative research effort might find it less problematic to not have all the parents' consent and to simply exclude children whose parents have not provided their permission for, say, an interview. It is not as simple, however, to exclude youths from school-based observational studies. Thus, if an investigator desires to undertake this type of research, under the New Jersey law of active consent, he or she would not be able to do so. Naturally this suggests, once more, the push toward what some might call *vanilla* research or "research of the sterile and mundane."

Active Versus Passive Consent in Internet Research

The Internet is an enormously comprehensive electronic archive of written and audible materials representing a vast array of peoples' opinions, concerns, life stories, hobbies, and lifestyles. Novice researchers who surf the Internet are sometimes shocked to see the varied Web sites established by laypeople, physicians, lawyers, academicians, musicians, and individuals and groups from all walks of life and representing most (if not all) social roles one can think of. Materials on these sites can be a rich source of data for social scientists interested in understanding the lives, experiences, and views of people. As discussed later in this book, there are a number of ways researchers can access and use data via the Internet. Among the several ways data can be solicited via the Internet are electronic surveys and electronic interviews (Bachman & Schutt, 2003; Eysenbach & Wyatt, 2002). Dillman (2000) suggests the e-mail survey is one method by which researchers can provide potential subjects with an instrument to complete via e-mail address and ask them to return the completed device. In terms of consent, one can certainly send along the survey with a description of the study and a statement to be checked off to indicate *informed consent.*

Web surveys, according to Bachman & Schutt (2003), are a variation on this data-collection strategy. Surveys are placed on a server controlled by the researcher, and potential respondents are invited to visit the Web site and complete the instrument. A description of the study can be provided, and the act of the subject going to the site and completing the survey can serve as a variation on passive consent.

Electronic interviews (see Chapter 4), once the interviewer and subject agree and informed consent is obtained either in person or online, can be undertaken through the use of private chat rooms where both the interviewer and the subject interact in real time, asking and answering questions over the Internet. Again, with regard to informed consent, information about the study can be transmitted to the subject's e-mail, and agreement to take part in the interview can be obtained at that time or, to maintain anonymity, during the course of the interview, once the interviewer directs the subject to the chat room. The inclusion of the Internet in qualitative research certainly opens innovative doors for research strategies. However, it also presents new problems for IRBs. Members of IRBs must now be versed in both traditional research orientations and those involving variations on Internet technology; they also must deal with an assortment of ethical and even moralistic problems. A reasonable question to ask is, Who in his or her right mind would want to serve on such a panel? This, however, brings us to the question of exactly who does serve on the review boards.

Membership Criteria for IRBs

The federal regulations specify that "each IRB shall have at least five members with varying backgrounds to promote complete and adequate review of research activities commonly conducted by the institution" (*Code of Federal Regulations*, 1993, p. 7). There are also provisions that IRBs should not be composed entirely of women, men, single racial groups, or one profession. Furthermore, each IRB should contain at least one member whose primary work does not include the sciences or social sciences (e.g., lawyers, ethicists, or members of the clergy). However, federal guidelines do not articulate how to select or locate IRB members, what research qualifications members should have, what lengths members' terms should be, or how to establish an IRB chairperson. The federal regulations do require that "assurances" be submitted to the Office for Protection from Research Risks, National Institutes of Health.

Among these assurances must be a list of IRB members' names, their "earned degrees; representative capacity; indications of experience such as board certifications, licenses, etc." (*Code of Federal Regulations*, 1993, p. 6). While no suggestion is given about what types of degrees people should have in order to sit on the IRB, the allusion to board certification or licenses does convey the notion of clinicians rather than social scientists. While many social scientists may believe that their institution's IRB is composed of clinicians, it is likely that it is not. The possibility may exist, however, that members of IRBs themselves have never conducted research on human subjects or, for that matter, conducted any research. The federal regulations do not require that IRB members have a research history; hence, the situation that some do not is quite conceivable.

Institutional review boards are really still in their infancy. They are certainly a necessary element in maintaining safe and ethical research in the social sciences. Exactly what their role should be, who should hold board positions, and what scientific role they should play in the research community remain to be worked out.

There are no quick fixes for establishing IRBs that are able to ensure both safety to human subjects and unhampered research opportunities for investigators. As the serious ethical infractions that occurred before the advance of IRBs demonstrate, social scientists left to their own designs sometimes go astray. On the other hand, researchers may be correct in their stance that IRBs left to their own devices may grow too restrictive. Nonetheless, IRBs should be able to operate in concert with researchers rather than in opposition to them. Social scientists need to become more involved in the IRB process and seek ways to implement board goals and membership policies that are responsive to changing times, social values, and research technologies.

Ethical Codes

During the past several decades, changing social attitudes about research as well as changing legislation have led professional associations to create codes of ethical conduct. For example, the American Nurses' Association developed *Human Rights Guidelines for Nurses in Clinical and Other Research* (1975). The American Sociological Association produced its code of ethics during the early 1980s (American Sociological Association, 1984, 1992). Ethical guidelines for psychologists emerged in the American Psychological Association (1981) in a document entitled "Ethical Principles of Psychologists" and again in a document entitled "Ethical Principles in the Conduct of Research with Human Participants" (1984). As of 2005, the American Society of Criminology had not formally adopted, but continue to develop, an acceptable code of ethics. Hagan (2006) implies that most criminologists and criminal justice researchers tend to borrow from cognate disciplines for their ethical guidelines. Paramount among these borrowed ethical tenets is the avoidance of harm to human subjects.

Some Common Ethical Concerns in Behavioral Research

Among the most serious ethical concerns that have received attention during the past two decades is the assurance that subjects are voluntarily involved and informed of all potential risks. Yet even here there is some controversy.

In general, the concept of voluntary participation in social science research is an important ideal, but ideals are not always attainable. In some instances—such as the one illustrated by Humphreys's (1970) study—violating the tenet of voluntary participation may appear justified to certain researchers. Typically, such justifications are made on the basis of an imaginary scale described as tipped toward the ultimate social good as measured against the possible harm to subjects.

Another argument against arbitrary application of this notion of voluntary participation concerns the nature of volunteering in general. First, if all social research included only those persons who eagerly volunteered to participate, little meaningful understanding would result. There would be no way of determining if these types of persons were similar to others who lacked this eagerness to volunteer. In other words, both qualitative and aggregated statistical data would become questionable.

Second, in many cases, volunteer subjects may in reality be coerced or manipulated into volunteering. For instance, one popular style of sample identification is the college classroom. If the teacher asks the entire class to voluntarily take part in a research project, there may be penalties for not submitting even if the teacher suggests otherwise. Even if no punishments are intentionally planned, if students believe that not taking part will be noticed and might somehow be held against them, they have been manipulated. Under such circumstances, as in the case of the overeager volunteers, confidence in the data is undermined.

Babbie (1992) similarly notes that offering reduced sentences to inmates in exchange for their participation in research—or other types of incentives to potential subjects—represents yet another kind of manipulated voluntary consent. As Martin, Arnold, Zimmerman, & Richard (1968) suggest, voluntary participation in studies among prisoners results from a strange mix of altruism, monetary gain, and hope for a potential way of enhancing their personal prestige and status.

A third justification for not gaining the voluntary consent of subjects is suggested by Rainwater and Pittman (1967). They believe that social science research enhances accountability in public officials. Consequently, research in many public institutions must be conducted covertly (thus, without voluntary participation on the part of subjects) if it is to be meaningful—and in some instances if it is to be conducted at all.

In contrast to these justifications for not obtaining voluntary participation, Kelman (1972) outlines how various invasions of privacy and manipulations of research subjects occur in fairly powerless segments of society and organizations. On the one hand, researchers might justify this invasion as the conduct of do-gooders who focus on such disadvantaged groups as drug abusers, the unemployed, and the poor because social service agencies are interested in helping people with social problems. On the other hand, researchers can create as strong a case for social agencies' desires to get a firmer grip on these disadvantaged groups, and certainly government agencies use social science research to formulate policies (Lakoff, 1971).

Regardless of the justification, because of their lack of political, social, and financial power, these disadvantaged groups are more accessible to researchers than many more powerful groups are. In consequence, researchers must be responsive to these conditions and clearly explain to subjects the rights and responsibilities of both the researchers and the participants.

No hard-and-fast answers exist for resolving the dilemma of voluntary participation. Researchers must balance how voluntary subjects' participation will be against their perceptions of personal integrity; their responsibilities to themselves, their profession, and their discipline; and the ultimate effects for their subjects. In other words, in the end, researchers must define for themselves what is ethical in research.

New Areas for Ethical Concern: Cyberspace

During the past few years, many areas of social scientific inquiry have benefited by extending their data-collection strategies to include the Internet. For instance, surveys have managed to take advantage of the geographical reach offered by the Web, as well as the fact that data can potentially be collected all hours of the day or night. Qualitative researchers can also take advantage of various benefits afforded by the Web. For instance, focus groups (to be discussed in detail in Chapter 5) can be formed via the Internet to undertake data collection among small groups composed of individuals in several distant locations simultaneously. Oral historians are now able to reach archives located on the Web in minutes, whereas previously it might have taken days or weeks to reach their sources. What may be the most surprising thing about the current Web-based research is not that there have been so many egregious violations of ethics but that there appear to have been so few (Thomas, 1999). Although problems have been identified and various solutions have been offered, concerns about the potential use and misuse of the Internet continue to move scholars toward finding ways to maintain ethical integrity in research when using the Internet as a research tool.

One of the interesting ethical elements of Web-based research is that it is potentially far more anonymous than many other types of invasive data-collecting strategies. Thus, a greater sense of security and anonymity may be permitted for some research subjects. The investigator and the subject need not ever engage in face-to-face interactions, be concerned over being appropriately dressed, or even necessarily have concerns about the investigator's gender, removing several major traditional sources of researcher reactivity. For example, in a study by Nicola Illingworth (2001, par. 7.1), which examined women's views on assisted reproductive technologies, she found the use of what she terms *computer-mediated communications* provided an effective means for collecting her data. As she explained it:

> Firstly, online participation offered personal anonymity in a very emotive field. Secondly, because of the sensitive nature of this research, a number of respondents emphasized their reluctance to participate had this research been conducted in a more conventional, face-to-face setting.

Of course, from a qualitative researcher's point of view, this absence of face-to-face engagement could also be considered a loss of potential data (in the various forms of visual cues and symbolic information contained in grimaces, winces, body movements, and the like).

There are at least two areas of potential ethical concern, which are produced by the freedom and anonymity created by Web-based data-collection strategies. These include greater needs to protect children and the need for debriefing subjects (Nosek, Banaji, & Greenwald, 2002).

Protection for Children

Whether or not the research being undertaken on the Internet is designed to include children, one must be mindful that children are out there. In a standard interview or focus group, the investigator is likely to notice a child's response when the research is designed for adults. On the other hand, merely asking the subject's age over the Internet does not necessarily ensure a truthful response. There are several precautions that one can take, however, to better ensure that participants are adults when using a Web-based data-collection strategy. First, recruit potential participants from list servers, chat rooms, Web sites, and organizations having an adult target audience.

Second, avoid using cutesy images or cartoons on the survey Web site in order to increase its appeal to adults and reduce its entertainment value to children.

Third, like some adult triple-X Web sites, you can require that the participant register with an *adult check* system prior to entering the research Web site. Although this procedure generally requires the subject to enter a credit card number and/or a driver's license, the individual's identity is kept confidential from the researcher. The obvious drawback to this restriction, of course, is that many would-be participants will leave abruptly rather than enter a credit card or driver's license number over the Web—no matter how secure you make the site.

Fourth, you might include a brief set of screening questions that is likely to tap into the memory of an adult but not likely to be common information known by most children. For example, you might ask where the Los Angeles Dodgers played before they moved to Los Angeles (answer: Brooklyn), or you might ask what color Howdy Doody's hair was (answer: red) or even who sang "Alice's Restaurant" (answer: Arlo Guthrie). Although these screening questions may not be foolproof, they are an added safeguard intended to better ensure that the average minor will not be allowed to take part in the research. If a few adults cannot answer your questions and are eliminated as a result, following such a procedure may still be in the best interest of protecting children and maintaining the ethical integrity of the research as a whole.

Debriefing the Subjects

It is not uncommon during the course of a face-to-face interview or a focus group interview to notice when a subject is becoming upset, agitated, or otherwise unsettled. However, given the nature of the Internet (and the loss of symbolic visual cues), it is not equally possible. Therefore, in the interest of ensuring no harm to participants, it is important to debrief the subjects and to determine if they require any assistance, counseling, or explanations for questions they have been asked during the course of the interview. The problems here include the innate difficulties of the technology itself. Internet participants may become involuntarily disconnected because of their server timing out, a server crash, the computer locking up or crashing, a program error, or even a power surge or outage. Or they may voluntarily and abruptly withdraw from participation because they become bored, angry, frustrated, or even simply because their doorbell or telephone rings. Whatever the cause, early withdrawal from the study is a threat not only to the quality of the research but also to the ability of the researcher to adequately debrief the subject and ensure that no harm has come to the participant.

There are a number of precautions the investigator can take to improve the likelihood of providing subjects with a debriefing. First, to ensure debriefing (even if it requires little more than to ask if the subject is okay or has any questions) it may be a good idea to secure the participant's e-mail address at the beginning of the study (Nosek, Banaji, & Greenwald, 2002).

Second, the Web site might include an *exit study* button clearly apparent on each page of the study, which might automatically direct participants to a debriefing page or a page outlining how to get directly in touch with the researcher if they have any concerns or questions.

Third, the researcher could provide his or her own e-mail address at the beginning of the interview and indicate that subjects should feel free to contact him or her if they have any concerns after completing the interview or at a later time should they need to discontinue the interview suddenly.

Fourth, if the Web site is not already a chat room–based medium (which works well for both interviews and focus group strategies), subjects might be directed to a chat room to have a real-time conversation with the interviewer about any concerns or questions they have.

Physical and Ethical Dangers in Covert Research

Another decision that the researcher must make is whether to enter the field as an overt (announced) or secret investigator. The highly illegal nature of certain deviant careers and activities—the very thing that may make them sociologically interesting—may preclude overtly investigating them. The adoption of a cover research role, however, must be carefully considered, for in addition to potentially violating the rights of the subjects, there is a real possibility that the researchers themselves might come to some harm or legal complication. Patricia Adler, for example, explains her attempt to strike a balance between overt and covert researcher roles (Adler, 1985, pp. 17, 27):

> In discussing this issue [whether to overtly or covertly investigate drug trafficking] with our key informants, they all agreed that we should be extremely discreet (for both our sakes and theirs). We carefully approached new individuals before we admitted that we were studying them. With many of these people, then, we took a covert posture in the research setting. . . . Confronted with secrecy, danger, hidden alliances, misrepresentations and unpredictable changes of intent, I had to use a delicate combination of overt and covert roles.

There is also the problem, particularly when conducting covert field research on deviants, that one will necessarily break the law (Adler, 1985; Becker, 1963; Carey, 1972; Polsky, 1969; Tunnell, 1998). Again, Patricia Adler (1985, p. 23) provides an excellent illustration of the various levels of illegality one might become guilty of:

> This [law violation] occurs in its most innocuous form from having "guilty knowledge": information about crimes that are committed. Being aware of major dealing and smuggling operations made us an accessory to their commission, since we failed to notify the police. We broke the law, secondly, through our "guilty observations," by being present at the scene of a crime and witnessing its occurrence. . . . Lastly, we broke the law through our "guilty actions," by taking part in illegal behavior ourselves. Although we never dealt drugs (we were too scared to be seriously tempted) we consumed drugs and possessed them in small quantities.

Kenneth Tunnell (1998, p. 208) makes a similar observation:

> Whenever we as researchers gain entry into the world of deviants and personally learn the activities of hustlers, thieves, and drug peddlers, for example, we become privy to information normally accessible only to occupants of such trades. A resultant problem, and one described by other ethnographers, is that legal authorities may learn of the research and exact damning information from researchers.

Although deception may be seen as a minor ethical violation by some investigators, it remains a serious breach of ethical conduct for others (Barnbaum & Byron, 2001; Kelman, 1967). Esterberg (2002, p. 52) states that she believes that covert research is almost never ethical, although she admits that some deception may at times be necessary. The decision about whether to assume an overt or a covert researcher role, then, involves a negotiated and balanced weighing of the potential gains against the potential losses.

Some social scientists, such as Kai Erikson (1967, 1995), argue that covert research and its associated deception jeopardize the ability of future researchers to undertake investigations by violating the trust and goodwill of similar subjects and the public. Other social scientists such as Jay Mitchell Miller (1998), and Tewksbury (Miller & Tewksbury, 2001) counter this argument by maintaining that many of the kinds of settings that would interest researchers and that require covert investigations tend to be restricted areas occupied by people who are already suspicious of strangers because of the potential threat of sanctions associated with their behaviors (see also Miller & Tewksbury, 2005). In effect, researchers interested in various aspects of deviance, sexual behaviors, drugs, or various criminal behavior already deal with resistant and distrustful populations.

Regarding research ethics, researchers must counterbalance their various social responsibilities. These include responsibilities to themselves, their discipline or profession, to the pursuit of knowledge, the society, and their subjects.

The orientation supported in this text is that there are situations in which covert research is both necessary and ethically justified. The determination depends on what you are studying, how you plan to conduct the study, and what you plan to do with the results. For example, powerful and elite groups in society are difficult to access; consequently, social scientists tend to avoid them and concentrate their research efforts on more powerless groups (Hertz & Imber, 1993; Miller, 1998; Taylor & Bogdan, 1998). To be sure, there are far more studies of poor people than there are of politicians, nurses than doctors, employees of corporations than CEOs of corporations, the working class than celebrities, and so forth. Researchers reveal the faults and frailties of these *undergroups,* while the powerful and elite go unscathed. Covert strategies of research may be the only means by which to investigate the powerful and elite. Such research, then, may well be morally and ethically justified. Nonetheless, the orientation supported here is to be cautious about the use of deception. I am especially cautious about outright deception of anyone merely for the sake of conducting a study that is only adding another *research notch* to an investigator's metaphoric gun handle, or simply to expedite the research, or because the research study will allow one to complete a degree requirement.

Other concerns related to decisions about ethical research practices can more easily be detailed and considered. Elaboration of each of these elements may assist researchers (particularly the inexperienced) in determining how to deal with ethical concerns in research. These elements include informed consent and implied consent, confidentiality and anonymity, securing the data, and objectivity and careful research design.

Informed Consent and Implied Consent

Issues surrounding informed consent grow out of the concern to avoid—or at least identify and articulate—potential risk to human subjects. Risks associated with participation in social scientific research include exposure to physical, psychological, or social injury.

Informed consent means the knowing consent of individuals to participate as an exercise of their choice, free from any element of fraud, deceit, duress, or similar unfair inducement or manipulation. In the case of minors or mentally impaired persons, whose exercise of choice is legally governed, consent must be obtained from the person or agency legally authorized to represent the interests of the individual.

In most institutionally sponsored research, consent must be ensured in writing. Typically, *informed consent slips* contain a written statement of potential risk and benefit and some phrase to the effect that these risks and benefits have been explained. As a rule, these slips are dated and signed by both the potential subject and the researchers or their designated representative.

There are chiefly two rationales behind the requirement to obtain signed informed consent slips. First, they systematically ensure that potential subjects are *knowingly* participating in a study and are doing so of their own choice. Second, signed consent slips provide IRBs a means by which to monitor (by examining signed slips) the voluntary participation of subjects.

Obtaining a signed informed consent slip, as may be obvious, presents in itself a slight ethical dilemma. A written record of the subjects' names (and frequently their addresses as well) means that a formal record of participants exists. In order to preserve privacy, these slips are usually kept under very careful guard by the principal investigator(s) and are revealed to IRBs only if questions arise concerning ethical practices in a given study.

Sometimes in large-scale survey questionnaire studies, separate signed informed consent slips are eliminated and replaced with implied consent. *Implied consent* is indicated by the subject taking the time to complete the lengthy questionnaire. In these circumstances, explanations of the study's purpose and potential risks and benefits are explained at the beginning of the survey.

A similar kind of implied consent can replace a signed consent slip when researchers conduct tape-recorded in-depth interviews. In this instance, the interviewers fully explain the nature of the project and the potential risks and benefits at the beginning of each interview. Next, the interviewers ask the subjects if they understand the information and are still willing to take part in the interview.

Affirmative responses and completed interviews serve the purpose of implying consent in the absence of a signed consent slip. The benefit of this particular style of informed consent is the elimination of any record of the subjects' names. This procedure is particularly helpful when interviewing people who might otherwise refuse to take part in a study. To a large measure, this type of implied consent is related to the next topic—namely, confidentiality and anonymity.

Confidentiality and Anonymity

Although *confidentiality* and *anonymity* are sometimes mistakenly used as synonyms, they have quite distinct meanings. *Confidentiality* is an active attempt to remove from the research records any elements that might indicate the subjects' identities. In a literal sense, *anonymity* means that the subjects remain nameless. In some instances, such as self-administered survey questionnaires, it may be possible to provide anonymity. Although investigators may know to whom surveys were distributed, if no identifying marks have been placed on the returned questionnaires, the respondents remain anonymous.

In most qualitative research, however, because subjects are known to the investigators (even if only by sight and a street name), anonymity is virtually nonexistent. Thus, it is important to provide subjects with a high degree of confidentiality.

Researchers commonly assure subjects that anything discussed between them will be kept in strict confidence, but what exactly does this mean? Naturally, this requires that researchers systematically change each subject's real name to a pseudonym or case number when reporting data. But what about changing the names of locations? Names of places, stores, or streets, in association with a description of certain characteristics about an individual, may make it possible to discover a subject's identity (Babbie, 2004; Gibbons, 1975; Morse & Richards, 2002). Even if people are incorrect about their determination of who is being identified, the result may nonetheless make people wary of cooperating in future research. Researchers, therefore, must always be extremely careful about how they discuss their subjects and the settings (Hagan, 1993, 2006; Hessler, 1992).

Keeping Identifying Records

It is not unusual for researchers, particularly ethnographers, to maintain systematically developed listings of real names and pseudonyms for people and places. As discussed in detail in Chapter 6, the use of such systematic lists ensures consistency during later analysis stages of the data. However, the existence of such lists creates a potential risk to subjects. Although court battles may eventually alter the situation, social scientists are presently unable to invoke professional privilege as a defense against being forced to reveal names of informants and sources during criminal proceedings. John Van Maanen (1983) once refused to turn over subpoenaed materials in a case of alleged police brutality on the questionable grounds of *research confidentiality;* he does not indicate that his efforts were successful. In other words, under normal conditions, lists of names and places can be subpoenaed along with other relevant research notes and data.

Strategies for Safeguarding Confidentiality

In effect, researchers may be placed in an ethical catch-22. On one hand, they have a professional obligation to honor assurances of confidentiality made to subjects. On the other hand, researchers, in most cases, can be held in contempt of court if they fail to produce the subpoenaed materials. Still, investigators can take several possible steps to safeguard their reputations for being reliable concerning confidentiality.

First, as discussed in Chapter 6, researchers may obtain a Federal Certificate of Confidentiality. Under provisions set forth as conditions of award, investigators cannot be forced to reveal notes, names, or pertinent information in court. Unfortunately, few of the many thousands of researchers who apply are awarded a Federal Certificate of Confidentiality.

A second tack, which is more effective, is to avoid keeping identifying records and lists any longer than is absolutely necessary. Although this may not prevent the courts from issuing a subpoena and verbally questioning investigators, the likelihood of this occurring is reduced in the absence of written records. In the mid-1980s, a court case resulted in a federal judge ruling in favor of a sociologist's right to protect subjects by refusing to release his field notes to a grand jury investigating a suspicious fire at a restaurant where he worked and conducted covert research (Fried, 1984). This case, however, has yet to result in significant changes in judicial attitudes about the nature of research and field notes. Certainly, the potential for legal problems is likely to persist for some time.

Because of the various precedents and differing state statutes, speculating or generalizing about how a particular case may be resolved is impossible (see Boruch & Cecil, 1979; Carroll & Knerr, 1977). For instance, Rik Scarce (1990) published a book based on his research on animal rights activists entitled *Ecowarriors: Understanding the Radical Environmental Movement*. In 1993, Scarce was ordered to appear before a grand jury and asked to identify the activists involved in his research. In order to maintain the confidentiality he had promised these individuals, Scarce refused to reveal who they were. Scarce was held in contempt and confined to jail for 159 days. Even if researchers choose to risk imprisonment for contempt, the fact that there exists a moral obligation to maintain their promise of confidentiality to the best of their ability should be apparent.

Securing the Data

Although court-related disclosures provide particularly difficult problems, they are rare cases. A more likely—as well as more controllable—form of disclosure comes from careless or clumsy handling of records and data. In other words, researchers must take intentional precautions to ensure that information does not accidentally fall into the wrong hands or become public.

Researchers frequently invent what they believe are unique strategies to secure pieces of research information. More often than not, though, these innovations simply represent attempts to separate names or other identifiers from the data. Regardless of whether you store data in multiple locations or place them in metal boxes inside locked closets or a locked desk drawer, precautions against accidental disclosure must be taken.

Precautions should also be taken to ensure that research-related information is not carelessly discussed. Toward this end, signing a *statement of confidentiality* is common for each member of a research team. This is sometimes referred to as a *personnel agreement for maintaining confidentiality* (see Figure 3.2).

Figure 3.2 Personnel Agreement for Maintaining Confidentiality

This form is intended to further ensure confidentiality of data obtained during the course of the study entitled "Drinking by American College Students During Social Gatherings." All parties employed in this research will be asked to read the following statement and sign their names indicating they agree to comply.

I hereby affirm that I will not reveal or in any manner disclose information obtained during the course of this study. I agree to discuss material directly related to this study only with other members of the research team. In any reports, papers, or published materials I write, I agree to remove obvious identifiers.

Name: _____

Signature: _____

Project Director's Signature: _____

These statements typically indicate the sensitive nature of the research and offer a promise not to talk to anybody about information obtained during the study.

While it is true that a signed statement of confidentiality is not likely to stand up in court if an investigator is subpoenaed, it does provide at least some assurance that personnel on the research team will not indiscriminately discuss the study.

Objectivity and Careful Research Design

A researcher may use an assortment of complicated measures to ensure confidentiality, but perhaps the most effective strategy is to think through the project carefully during the design stage. During the design stage of any study, the researcher can safely consider what actions must be taken to safeguard the identities of subjects as well as the data once it is collected, used, and stored.

In addition to these general safeguard issues, nurse researchers may have other ethical problems to consider because some of their research endeavors overlap into the biomedical realm. Polit and Hungler (1995, pp. 132–133), for example, outline a number of research problems and potential ethical dilemmas that each may involve. Two of these sample problems follow (Polit & Hungler, 1995, p. 132):

Research Problem

How empathic are nurses in their treatment of patients in intensive care units?

Ethical Dilemma

To address this question, the researcher would likely want to observe nurses' behavior while treating patients. Ethical research generally involves explaining the study to participants and obtaining their consent to participate in the study. Yet if the researcher in this example informs the participating nurses that their treatment of patients will be observed, will their behavior be "normal"? If the nurses' behavior is altered because of their awareness of being observed, the entire value of the study would be undermined.

Research Problem

What are the feelings and coping mechanisms of parents whose children have a terminal illness?

Ethical Dilemma

To answer this question fully, the researcher may need to probe intrusively into the psychological state of the parents at a highly vulnerable time in their lives; such probing could be painful and even traumatic. Yet knowledge of the parents' coping mechanisms could help to design more effective ways of dealing with parents' grief and anger.

As these examples suggest, some research situations place the researcher in an ethical bind. On the one hand, researchers want to advance scientific knowledge and understanding in the most rigorous manner possible. On the other hand, they must be careful not to violate the rights of subjects or to place them in harm's way.

Even if researchers can protect subjects from harm during the course of research, they must also consider what happens thereafter as a direct result of the research. Particularly when conducting policy-laden research on various drug- or crime-involved subjects, what investigators learn from these subjects may change the subjects' lives—and not necessarily for the better. Disseminating results that provide law enforcement agencies with improved techniques for interception could be construed as causing harm to the subjects (Lakoff, 1971).

In addition to deciding against a given project during the design stage, researchers may consider possible ways of protecting the interests of subjects both during and following the actual study. By carefully considering possible harm to subjects in advance, researchers can sometimes avoid personal embarrassment and breaches of confidentiality.

The practice of researchers ensuring confidentiality in order to obtain the cooperation of subjects is likely to continue. It is quite important, therefore, that novice researchers recognize the potential tension between what might be called *academic freedom* and enforcement of the laws of the land. As Hofmann (1972) points out, social scientists must be responsible—and accountable—for their actions. With this firmly in mind, researchers ultimately may continue to question whether their ethical practices are justified by their ends. The ethical justification of research must be considered situationally, case by case.

TRYING IT OUT

You have been asked to sit on an institutional review board to consider a doctoral student's planned dissertation project. The summary for this research follows:

> My proposed research will involve an observational study of children's classroom behavior, and the effect of praise on student performance. I propose to use sixth grade students in a local public school. I plan to enter the setting as a student teacher (the teacher of record will be told what my real purpose is).

I will then divide the class into two separate groups. One group of children I will frequently compliment and praise for being smart, clever, intelligent, and good students. The other group I will largely ignore, or when pressed, comment that they are doing an adequate job. I will collect field notes on how members of each group tend to interact with each other and their teacher. I will additionally collect discrete data (their various exam and essay scores for the class) to see if my use of positive labels affects their class performance.

After reading the foregoing summary of the proposal, answer the following questions:

1. What are some of the important ethical concerns to consider regarding this proposed research project?
2. If you were the researcher, what might you do to respond to the comments made in question 1?
3. What safeguards should the researcher take to protect the subjects in this particular study?

REFERENCES

Adler, P. A. (1985). *Wheeling and Dealing*. New York: Columbia University Press.
American Nurses Association. (1975). *Human Rights Guidelines for Nurses in Clinical and Other Research*. Kansas City, MO: American Nurses Association.
American Psychological Association. (1981). Ethical principles of psychologists. *American Psychologist, 36,* 633–638.
American Psychological Association. (1984). *Ethical Principles in the Conduct of Research with Human Participants.* Washington, DC: American Psychological Association.
American Sociological Association. (1984). Code of Ethics. Washington, DC: American Sociological Association.
American Sociological Association. (March 1992). Code of ethics. *Footnotes 10,* 9–10.
Babbie, E. (1983). *The Practice of Social Research* (3rd ed.). Belmont, CA: Wadsworth.
Babbie, E. (1992). *The Practice of Social Research* (5th ed.). Belmont, CA: Wadsworth.
Babbie, E. (2001). *The Practice of Social Research* (9th ed.). Belmont, CA: Wadsworth.
Babbie, E. (2004). *The Practice of Social Research* (10th ed.). Belmont, CA: Wadsworth.
Bachman, E., & Schutt, R. K. (2003). *The Practice of Research in Criminology and Criminal Justice* (2nd ed.). Thousand Oaks, CA.: Pine Forge Press.
Bailey, C. A. (1996). *A Guide to Field Research*. Thousand Oaks, CA: Pine Forge Press.
Barber, B. (1973). Prepared Statements to the House Subcommittee on Health Hearing, Protection of Human Subjects Act. U.S. Congress, Washington, DC.
Barnbaum, D. R., & Byron, M. (2001). *Research Ethics Text and Readings*. Upper Saddle River, NJ: Prentice Hall.
Becker, H. S. (1963). *Outsiders: Studies in the Sociology of Deviance*. New York: Free Press.
Berg, B. L., Austin, W. T., & Zuern, G. A. (1992, March). Institutional review boards: Who, what, where, and why? Paper presented at the annual meeting of the Academy of Criminal Justice Sciences, Pittsburgh.

Berg, B., Sañudo, F., Hovell, M., Sipan, C., Kelley, N., & Blumberg, E. (2004). The use of indigenous interviewers in a study of Latino men who have sex with men: A research note. *Sexuality and Culture 8*(1), 87–103.

Berger, R. L. (1990). Nazi science: The Dachau hypothermia experiments. *New England Journal of Medicine, 322*(20), 1435–1440.

Bogdan, R., & Biklen, S. K. (1992). *Qualitative Research for Education* (2nd ed.). Boston: Allyn and Bacon.

Bogdan, B., & Biklen, S. K. (2003). *Qualitative Research for Education* (4th ed.). Boston: Allyn & Bacon, Inc.

Boruch, R. F., & Cecil, J. (1979). *Assuring the Confidentiality of Social Research Data.* Philadelphia: University of Pennsylvania Press.

Bower, R. T., & de Gasparis, P. (1978). *Ethics in Social Research.* New York: Praeger.

Brandt, A. M. (December 1978). Racism and research: The case of the Tuskegee syphilis study. *Hasting Center Report*, 21–29.

Burns, N., & Grove, S. (2000). *The Practice of Nursing Research* (4th ed.). Philadelphia: W. B. Saunders.

Burstein, A. G. (February 1987). The virtue machine. *American Psychologist*, 199–202.

Carey, J. T. (1972). Problems of access and risk in observing drug scenes. In J. D. Douglas (Ed.), *Research on Deviance*. New York: Random House.

Carroll, J. D., & Knerr, C. (1977). *The Confidentiality of Research Sources and Data.* Testimony presented to the Privacy Protection Study Commission. Washington, DC.

Cassell, J. (1978). Risk and benefit to subjects of fieldwork. *American Sociologist, 13,* 134–143.

Champion, D. J. (2006). *Research Methods for Criminal Justice and Criminology* (3rd ed.). Upper Saddle River, NJ: Pearson/Prentice Hall.

Clinton, W. (1997). Remarks by the President in apology for study done in Tuskegee. Press release. Washington, DC: Office of the Press Secretary, The White House.

Code of Federal Regulations. (1993). Protection of Human Subjects. Article 45, Part 46, Sections 101–110. Washington, DC: Office of the Federal Register, National Archives and Records Administration.

Department of Health and Human Services. (1989). *Code of Federal Regulations* (45 CFR 46). Protection of Human Subjects. Washington, DC: National Institutes of Health, Office for Protection from Research Risks.

Department of Health, Education, and Welfare. (1978a). *Report and Recommendations on Institutional Review Boards*, Pub. no. (05) 78-008. Washington, DC.

Department of Health, Education, and Welfare. (1978b). *Belmont Report.* Pub. no. (05) 78-0012. Washington, DC.

Deschenes, L. P., & Vogel, R. E. (1995). Ethical and practical issues in school-based research: A case study of active consent. Paper presented at the annual meeting of the American Society of Criminology, Boston.

Dillman, D. (2000). *Mail and Internet Surveys: The Tailored Design Method* (2nd ed.). New York: Wiley.

Eaton, D. K., Lowry, R., Brener, N. D., Grunbaum, J. A., & Kahn, L. (2004). Passive versus active parental permission in school-based survey research: Does the type of permission affect prevalence estimates of risk behaviors: *Evaluation Review 28,* 564–577.

Ellickson, P. L., & Hawes, J. A. (1989). An assessment of active versus passive methods for obtaining parental consent. *Evaluation Review 13*(1), 45–55.

Erikson, K. T. (1967). A comment on disguised observation in sociology. *Social Problems* *14*, 366–373.

Erikson, K. T. (1995). Commentary. *The American Sociologist 26*(2), 4–11.

Esterberg, K. G. (2002). *Qualitative Methods in Social Research.* Boston: McGraw Hill.

Eysenbach, G., & Wyatt, J. (2002). Using the Internet for surveys and health research. *Journal of Medical Internet Research 4*(2), 13–20.

Federal Register. (November 30, 1978). Protection of human subjects: Institutional review boards, 943 FR 56174.

Fields, C. M. (March 12, 1978). Universities fear impact of rules to protect research subjects. *Chronicle of Higher Education*, 5–6.

Fried, J. P. (April 8, 1984). Judge protects waiter's notes on fire inquiry. *New York Times*, p. A47.

Gibbons, D. C. (1975). Unidentified research sites and fictitious names. *American Sociologist 10*, 32–36.

Gray, B. G. (1977). The functions of human subjects review committees. *American Journal of Psychiatry 134*, 907–909.

Gray, F. D. (2002). *The Tuskegee Syphilis Study: The Real Story and Beyond.* Montgomery, AL: River City Publishing.

Hagan, F. E. (2006). *Research Methods in Criminal Justice and Criminology* (7th ed.). Boston: Allyn and Bacon.

Hagan, F. E. (1993). *Research Methods in Criminal Justice and Criminology.* New York: Macmillan.

Hershey, N., & Miller, R. (1976). *Human Experimentation and the Law.* Germantown, MD: Aspen.

Hertz, R., & Imber, J. B. (1993). Fieldwork in elite settings: Introduction. *Journal of Contemporary Ethnography 22*, 3–6.

Hessler, R. M. (1992). *Social Research Methods.* New York: West Publishing.

Hofmann, G. (1972). The quest for relevance: Some implications for social research. *ET AL. 3*, 50–57.

Holden, C. (1975). Privacy: Congressional efforts are coming to fruition. *Science 188*, 713–715.

Humphreys, L. (1970). *Tearoom Trade: Impersonal Sex in Public Places.* Chicago: Aldine.

Illingworth, N. (2001). The Internet matters: Exploring the use of the Internet as a research tool. *Sociological Research Online 6*(2). Available online at www.socresonline.org.uk/6/2/illingworth.html

Jacobs, B. A. (1998). Researching crack dealers: Dilemmas and contradictions. In J. Ferrell & M. S. Hamm (Eds.), *Ethnography at the Edge: Crime Deviance and Field Research* (pp. 160–177). Boston: Northeastern University Press.

Jones, J. H. (1993). *Bad Blood: The Tuskegee Syphilis Experiment.* New York: Free Press.

Katz, J. (1972). *Experimentation with Human Beings.* New York: Russell Sage.

Kearney, K., et al. (1983). Sample bias resulting from a requirement for written parental consent. *Public Opinion Quarterly 47*, 96–102.

Kelman, H. C. (1967). The human use of human subjects: The problem of deception in social psychological experiments. *Psychological Bulletin 67*, 1–11.

Kelman, H. C. (1972). The rights of the subjects in social research: An analysis in terms of relative power and legitimacy. *American Psychologist 27*, 989–1015.

Lakoff, S. A. (1971). Knowledge, power, and democratic theory. *Annals 394*, 5–12.

Levine, R. J. (1986). Declaration of Helsinki. *Ethics and Regulations of Clinical Research* (2nd ed.). Baltimore: Urban and Schwarzenberg.

Liemohn, W. (1979). Research involving human subjects. *Research Quarterly 50*(2), 157–163.

LoBiondo-Wood, G., & Haber, J. (2002). *Nursing Research: Methods, Critical Appraisal and Utilization* (5th ed.). St. Louis, MO: Mosby.

Martin, D. C., Arnold, J. D., Zimmerman, T. F., & Richard, R. H. (1968). Human subjects in clinical research—A report on three studies. *New England Journal of Medicine 279*, 1426–1431.

McSkimming, M. J. (1996). *Gaming and Gambling in Tavern Life.* Doctoral dissertation. Department of Criminology, Indiana University of Pennsylvania, Indiana, PA.

Meyer, R. E. (August 1977). Subjects' rights, freedom of inquiry, and the future of research in the addictions. *American Journal of Psychiatry 134*(8), 899–903.

Milgram, S. (1963). Behavioral study of obedience. *Journal of Abnormal and Social Psychology 67*(37), 1–378.

Miller, J. M. (1998). Covert participant observation: Reconsidering the least used method. In P. Tontodonato & F. E. Hagan (Eds.), *The Language of Research in Criminal Justice.* Boston: Allyn and Bacon.

Miller, J. M., & Tewksbury, R. (2001). *Extreme Methods: Innovative Approaches to Social Science Research.* Boston: Allyn and Bacon.

Miller, M. J., & Tewksbury, R. (2005). *Research Methods: A Qualitative Reader.* Upper Saddle River, NJ: Pearson/Prentice Hall.

Morse, J. M. (1994). *Critical Issues in Qualitative Research Methods.* Thousand Oaks, CA: Sage.

Morse, J. M., & Richards, L (2002). *Read Me First: For a User's Guide to Qualitative Methods.* Thousand Oaks, CA: Sage.

Nosek, B. A., Banafi, M. R., & Greenwald, A. G. (2002). E-research: Ethics, security, design, and control in psychological research on the Internet. *Journal of Social Issues 58*(1), 161–172.

Nguyen, T. H. (2003). *Video Gambling Vietnamese Cafés: An Observational Study of "Hot Line" Machines in Southern California.* Unpublished Masters Thesis, Department of Criminal Justice, California State University, Long Beach.

Polit, D. F., & Hungler, B. (1995). *Nursing Research: Principles and Methods.* Philadelphia: Lippincott.

Polsky, N. (1969). *Hustlers, Beats, and Others.* New York: Doubleday.

Punch, M. (1994). Politics and ethics in qualitative research. In N. K. Denzin & Y. S. Lincoln (Eds.), *Handbook of Qualitative Research* (pp. 83–98). Thousand Oaks, CA: Sage.

Rainwater, L., & Pittman, D. J. (1967). Ethical problems in studying a politically sensitive and deviant community. *Social Problems 14*, 357–365.

Scarce, R. (1990). *Ecowarriors: Understanding the Radical Environmental Movement.* Chicago: Noble Press.

Severson, H., & Ary, D. (1983). Sampling bias due to consent procedures with adolescents. *Addictive Behaviors 8*, 433–437.

Shalala, D. E. (June 17, 1997) "Ethics in human subjects research—Action." Memorandum from the Secretary of Health and Human Services, Washington, DC.

Smith, M. B. (1967). Conflicting values affecting behavioral research with children. *Children 14*, 53–58.

Sykes, G. M. (1967). Feeling our way: A report on a conference on ethical issues in the social sciences. *American Behavioral Scientist 10*, 8–11.

Taylor, R. B. (1994). *Research Methods in Criminal Justice*. New York: McGraw-Hill.

Taylor, S. J., & Bogdan, R. (1998). *Introduction to Qualitative Research Methods: A Guidebook & Resource*. New York: Wiley.

Tewksbury, R. (1990). Patrons of porn: Research notes on the clientele of adult bookstores. *Deviant Behavior 11*(3), 259–272.

Thomas, J. (1999). Balancing the ethical conundrums of Internet research—an existential view from the trenches. *Iowa Journal of Communications 31* (Spring), 8–20.

Thompson, T. (1984). A comparison of methods of increasing parental consent rates in social research. *Public Opinion Quarterly 48*, 779–787.

Tong, R. (2003). Feminist ethics. *Stanford Encyclopedia of Philosophy*. Available online at http://plato.stanford.edu/entries/feminism-ethics.

Trochim, W. M. K. (2001). *The Research Methods Knowledge Base* (2nd ed.). Cincinnati, OH: Atomic Dog Publishers.

Tunnell, K. D. (1998). Honesty, secrecy, and deception in the sociology of crime: Confessions and reflections from the backstage. In J. Ferrell & M. S. Hamm (Eds.), *Ethnography at the Edge: Crime Deviance and Field Research* (pp. 206–220). Boston: Northeastern University Press.

Van Maanen, J. (1983). The moral fix: On the ethics of fieldwork. In R. M. Emerson (Ed.), *Contemporary Field Research* (pp. 269–287). Boston: Little, Brown.

Viadero, D. (February 27, 2002). New student-survey policy worries some researchers. *Education Week*. Available online at www.edweek.org/ew/newstory.cfm?slug=24survey.h2l.

Wax, M. L. (1977). On fieldworkers and those exposed to fieldwork: Federal regulations and moral issues. *Human Organizations 36*(3), 321–327.

Wetzstein, C. (January 29, 2002). All that schools survey. *The Washington Times*.

Wexler, S. (1990). Ethical obligations and social research. In K. L. Kempf (Ed.), *Measurement Issues in Criminology* (pp. 78–107). New York: Springer-Verlag.

Zimbardo, P. G. (1972). "Pathology of Imprisonment." *Society* No. *9*, 4–6.

Chapter 4

A Dramaturgical Look at Interviewing

NTERVIEWING MAY BE DEFINED simply as a conversation with a purpose. Specifically, the purpose is to gather information. This standard definition of interviewing has been discussed by Denzin (1978), Spradley (1979), Patton (2001), Salkind (2003), Frankfort-Nachmias and Nachmias (2000), Babbie (2001, 2003), Leedy and Ormrod (2004), and Bogdan and Knopp Biklen (2002).

Unfortunately, the consensus on how to conduct an interview is not nearly as high. Interviewing and training manuals vary from long lists of specific do's and don'ts to lengthy, abstract, pseudotheoretical discussions on empathy, intuition, and motivation. The extensive literature on interviewing contains numerous descriptions of the interviewing process. In some cases, being a good interviewer is described as an innate ability or quality possessed only by certain people. Interviewing, from this perspective, has been described as an art rather than a skill or a science (Fontana & Frey, 1998). In other cases, interviewing has been described as a game in which the respondent receives intrinsic rewards for participation (Holmstrom, cited in Manning, 1967). In still other instances, interviewing has been described as a technical skill you can learn in the same way you might learn how to change a flat tire. In this case, an interviewer is like a laborer or a hired hand (Roth, 1966). Many sources describe interviewing as some sort of face-to-face social interaction, although exactly what distinguishes this type of interaction from others is often left to the imagination (Leedy & Ormrod, 2001, 2004; Salkind, 2002; Warren & Karner, 2005).

To be sure, there is some element of truth to each of these preceding characterizations. Certainly, anybody can be instructed in the basic orientations, strategies, procedures, and repertoire (to be discussed later in this chapter) of interviewing. Gorden (1992), for example, offers a clear, step-by-step description of how to go about the process of interviewing. To a large extent, Gorden (1992) and others offer the basic rules of the game. Furthermore, there is assuredly something extraordinary (if not unnatural) about a conversation in which one participant has an explicitly or implicitly scripted set of lines and the other participant does not. To judge any of these characteristics exclusively, however, seems inadequate. Just as some artists and actors are perceived by their peers to be exceptional while others in the field are viewed as mediocre, so can this assessment be made about interviewers. The previous characterizations have served little more than to circumscribe what might be termed the possible range of an interviewer's ability; they have not added appreciably to the depth of understanding about the process of interviewing or how you might go about mastering this process.

This chapter is devoted to the latter effort and draws on the symbolic interactionist paradigm, the stream of symbolic interaction more commonly referred to as *dramaturgy*.

Dramaturgy and Interviewing

This chapter attempts to illustrate dramaturgy's beneficial effects on interviewing beyond the interviewer training stage. Discussions will include types of interview structures, survey construction, the interviewer role and the role of the interviewer (social roles played by the investigator), rapport, reactivity, and accessing difficult or sensitive materials.[1]

It has been suggested by Denzin (2001, p. 26) that we inhabit a performance-based, dramaturgical culture. Indeed, even in research, the line between performer and audience sometimes blurs, and the whole process becomes a dramatic performance. In the broader context of society, there are likewise blurred boundaries between everyday life, theatrical performances on MTV, VH1, videotapes, television, and the movies. Reality-based television shows have significantly influenced what we now consider entertainment, further blurring the lines between performance, dramaturgy, and everyday life.

Research, then, is being swept along with the other aspects of culture, and it too is being significantly affected by the blurring of lines between performance and reality. Research, particularly field research, is sometimes divided into two separate phases—namely, getting in and analysis (Shaffir, Stebbins, & Turowetz, 1980). *Getting in* is typically defined as various techniques and procedures intended to secure access to a setting, its participants, and knowledge about phenomena and activities being observed. *Analysis* makes sense of the information accessed during the getting-in phase. As a consequence, the literal boundaries between these two phases may also become blurred—assuming they ever really existed during the process of research.

Nonetheless, this chapter will reclarify the two phases and consider each phase as distinct. In the case of the former, getting in means learning the ropes of various skills and techniques necessary for effective interviewing (Geer et al., 1968; Gorden, 1987; Lofland, 1976; Shaffir et al., 1980; Taylor & Bogdan, 1998). Regarding the latter, as this chapter will show, there are a number of ways you may go about making sense out of accessed information.

Let us look at the process of interviewing, specifically the notion of interviewing, as an "encounter" (Goffman, 1967), as a "social interaction" (Fontana & Frey, 1998), or as a "face-to-face interactionary performance" (Babbie, 1998, 2004). All discussions of interviewing are guided by some model or image of the interview situation, and here interviewing is perceived as a "social performance" (Goffman, 1959), organized around the premise that interviewing is best accomplished if guided by a dramaturgical model (Burke, 1957, 1966; see also Edgley, 2003).

Dramaturgy, as a theoretical perspective, involves the elements and language of theater, stagecraft, and stage management. This theoretical perspective is derived in part from the symbolic interactionists' general assumption that humans perceive and interact in reality through the use of symbols. Drama, then, is a mode of symbolic action in which some individuals act symbolically for others who watch symbolically. In the case of the former, the term used to describe acting individuals is usually simply *actors*. In the case of the latter, the reference typically is *social audience* or simply *audience*.

The symbolic action that passes between actor and audience is called a *social performance* or a *performance*. In this chapter, the language of dramaturgy is applied metaphorically to a concrete situation—namely, the interview. More theoretical and detailed discussions of dramaturgy may be found in Burke (1957, 1966), Goffman (1959), Messenger, Sampson, and Towne (1962), and more recently, Douglas (1985), and Peshkin (1988).

The dramaturgical orientation offered in this chapter is similar in some ways to what Douglas (1985) terms *creative interviewing*. Creative interviewing involves using a set of techniques to move past the mere words and sentences exchanged during the interview process. It includes creating an appropriate climate for informational exchanges and for mutual disclosures. This means that the interviewer will display his or her own feelings during the interview as well as elicit those of the subject. The dramaturgical model of interviewing presented here is also similar to what Butler (1997) and Mienczakowski (1995, 2000) refer to as performance-based or, simply, performance interviews. Performance interviews, then, can be situated in the complex system of discourse, where traditional, everyday, and avant-garde meanings of theater, film, video, ethnography, cinema, performance, text, and audience come together and inform one another (Denzin, 2001).

Also similar to the dramaturgical perspective presented here is what Holstein and Gubrium (1995) call active interviewing. From their perspective, the interview is not arbitrary or one-sided. Instead, the interview is viewed as a meaning-making occasion in which the actual circumstance of the meaning construction is important (Holstein & Gubrium, 1995). The proposed dramaturgical model differs most from the active interview in its emphasis on the interviewer *using* the constructed relationship of the interviewer and subject to draw out information from the subject. The various devices used by the dramaturgical interviewer, therefore, move this orientation slightly closer to the creative interviewing model and the more reflexive performance interview.

Types of Interviews

No consideration of interviewing would be complete without some acknowledgment of the major interview structures. These are sometimes referred to as "the family of qualitative interviews" (Rubin & Rubin, 1995). Some sources mention only two interview structures—namely, formal and informal (see, for example, Fitzgerald & Cox, 2002, pp. 118–119). Other sources refer to this research process as either structured or unstructured (Fontana & Frey, 1994; Leedy & Ormrod, 2001). However, at least three major categories may be identified (Babbie, 2001; Merriam, 2001; Nachmias & Nachmias, 2000; Nieswiadomy, 2002; Polit & Hungler, 1995): the standardized (formal or structured) interview, the unstandardized (informal or nondirective) interview, and the semistandardized (guided-semistructured or focused) interview. The major difference between these different interview structures is their degree of rigidity with regard to presentational structure. Thus, if we cast them onto an imaginary continuum of formality, they would look a little like the model in Figure 4.1.

The Standardized Interview

The *standardized interview*, as suggested in Figure 4.1, uses a formally structured schedule of interview questions. The interviewers are required to ask subjects to respond to each question, exactly as worded. The rationale here is to offer each subject approximately the same stimulus so that responses to questions, ideally, will be comparable (Babbie, 2001). Researchers using this technique have fairly solid ideas about the things they want to uncover during the interview (Merriam, 2001; Schwartz & Jacobs, 1979). In other words,

Figure 4.1 Interview Structure Continuum of Formality

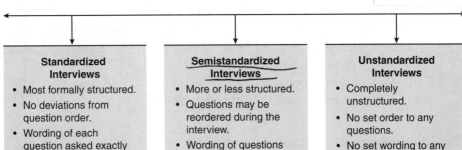

Standardized Interviews	Semistandardized Interviews	Unstandardized Interviews
• Most formally structured. • No deviations from question order. • Wording of each question asked exactly as written. • No adjusting of level of language. • No clarifications or answering of questions about the interview. • No additional questions may be added. • Similar in format to a pencil-and-paper survey.	• More or less structured. • Questions may be reordered during the interview. • Wording of questions flexible. • Level of language may be adjusted. • Interviewer may answer questions and make clarifications. • Interviewer may add or delete probes to interview between subsequent subjects.	• Completely unstructured. • No set order to any questions. • No set wording to any questions. • Level of language may be adjusted. • Interviewer may answer questions and make clarifications. • Interviewer may add or delete questions between interviews.

researchers assume that the questions scheduled in their interview instrument are sufficiently comprehensive to elicit from subjects all (or nearly all) information relevant to the study's topic(s). They further assume that all questions have been worded in a manner that allows subjects to understand clearly what they are being asked. Stated in slightly different terms, the wording of each question is equally meaningful to every subject. Finally, they assume that the meaning of each question is identical for every subject. These assumptions, however, remain chiefly "untested articles of faith" (Denzin, 1978, p. 114).

In sum, standardized interviews are designed to elicit information using a set of predetermined questions that are expected to elicit the subjects' thoughts, opinions, and attitudes about study-related issues. Standardized interviews, thus, operate from the perspective that one's thoughts are intricately related to one's actions. A typical standardized interview might look like this diet history (J. Berg, 1986):

1. When is the first time you eat or drink on a typical day?
2. What is the first thing you eat?
3. When is the next time you eat or drink?
4. What do you eat or drink?

5. When is the next time you eat or drink?
6. What do you eat or drink?
7. What else do you eat or drink on a typical day?
8. How many times a week do you eat eggs? Cheese? Milk? Fish? Beef? Pork? Beans? Corn? Grits? Bread? Cereal? Ice Cream? Fruits? Vegetables?
9. Which protein foods do you like best?
10. Which protein foods do you not eat?
11. What foods do you like to eat between meals?

The Unstandardized Interview

In contrast to the rigidity of standardized interviews, *unstandardized interviews* do not utilize schedules of questions and are located on the imaginary continuum (as depicted in Figure 4.1) at the opposite extreme from standardized interviews. Naturally, unstandardized interviews operate from a different set of assumptions. First, interviewers begin with the assumption that they do not know in advance what all the necessary questions are. Consequently, they cannot predetermine fully a list of questions to ask. They also assume that not all subjects will necessarily find equal meaning in like-worded questions—in short, that subjects may possess different vocabularies.

In an unstandardized interview, interviewers must develop, adapt, and generate questions and follow-up probes appropriate to each given situation and the central purpose of the investigation. Schwartz and Jacobs (1979, p. 40) note that this will result in appropriate and relevant questions arising from interactions during the interview itself.

Unstandardized interviews are sometimes used during the course of field research to augment field observations. For example, Diane Barone (2002) undertook a field study that examined literacy teaching and learning in two kindergarten classes at a school considered to be *at risk* and inadequate by the state. Barone conducted observations in the classrooms and wrote weekly field notes. In addition, however, she included ongoing informal interviews with the teachers throughout the yearlong study. Such unstructured interviews permit researchers to gain additional information about various phenomena they might observe by asking questions. Unstandardized interviews, however, are not restricted to field research projects, as illustrated by an archival study recently undertaken by Horowitz and her associates (2000). In this study, the researchers were interested in examining the sociocultural disparities in health care. Toward this end, the investigators examined the contents of health care and health articles with regard to racial, ethnic, and socioeconomic disparities. Their research, in some ways, might even be considered chiefly metatheoretical (where literature serves as the data of the study). But, in addition to this more archival approach, they also included informal interviews with research, policy, and program experts to assist in developing a framework of programs that addressed disparities (Horowitz, Davis, Palermo, & Vladeck, 2000). Thus, the informal interviews provided important information for these investigators along with the data culled from various published and unpublished articles and documents.

The Semistandardized Interview

As drawn in Figure 4.1, the *semistandardized interview* can be located somewhere between the extremes of the completely standardized and the completely unstandardized interviewing structures. This type of interview involves the implementation of a number of predetermined questions and special topics. These questions are typically asked of each interviewee in a systematic and consistent order, but the interviewers are allowed freedom to digress; that is, the interviewers are permitted (in fact, expected) to probe far beyond the answers to their prepared standardized questions.

Again, certain assumptions underlie this strategy. First, if questions are to be standardized, they must be formulated in words familiar to the people being interviewed (in vocabularies of the subjects). Police officers, for example, do not speak about all categories of persons in a like manner. Special terms they use include "scrots" (derived from the word *scrotum*), used as a derogatory slur when describing an assortment of bad guys; "skinners," used to describe rapists; "dips" to describe pickpockets; and "clouters," used to describe persons who break into automobiles to steal things. Questions used in a semistandardized interview can reflect an awareness that individuals understand the world in varying ways. Researchers, thus, approach the world from the subject's perspective. Researchers can accomplish this by adjusting the level of language of given scheduled questions or through unscheduled probes (described in greater detail in the following interview excerpt) that arise from the interview process itself.

One study of Latino men who have sex with other men (B. Berg et al., 2004) used a semistandardized interview schedule. Although many of the primary questions asked each of the 35 subjects derived from the predetermined schedule, the men's perceptions were often more fully elaborated after being asked an unscheduled probe. For example, after being asked a question, the subject might have responded with a brief "yes" or "no." In order to elicit additional information, the interviewer would then ask, "And then?" or "Uh huh, could you tell me more about that?" or some similar simple inquiry.

On other occasions the interviewer might have asked another full question seeking additional information. An example of these scheduled and unscheduled probes from interview number 14 illustrates this (B. Berg, 2002). All questions were asked and answered in Spanish and later translated into English.

Interviewer [Scheduled Question]: How about your family, do they know about your sexual activities?

Subject: Yes, yes, they do know how I am, how I see myself. But they do not like it. On some occasions they tell me that they are going to send me to Mexico. They wanted to bribe me, but that is why I work, so I do not have to depend on them economically.

Interviewer [Scheduled Question]: What do your parents (brothers, sisters, etc.) think about your participation with sex between same masculine genders?

Subject: Okay, my parents found out because I told my sister that I was homosexual, because one of my father's brothers had raped me. My sister then told my father and my parents supported me. If the rest of my family does not support me, I do not care, just as long as my parents accept me, that is enough for me.

Interviewer [Unscheduled Probe]: When your uncle raped you, did he know you were gay?

Subject: Yes.

Interviewer [Unscheduled Probe]: How old were you at the time of the rape?

Subject: I was only eight years old when he raped me.

Interviewer [Unscheduled Probe]: Yes, and then? (pause)

Subject: I was eight years old when my uncle raped me, we were at the ranch, my mother and father went to make a phone call to my brothers who were in the United States so I was left alone with him. I already showed signs of being gay, my uncle took off my clothes, hit me and raped me. I still do not know why he did this to me; after all we were family. He threatened me, and told me to not say anything or he was going to hurt my parents. But at age thirteen I exploded, I could not keep it in any longer, so I told my sister what was happening. It was already the second time he had raped me. My sister was crying, she hugged me and said that she loved me. She then told my father and he made me confront my uncle. My father thought I was lying to him, but my uncle could not lie, he lowered his head and admitted that he had raped me. My father questioned him on why he did it and his response was that I wanted to do it with a homosexual. But I always ask myself, "Why me?"

Interviewer [Unscheduled Probe]:   How old was your uncle?

Subject: He was twenty-six years old and I was eight the first time he raped me. I already knew I was homosexual, but I would have preferred to experience that with the person that I loved, not by being raped. That gets me so upset and I will never forget it. I do not even wish for it to happen to my worst enemy.

The Interview Schedule

Traditionally, the term *survey* refers to both interviews and pencil-and-paper questionnaires. In this text, the term *survey,* unless otherwise indicated, is exclusively used in the context of interviewing. Typically, the choice to use an interviewing technique rather than a survey questionnaire technique is based on the selected procedure's ability to provide maximum opportunity for complete and accurate communication of ideas between the researcher and the respondent (Cannell & Kahn, 1968, p. 554). Among other things, this notion of accurate communication of ideas implies that researchers have clear ideas about the type of information they want to access and about the purpose and aims of their research.

The interview is an especially effective method of collecting information for certain types of research questions and, as noted earlier in this chapter, for addressing certain types of assumptions. Particularly when investigators are interested in understanding the perceptions of participants or learning how participants come to attach certain meanings to phenomena or events, interviewing provides a useful means of access (Taylor & Bogdan, 1998, p. 98). However, interviewing is only one of a number of ways researchers can obtain answers to questions. The determination of which data-gathering technique to use is necessarily linked to the type of research question being asked.

For instance, Becker (1963) suggests that if you are interested in knowing how frequently a subject smokes marijuana (how many times daily, weekly, monthly, and so on), then you may effectively use a questionnaire survey. If, however, you are interested in the sensation of marijuana smoking (the emotion-laden sensory experience as perceived by the subject), a more effective means of obtaining this information might be an open-ended interview question (Mutchnick & Berg, 1996).

A similar consideration is necessary when you determine what sort of structure an interview should have. For example, Rossman (1992) used semi-structured interviews in his examination of the development of Superfund community relations plans (Superfunds are federal funds offered to assist communities in environmental clean-up activities). Rossman (1992, p. 107) explains:

> Because of the nature of the information collected, applied researchers who develop community relations plans are best advised to use interviews and interviewers. Questionnaires lack the flexibility that is required to capture the subtle character of risk definition, especially a risk that is often defined ambiguously within a community. Risks such as those associated with Superfund sites are a major part of the community's social structure, but are less crystallized than risk associated with crime, or even natural environmental risk.

Conversely, Miller (1986) found that in her study of female street hustlers, an unstructured interview served her purposes best. Miller (1986, p. 26) writes:

> Seventy women agreed to taped interviews with me during which they shared with me the details of their lives. Special attention was paid to the initiation of these women into street hustling and the development of a career as a street hustler. Although the same broad topics were introduced during each interview, many of my questions changed over time.

Ellis, Kiesinger, and Tillmann-Healy (1997, p. 121) wanted to gain a more reflexive and intimate understanding of women's emotional experiences, and decided to use an interactive approach and a more or less unstructured interviewing style:

> [We] view interviewing as a collaborative communication process occurring between researchers and respondents, although we do not focus on validity and bias. For us, interactive interviewing involves the sharing of personal and social experiences of both respondents and researchers, who tell (and sometimes write) their stories in the context of a developing relationship.

Thus, when determining what type of interview format to use, you must consider the kinds of questions you want to ask and the sorts of answers you expect to receive. This line of thought naturally leads to consideration of how to create questions and an interview schedule.

Schedule Development

The first step to interview construction has already been implied: Specifically, researchers must determine the nature of their investigation and the objectives of their research. This determination provides the researchers with a starting point from which to begin developing a schedule of questions.

Selltiz et al. (1959), Spradley (1979), Patton (2002), and Polit and Hungler (1995) suggest that researchers begin with a kind of *outline*, listing all the broad categories they feel may be relevant to their study. This preliminary listing allows them to visualize the general format of the schedule. Next, researchers should develop sets of questions relevant to each of the outlined categories. The interview schedule for a study of volunteer police officers (Berg & Doerner, 1987) was developed by first listing general relevant areas gleaned from a reading of the literature. (See Chapter 2 on the spiraling nature of the research process.) These included:

1. Demographics
2. Police-related questions
3. Organizational memberships
4. Friends and family involved in police work
5. Personality style (passive, aggressive, authoritative, and so on)
6. Leisure activities

Following this, separate lists of questions for each of the six major thematic categories were developed. For instance, under demographics, we listed questions about birth date, level of education, marital status, and so forth. Under police-related questions we asked, "What would you say are the reasons you joined the reserve officers unit?" "How long have you been a reserve officer?" "Have you ever served as a regular police officer anywhere?" and so on. The purpose of these questions was to elicit information about how the subjects' relationships corresponded to various attitudes and behaviors described elsewhere in the interviews.

Question Order, Content, and Style

The specific ordering (sequencing), phrasing, level of language, adherence to subject matter, and general style of questions depend on the educational and social level of the subjects as well as their ethnic or cultural traits, age, and so forth. Additionally, researchers must take into consideration the central aims and focuses of their studies.

In order to draw out the most complete story about various subjects or situations under investigation, four types or styles of questions must be included in the survey instrument: essential questions, extra questions, throw-away questions, and probing questions.

Essential Questions   *Essential questions* exclusively concern the central focus of the study. They may be placed together or scattered throughout the survey, but they are geared toward eliciting specific desired information. For example, Glassner and Berg (1980, 1984) sought to study drinking patterns in the Jewish community. Consequently, essential questions addressing this specific theme were sprinkled throughout the 144-structured-question survey instrument. For instance, among a series of questions about friends and people the family feels proud of, the following question was introduced: "Has anyone in the family ever thought anyone else drank too much?" Later during the interview, among general questions about ceremonial participation in the Jewish holiday of Passover, the interviewer systematically asked:

> There is a question that we are a little curious about, because there seems to be some confusion on it. During the Passover story, there are seven or eight places it speaks about lifting a glass of wine. And there are three or four places which speak directly of drinking the wine. In some people's homes they drink a cup each time, and in some people's homes they count a sip as a cup. How is it done in your home?

Another regularly scheduled question during this segment of the interview asked: "Another question that interests us is, what becomes of the cup of wine for Elijah [ceremonially poured for the Angel Elijah]?" Later, during a series of questions centering on Chanukkah observance styles, the interviewer asked: "What drinks are usually served during this time?"

Separating these essential questions, however, were numerous other essential questions addressing such other research concerns as ritual knowledge and involvement, religious organization membership, leisure activities, and so on. In addition, there were three other types of questions intended for other purposes.

Extra Questions   *Extra questions* are those questions roughly equivalent to certain essential ones but worded slightly differently. These are included in order to check on the reliability of responses (through examination of consistency in response sets) or to measure the possible influence a change of wording might have.

Throw-Away Questions   Frequently, you find throw-away questions toward the beginning of an interview schedule. *Throw-away questions* may be essential demographic questions or general questions used to develop rapport between interviewers and subjects. You may also find certain throw-aways sprinkled throughout a survey to set the interviewing pace or to allow a change in focus in the interview. Throw-away questions, as the term implies, are incidental or unnecessary for gathering the important information being examined in the study. Nonetheless, these throw-away questions may be invaluable for drawing out a complete story from a respondent.

On occasion, throw-away questions may serve the additional purpose of cooling out the subject (Becker, 1963; Goffman, 1967). On these occasions, a throw-away question (or a series of them) may be tossed into an interview whenever subjects indicate to the interviewers that a sensitive area has been entered. The interviewer offhandedly says something to the effect of, "Oh, by the way, before we go any further, I forgot to ask you. . . ." By changing the line of questions, even for only a few moments, the interviewer moves away from the sensitive area and gives the interviewee a moment to cool out.

Probing Questions   *Probing questions,* or simply *probes,* provide interviewers with a way to draw out more complete stories from subjects. Probes frequently ask subjects to elaborate on what they have already answered in response to a given question—for example, "Could you tell me more about that?" "How long did you have that?" "What happened next?" "Who else has ever said that about you?" or simply, "How come?" Along similar lines, Lofland and Lofland (1984, p. 56) write:

> In interview[s]. . . the emphasis is on obtaining narratives or accounts in the person's own terms. You want the character and contour of such accounts to be set by the interviewees or informants. You might have a general idea of the kinds of things that will compose the account but still be interested in what the interviewees provide on their own and the terms in which they do it. As the informants speak, you should be attentive to what is mentioned and also to what is not mentioned but which you feel might be important. If something has been mentioned about which you want to know more, you can ask, "You mentioned_____; could you tell me more about that?" For things not mentioned, you might ask, "Did_____?" or "Was_____a consequence?"

Often interviewers incorporate a structured series of probes triggered by one or another type of response to some essential question. Probes, then, are intended to be largely neutral. Their central purpose is to elicit more information about whatever the respondent has already said in response to a question.

Wording of Questions   In order to acquire information while interviewing, researchers must word questions so that they will provide the necessary data. Thus, you must ask questions in such a manner as to motivate respondents to answer as completely and honestly as possible. As in the saying about computers, "garbage in, garbage out," so it is in interviewing. If the wrong questions are asked or if questions are asked in a manner that inhibits or prevents a respondent from answering fully, the interview will not be fruitful—garbage will come out. Denzin offers the following guidelines for formulating interview questions (Denzin, 1970, p. 129):

> Questions should accurately convey meaning to the respondent; they should motivate him to become involved and to communicate clearly his attitudes and opinions; they should be clear enough so that the interviewer can easily convey meaning to the respondent; they should be precise enough to exactly convey what is expected of the respondent. . . ; any specific question should have as a goal the discerning of a response pattern that clearly fits the broad contents of the investigation. . . ; if questions raise the possibility of the respondent's lying or fabricating (which is always a possibility), care should be taken to include questions that catch him up, or reveal to him and the interviewer that his previous answers have been incorrect.

Communicating Effectively

Perhaps the most serious problem with asking questions is how to be certain the intentions of the questions have been adequately communicated. Researchers must always be sure they have clearly communicated to the subjects what they want to know. The interviewers' language must be understandable to the subject; ideally, interviews must be conducted at the level or language of the respondents.

Becker and Geer (1957, pp. 28–29) note the seriousness of knowing the language of the interviewee both in order to ask understandable questions and to interpret correctly what the interviewee says in response. They state:

> Although we speak one language and share in many ways in one culture, we cannot assume that we understand precisely what another person, speaking as a member of such a group, means by any particular word. In interviewing members of groups other than our own, then, we are in somewhat the same position as the anthropologist who must learn a primitive language, with the important difference that, as Icheiser has put it, we often do not understand that we do not understand and are thus likely to make errors in interpreting what is said to us.

When developing surveys that will be applied to a large and diverse general population, many researchers choose what may be termed the *zero-order level of communications.* In such instances, the words and ideas conveyed by survey questions are simplified to the level of the least sophisticated of all potential respondents. Although this should tend to minimize potential communication problems with a range of respondents, it may also create some problems: The more sophisticated respondents may react negatively to questions asked in too simplistic a manner. When you are investigating a homogeneous subculture, this problem becomes somewhat less critical. However, when interviewing a cross section of subjects on the same topic, you may need to consider varying levels of language.

Similarly, you must allow for special languages (both real and symbolic) that certain groups may use. For example, in the Glassner and Berg (1980, 1984) study, the interviewer needed to be moderately versed in Yiddish idioms in order both to conduct many of the interviews and to assist transcribers in accurately reproducing interview transcripts. In another instance, when Berg and Doerner (1987) conducted a study of volunteer police officers, the interviewer needed a general understanding of "cop speak," the jargonized symbolic language frequently used by police officers as illustrated earlier in this chapter.

It is important during the course of the interviews that the interviewer shares meanings for terms commonly held by members of the research population. This sometimes goes beyond mere language barriers. For example, in a recent study (Berg et al., 2002) of risk factors associated with men who have sex with other men (MSM), one obstacle was that the subjects spoke Mexican street Spanish. Another was that within the MSM community, certain words and terms are used with specific connotations. To the average outsider these terms hold one meaning, but to the MSM community member such terms hold a dramatically different meaning. It was important, therefore, that the researchers be versed in these special words and terms.

The last point is underscored by Murray (1991), who suggests that researchers must be aware of what he refers to as *language codes* in linguistics. These include various phrases used in Black English (sometimes referred to as Ebonics) and Chicano or Mexican street Spanish. If the interviewer is not knowledgeable about a group's special language use, various nuances of dialect may be lost during the interview.

A Few Common Problems in Question Formulation

Several other problems arise when constructing interview questions. Among the more serious ones are affectively worded questions, double-barreled questions, and overly complex questions.

Affectively Worded Questions

Affective words arouse in most people an emotional response that is usually negative. Although these questions may not be intended as antagonistic, they nonetheless can close down or inhibit interview subjects. For instance, the word *why*, in American culture, tends to produce in most people a negative response. One possible explanation has to do with the punitive connotation of this question, as in "Why did you do that wrong thing?" Consequently, when subjects mention some form of conduct or an attitude and are then asked by the interviewers, "Why?" they may not respond accurately or completely. On the other hand, if asked in response to these same statements, "How come?" they may offer complete responses in a relaxed manner.

Kinsey, Pomeroy, and Martin (1948) similarly found that when affective topics were considered, neutralizing the sense of the questions (reducing their affects) improved the likelihood of a full answer. They cite, as an example, asking subjects in a study of human sexuality, "Do you masturbate?" Virtually all the initial respondents answered immediately, "I never masturbate." Yet, when the question was reworded—"About how many times a week would you say you masturbate?"—suddenly many respondents were willing to offer responses. The second version of the question tends to neutralize or normalize the affect (sensitivity) of the question. Asking how often one masturbates implies that others do so as well, thereby reducing the affect of the word and concept *masturbate*.

The Double-Barreled Question

Among the more common problems that arise in constructing survey items is the double-barreled question. This type of question asks a subject to respond simultaneously to two issues in a single question. For instance, one might ask, "How many times have you smoked marijuana, or have you only tried cocaine?" It should be noticed that the two issues in this single question are slightly unrelated. In the first clause, the question asks the frequency of marijuana usage. The second clause confuses the issue and asks whether marijuana or cocaine has ever been used by the subject.

The logical solution to the double-barreled question, of course, is to separate the two issues and ask separate questions. Failure to separate the two issues may yield some answers, because people tend to be obliging during interviews and may answer almost anything they are asked, but analysis of a response to a double-barreled question is virtually impossible.

Complex Questions

The pattern of exchange that constitutes verbal communication in Western society involves more than listening. When one person is speaking, the other is listening, anticipating, and planning how to respond. Consequently, when researchers ask a long, involved question, the subjects may not really hear the question in its entirety. Their response, then, may be only to some small portion of a greater concern woven into the complex question. Thus, keeping questions brief and concise allows clear responses and more effective analysis of the answers.

Question Sequencing

The arrangement or ordering of questions in an interview may significantly affect the results. Interviews typically begin with mild, nonthreatening questions concerning demographic matters. These questions tend to be easy for the subjects to answer and allow interviewers to develop rapport through eye contact and general demeanor. As the interview conversation proceeds, more complex and sensitive questions may be introduced.

Pretesting the Schedule

Once researchers have developed the instrument and are satisfied with the general wording and sequencing of questions, they must pretest the schedule. Ideally, this involves at least two steps. First, the schedule should be critically examined by people familiar with the study's subject matter—technical experts, other researchers, or persons fitting the type to be studied. This first step facilitates the identification of poorly worded questions, questions with offensive or emotion-laden wording, or questions revealing the researchers' own biases, personal values, or blind spots.

The second step in pretesting before the instrument can be used in a real study involves several practice interviews to assess how effectively the interview will work and whether the type of information being sought will actually be obtained. Chadwick, Bahr, and Albrecht (1984, p. 120) suggest five questions for assessing an instrument:

1. Has the researcher included all of the questions necessary to test the research hypothesis?
2. Do the questions elicit the types of response that were anticipated?

3. Is the language of the research instrument meaningful to the respondents?
4. Are there other problems with the questions, such as double meaning or multiple issues embedded in a single question?
5. Finally, does the interview guide, as developed, help to motivate respondents to participate in the study?

A careful pretest of the instrument, although time consuming in itself, usually saves enormous time and cost in the long run.

Long Versus Short Interviews

Interviewing can be a very time-consuming, albeit valuable, data-gathering technique. It is also one that many uninitiated researchers do not fully understand. This is particularly true when considering the length of an interview. Many quantitative researchers who dabble at interviewing are convinced that interviews must be short, direct, and businesslike. Some who use interviews over the telephone even recommend keeping them to no more than about five minutes (Hagan, 1995). As a result, one issue surrounding interviews is exactly how long or short they should be.

There are several ways to answer this question, but all will immediately direct your attention back to the basic research question(s). If potential answers to research questions can be obtained by asking only a few questions, then the interview may be quite brief. If, on the other hand, the research question(s) are involved or multilayered, it may require a hundred or more questions. Length also depends on the type of answers constructed between the interviewer and the subject. In some cases, where the conversation is flowing, a subject may provide rich, detailed, and lengthy answers to the question. In another situation, the subject may respond to the same question with a rather matter-of-fact, short, cryptic answer.

Obviously, the number of questions on the interview schedule is at least partially related to how long an interview is likely to take. On the average, an interview schedule with 165 questions is likely to take longer than one with only 50 questions. Yet, there are several misconceptions about long interviews that sometimes creep into research methods class lectures. For instance, some researchers believe that most subjects will refuse to engage in an interview once they know it may last for two or more hours. Others maintain that subjects may not remain interested during a long interview, and it will end in a withdrawal. Or, conversely, some researchers believe that short interviews do not provide any useful information. In fact, I am certain that such conditions do occasionally occur. However, they do not represent binding rules or even terribly viable guidelines.

Interviews, unlike written surveys, can be extremely rewarding and interesting situations for both the interviewer and the subject. Believing that subjects would quickly weary with a written survey containing 175 questions may be true. I for one believe such a situation is boring. However, talking with an interviewer about things that matter to the interviewee and doing so in a way that provides him or her with appropriate feedback often provides subjects with a kind of intangible yet intrinsic reward. For subjects to comment after a long interview that they did not actually realize so much time had already passed is common. I will liken this to reading a good book. At some time or another, most of us have begun reading some exciting or engaging novel and not realized that hours had actually passed. So it is with a well-run long interview. Even after several hours, there is often a feeling that only minutes have passed.

Certain types of research lend themselves to longer interviews than others. For example, when one conducts a *life history,* the researcher is interested in the life events of those being interviewed (Rubin & Rubin, 1995). In this case, the interview may go on for a very long time, perhaps carrying over to several separate sessions on different days. On the other hand, the interview may involve a single topic and require only a brief interview situation.

To suggest that all interviews must be lengthy if they are to yield useful information is not accurate. In 1989, Cal Larson and I conducted interviews in a maximum security prison among an assortment of inmates (Berg & Larson, 1989). Our research question involved an interest in the ways inmates perceived predetermined or fixed sentences—a flat length of time such as 5 years or 10 years—compared to their view of indeterminate sentences—a time range such as 5 to 10 years or 10 to 20 years. We were not interested in the family backgrounds or social experiences of inmates who committed particular categories of crime. We were not interested in determining explanations for why or how inmates committed their particular crimes nor whether inmates had received deals or plea bargains, or any of an assortment of other interesting but unconnected issues. We simply wanted to know about their views of determinate and indeterminate sentences and a number of related questions. As a result, we focused directly on these issues, and the interviews lasted an average of about 45 minutes.

What we learned, however, was very interesting and important information. First, inmates reported they seldom think about getting caught when they commit a crime. As a result, the idea of a particular crime carrying a long fixed sentence did not offer any deterrence to their committing the crime (Berg & Larson, 1989). Second, several armed robbers indicated that if they did become concerned about lengthy fixed sentences, they would likely leave no witnesses, whereas their previous criminal style was to avoid harming bystanders. In short, we learned that fixed sentences might have the unintended effect of increasing the level of violence associated with some crimes.

You should understand that length is a relative concept when conducting interviews. Some topics and subjects will produce long interviews while others will create short ones. Furthermore, different styles of interviewing, such as interactive or interpretive orientations, that require the development of a *relationship* between researcher and subject, may last not only long durations but multiple sessions (Hertz, 1995; Kvale, 1996; Miller, 1996). What is important to remember is that simply because an interview contains many questions or only a few does not in itself immediately translate into a long or short interview.

Telephone Interviews

Related to the question of interview length is the role of telephone interviews in qualitative research. Telephone interviews are not a major way of collecting qualitative data. To be sure, telephone interviews lack face-to-face nonverbal cues that researchers use to pace their interviews and to determine the direction to move in. Yet, researchers have found that, under certain circumstances, telephone interviews may provide not only an effective means for gathering data but also in some instances—owing to geographic locations—the only viable method. In fact, the primary reason that one might conduct a qualitative telephone interview is to reach a sample population that is in geographically diverse locations. For example, if an investigator is interested in studying how nursing home directors define elder abuse, he or she might consider conducting in-person interviews with some sample of nursing home directors. However, given that nursing home facilities may be at some distance from one another, as well as from the location of the interviewer, conducting interviews by telephone may be a logical resolution.

Qualitative telephone interviews are likely to be best when the researcher has fairly specific questions in mind (a formal or semistructured interview schedule). Qualitative interviews are also quite productive when they are conducted among people with whom the researcher has already conducted face-to-face interviews or with whom he or she may have developed a rapport during fieldwork (Rubin & Rubin, 1997). There are several important, necessary steps to accomplish a qualitative telephone interview. First, the investigator must establish legitimacy; next, the researcher must convince the potential subject that it is important for the subject to take part in the research; and finally, the researcher must carefully ensure that the information he or she obtains is sufficiently detailed to contribute meaningfully to the study.

This first step can be accomplished in several ways. For example, the interviewer might mail a letter to the prospective subject explaining the nature of the research and that the subject will be called to set an appointment for the actual interview. The letter should be on official letterhead and may contain supportive documentation (letters of support from relevant or significant people in the community, newspaper stories about the researcher or the study, etc.).

The second step will arise when the investigator initially contacts potential subjects and attempts to convince them to take part. This call will actually accomplish several things. It will allow the subjects to ask questions and raise any concerns they might have about the study or their participation. It will also provide an opportunity for the investigator to gain some sense of the individual and to begin developing a kind of relationship and rapport as well as an opportunity to convince the individual to participate in the study if the individual is resistant.

These calls should be made during normal working hours and researchers should *break the ice* by introducing themselves and ascertaining whether the individual has received the letter and accompanying materials. Calls should be made approximately one week to 10 days following the mailing of the letters of introduction. After the initial introduction, the researcher might ask if the individual has any questions. Next, using a polite and friendly but firm affirmative statement, the researcher should ask, "When would it be convenient for me to call you back to conduct the interview?" Recognize that not all subjects will immediately agree to take part, and the researcher may need to do a little convincing. This may offer the additional benefit of forging a rapport with the subject.

Advantages of the Telephone Interview

Hagan (2006) outlines a series of advantages associated with undertaking telephone interviews. These include reduced staff requirements, a method by which the investigator can easily monitor ongoing interviews to assure quality and avoid interviewer bias, and the ability to reach widespread geographic areas at an economical cost. In addition, interviews can be recorded via an inexpensive patch between the telephone and the recording instrument. If a digital recorder is used, the interview can later be transcribed in the traditional fashion or downloaded into a computer and converted to text (which may need light editing) by a speech-to-text program (Halbert, 2003). Some researchers argue that telephone interviews and surveys, because they provide a kind of instant anonymity, are effective for obtaining hard-to-locate individuals or when asking highly sensitive questions (Champion, 2006; Hagan, 2006).

Disadvantages of the Telephone Interview

There are, of course, disadvantages to using telephone interviews, which for many researchers outweigh the potential advantages. For example, some people have no telephone, and others have unlisted numbers—both groups are effectively eliminated as potential interviewees. Also excluded from the subject pool are those who screen their calls through caller ID or an answering machine and avoid taking calls from researchers. From a symbolic interactionist perspective, an important disadvantage is that current telephone technology lacks the ability for the interviewer and interviewee to use full channels of communication. In other words, neither can read visual cues offered by the other (either those unintentional cues by the respondent or those intentionally transmitted by the interviewer).

Computer Assisted Interviewing

As pointed out in Chapter 1 of this book, among the fascinating changes occurring in the world of social research is the increased and innovative use of computer technology. Here I discuss two major technological innovations that impact interviewing. One is commonly referred to as *Computer Assisted Telephone Interviewing* (CATI) and the other as *Computer Assisted Personal Interviewing* (CAPI). Both of these strategies have long been used in traditional survey research, but both also have potential qualitative applications.

Computer Assisted Telephone Interviewing (CATI)

When conducting qualitative telephone interviews, CATI can be very useful. Earl Babbie (2001, p. 265) offers an excellent image of the basic process. He states:

> Imagine an interviewer wearing a telephone headset, sitting in front of a computer terminal and its video screen. The central computer has been programmed to select a telephone number at random and dials it. (Random-digit dialing avoids the problem of unlisted telephone numbers.) On the video screen is an introduction ("Hello, my name is . . .") and the first question to be asked ("Could you tell me how many people live at this address?").

When the subject answers the telephone, the interviewer begins with an introduction, explains the purposes of the study, and invites the person to take part. Once the subject consents to participate, the interview begins. As the subject answers each question, the interviewer immediately types the response into the computer. In computer-assisted, *pencil-and-paper* surveys, the interviewer chiefly asks the questions, lists the possible answers, and then inputs the subject's responses.

In a qualitative version of CATI, the interviewer asks open-ended questions and types in the full accounts offered by the subject. The advantages to this version include skipping the need to later transcribe the data and allowing the information to be immediately input into a textual data manager (a computer program designed for qualitative textual analysis) or to be coded. Naturally, this requires an interviewer who is skilled in typing and is able to take the equivalent of dictation. However, because not all interviewers have this typing capacity and because it can become quite expensive to hire and train someone to do this, an investigator might opt to employ a system known as *Voice Capture*. This process has been extensively used in marketing research for over 10 years and involves digitally recording the voice of the subject during the course of the CATI (Tallal, 1998). Later, this recording can be transcribed, but during the course of the interview the subject is permitted to speak openly and freely with an added sense of anonymity, since the interviewer does not know what the subject looks like. Again, there is the obvious loss of visual cues because of the absence of face-to-face contact. This can be rectified with CAPI.

Computer Assisted Personal Interviewing (CAPI)

Like CATI, CAPI employs a computer to provide the questions and capture the answers during an interview. In this case, the interviews are conducted face-to-face, thereby restoring the visual cues lost during a typical CATI-type interview. Again, the process can involve either the interviewer asking the questions and typing in the response (as with dictation) or with Voice Capture or similar type system to record the answers. There is also a second style of computer-assisted interviewing called Computer Assisted Self-Administered Interviewing (CASI). In this version of the process, the subject is provided with a computer (a laptop or access to a desktop computer) and allowed to read the interview schedule and type in his or her responses. Again, the advantages to this strategy include having the data ready to be placed into a data manager or coded, as well as offering the subject privacy while responding (there is no interviewer present while the subject types his or her answers).

The disadvantages, unfortunately, are numerous and include the fact that many people cannot type and will take a long time to hunt and peck at the keyboard. Some people may feel self-conscious about being poor spellers or writers and, thus, use only cryptic responses rather than fluid full accounts. Other subjects may be in a hurry and choose to either skip questions or write only very short answers. Some subjects may be weak readers or illiterate, further complicating the process. For this last category of subjects, some advances have been offered. Turner and his associates (1998), for example, have employed what they coined *Audio-CASI* (Audio Computer Assisted Self-Interview) as a strategy. This technique similarly employs a laptop computer with the questions on it and the ability of the subject to provide answers, but in addition this technique uses a headset and an audio version of the survey that is played for the subject to hear. Although Turner and colleagues (1998) used this technique with a survey-type questionnaire, the same process could be adapted for a more open-ended qualitative interview.

Web-Based In-Depth Interviews

As noted in this and the previous edition of *Qualitative Research Methods for the Social Sciences*, as technology advances, methods used in qualitative research must strive to keep up—or at least seek ways to take advantage of these technological advancements. As suggested, one way qualitative researchers can capitalize on the advancing computer age is through the use of a type of "digitized convergence" (Brown, 2002) by which investigators integrate or co-opt the more traditional survey-based procedures of CAPI and use them in a qualitative interview. Another method is to simply go online and use the Internet as a research tool for conducting in-depth interviews. This can be accomplished either in synchronous (real-time) or asynchronous (not real-time) interview environments (Stromer-Galley, 2003).

Synchronous environments include real-time chat rooms, instant messenger protocols, and real-time threaded communications. Such environments provide the researcher and respondent an experience similar to face-to-face interaction insofar as they provide a mechanism for a back-and-forth exchange of questions and answers in what is almost real time. In some cases, "vid-cams" (computer-linked video cameras) can be used to allow the researcher and respondent to actually see one another.

While this type of interview interaction is not identical to a more traditional face-to-face interview, it does approach it in a number of ways. For example, when a respondent answers a question, the interviewer has the ability to ask probing questions to elicit additional information, or to run in an entirely different direction, similar to the interviewer's ability in a face-to-face interview. Consequently, a researcher can delve as deeply as he or she chooses into an area either structured into the interview schedule or arising spontaneously in the course of the interview exchange.

Asynchronous environments include the use of e-mail, message boards, and privately hosted bulletin posting areas. Asynchronous environments are commonly used by investigators undertaking survey-based research (Bachman & Schutt, 2003; Champion, 2006). Bampton and Cowton (2002, p. 1) suggest that qualitative researchers can also take advantage of what they term the "e-interview." They describe the benefits of conducting e-mail-based qualitative interviews:

> The asynchronicity of the e-interview has several consequences. There can be pauses in face-to-face interviews, of course, but in an e-interview the delay in interaction between researcher and subject can range from seconds (virtually real time) to hours or days. In our own research some of the replies came back surprisingly quickly, but the important thing is that the interviewee was not committed to replying promptly. In this lies one of the major benefits of the e-interview, in that busy subjects—and busy researchers, for that matter—do not have to identify a mutually convenient time to talk to each other. Nor do they each need to find a single chunk of time in which to complete the full interview, since as an interview—rather than something more akin to an e-mailed questionnaire—there should normally be more than one episode of question and answer. Indeed, such iterations are fundamental to the communication having the dialogic or conversational characteristics of a good interview.

For many people, the use of e-mail has become a common and comfortable activity. Transferring this comfort to the interview situation, then, can similarly provide a benefit for qualitative interviewing (Stromer-Galley, 2003). Another advantage of the e-interview is that e-mail questions transmitted to an individual are effectively private: no one else online can add to, delete, or interrupt the exchange.[2]

Setting meeting times for interviews and conquering distance problems have long been problems when conducting qualitative interviews. E-mail interviews eliminate these issues by permitting subjects to answer in their own time and literally from across the country or even the world. Lindlof and Taylor (2002) also suggest that fatigue can be a problem in lengthy interviews, and this too is eliminated in the e-interview.

Asynchronous environments such as e-mail and bulletin boards naturally have drawbacks when it comes to conducting qualitative interviews. The obvious drawback is the loss of visual cues—both those that occur between interviewer and respondent as part of the conversational flow of the interview and those that serve as social markers in the interactionary process (e.g., age, gender, race, dress style). Also lacking is the spontaneity of prob-ing and chasing down interesting topics that inadvertently arise in the course of the interview. Finally, interview subjects are limited to those who have access to both a computer and an e-mail account, as well as to those who are literate enough to express themselves in an e-mail format.

While I am not arguing that the e-interview should replace the face-to-face interview in all future research endeavors, it seems prudent to include this and other technological data-collecting strategies in the arsenal of lines of action for conducting qualitative research.

Conducting an Interview: A Natural or an Unnatural Communication?

Everyone actually has received some training and has experience in inter-viewing. Children, for example, commonly ask their mom or dad questions whenever they see or experience something different, unusual, or unknown. In school, students ask their teachers questions and respond to questions put to them by teachers. People regularly observe exchanges of questions and answers between teachers and other students, siblings and parents, employ-ers and employees, and among friends. Thus, one might assume that since everyone has received tacit training in both asking questions (sending mes-sages) and answering questions (receiving messages), the research interview is just another natural communication situation. But the research interview is not a natural communication exchange.

Beyond acquiring the ability to send and receive messages while growing up in society, people also learn how to avoid certain types of messages. Goffman (1967) has termed this sort of avoidance *evasion tactics*. Such tactics may involve a word, phrase, or gesture that expresses to another participant that no further discussion of a specific issue (or in a particular area) is desired. Conversely, people also usually acquire the ability to recognize these evasion tactics and, in a natural conversational exchange, to respect them. This sort of deference ceremony (Goffman, 1967, p. 77) expresses a kind of intrinsic respect for the other's avoidance rituals. In return, there is the unspoken expec-tation that this respect will be reciprocated in some later exchange.

As anyone who has ever conducted an interview already knows, this sort of deference ceremony simply cannot be permitted during the course of a research interview. In fact, a subject's evasion tactics during the course of an interview are among the most serious obstacles to overcome—but overcome them you must! At the same time, you do not want to jeopardize the evolving definition of the situation, the potential rapport with the subject, or the amount of falsification and gloss a subject may feel compelled to use during the interview. As Gorden (1987, p. 70) suggests, "If all respondents said nothing, responded with truth, or said 'I won't tell you!' the task of the interviewer would be much simpler. Unfortunately, the respondent can avoid appearing uncooperative by responding voluminously with irrelevancies or misinformation, and this presents a challenge to the interviewer." In other words, the interviewer must maneuver around a subject's avoidance rituals in a manner that neither overtly violates social norms associated with communication exchanges nor causes the subject to lie.

Qualitative interviews may appear to be similar to ordinary conversations in some ways, but they differ in terms of how intensely the researcher listens to pick up on key words, phrases, and ideas (Rubin & Rubin, 1997). They differ also in terms of the kinds of nonverbal cues that the investigator will watch for in order to effectively identify the interviewee's emotional state, deference ceremonies, and even lies. One way these obstacles can be handled is through use of the dramaturgical interview.

The Dramaturgical Interview

There are a number of necessary terms and elements connected with understanding the dramaturgical interview and learning how to maneuver around communication-avoidance rituals. Central to these is the differentiation between the *interviewer's role* and the *roles an interviewer may perform*. As De Santis (1980, p. 77) suggests, the interviewer may be seen as "playing an occupational role," and "society can be expected to have some knowledge, accurate or inaccurate, about the norms which govern the role performance of various occupations." For instance, in our society, one might expect a farmer to wear jeans, not a fine three-piece suit, while working in the field. Similarly, one can expect certain things about appearance, manner, style, and language connected with other occupational roles, including that of an interviewer. For example, Maccoby and Maccoby (1968, p. 462) state:

> What are some of the roles in which respondents may perceive an interviewer? Much depends, of course, on the auspices of the study and the setting of the interview. If the study has been sponsored by a prestigeful institution and covers topics on which the interviewer might be assumed to have expert knowledge, the interviewer may find himself placed in a role similar to that of the family doctor; he is consulted for advice on the respondent's problems.

The implication of the preceding description of the role of an interviewer is that preconceived notions do exist among interviewees, but these notions are malleable. There can also be preconceived notions of subjects on the part of interviewers. Whether acknowledged or not, "There is always a model of the research subject lurking behind persons placed in the role of interview respondent" (Holstein & Gubrium, 1995, p. 7). In a study seeking to examine the isolation and vulnerability of elders, Cherry Russell (1999) found that her preconceived understandings of older people affected how she planned to research them, and this preconceived notion negatively affected the study. Because a subject's and an interviewer's preconceptions about one another may be based on both correct and incorrect information, the actual conception of the interviewer role rests on the definition of the situation established during the course of the interview itself.

In a number of sources on interviewing, the interviewer's role is discussed in terms of *biasing effects* or *reactivity* (Babbie, 1995; Chadwick et al., 1984). But the role of the interviewer is not necessarily established in granite, nor do the interviewer and interviewees operate within a vacuum! As Kahn and Cannell (1957, p. 62) suggest, "The role of the interviewer . . . is determined in part by the expectations of others." It is, therefore, within the capacity of an interviewer to affect (without biasing results) even the preconceived notions that subjects may have about the interviewer's role.

Many roles are available to an interviewer. Regardless of any preconceived notion and expectation about the interviewer's role as perceived by the interviewee, it is possible (within certain limits) for the interviewer to shape, alter, and even create desired role images. Gorden (1987, p. 213) describes this as *role-taking*. He explains that "role-taking is a conscious selection, from among one's actual role repertory, of the role thought most appropriate to display to a particular respondent at the moment."

As explained in the next section, by changing roles, the interviewer can also circumvent many of the avoidance tactics an interviewee might otherwise effectively use.

Interviewer Roles and Rapport

The model of the dramaturgical interview is intended to convey the notion of a very fluid and flexible format for conducting research interviews. With regard to rapport, which can be defined as the positive feelings that develop between the interviewer and the subject, it should not be understood as meaning there are no boundaries between the interviewer and the subject. The model of the dramaturgical interview should be interpreted as a conversation between two people conversing on one person's perceptions on the events of daily life, but, as Kvale (1996, pp. 5–6) similarly explains, "It is not a conversation between equal partners." The dramaturgical interview should not be a dialogue, with more or less equal time allocated to each participant, because the whole point is to obtain information from the subject. In many ways, the ideal situation would be to assist the subject in conveying almost a monologue on the research topic. When this is not possible, the dramaturgical interview provides pathways to help the subject to offer his or her accounts.

To accomplish this, the interview must rely on the establishment and maintenance of good rapport. Just as no two people in society are exactly alike, no interviewer and his or her subject are exactly alike. However, if the interviewer is able to establish some sense of common ground, then one avenue of rapport building could be opened. For example, during the course of the Berg (2002) study of risk factors associated with men who have sex with other men, one of the interviewers, Jose (a pseudonym), regularly made reference to the fact that he was a member of the MSM community. A second interviewer, Rosa, a heterosexual Latina, found common ground by referring to familiar Mexican cultural elements and events she and the subjects both understood. Similarly, in a study of Appalachian women and domestic violence, Patricia Gagne found common ground by alluding to her own experiences in an abusive relationship (Tewksbury & Gagne, 1997).

It is important to note that the interviewer does not necessarily always have to possess similar characteristics or experiences to that of the subjects— although some degree of understanding would certainly be a good thing to possess. In some situations, such as a study of the Ku Klux Klan, it would be unwise to send an African American in to conduct interviews. On the other hand, almost any Caucasian (who did not have significant ethnic facial characteristics) would likely work.

A number of feminist approaches to research in the social sciences seek in interviewing to emphasize the importance of building rapport with the respondents in order to achieve a successful interview outcome. Toward this end, some feminist researchers argue that interviewers must be willing to offer self-disclosures of personal information and develop genuine relationships with their interviewees beyond the boundaries of the roles of interviewer and interviewees (Cotterill, 1992; Oakley, 1981). This gives way to what may be referred to as a participatory model of interviewing (Lyons & Chipperfield, 2000). Participatory models of interviewing address the power differential between the researcher and the subject, thereby creating a nonhierarchical, nonmanipulative research relationship. Unfortunately, most interview situations, and notably the dramaturgical model, require the interviewer to maintain a certain amount of intentional control over the interview process—no matter how deferential, open, or self-disclosing he or she might choose to be during the course of the interview or when developing rapport.

Much of the literature of interviewing, especially in relation to the concepts of reactivity and rapport, suggests that the interviewee's conception of the interviewer centers around aspects of appearance and demeanor. Overt, observable characteristics such as race, gender, ethnicity, style of dress, age, hairstyle, manner of speech, and general demeanor provide information used by an interviewee to confirm or deny expectations about what an interviewer ought to be like. The negative, reactive effects of an interviewer's observable social characteristics and personal attributes are extensively discussed in the literature on interviewing (see Burns & Grove, 1993; De Santis, 1980; Gorden 1975, 1980, 1987; Nieswiadomy, 2002; Patton, 2001). In each source, however, the emphasis is on the effect an interviewer's characteristics have on obtaining the interviewee's consent to participate in an interview. Another theme emphasized in the literature is the potential bias arising from the effects of the interviewer's attributes.

There is little question that, as Stone (1962, p. 88) states, "Basic to the communication of the interview meaning is the problem of appearance and mood. Clothes often tell more about the person than his conversation." Is it really sufficient merely to look the part? If a man dons an ermine cape and robe, places a gold crown on his head, attaches a perfectly sculpted crepe beard to his face, and regally struts about, is this a guarantee that he will perform *King Lear* in a convincing or even adequate fashion? To be sure, the interviewer's appearance, accreditation, sponsorship, and characteristics are important to interviewing (see, for example, Benny, Riesman, & Star, 1956). All of these, of course, are within the absolute control of the interviewer. Attributes of appearance are in many ways analogous to the old door-to-door vacuum cleaner salesman's trick of placing a foot between the open door and its jamb—a trick that neither ensured a sale nor prevented the injury of the salesman's foot as the door was slammed shut.

The Role of the Interviewee

It is important to keep in mind that throughout the interview process, there are two individuals involved: the interviewer and the interviewee. While this text and others spend considerable time discussing the role of the interviewer, little if any direct attention is given to the impression-management activities of the interviewee (Collins, Shattell, & Thomas, 2005). In our everyday conversations with others, it is common to consider how each party in the conversation seeks to present his or her best face, so to speak. But it is less common to think about such impression management going on in the interview relationship between the interviewer and the interviewee (Dingwall, 1997).

Individuals who agree to take part in an interview usually have a complex set of reasons for doing so. Perhaps they expect to gain some sort of therapeutic benefit or are curious about the topic to be addressed. They may desire to share some personal experiences they have not felt comfortable sharing with others before, or their reason may be as mundane as a desire to spend time with someone because they are lonely. Each of these is an element, or facet, of the interviewee that he or she may want to either show or shield from the interviewer. Particularly because social scientists may be interviewing various deviants, criminals, abusers, or victims of abuse, the interviewee may desire to construct himself or herself in the most positive (or perhaps most negative) light possible in relation to the study topic (Rapley, 2001).

While interviewees often experience a kind of intangible gratuitous reward as a consequence of talking with a trained listener, they may also experience considerable apprehension about how the interviewer perceives them or the behaviors they are discussing (Collins, Shattell, & Thomas, 2005; Thomas & Pollio, 2002). The solution, then, is for the interviewer to become somewhat more reflexive in his or her efforts throughout the interaction and to become a more *self-conscious performer* during the interview.

The Interviewer as a Self-Conscious Performer

The performance of the interviewer, as illustrated in the preceding anecdotes, is not at all haphazard. Actions, lines, roles, and routines must be carefully prepared and rehearsed in advance and, thus, constitute a *self-conscious performance*.

The literature on interviewing techniques often describes interviewers who react spontaneously to responses offered by interviewees in areas not scheduled on the interview instrument. Interviewers are described as using their insight and intuition to formulate the next question or probe almost instinctively. However, even though following up subject areas initiated by interviewees is important (even when the areas may not have been seen as relevant during the interview's design stage), the notion that interviewers respond spontaneously is faulty. The use of terms such as *intuition* likewise seems loose and inaccurate.

Goode and Hatt (1952, p. 186) voiced a similar concern more than 50 years ago. They stated, "This is an unfortunate term [intuition] since for many it possesses overtones of vagueness, subjectivity and even mysticism."

Perhaps a more accurate understanding of the meaning of interviewer's intuition is what Archer (1980) calls *social interpretations*. The process of social interpretation, although not fully understood, is nonetheless evidenced by convincing empirical research (see Archer & Akert, 1977, 1980). Even when interviewers are presented with a unique response by an interviewee, it is highly unlikely that a similar (spontaneously created) action or statement is required from the interviewers. In the majority of interview situations, even novice interviewers will use some version of social interpretation and draw on a response taken from their repertoire of tactics (discussed in detail in a following section). Lincoln and Guba (1985) have similarly mentioned the effects of tacit knowledge with regard to nonverbal cues relevant to communications between senders and receivers—in other words, subtly and often implicitly learned pieces of knowledge that trigger associations between actions and meanings.

More recently, Holstein and Gubrium (1995, p. 7) indicate that interviewers often have some preconceived notion about their subjects:

> If only tacitly, there is always a model of the research *subject* lurking behind persons placed in the role of interview respondent. Considering the epistemological activity of the interview requires us to ask how interviewers relate to respondents, as imagined subjects, and to the conversations they have with those subjects.

Social Interpretations and the Interviewer

Social interpretations are defined as the affected messages transferred from one acting individual to another through nonverbal channels. These nonverbal channels include body gestures, facial grimaces, signs, symbols, and even some phonemic sounds such as tongue clicks, grunts, sighs, and similar visible indicators of communication (e.g., physical proximity between participant actors, their blocking, and so forth). As Gorden (1987, p. 75) suggests, interviewers must hear not only *what* the subjects say but also *how* they say it.

Nonverbal channels include a variety of diverse elements. Each of these elements, taken individually, provides only a fragment of the information necessary for an accurate social interpretation. When rendered in combination, or as Archer and Akert (1980, p. 396) describe it, "in symphony," they provide sufficient cues and clues to convey clear messages and social meanings.

These nonverbal channels of communication, together with more obvious verbal channels, make up the conversational interaction situation or what has been called *full-channel communication*.

Social interpretations are not instinctive but learned and can be accurately made in a matter of seconds (Archer & Akert, 1977, 1980; Rosenfeld & Civikly, 1976; Rosenthal, Hall, Dimatteo, Rogers, & Archer, 1979). Social interpretations are formed by observing the complex presentation of clues in real-life situations, from filmed versions of these interactions, or from still photographs in which even the nonverbal channels have been frozen in motionlessness as well as silence.

Throughout the interview process, the interviewer and the interviewee simultaneously send and receive messages on both nonverbal and verbal channels of communication. This exchange is in part a conscious social performance. Each participant is aware of the other's presence and intentionally says something and/or acts in certain ways for the other's benefit. However, to some extent, the interactions in an interview are also *unconscious,* which does not necessarily mean *unintended.* Unconscious behaviors should be understood as second-nature behaviors. An illustration of this sort of second-nature (automatic) interaction can often be observed when someone answers the telephone. The telephone voice is frequently almost melodic, even when only moments before the same voice may have been raised in angry shrieks directed toward a spouse or child. The social performance, of course, is for the benefit of whoever has just telephoned. Following the call, this individual's voice may again be raised in tones of anger—just as quickly and unconsciously.

Whenever interviewers realize they have trespassed on some unpleasant area of a respondent's life or an area the respondent does not want to talk about, it is not due to intuition or insight. This realization is derived from a social interpretation of the messages sent by the interviewee. The ways interviewers respond to these messages, however, will have a profound effect on the quality of the interview as a whole. For example, if interviewers ignore what they have interpreted as a very sensitive area and plunge ahead, they may force the respondent to lie, change the subject, not respond, or withdraw from the interview. If, on the other hand, interviewers do defer to the avoidance rituals used by the respondent, they may lose valuable information necessary to the study.

However, if an interviewer, in response to the clues, offers some demonstration that he or she has received the message and will at least, to some extent, respect the interviewee's desires, the interview will probably continue. It is also likely that the interviewer will be able to direct the respondent back to this unpleasant area at a later point in the interview.

The use of social interpretations as described earlier certainly resembles Goffman's (1967) deference ceremony. There are, however, several critical distinctions, perhaps the most significant being that the deference is only temporary.

It has been suggested previously that throughout the performance you as an interviewer must be conscious and reflective. You must carefully watch and interpret the performance of the subject. Your interpretations must be based on the cues, clues, and encoded messages offered by the interviewee. Included in the information these interactions supply may be the communication of a variety of moods, sentiments, role portrayals, and stylized routines, which represent the interviewee's script, line cues, blocking, and stage directions. You, the interviewer, then must play several other roles simultaneously with that of interviewer. You must participate as an actor but must serve as director and choreographer as well.

The Interviewer as Actor   As an actor, you must perform your lines, routines, and movements appropriately. This means that in addition to reciting scripted lines (the interview questions), you must be aware of what the other actor (the interviewee) is doing throughout the interview. You must listen carefully to line cues in order to avoid stepping on the lines of the interviewee (interrupting before the subject has completely answered a question). In addition, as actor, you must remain nonjudgmental regardless of what the interviewee may say. If you want people to openly talk about their feelings and views, you must refrain from making any negative judgments—either verbally or through visual cues. The best way to accomplish this is to accept people for who and what they are; avoid making judgments of their actions, beliefs, or life styles, even in your mind.

The Interviewer as Director   At the same time as you are performing as actor, you must also serve as director. In this capacity, you must be conscious of how you perform lines and move, as well as of the interviewee's performance. As an interviewer, you must reflect on each segment of the interview as if you were outside the performance as an observer. From this vantage point, you must assess the adequacy of your performance (for example, whether you are responding correctly to line cues from the interviewee and whether you are handling avoidance messages appropriately). This may include demonstrating both verbally and visually that you are empathic to things the interviewee has said. An approving nod or a brief comment, such as "I understand what you mean" or "I see," may offer sufficient positive reinforcement.

The Interviewer as Choreographer   The various assessments made in the role of director involve a process similar to what Reik (1949) described as "listening with the third ear." By using what you have heard (in the broadest sense of this term) in a self-aware and reflective manner, you as interviewer manage to control the interview process. As a result, as choreographer, you can effectively block (choreograph) your own movements and gestures and script your own response lines.

From this dramaturgical perspective, you as interviewer do not respond to any communication, verbal or nonverbal, scheduled (on the interview) or initiated by the subject, by means of spontaneous intuition or innate insight. Instead, the entire interview performance is a self-conscious social performance. You and the interviewee are constantly in the process of performing and evaluating your own and each other's performance. Using these assessments, both participants are able to adjust scripts and movements in response to messages sent and received throughout the interview.

The Interviewer's Repertoire

Interviewers make adjustments throughout the interview consisting largely of switching from one role to another or altering their style of speech, manner, or set of lines. These devices comprise the interviewer's *repertoire*. Interviewers seldom genuinely improvise a spontaneous technique or strategy during the course of an actual interview. Certainly, a new technique would hardly be tried unless the repertoire of standard strategies had already been exhausted.

Preparation is a major guideline in interviewing. This is not to say that you should not actively pursue a topic initiated by the interviewee. However, even when interviewers pursue unplanned leads, they still can do it in a consistently scripted, rather than novel, fashion. At the very least, interviewers should be prepared with a series of scripted questions that may be triggered by virtually any possible topic area. These questions, very simply, include "Who with?" "Where?" "How come?" "How often?" "How many?" and a variety of similar questions relevant to the specifics of the study. In other words, during the design stages of the research, one must think about the possibility that unanticipated subject areas might arise. Consequently, even the unanticipated can be planned for!

For example, although one of the major foci in the Jewish drinking study conducted by Glassner and Berg (1980, 1984) was alcohol use, we were also interested in our subjects' possible involvement in other drugs. However, this interest was incidental, and we were thus only interested in drug use if the subjects raised the issue. For example, whenever a subject initiated a discussion connected with marijuana use, regardless of where in the structured interview it occurred, the interviewer pursued the topic through use of a series of systematically scripted questions. Following the completion of the question series, the interviewer returned to the place in the interview schedule from which he had digressed. The use of a consistent and systematic line of questions for even unanticipated areas is particularly important for reliability and for possible replication of a study. This is especially true when interviewing from a dramaturgical perspective. Since interviewers as actors, directors, and choreographers may not be able to provide future researchers with detailed descriptions of the various character portrayals, routines, and devices they used during individual interview performances, it is crucial that, at least, a comparable script exists.

The idea of interviewers possessing a repertoire of prepared lines, routines, and communication devices sometimes conjures up the image of a little black bag of dirty tricks. It should not. As suggested earlier in this chapter, the research interview is not a natural communication interaction. It is necessary when interviewing to remain in control of the interaction. Similarly, the interviewers' ability to move gracefully into and out of a variety of characterizations should not be seen as phony behavior. The characterizations are also components of the interviewers' repertoire, and they provide interviewers with the means of effectively conducting research interviews without violating social norms or injuring subjects.

An interviewer's ability to accurately read lines and cues offered by an interviewee and to play effectively to them is not some insincere ploy intended only to obtain desired information. Quite the contrary—if these were the only objectives, there would be no reason to vary roles and/or characters to adjust to the subject's responses. The various tactics and characterized roles used by dramaturgical interviewers allow interviewees to feel more comfortable. The performance is, thus, not a phony one. Zurcher (1983, p. 230) writes:

> Why do we select a particular role for enactment? Why do we conform to some roles and modify or create others? What influences our choices or strategy for resolving role conflict or marginality? Why do we accept some identities and reject others? The circumstances of the social setting and the socialization process in which we find ourselves instrumentally affect the character of our role selections and enactments.

Extending Zurcher's (1983) notions on role enactments, one can see that in many situations, character projections present effective opportunities to develop or increase rapport. For example, one rapport-building tool that can be used before beginning an interview is *chatting* (Berg & Glassner, 1979; Douglas, 1985; Silverman, 2000). By briefly speaking with the subject on non-study-related issues, such as the weather, sports, family, cars, television, the movies, and so forth, the interviewer develops rapport with the interviewee even before the interview has begun. It is an opportunity, also, for the interviewee to adjust his or her projection of self in an effort to be more comfortable with whatever impression he or she chooses to manage (Rapley, 2001).

As Goffman (1967) aptly states, the initial self-projection of the interviewers commits them to being what and who they purport to be. Thus, when interviewers identify themselves as such, namely, as research interviewers, they are committed to portraying a convincing characterization of this role. How they develop the character is variable and dependent on the other participant(s) in the interview performance.

As the interview unfolds from the initial encounter, various modifications, alterations, and adaptations used by the interviewer may be added to the initial projection of the interviewer's character. It is essential, of course, that these additions neither contradict nor ignore earlier character developments or the initial projection of self. Instead, these additions should be built on previous expressions of the interviewer's projected image.

For example, during the Glassner and Berg (1980, 1984) study, while arranging for initial interview appointments by telephone, I found it was important to amend my initial projection as simply an interviewer: I needed to express the fact that I was a *married* interviewer. I came to add this element intentionally to my character projection as a result of a number of line cues expressed to me by female potential interviewees. They usually asked what sex the interviewer was and then paused after learning that I was the interviewer. Many of these women then amended their character projections. Each explained that she would consent to the interview provided that her husband could be present. Picking up on this line cue, I originally went into a well-rehearsed series of lines on the confidential nature of the interview and my concern that she be comfortable to speak freely throughout the interview. I carefully added that her husband could certainly be present but would have to refrain from answering any questions I put to her, at least until she had completed her own answers. Although this tended to work effectively (these women did conditionally consent to the interview), it was a long and somewhat involved script.[3]

Almost by accident, I discovered I could easily indicate that I was married. I accomplished this by simply pausing in my conversation with female interviewee prospects and asking my wife a question (usually having to do with booking an interview date). In most cases, I would carefully attempt to have the telephone pick up my wife's voice when she answered. In some cases, however, I put the questions to my wife when she was not even at home, and the performance was nonetheless effective in altering my character projection. Suddenly, I no longer posed any further threat to these female subjects (at least not on the basis of my possibly being an unmarried male).

My character amendment had not contradicted or ignored my original and initial role projection. I was still the interviewer, but I was now additionally known to be married. My performance did not trick the subjects into doing something they fundamentally did not want to do. Rather, the performance was a sincere attempt to reduce the potential interviewees' fears and anxieties—in short, to make them feel more comfortable with the idea of being interviewed.

Interviewers' Attitudes and Persuading a Subject

Attitudes toward the interview process strongly affect the quality of the resulting research. One interesting and fairly common assumption novice interviewers make is that subjects will not discuss certain topics with them.

Interestingly, however, once subjects have been persuaded to participate in an interview, they often tell far more intimate details than the interviewers would ever want to know.

The problem actually involves getting novice interviewers over the first few nervous moments when they attempt to persuade potential subjects to take part in the research. Naturally, if everybody always happily participated in research projects, there would be no problem for novice interviewers. Unfortunately, people often resist or are skeptical and need to be convinced.

When they meet this sort of resistance, novice interviewers are often panic-stricken. Nervousness is to be expected, especially if you are unprepared. On the other hand, countless interviewers have already encountered this situation and have developed a number of effective responses. Knowledge of these responses should both reassure novice interviewers and provide a means of persuading the majority of resistant individuals to take part in a research project.

Some individuals will not cooperate regardless of how persuasive one is or how they are approached. Backstrom and Hursh (1981) offer a variety of typical statements by skeptical potential subjects, along with sample responses. As they suggest, subjects tend to ask, "Why me and not someone else?" and insist, "I simply don't have the time." For example, a potential subject might ask, "Why [or how] was I picked?" The best answer is a simple and direct one: "You were chosen by chance according to a random selection procedure."

It is also sometimes necessary to convince subjects that what they have to say is important. For instance, a common response from a potential subject is, "Gee, I don't know too much about [whatever the subject is]; maybe you should interview someone else." Again, simplicity is the key: "It isn't what you know about [whatever the subject is], just what you think about it. I'm interested in your opinions."

If potential respondents insist that they simply have no time, researchers may be faced with a somewhat more difficult problem. Several strategies may be necessary. First, depending on the actual length of time required for the interview, interviewers may volunteer to conduct it during late evening hours (if that is convenient for the subject). Or they may suggest conducting the interview in several segments, even during lunch breaks at the work site, if that is possible. Frequently, if interviewers simply indicate that they realize time is an important commodity and they really appreciate the sacrifice the potential subject will be making, some accommodation will be made. In the Glassner and Berg (1980, 1984) study, for example, interviews were conducted at the homes of individuals or in their offices, and periodically began as late as 11:30 at night or as early as 5:30 in the morning. In other words, it is important to be flexible.

Developing an Interviewer Repertoire

One final question that naturally arises is how neophyte interviewers develop their repertoires. People do not usually wake up one morning and suddenly decide, that they are going to run out and conduct research using interviews to collect data! People also do not become expert interviewers immediately after reading books on interviewing. Interviewing requires practice. Whether first attempts at conducting interviews are called pilots, role-playing, pretests, practice interviews, mock interviews, or any other euphemism, they all mean interviews. Certainly, reading about how to interview, particularly ethnographic accounts, offers neophyte interviewers some necessary strategies and tactics. However, without actually conducting interviews, students cannot manage to develop appropriate repertoires.

Perhaps the most effective way to learn how to interview is by role-playing with more experienced interviewers. Although many sources on interviewing recommend role-play, few specify that at least one participant should be experienced. To have two inexperienced interviewers role-play with each other seems analogous to having two plumbers teach each other neurosurgery. It is particularly fruitless, furthermore, to have neophyte interviewers assume the role of interviewees. Although it would be impossible for even the most experienced interviewer to characterize all the different kinds of individuals and sorts of responses neophytes will encounter in the field, it is, however, far less likely that neophytes could perform the role of interviewee adequately. It is, however, possible for experienced interviewers to draw on their actual past performances and to develop composite characterizations of different interviewee types. By working with these projected characterizations in the process of a mock interview, neophytes are afforded an opportunity to acquire various lines and routines necessary for maintaining control over the entire interview performance.

Techniques to Get New Researchers Started

Sometimes, during the course of an interview, you will notice that the interviewee answers only in single-word responses or in very short statements. In order to create more complete and detailed interviews (to literally draw out the depth) interviewers must use various strategies and devices from their repertoire. In an effort to give new interviewers a few techniques to start their repertoire, I will address the uncomfortable silence, echoing, and letting people talk.

Uncomfortable Silence   The technique of uncomfortable silence involves consciously creating a long, silent pause after asking the interviewee a question, even if the interviewee offers only a word or a cryptic response. Indeed,

Kvale (1996) also points to the possible utility of silence as a strategic device to enhance data collection. Specifically, he suggests that interviewers employ silence to further the interview in a manner analogous to that used by therapists. "By allowing pauses in the conversation the subjects have ample time to associate and reflect and then break the silence themselves with appropriate information" (Kvale, 1996, pp. 134–135).

In normal conversational interactions, particularly in Western society, people have a difficult time with silence while talking with someone. The natural reaction when such a silence continues for a prolonged period is for interviewees to say something. In some cases, they will repeat their brief answer. In other cases, they will provide additional and amplifying information. In still other situations, they will state, "I have nothing else to say," or some similar comment. Rarely, however, will they simply sit silently for too long. I recommend that this period of silence extend only for a maximum of 45 seconds. Try to count slowly to yourself ("one, Mississippi, two Mississippi," and so forth) while offering the interviewee good eye contact.

Echoing   There is a tendency in interviewing to try and communicate that you understand what the interviewee is talking about. Some sources will even recommend that the interviewer periodically state "I know what you mean," or "that happened to me too," (Taylor & Bogdan, 1998, p. 100). I will argue that this can be disastrous, especially for a new interviewer because it is unlikely that a novice will make a short statement and leave it at that. The greater probability will be (and to a large extent the more natural conversational response) the interviewer will discuss in detail his or her similar experience, shifting the focus from the interviewee to the interviewer. This does not effectively convey that the interviewer is paying attention to the interviewee. Instead, it says, "Listen to me. I have something more important to say than you do."

However, it is important to convey the idea that you as interviewer are hearing what is being said and that you are genuinely listening and understand. This can be accomplished through echoing what the interviewee has just said. For example, consider the following exchange.

> *Jack:* When I first tried using marijuana, I felt really scared. I was, like, really out of control. I was all alone and I really didn't like how it felt.
>
> *Interviewer:* That must have been a scary feeling.
>
> *Jack:* Yeah, I was not really interested in trying marijuana again too soon. At least, I wasn't going to do it alone. I figured it would be better with a group of friends.

Although the interviewer has added nothing new to the exchange, he or she has conveyed that he or she was listening. In turn, the interviewee is encouraged to continue.

Letting People Talk   From a dramaturgical perspective this actually means the interviewer must not *step on the interviewee's lines*. In other words, avoid unintentional interruptions. People speak at different paces and with varying breathing and pausing rates. Just because a subject has made a one-sentence statement and paused does not mean he or she may not intend to continue with eight or ten more sentences. The interviewer must assess the way a subject tends to answer questions and adjust his or her own pace and desire to ask probing questions. Inexperienced interviewers frequently cut off their interviewees simply because they are anxious to get through their schedule of questions. This can be a serious mistake that will radically reduce the quality of the resulting interview. The answer is: *Let people talk!* Better to be a little slow at first with your questions than to constantly cut off interviewees by stepping on their lines.

Taking the Show on the Road

After neophyte interviewers have become novices and have developed their repertoire, they are ready to play their role before an audience. Just as a musical show seldom opens on Broadway until it has played smaller cities such as Boston or New Haven, novice interviewers should also not run immediately into the field. Broadway productions take the show on the road in order to obtain feedback from critics and audiences. In a similar manner, novice interviewers must try out their performances in front of an audience of competent critics, who may include experienced interviewers or the kinds of people they may be interviewing for a given study.

This sort of going on the road should allow interviewers to polish their performances. The most effective way to accomplish this is a dress rehearsal—that is, conducting an interview as if it were the real thing. This will also provide the novice with an opportunity to try out various strategies for drawing out fuller and more complete details. Following this dress-rehearsal period, novice interviewers should be ready to enter the field.

The Ten Commandments of Interviewing

Borrowing an idea from Salkind (1991, p. 135, 1996), I have constructed the following ten points or ten commandments of interviewing. I believe they nicely summarize the basic rules for conducting a decent interview. Better interviews will result only from practice and interviewer self-development.

1. *Never begin an interview cold.* Remember to spend several minutes chatting and making small talk with the subject. If you are in the subject's home, use what's there for this chatting. Look around the room and ask about such things as photographs, banners, books, and so forth. The idea here is to set the subject at ease and establish a warm and comfortable rapport.

2. *Remember your purpose.* You are conducting an interview in order to obtain information. Try to keep the subject on track, and if you are working with an interview schedule, always have a copy of it in front of you—even though you should have your questions memorized.

3. *Present a natural front.* Even though your questions are memorized, you should be able to ask each one as if it had just popped into your head. Be relaxed, affirmative, and as natural as you can.

4. *Demonstrate aware hearing.* Be sure to offer the subjects appropriate nonverbal responses. If they describe something funny, smile. If they tell you something sad, look sad. If they say that something upset them, try to console them. Do not present yourself as uninterested or unaware.

5. *Think about appearance.* Be sure you have dressed appropriately for both the setting and the kind of subject you are working with. Generally, business attire is most appropriate. If you are interviewing children, a more casual appearance may be more effective. Remember to think about how you look to other people.

6. *Interview in a comfortable place.* Be sure that the location of the interview is somewhere the subject feels comfortable. If the subject is fearful about being overheard or being seen, your interview may be over before it ever starts.

7. *Don't be satisfied with monosyllabic answers.* Be aware when subjects begin giving yes-and-no answers. Answers like these will not offer much information during analysis. When this does occur, be sure to probe with questions such as, "Can you tell me a little bit more about that?" or "What else happened?" Even a simple pause and an *uncomfortable silence* might yield additional information.

8. *Be respectful.* Be sure the subject feels that he or she is an integral part of your research and that any answer offered is absolutely wonderful. Often subjects will say things like, "You don't really want to know how I feel about that." Assure them that you really do!

9. *Practice, practice, and practice some more.* The only way to actually become proficient at interviewing is to interview. Although this book and other manuals can offer guidelines, it is up to you as a researcher to develop your own repertoire of actions. The best way to accomplish this task is to go out and do interviews.

10. *Be cordial and appreciative.* Remember to thank the subject when you finish and answer any questions he or she might have about the research. Remember, you are always a research emissary. Other researchers may someday want to interview this subject or gain access to the setting you were in. If you mess things up through inappropriate actions, you may close the door for future researchers.

Know Your Audience

If you have ever attended the live performance of a pretty good comedian, you may have noticed that he or she seemed to know the audience. The comedian seemed to know how much *blue material* the audience wanted and would tolerate. He or she even may have used local names of people or places in the routine. In fact, in the case of really good comedians, they may even have incorporated certain local *insider* jokes during the course of the routine. All of these things were because the comedian had taken the time to prepare and get to know the audience.

When interviewing, it is likewise advisable to *know your audience.* In this case, however, it means understanding the group or groups from which you draw your subjects. During the past several years, I have worked with a number of Asian and Middle Eastern graduate students. They are a constant reminder to me that it is very important to understand the culture of your research subjects. Often the kinds of questions that we in the West take for granted create significant cultural dilemmas for certain groups.

For instance, one of my graduate students was developing a dissertation project to examine delinquency in Taiwan. The student, who was Chinese, began developing questions from information he found in the literature.

Among the original questions we discussed was what seemed to be a fairly innocuous one: "About how often do you date?" The student explained that he could not ask Chinese adolescents this question. I was a bit surprised, being somewhat ignorant about Chinese culture. He went on to explain that proper Chinese adolescents do not date as we Westerners think about dating. In other words, an adolescent boy and girl would never go off on their own to the movies, or roller skating, or any other traditional *date.* In fact, such an activity would be viewed by most proper adults as indecent since dating tends to have sexual connotations in Taiwan. Furthermore, it would be impolite to ask adolescents such a question. He also explained that this did not mean that Taiwanese adolescents did not have their own form of dating. This variation in dating might be called *group dating*. In this form, five or six male friends will meet five or six girls at a skating rink—not so much by chance as by design. Once there, the groups tend to pair off, but they would never describe this as a *date*.

The solution to this problem was to craft a question that asked whether the youths ever intentionally went to certain locations with friends of the same gender to meet with groups of friends of the opposite gender.

In another situation, one of my students from Jordan was interested in examining issues of delinquency among a population of incarcerated Jordanian youths. His study population included both male and female delinquents. Among the questions commonly asked, according to the literature he reviewed, pertained to sexual activity. He came to me quite upset. He explained that under Islamic law he simply could not discuss sexual activity with young girls. Not only would it be improper for him and embarrassing to the girls, but it also might actually force these girls to lie if they were, in fact, sexually active. Ironically, we circumvented this problem by asking these girls about dating practices.

These examples suggest a very important issue that must not be under-played. This issue is understanding the culture of the subjects you work with. It is of critical importance that when you develop interview schedules the language as well as the nature of the questions remain inoffensive. In the ever-shrinking electronic world we currently live in, it is becoming more and more possible to conduct comparative research projects. As a result, many researchers are dealing with a wide variety of different and literally foreign cultures. It is critical, then, that you carefully plan out the types of questions you want to ask and the types of individuals you use to conduct interviews in these situations. In short, know your audience before your performance!

Curtain Calls

In concluding this section on learning the ropes of dramaturgical interviewing, it is important to note that some individuals may never achieve the status of highly skilled interviewer. However, just as there are B-movie actors who make their entire careers by acting in dozens of low-budget films and never achieve stardom, so too can there be effective B-movie interviewers. Put simply, some individuals will be able to obtain sufficient information from an interview to conduct viable research, yet will always remain awkward or clumsy in their performance.

Other individuals will completely fail to conduct interviews successfully. These individuals fail to become even B-level interviewers not because of interpersonal limitations but because of their failure to achieve a self-aware performance. These individuals are unable to adapt their scripts and blocking in order to accommodate the interviewee while continuing to maintain effective control over the interview process.

Analyzing Data Obtained from the Dramaturgical Interview

When novice interviewers have mastered to some extent interviewing strategies and practices and have conducted a number of interviews, the next problem is how to organize all the data accumulated in the interviews. How should the interviewers proceed with the task of taking many hours of tape-recorded interviews, for example, and analyzing them? Janice Morse (1994, p. 23) observes that despite the proliferation of qualitative research methodology texts, the process of data analysis remains fairly poorly described.

Although analysis is without question the most difficult aspect of any qualitative research project, it is also the most creative. Because of the creative component, it is impossible to establish a complete step-by-step operational procedure that will consistently result in qualitative analysis. Unlike quantitative research, qualitative analysis does not lend itself to this sort of certainty. One cannot pull out numbers (operationally reduce responses) from the interviews and expect to plug them into a qualitative analysis computer program—none exists! For these reasons, the following points are intended more as recommendations, tips, and hints on how to organize interview data rather than as a specific, rigid guide. Although some of the suggestions may suit certain projects nicely, the analysis of data is primarily determined by the nature of the project and the various contingencies built in during the design stages.

It is important to note that while qualitative analysis is sometimes thought to lack the precision assumed to be present in quantitative research, this is not necessarily the case. Good qualitative research, like good quantitative research, is based on calculated strategies and methodological rigor. Insights obtained from qualitative research cannot only add texture to an analysis but also demonstrate meanings and understandings about problems and phenomena that would otherwise be unidentified. Qualitative analysis cannot be undertaken quickly, neatly, or lightly, but this should never be viewed as a liability or limitation. Instead, this characteristic of qualitative analysis is perhaps its greatest strength. When qualitative analysis is undertaken, certain priorities must be established, assumptions made during the design and data-collection phases must be clarified, and a particular research course must be set. Quantitative data are sometimes incorrectly leaf raked (particularly by computer programs) in order to find results, but qualitative analysis cannot be conducted in this manner.

From an interactionist position, interviews are essentially symbolic interactions. From the dramaturgical interview's perspective, these interactions can be described along the lines of performances. The social context of the interview, therefore, is intrinsic to understanding the data that were collected (Silverman, 1993).

Beginning an Analysis

Analysis of interview data cannot be completely straightforward or cut and dry, but it is still necessary to understand what to do when you reach this phase in the research. The most obvious way to analyze interview data is *content analysis*. Although you may certainly abstract reducible items from interview data in order to quantify them, your analysis immediately ceases to be qualitative. A comprehensive consideration of content analysis is the subject of Chapter 11. This section outlines how to organize and prepare for analyzing the data collected from depth interviews. In order to analyze data, you must first arrange them in some ordered fashion. In the next section, some suggestions about ordering data are offered.

Systematic Filing Systems

As Lofland and Lofland (1984) suggest, "First, and perhaps foremost is the establishment of some kind of filing system." By *filing,* Lofland and Lofland literally mean a physical (mechanical) means of maintaining and indexing coded data and sorting data into coded classifications. Files may involve placing material into boxes, file cabinets, or envelopes, or even on floppy disks. The obvious purpose of a filing system is to develop a means by which to access various aspects of the data easily, flexibly, and efficiently. Of course, the central issue is what should be filed. In Chapter 11, a related and comprehensive examination of what Strauss (1987) calls *open coding* is offered. In this chapter, however, it is assumed that each interview was recorded on tape and transcribed verbatim and is ready for a thorough reading and annotating of codable topics, themes, and issues.

To begin, you simply seek naturally occurring classes of things, persons, and events, and important characteristics of these items. In other words, you look for similarities and dissimilarities—patterns—in the data. But you must look for these patterns systematically!

Typically, a systematic indexing process begins as researchers set up several sheets of paper with major topics of interest listed separately. Below these major interest topics are usually several other subtopics or themes. For example, Glassner and Berg (1980) began analysis with 16 separate major thematic topic sheets, each containing from 2 to 13 minor topics or subthemes (Berg, 1983, p. 24). A total of 80 specific subthemes were consistently sought, coded, and annotated on interview transcripts.

Ideally, this process should be accomplished by two or more researchers/coders, independently reading and coding each of several transcripts. This process is intended to establish the various topics to be indexed in the filing system. Using two or more independent coders ensures that naturally arising categories are used rather than those a particular researcher might hope to locate—regardless of whether the categories really exist. The consequence of this process, if correctly executed, is a precise, reliable, and reproducible coding system.

These *index sheets* should contain some type of code identifying the transcript in which it has been located, the page number of the specific transcript, and a brief verbatim excerpt (no more than a sentence). Traditionally, codes used to identify transcripts are pseudonyms or case numbers (randomly assigned). A typical index sheet might look something like the one in Table 4.1.

As implied in the preceding example, every subtheme is annotated from each transcript. When more than one subtheme is mentioned in the same passage, it is nonetheless shown under each subtheme (see the entries for #6 under the headings *Beer* and *Wine*). Cross-referencing in this fashion, although extremely time consuming during the coding stage, permits much easier location of particular items during the later stages of analysis.

Table 4.1   Alcohol Use [Major Topic/Theme]

Subthemes		
Beer	*Wine*	*Hard Liquors*
#12, pp. 3–6: I only drink beer when I am with my. . . .	#6, pp. 2–4: I love the taste of wine, but I hate beer.	#7, pp. 22–25: When I'm feeling real up, I'll have a drink.
#6, pp. 2–4: (see wine)	#5, p. 8: I only drink wine during the ceremonies, you know, the religious ceremonies.	#5, p. 23: I almost never drink liquor, just that one I told you about.
#9, pp. 3–4: Whenever I am really warm, like in the summer, I'll have a beer.		

When every interview transcript has been read and index sheets have been appropriately annotated, researchers should have a comprehensive means for accessing information. Additionally, the index sheets provide a means for counting certain types of responses in order to suggest magnitudes in response sets or for beginning content analysis of various specific themes.

Short-Answer Sheets

In addition to developing a comprehensive filing and indexing system, researchers may want to create a *quick response* or short-answer sheet to include in their files. Particularly when conducting standardized interviews, it is possible to complete brief responses for each of the questions asked as you read through and code each transcript. In essence, the questions become the interview schedule, and coders simply write short responses for each. Frequently this can be accomplished by reducing many of the responses to either affirmative (yes), negative (no), no clear response (unclear), or a very brief excerpt (no more than one sentence) including page reference.

Short-answer sheets are included primarily for convenience. They can be stored in separate files or with each interview transcript. They summarize many of the issues and topics contained in each transcript (for example, a respondent's income, age, gender, occupation, and so forth). Since answers for which more detail was provided have been captured and coded in the indexing sheet procedure, these short-answer sheets offer another type of cross-reference summary.

Analysis Procedures: A Concluding Remark

Stacy (1969) suggests that the collection of qualitative data is often so extensive that researchers can feel that their jobs must be complete when they have gathered it all in. This conclusion, of course, is far from accurate. As they listen to the interviewees, researchers frequently develop many interesting (and sometimes unreliable) impressions about possible patterns. After the interviews are completed, however, researchers must closely examine potential patterns to see what findings actually emerge directly from the data (Glaser & Strauss, 1967; Schatzman & Strauss, 1973). Such grounded findings, emerging from the data themselves, are frequently among the most interesting and important results obtained during research, even though they may have gone unnoticed during the data-collecting phase. Procedures used to identify these grounded concepts and patterns are discussed in greater detail in Chapter 11.

TRYING IT OUT

Naturally a certain amount of mental effort is required to learn the skills necessary for conducting effective interviews. These mental juices may have been flowing as you read this chapter on interviewing. But, as previously mentioned, there is no substitute for practice. You will have to go out and conduct several interviews. There are many public places where you can practice interviewing. Consider, for example, conducting several unstructured interviews with people at your local public library, on a busy downtown street corner, or even while feeding pigeons in a public park.

You might also consider creating a brief semistructured instrument (either individually or as a class) on some timely issue. These instruments can then be used as practice schedules during interviews either among classmates or in public places. Some possible topics include how the threat of AIDS may have affected dating practices, whether all workers should be subject to urine analysis as a condition of employment, or whether elementary and secondary school teachers should be required to pass competency examinations as conditions of their retention in schools. Or simply select a topic from the headlines of the local newspaper. Remember, your purpose is to practice interviewing skills, not to derive actual scientific empirical research.

Good interviewers work on improving their listening skills. The better an interviewer hears what is being said by the subject, the more effectively he or she can play the interviewer role. Classrooms are excellent places to practice *aware hearing* techniques. In our culture, we have a tendency to interrupt speakers in order to interject our own views or comments. It is, in fact, quite difficult for novice interviewers to learn that they cannot say such things as, "Oh yeah, I did that once," or "Gee, that's really something, but have you ever tried . . . ," or similar interruptions. Remember, when interviewing, the ideal is to have the subject speaking 80 to 90 percent of the time. When interviewers take up too much of the conversation, little research information is gained.

It is likewise important to demonstrate to the subject that you are really listening—*aware listening*, as it may be called. This means you are not thinking about your next question or about how smart you can make yourself look with some comment—the usual style of natural conversational exchange.

Try the following in order to practice aware listening skills: The instructor pairs off all the students in the class. Each pair is positioned so that their seats are facing each other, but not too close together. The teacher arbitrarily assigns a listener and a speaker in each pair. Now the teacher asks each speaker to talk for 30 seconds on some mundane topic—for example, "my favorite color," "my favorite food," or "the best day in my life." The instructor times this exercise and, after 30 seconds have elapsed, calls out "Stop!" At this point, the *listener* repeats verbatim everything he or she heard. This includes using first person singular ("I" statements) if the original speaker used them.

Following this, the participants reverse roles. The original speaker becomes the listener and vice versa. The teacher again times a 30-second mundane-topic exchange. After this is complete, the time is increased to 60 seconds, and the teacher suggests a slightly more personal topic, such as "the most embarrassing thing that ever happened to me," "something I really like about myself," "something I would change about myself if I could," or "something I dislike about myself."

It is important to be sure you do not make any verbal statements, responses, or comments when in the role of the listener. You may make nonverbal gestures, such as a nod or use of eyes or eyebrows, to show appropriate response to statements.

When you have completed the exchanges, consider the following questions:

1. Did your body language change during the exchanges? For example, did you move closer or further apart? Did you cross or uncross your legs or arms?
2. Did the level of sound change at all when you went from the mundane question to the more revealing personal one?
3. Was there less (if any) giggling and movement during the more self-revealing questions as compared with the mundane questions?
4. Was it difficult to sit silently and concentrate on listening?

NOTES

1. Few accounts of the interviewing process directly make use of a dramaturgical mode. One notable exception is Douglas (1985), who uses dramaturgy to describe creative interviewing. Another exception is Denzin (1973, 1978), who applies several dramaturgical elements to his description of the interview situation. However, traditional descriptions of the interviewing process ignore, or at most, make rudimentary use of the notion of role-playing. The description of role-playing itself is usually isolated from the actual interviewing process and appears under such headings as "training interviewers" or "piloting surveys" (Benny & Hughes, 1956; Bingham & Moore, 1959; Denzin, 1970, 1973, 1978; Kahn & Cannell, 1957; Smith, 1975). Occasionally, more knowledgeable authors correctly identify Moreno (1977) as a major contributor to the development of role-playing as a means of training researchers and therapists. Yet, these same sources fail to recognize the benefit of role-playing and other dramaturgical elements beyond the interviewer-training stage.

2. A slight risk does exist, of course, should these e-mails be transmitted via a wireless network. A well-versed hacker could conceivably hijack the entire communication. The likelihood of this occurring is rather small, and encrypting wireless transmissions would even further reduce the risk.

3. Very few of the women actually had their husbands sit through any portion of the interview. In most cases, it seemed sufficient for their husbands to look over the interviewer and be present in the house.

REFERENCES

Archer, D. (1980). *Social Intelligence*. New York: Evans.

Archer, D., & Akert, R. M. (1977). Words and everything else: Verbal and nonverbal cues in social interpretation. *Journal of Personality and Social Psychiatry 35*, 443–449.

Archer, D., & Akert, R. M. (1980). The encoding of meaning: A test of three theories of social interaction. *Sociological Inquiry 50*(3–4), 393–419.

Babbie, E. (1995). *The Practice of Social Research* (7th ed.). Belmont, CA: Wadsworth.

Babbie, E. (1998). *The Practice of Social Research* (8th ed.). Belmont, CA: Wadsworth.

Babbie, E. (2001). *The Practice of Social Research* (9th ed.). Belmont, CA: Wadsworth.

Babbie, E. (2004). *The Practice of Social Research* (10th ed.). Belmont, CA: Wadsworth.

Bachman, E., & Schutt, R. K. (2003). *The Practice of Research in Criminology and Criminal Justice* (2nd ed.) Thousand Oaks, CA: Pine Forge Press.

Backstrom, C. H., & Hursh, G. D. (1981). *Survey Research*. New York: Wiley.

Bampton, R., & Cowton, C. J. (2002). The e-interview. *Forum: Qualitative Social Research* Vol. 3, No. 2. Available online at: http://www.qualitative-research.net/fqs-texte/2-02/2-02bamptoncowton-e.htm.

Barone, D. (2002). Literacy teaching and learning in two kindergarten classrooms in a school labeled at-risk. *The Elementary School Journal 102*(5), 415–442.

Becker, H. S. (1963). *Outsiders: Studies in the Sociology of Deviance*. New York: Free Press.

Becker, H. S., & Geer, B. (1957). Participant observation and interviewing: A comparison. *Human Organization 16*, 28–32.

Benny, M., & Hughes, E. C. (1956). Of sociology and the interview: Editorial preface. *American Journal of Sociology 62*, 137–142.

Benny, M., Riesman, D., & Star, S. (1956). Age and sex in the interview. *American Journal of Sociology 62*, 143–152.

Berg, B. L. (1983). *Jewish identity: Subjective declarations or objective life styles*. Doctoral dissertation, Syracuse University.

Berg, B. L. (2002). *Risk factors associated with Latino men who have sex with other men*. Interview number 14. Unpublished interview.

Berg, B. L., & Doerner, W. G. (1987, November). *Volunteer police officers: An unexamined aspect of police personnel*. Paper presented at the annual meeting of the American Society of Criminology, Montreal, PQ.

Berg, B. L., & Glassner, B. (1979). *Methodological strategies for a study of Jews and drinking*. Paper presented at the annual meeting of the American Sociological Association, Boston, MA.

Berg, B. L., & Larson, C. (1989). Inmates' perspectives on determinate and indeterminate sentencing. *Journal of Behavioral Science and the Law 7*(1), 127–137.

Berg, B., Sañudo, F., Hovell, M., Sipan, C., Kelley, N., & Blumberg, E. (2004). The use of indigenous interviewers in a study of Latino men who have sex with men: A research note. *Sexuality and Culture 8*(1), 87–103.

Berg, J. P. (1986). *Dietary protein intake: Compliance and knowledge in hemodialysis patients*. Master's thesis, University of Florida, Gainesville.

Bingham, W., & Moore, B. V. (1959). *How to Interview* (4th ed.). New York: Harper and Bros.

Bogdan, R., & Knopp Biklen, S. (2002). *Qualitative Research for Education* (4th ed.). Boston: Allyn and Bacon.

Brown, D. (2002). Going digital and staying qualitative: Some alternative strategies for digitizing the qualitative research process. *Forum: Qualitative Social Research*.

Vol. 3, No. 2. Available online at: http://www.qualitative-research.net/fqs-texte/2-02/2-02brown-e.htm.

Burke, K. (1957). *The Philosophy of Literary Form: Studies in Symbolic Action.* New York: Vintage.

Burke, K. (1966). *Language as Symbolic Action: Essays on Life, Literature, and Method.* Berkeley: University of California Press.

Burns, N., & Grove, S. K. (1993). *The Practice of Nursing Research* (2nd ed.). Philadelphia: W. B. Saunders.

Butler, J. (1997). *Excitable Speech: A Politics of the Performative.* New York: Routledge.

Chadwick, B. A., Bahr, H. M., & Albrecht, S. L. (1984). *Social Science Research Methods.* Englewood Cliffs, NJ: Prentice Hall.

Champion, D. J., (2006). *Research Methods for Criminal Justice and Criminology* (3rd ed.). Upper Saddle River, NJ: Pearson/Prentice Hall.

Collins, M., Shattell, M., & Thomas, S. P. (2005). Problematic Interviewee behaviors in qualitative research. *Western Journal of Nursing Research 27*(2), 188–199.

Cotterill, P. (1992). Interviewing women: Issues of friendship, vulnerability, and power. *Women's Studies International Forum 15,* 593–606.

De Santis, G. (1980). Interviewing as social interaction. *Qualitative Sociology* 2(3), 72–98.

Denzin, N. K. (1970). *Sociological Methods: A Sourcebook.* Chicago: Aldine.

Denzin, N. K. (1973). *The Research Act.* Chicago: Aldine.

Denzin, N. K. (1978). *The Research Act* (5th ed.). New York: McGraw-Hill.

Denzin, N. K. (2001). The reflexive interview and a performative social science. *Qualitative Research 1,* 23–46.

Dingwall, R. (1997). Accounts, interviews, and observations. In G. Miller & R. Dingwall (Eds.), *Context and Method in Qualitative Research* (pp. 51–65). Thousand Oaks, CA: Sage.

Douglas, J. D. (1985). *Creative Interviewing.* Beverly Hills, CA: Sage.

Edgley, C. (2003). The dramaturgical genre. In L. T. Reynolds & N. J. Herman-Kinney (Eds.), *Handbook of Symbolic Interactionism.* New York: Rowman & Littlefield.

Fitzgerald, J. D., & Cox, S. M. (2002). *Research Methods and Statistics in Criminal Justice: An Introduction* (3rd ed.). Belmont, CA: Wadsworth.

Fontana, A., & Frey, J. H. (1994). Interviewing: The art of science. In N. K. Denzin & Y. S. Lincoln (Eds.), *Handbook of Qualitative Research.* Thousand Oaks, CA: Sage.

Fontana, A., & Frey, J. (1998). Interviewing: The art of science. In Norman K. Denzin & Yvonna S. Lincoln (Eds.), *Collecting and Interpreting Qualitative Materials.* Thousand Oaks, CA: Sage.

Frankfort-Nachmias, C., & Nachmias, D. (2000). *Research Methods in the Social Sciences* (6th ed.). New York: St. Martin's Press.

Geer, B., Haas, J., ViVona, C., Miller, S. J., Wood, C., & Becker, H. S. (1968). Learning the ropes: Situational learning in four occupational training programs. In I. Deutscher & E. Thompson (Eds.), *Among the People: Encounters with the Poor* (pp. 209–233). New York: Basic Books.

Glaser, B., & Strauss, A. (1967). *The Discovery of Grounded Theory: Strategies for Qualitative Research.* Chicago: Aldine.

Glassner, B., & Berg, B. L. (1980). How Jews avoid alcohol problems. *American Sociological Review 45*(1), 647–664.

Glassner, B., & Berg, B. L. (1984). Social locations and interpretations: How Jews define alcoholism. *Journal of Studies on Alcohol 45*(1), 16–25.

Goffman, E. (1959). *The Presentation of Self in Everyday Life.* Garden City, NJ: Doubleday.

Goffman, E. (1967). *Interaction Ritual.* New York: Anchor Books.

Goode, W. J., & Hatt, P. K. (1952). *Methods in Social Research.* New York: McGraw-Hill.

Gorden, R. L. (1975). *Interviewing* (2nd ed.). Chicago: Dorsey Press.

Gorden, R. L. (1980). *Interviewing* (3rd ed.). Chicago: Dorsey Press.

Gorden, R. L. (1987). *Interviewing* (4th ed.). Chicago: Dorsey Press.

Gorden, R. L. (1992). *Basic Interviewing Skills.* Itasca, IL: F. E. Peacock Publishers.

Hagan, F. (1995). *Research Methods in Criminal Justice and Criminology* (4th ed.). New York: Macmillan.

Hagan, J. E., (2006). *Research Methods in Criminal Justice and Criminology.* Boston, MA: Allyn and Bacon.

Halbert, S. C. (2003). Rhythm and reminiscence: Popular music, nostalgia, and storied self. *Senior Thesis,* Department of Sociology, University of Houston. Cited by Carol A. B. Warren and Tracey X. Kamer (2005, p. 153) in *Discovering Qualitative Methods.* Los Angeles, CA: Roxbury.

Hertz, R. (1995). Separate but simultaneous interviewing of husbands and wives: Making sense of their stories. *Qualitative Inquiry 1,* 429–451.

Holstein, J. A., & Gubrium, J. F. (1995). *The Active Interview.* Thousand Oaks, CA: Sage.

Horowitz, C. R., Davis, M. H., Palermo, A. S., and Vladeck, B. C. (2000). Approaches to eliminating sociocultural disparities in health. *Health Care Financing Review 21*(4), 57–75.

Kahn, R. L., & Cannell, C. F. (1957). *The Dynamics of Interviewing.* New York: Wiley.

Kinsey, A. C., Pomeroy, W. B., & Martin, C. E. (1948). *Sexual Behavior in the Human.* Philadelphia: W. B. Saunders.

Kvale, S. (1996). *Interviews: An Introduction to Qualitative Research Interviewing.* Thousand Oaks, CA: Sage.

Leedy, P., & Ormrod, J. E. (2001). *Practical Research: Planning and Design* (7th ed.). Upper Saddle River, NJ: Prentice Hall.

Leedy, P., & Ormrod, J. E. (2004). *Practical Research: Planning and Design.* (8th ed.). Upper Saddle River, NJ: Prentice Hall.

Lincoln, Y. S., & Guba, E. G. (1985). *Naturalistic Inquiry.* Beverly Hills, CA: Sage.

Lindlof, T. R., & Taylor, B. C. (2002). *Qualitative Communication Research Methods* (2nd ed.). Thousand Oaks, CA: Sage.

Lofland, J. A. (1976). *Doing Social Life: The Qualitative Study of Human Interaction in Natural Settings.* New York: Wiley.

Lofland, J. A., & Lofland, L. H. (1984). *Analyzing Social Settings: A Guide to Qualitative Observation and Analysis.* Belmont, CA: Wadsworth Publishing.

Lyons, L., & Chipperfield, J. (Spring–Summer 2000). (DE)constructing the interview: A critique of the participatory model. *Resources for Feminist Research,* 33–49.

Maccoby, E., & Maccoby, N. (1968). The interview: A tool of social science. In G. Lindzey & E. Aaronson (Eds.), *Handbook of Social Psychology* (Vol. 2, pp. 459–470). Reading, MA: Addison-Wesley.

Mann, C., & Stewart, F. (2000). *Internet Communication and Qualitative Research: A Handbook for Researching Online.* London: Sage.

Manning, P. K. (1967). Problems of interpreting interview data. *Sociology and Social Research 15*, 302–316.

Marshall, C., & Rossman, G. B. (1999). *Designing Qualitative Research* (3rd ed.). Thousand, Oaks, CA: Sage.

Merriam, S. B. (2001). *Qualitative Research and Case Study Applications in Education.* San Francisco: Jossey-Bass.

Messenger, S. L., Sampson, H., & Towne, R. D. (1962). Life as theater: Some notes on the dramaturgical approach to social reality. *Sociometry 25*(1), 988–110.

Mienczakowski, J. (1995). The theatre of ethnography: The reconstruction of ethnography into theatre with emancipatory potential. *Qualitative Inquiry 1*(3), 360–375.

Mienczakowski, J. (2000). Ethnodrama: Performed research: Limitations and potential. In P. Atkinson et al. (Eds.), *Handbook of Ethnography.* London, Sage.

Miller, E. M. (1986). *Street Woman.* Philadelphia: Temple University Press.

Miller, M. (1996). Ethics and understanding through interrelationship: I and thou in dialogue. In R. Josselson (Ed.), *Ethics and Process in the Narrative Study of Lives* (Vol. 4, pp. 129–147). Thousand Oaks, CA: Sage.

Moreno, J. L. (1977). *Psychodrama* (Vol. 1). Beacon, NY: Beacon House.

Morse, J. M. (1994). *Critical Issues in Qualitative Research Methods.* Thousand Oaks, CA: Sage.

Murray, S. O. (1991). Ethnic differences in interpretive conventions and the reproduction of inequality in everyday life. *Symbolic Interaction 14*(2), 165–186.

Mutchnick, R. J., & Berg, B. L. (1996). *Research Methods for the Social Sciences: Practice and Applications.* Boston: Allyn and Bacon.

Nachmias, C. F., & Nachmias, D. (2000). *Research Methods in the Social Sciences* (6th ed.). New York: Worth Publishing.

Nieswiadomy, R. M. (2002). *Foundations of Nursing Research* (4th ed.). Upper Saddle River, NJ: Prentice Hall.

Oakly, Ann. (1981). Interviewing women: A contradiction in terms. In H. Roberts (Ed.), *Doing Feminist Research* (pp. 30–61). London: Routledge & Kegan Paul.

Patton, M. Q. (2001). *Qualitative Research and Evaluation Methods* (3rd ed.). Beverly Hills, CA: Sage.

Peshkin, A. (1988). The researcher and subjectivity: Reflections on an ethnography of school and community. In G. Spindler (Ed.), *Doing the Ethnography of Schooling* (pp. 48–67). Prospect Heights, IL: Waveland Press.

Polit, D. F., & Hungler, B. (1995). *Nursing Research: Principles and Methods.* Philadelphia: Lippincott.

Rapley, T. J. (2001). The art(fullness) of open-ended interviewing: Some considerations on analyzing interviews. *Qualitative Research 1*, 303–323.

Reik, T. (1949). *Listening with the Third Ear.* New York: Farrar, Straus.

Rosenfeld, L. B., & Civikly, J. M. (1976). *With Words Unspoken: The Nonverbal Experience.* New York: Holt, Rinehart, & Winston.

Rosenthal, R., Hall, J., Dimatteo, M. R., Rogers, P. L., & Archer, D. (1979). *Sensitivity to Nonverbal Communication: The PONS Test.* Baltimore: Johns Hopkins University Press.

Rossman, E. J. (1992). The use of semistructured interviews in developing Superfund community relations plans. *Sociological Practice Review 3*(2), 102–108.

Roth, J. (1966). Hired hand research. *The American Sociologist 1*, 190–196.

Rubin, H. J., & Rubin, I. S. (1995). *Qualitative Interviewing: The Art of Hearing Data.* Thousand Oaks, CA: Sage.

Rubin, H. J., & Rubin, I. S. (1997). *Qualitative Interviewing: The Art of Hearing Data* (2nd ed.). Thousand Oaks, CA: Sage.

Salkind, N. J. (1991). *Exploring Research.* New York: Macmillan.

Salkind, N. J. (1996). *Exploring Research* (3rd ed.). Englewood Cliffs, NJ: Prentice Hall.

Schatzman, L., & Strauss, A. (1973). *Field Research: Strategies for a Natural Sociology.* Englewood Cliffs, NJ: Prentice Hall.

Schwartz, H., & Jacobs, J. (1979). *Qualitative Sociology: A Method to the Madness.* New York: Free Press.

Selltiz, C., Jahoda, M., Deutsch, M., & Cook, S. W. (1959). *Research Methods in Social Relations.* New York: Holt, Rinehart & Winston.

Shaffir, W. B., Stebbins, R. A., & Turowetz, A. (1980). *Fieldwork Experience: Qualitative Approaches to Social Research.* New York: St. Martin's Press.

Silverman, D. (2000). *Doing Qualitative Research.* London: Sage.

Silverman, D. (1993). *Interpreting Qualitative Data.* Thousand Oaks, CA: Sage.

Smith, H. W. (1975). *Strategies of Social Research.* Englewood Cliffs, NJ: Prentice Hall.

Spradley, J. P. (1979). *The Ethnographic Interview.* New York: Holt, Rinehart & Winston.

Stacy, M. (1969). *Methods of Social Research.* New York: Pergamon.

Stone, G. P. (1962). Appearance and the self. In A. Rose (Ed.), *Human Behavior and Social Processes.* Boston: Houghton Mifflin.

Strauss, A. L. (1987). *Qualitative Analysis for Social Scientists.* New York: Cambridge University Press.

Stromer-Galley, J. (2003). Depth interviews for the study of motives and perceptions of Internet use. Presented at the International Communication Association Conference, San Diego, CA.

Tallal, S. (May 1998). Digital audio gives a real voice to respondents. *Quirk's Marketing Research Review.* Available online at: http://www.quirks.com/articles/search.asp.

Taylor, S., & Bogdan, R. (1998). *Introduction to Qualitative Research Methods* (3rd ed.). New York: Wiley.

Tewksbury, R., & Gagne, P. (1997). Assumed and presumed identities: Problems on self-presentation in field research. *Sociological Spectrum 17,* 127–156.

Thomas, S. P., & Pollio, H. R. (2002). *Listening to Patients: A Phenomenological Approach to Nursing Research and Practice.* New York: Springer.

Turner, C. F., Ku, L., Rogers, M., Lindberg, D. L., Pleck, J. H., & Sonenstein, F. L. (1998). Adolescent sexual behavior, drug use, and violence: Increased reporting with computer survey technology. *Science 280,* 867–873.

Warren, C., & Karner, T. (2005). *Discovering Qualitative Methods.* Los Angeles, CA: Roxbury.

Zurcher, L. A. (1983). *Social Roles.* Beverly Hills, CA: Sage.

Chapter 5

Focus Group Interviewing

What Are Focus Group Interviews?

The focus group is an interview style designed for small groups of unrelated individuals, formed by an investigator and led in a group discussion on some particular topic or topics (Schutt, 2003). Using this approach, researchers strive to learn through discussion about conscious, semiconscious, and unconscious psychological and sociocultural characteristics and processes among various groups (Larson, Grudens-Schuck, & Lundy, 2004; Lengua et al., 1992; Stewart & Shamdasani, 1990). Group interviews are sometimes used to quickly and conveniently collect data from several people simultaneously; however, focus group interviews explicitly use group interactions as part of the data-gathering method. To be more specific, focus group interviews are guided or unguided group discussions addressing a particular topic of interest or relevance to the group and the researcher (Edmunds, 2000).

Focus group interviews are a useful strategy either as a standalone data-gathering strategy or as a line of action in a triangulated project (see Chapter 2). Stewart and Shamdasani (1990, p. 15) offer a number of appropriate uses for focus groups interviews:

1. Obtaining general background information about a topic of interest.
2. Generating research hypotheses that can be submitted to further research and testing using more quantitative approaches.
3. Stimulating new ideas and creative concepts.
4. Diagnosing the potential for problems with a new program, service, or product.
5. Generating impressions of products, programs, services, institutions, or other objects of interest.

6. Learning how respondents talk about the phenomenon of interest, which may facilitate quantitative research tools.
7. Interpreting previously obtained qualitative results.

The focus group may be defined as an interview style designed for small groups. Using this approach, researchers strive to learn through discussion about conscious, semiconscious, and unconscious psychological and sociocultural characteristics and processes among various groups (Basch, 1987; Lengua et al., 1992). It is an attempt to learn about the biographies and life structures of group participants. To be more specific, focus group interviews are either guided or unguided discussions addressing a particular topic of interest or relevance to the group and the researcher (Edmunds, 2000).

A typical focus group session consists of a small number of participants under the guidance of a facilitator, usually called the *moderator*. Krueger (1994) suggests that for complex problems focus group size should be kept to no more than about seven participants.[1] Thus, larger groups of subjects may be divided into a series of smaller focus groups. The moderator's job, like the standard interviewer's, is to draw out information from the participants regarding topics of importance to a given research investigation. The informal group discussion atmosphere of the focus group interview structure is intended to encourage subjects to speak freely and completely about behaviors, attitudes, and opinions they possess. Therefore, focus groups are an excellent means for collecting information from young children and teens, as well as from elderly adults.

Focus group interviews also provide a means for collecting qualitative data in some settings and situations where a one-shot collection is necessary. Although one-shot data collections usually are associated with survey questionnaires, in some cases, focus group interviews may serve a similar purpose. Certain groups of interest to social scientists may remain available for study only for limited amounts of time. For example, say you are interested in studying battered women. You might decide that access to a sample of such women can be best obtained through a battered women's shelter. However, women typically remain in such shelters only for short periods of time, perhaps as little as a month. Now imagine there are 40 or 50 women residing in the shelter at any given time. Individual interviews would not be a practical strategy for data collection, considering the amount of time that would be required to conduct that many interviews. Focus group interviews, however, might work well. You could easily hold four or five sessions during the course of a single week and collect necessary research information.

Along with more traditional populations, then, semitransient ones such as prisoners; hospital, clinic, and HMO patients; students and children in special courses; migrant workers; parents at PTA or PTO meetings; and even conventioneers may be suitable for focus group interviews. Even the settings where these semitransient groups are found lend themselves to data-collection plans that are faster than traditional individual face-to-face interviews.

When focus groups are administered properly, they are extremely dynamic. Interactions among and between group members stimulate discussions in which one group member reacts to comments made by another. This group dynamism has been described as a "synergistic group effect" (Stewart & Shamdasani, 1990; Sussman, Burton, Dent, Stacy, & Flay, 1991). The resulting synergy allows one participant to draw from another or to *brainstorm* collectively with other members of the group. A far larger number of ideas, issues, topics, and even solutions to a problem can be generated through group discussion than through individual conversations. Indeed, it is this group energy that distinguishes focus group interviews from more conventional styles of one-on-one, face-to-face interviewing approaches.

By this time, some readers are asking themselves one central question about focus group interviews: If focus group interviews are so compelling, why haven't they been more widely used in the social sciences? The answer to this question requires a little background on how focus group interviews have evolved over the past 50 or so years.

The Evolution of Focus Group Interviews

As a research technique, focus group interviews or discussions have existed since the beginning of World War II (Libresco, 1983; Merton, 1987; Morgan, 1989).[2] At that time, military psychologists and civilian consultants used group interviews to determine the effectiveness of radio programs designed to boost army morale. Although social scientists did originally make active use of this technique, until recently it was more extensively used and developed by marketing researchers.

At the 1986 meeting of the American Association of Public Opinion Research (AAPOR), Robert K. Merton described his introduction to focus group interviewing (Merton, 1987). Merton explained that in November 1941, he was invited to dinner at the home of a colleague, Paul Lazarsfeld, who had just been asked by the Office of Facts and Figures—predecessor to the Office of War Information and later the Voice of America—to test responses to several radio morale programs.

Lazarsfeld invited Merton to attend a session and witness how audience responses were tested. Merton (1987, p. 552) explains his first reactions:

> Do try to see it through my then naïve eyes and remember that your present sophistication is the legacy of almost half a century of evolving inquiry. I entered a radio studio for the first time, and there I see a smallish group—a dozen, or were there twenty?—seated in two or three rows. Paul and I take our places as observers at the side of the room as unobtrusively as we can; there is no one-way mirror or anything of that sort. These people are being asked to press a red button on their chairs when anything they hear on the recorded radio program evokes a negative response—irritation, anger, disbelief, boredom—and to press a green button when they have a positive response. . . . Thereafter, we observe one of Paul's assistants questioning the test-group—the audience—about their "reasons" for their recorded likes and dislikes.

Merton was intrigued by this strategy for gathering information about people's attitudes. Lazarsfeld persuaded Merton to work with him on the radio response project (Merton, 1987). Later, Merton, with Patricia Kendall (1946), published an article in the *American Journal of Sociology* entitled "The Focused Interview." In 1956, Merton published a book by the same title (Merton, Fiske, & Kendall, 1956). The book sold only a few thousand copies and quickly went out of print (Merton, 1987). And, in many ways, so did the technique of focused group interviews go out of print for many of the social sciences.

Focus group interviews found a home within the confines of marketing research. In fact, focus groups remain the predominant form of qualitative research for marketing researchers (e.g., Bartos, 1986; Edmunds, 2000; Hayes & Tathum, 1989; Moran, 1986; Morgan, 1989, 1997). Today, with the technological advances made in computers and the Internet, marketing researchers have expanded their focus group strategies to harness the power of the Web via the *virtual focus group* (Nadilo, 1999; Nucifora, 2000; Whiting, 2001).

Among most social scientists, however, little attention was paid to focus group interviewing as a technique until its reemergence during the 1980s (Hamel, 2001). During the 1980s and early 1990s, focus group interviewing conducted in the social sciences was sometimes labeled *group interviewing*. Yet, the basic elements of these group interviews closely resemble the purpose and procedures of focus group interviews. During this new millennium, it behooves social scientists to begin seriously looking toward the Internet as a means of securing and conducting a variation of marketing research's virtual focus group by improving on what some have already termed the *online focus group* (see, e.g., Clarke, 2000).

Advantages and Disadvantages of Focus Group Interviewing

Various sources in the literature describe a number of significant advantages associated with the use of traditional focus groups as a data-gathering strategy (see, e.g., Edmund, 2000; Hagan, 2006; Salkind, 2003). A conglomeration of these various advantages suggests the following:

1. It is highly flexible (in terms of number of participants, groups, costs, duration, etc.).
2. It permits the gathering of a large amount of information from potentially large groups of people in relatively short periods of time.
3. It can generate important insights into topics that previously were not well understood.
4. It allows researchers to better understand how members of a group arrive at, or alter, their conclusions about some topic or issue and provides access to interactionary clues.
5. It can be used to gather information from transient populations.
6. It places participants on a more even footing with each other and the investigator.
7. The moderator can explore related but unanticipated topics as they arise in the course of the group's discussion.
8. Focus groups do not require complex sampling strategies.

There is also a set of accompanying disadvantages one can cull from the existing literature on focus groups:

1. The quality of the data is deeply influenced by the skills of the facilitator to motivate and moderate.
2. Focus groups lend themselves to a different kind of analysis than might be carried out with surveys or even individual interviews.
3. Focus group attendance is voluntary, and an insufficient number may attend a given planned session.
4. The length (duration) of each focus group needs to be fairly brief (ideally between 30 to 60 minutes, although longer focus groups do occur).
5. A limited number of questions can be used during the course of any focus group session.
6. Only group, not individual, opinions are obtained in the results.

7. Dominant personalities may overpower and steer the group's responses unless the moderator is active.
8. The researcher must be careful about how he or she uses (or attempts to generalize) information obtained from focus groups.

The information obtained from focus groups provides elements of data similar to those of traditional interviewing, direct observation, and even certain unobtrusive measures commonly used in qualitative research. Yet, I caution that focus group data does not actually offer the same depth of information as, for example, a long semistructured interview. Nor does it provide as much rich observational data as one might obtain, for instance, by observing a class of sixth graders on the playground over a period of several weeks. In effect, to best assess the benefits and limitations of focus group interviewing, we should actually compare it directly with several conventional qualitative data-collection approaches. The following sections undertake such a series of comparisons.

Focus Group Interviewing and Face-to-Face Interviewing

One important distinction between focus group and face-to-face interviewing is the ability to observe interactions about a discussion topic during the focus group session. Researchers can observe session participants interacting and sharing specific attitudes and experiences, and they can explore these issues. In truth, traditional interviewing styles permit a more detailed pursuit of content information than is possible in a focus group session. Traditional interviewing approaches, however, sacrifice the ability to observe interaction for greater amounts of detail on various attitudes, opinions, and experiences. As a consequence, researchers may never learn how subjects might have discussed these issues among themselves.

In many ways, it is the very give-and-take interactions characteristic of focus group interviews that lead to spontaneous responses from session participants. Hearing how one group member responds to another provides insights without disrupting underlying normative group assumptions. Meanings and answers arising during focus group interviews are socially constructed rather than individually created. Situations such as focus group interviews provide access to both actual and existentially meaningful or relevant interactional experiences. Such naturally arising glimpses into people's biographies are necessary for *interpretive interactionism* (Denzin, 1989).

As Rubin and Rubin (1995, p. 140) explain:

> In focus groups, the goal is to let people spark off one another, suggesting dimensions and nuances of the original problem that any one individual might not have thought of. Sometimes a totally different understanding of a problem emerges from the group discussion.

In the same way that face-to-face interviews should be understood as social interaction, focus group interviews should be seen in terms of group dynamics (Taylor & Bogdan, 1998). Because interactions between group members largely replace the usual interaction between interviewer and subject, greater emphasis is given to the subjects' viewpoints. As with informal interviewing, focus groups can sometimes be undertaken without preconceived questions, focus questions, or guidelines (Morgan, 1989, 1997; Morgan & Spanish, 1984). This can effectively eliminate the researcher's perspective from the resultant data. Conversely, should more guided responses be desired, focus group interviews, like individual ones, can be made more formal and structured.

David Morgan (2002, p. 148) offers a description of what he terms his "ideal focus group," which demonstrates the difference in flow between a face-to-face interview and a focus group session:

> The ideal group would start with an opening question that was designed to capture the participants' interest, so that they themselves would explore nearly all the issues that a moderator might have probed. Then, just as the allocated time for that question was running out, one of the participants in the ideal group would spontaneously direct the others' attention to the topic for the second question by saying something like, "You know what really strikes me is how many of the things we're saying are connected to . . . ".

Naturally, such an ideal type of focus group is unlikely to unfold, especially when facilitated by novice moderator. However, Morgan's illustration should serve as the model to strive toward in undertaking focus group interviews.

Another perceived benefit of focus group interviews is the belief by some that they are less expensive to conduct than individual interviews. This may be the case in some study situations but is not an accurate blanket rule. Much will depend on the way the investigator designed his or her study. (Design is discussed extensively in Chapter 2.) Certainly, if a researcher plans to pay subjects, hire a professional moderator, employ transcribers and coders, and purchase specialized equipment, costs could soar. On the other hand, costs could be low if the investigator conducted his or her own focus group interviews and did the data organization and analysis himself or herself.

Similarly, in face-to-face interviewing, costs largely depend on how much of the work is done by "hired hands" (Roth, 1966) and how much by the researcher. Likewise, costs will be affected by whether or not subjects are paid for their involvement in the study.

A more relevant comparison between focus group interviewing and individual interviewing is time costs. As suggested earlier, focus group interviews can be undertaken among temporary or transient populations. This is because they require far less time than individual interviews do to involve the same number of participants. At the same time, of course, these focus group interviews will produce substantially less data than individual interviews. Fern (1982), in a controlled experiment, showed that group interviews did not produce significantly more or better ideas than an equivalent number of one-on-one interviews. In fact, Fern found that the group interviews produced only about 70 percent as many original ideas as the individual interviews (those not duplicated in either the real group or the one-on-one interviews).

Sussman et al. (1991) found that focus group data tended to make subjects' responses more extreme when compared to responses offered in survey questionnaires. Taken together with Fern's (1982) earlier work, this suggests that an interviewer must be willing to give up some degree of data precision in exchange for time savings.

Focus Group Interviewing and Participant Observation

When you are involved with participant observation, you are able to observe the naturally unfolding worlds of the population under study. This includes those times when several parties in the field come together to spontaneously hold a conversation, discussion, or argument. This natural evolution, of course, is not present in the artificially created situation of the focus group. Focus groups frequently contain members who might never have come together were it not for the creation of the group. Furthermore, the facilitator or moderator can control the assembly, alter the pace of discussions, change the direction of comments, interrupt or stop conversations, and so forth. Focus groups, then, like other forms of interviewing, are not truly natural conversations.

If you are interested in observing behaviors and meanings as they emerge in their natural setting, you may find that the simulated conversations of focus groups are insufficient. More traditional forms of participant observations and various sorts of field ethnography might prove more fruitful. However, if you are interested in collecting data on a large range of behaviors, a wide variety of interactions, and comprehensive and open discussions about certain topics or issues, focus group interviews work well.

For the most part, focus group interviews are further limited by the fact that the bulk of the behavior is verbal. During the group sessions, you should take notes on various behaviors and physical expressions of participants. However, these notes will represent only a small portion of the basic verbal data typically collected during a focus group interview.

Morgan (1989) suggests that focus groups are also useful when investigating research areas that do not have dense sets of observations readily available. In effect, researchers tend to conduct participant observation studies in settings where there is something available to observe. Organizations and organizational structures, social roles among group members, normative values among deviants, and similar topics become typical fodder for participant observers. Topics like these seem especially well suited for the structure of participant observation. Yet topics of a more psychological, cognitive, or deep attitudinal nature seem less effectively studied through participant observation. Such topics could, however, be examined during focus group interviews.

Since both participant observation and focus groups seek to examine group interaction of some sort, there are many times and many topics in which either might be used. The decision you make when selecting one over the other, of course, is based on what you are willing to give up or trade off. You must be willing to trade off emergent observations in a natural setting for concentrated interactions in a short time frame. This is likely not the sort of decision that you will make strictly on the basis of financial and time costs. Largely, such decisions are made on the basis of the value placed on the advantages or disadvantages of each technique. Also, decisions will be affected by the research topic itself and the specific interests, values, background, and training of the investigator. Certainly, among many social scientists, focus group interviews remain tainted by their long-standing relationship with marketing research. This association may also have an impact on decisions about whether to use one technique over another.

Focus Group Interviewing and Unobtrusive Measures

One main advantage to unobtrusive measures is that, by definition, they do not require intrusion into the lives of participants by investigators. This is because most unobtrusive data have been created by people and left as either residue or erosion—but without the intention of leaving research data. Other data-collection strategies, including focus group interviews, are quite intentional and invasive.

In order to conduct focus group interviews, you must first locate some population from which to select participants. Next, you must contact potential participants and convince them that their participation is important and necessary. Finally, you must actually hold the focus group session. With most unobtrusive data strategies, no subjects need be involved during the actual course of the research. There are some types of unobtrusive data collection, however, in which subjects may be more actively involved than in others. For example, if researchers ask a group of individuals to intentionally create daily diaries, the lives of subjects have been intruded upon.

Unobtrusive data may include limited elements that provide insight into the cognitive or psychological lives of individuals. However, there is no interaction between subjects or between subject and investigator. Unlike focus groups, participant observation, or other forms of interviewing, unobtrusive strategies are passive rather than dynamic. If you are interested in examining how people have lived under certain circumstances or in specific settings, there may be a number of viable unobtrusive strategies available. Even if you wanted to know how people acted and their attitudes during some event or time, unobtrusive tactics could be used. But, by their very nature, unobtrusive data usually are historical. That is, information is created at one time but identified as data at some later time.

Reinharz (1992) described a computer group diary, a strategy that in some ways resembles an unobtrusive data strategy but is also akin to focus group interviewing. Reinharz tells how women graduate students in the department of sociology at Boston College established a computer-based group diary. The original intention of this activity was to allow students, anonymously and without fear of reprisal, to communicate incidents of sexism.

The diary text was open only to the contributors and provided a means for women both to express their own thoughts and to read the thoughts of others. Reinharz (1992, p. 222) provides a glimpse of the introduction to a document produced in the department as a result of this group diary:

> Who is writing this?: The Graduate Women's Forum agreed last fall to develop a document which described incidents of sexism within the department. Women participating in its writing include virtually all the graduate women currently doing course work.
>
> Working anonymously and individually, women began the report by entering on the computer our descriptions and comments about being women students in the department. In some cases, a woman would write about an experience of another woman who found it impossible to write about it herself; sometimes passages were written together by two women. The process of writing, reading, responding, and rewriting was simultaneously an individual and a collective task, both a spontaneous and a reflective effort. The report grew quickly away from its original circumscribed goal of citing individual sexist incidents. It became a collaborative work generated by the unexpressed breadth of our experience and analysis of sexism in the department, and by the unexpected synergy of writing with each other.

Kramer (1983, pp. 3–4) has specifically called for the combined use of group sessions and diary research. In this case, Kramer refers to consciousness-raising groups: "Numerous studies have utilized the small group and consciousness-raising group . . . for information gathering, yet few have utilized the methodology as a complement to diary research."

What the unobtrusive tactic of solicited diaries lacks in interaction can be adjusted through use of focus-group-like activities of a group diary. By sharing information, thoughts, and common problems and suggesting solutions one to the other, group diaries effectively become unguided focus groups. Their discourse, then, amounts to a similar synergistically created convergence of ideas and experiences. Such biographical information provides researchers with the structure of the writers' lives. Biographical experiences are culturally influenced and created. Every culture affects its members' self-perceptions and understanding about social roles, social institutions, and social structures.

Denzin (1989, p. 39) suggests that biographical experiences have effects at two levels in a person's life: the surface level and the deep level. On the surface level, effects may be barely felt or noticed. They are often taken for granted and are nondisruptive. Picking up a container of milk on the way home from work might be an example. Effects at the deep level, however, strike at the core of an individual's life. They have a strong hold over us as individuals and affect how we behave, think, and understand things. Acceptance of our sexuality, self-hate, grief, and other deep-rooted epiphanies serve to illustrate deep-level life structures. Although unobtrusive strategies are quite good at identifying surface-level structures of life, most are not adequate for uncovering deep-level life structures.

Focus groups, on the other hand, provide avenues to understand a variety of deep structural elements. For instance, Twiggs (1994) and Grant (1993) suggest that focus groups can be used to evaluate the strengths and weaknesses of court cases and even to determine important issues in particular cases. Grant further suggests that information culled from focus groups may assist attorneys in selecting juries during *voir dire*.

Unobtrusive strategies and focus group interviews share an overlapping interest in the biographical experiences of group members. For the most part, unobtrusive measures remain in the realm of the surface level. On the other hand, focus group interviews possess the ability to effectively alternate between surface and deep levels. Decisions about whether to use unobtrusive measures or focus groups will be made for several reasons. The most obvious is the level of life structure you wish to examine. Another, again, may be financial. Here, however, you are likely to find that unobtrusive measures, like focus group interviews, can be created at fairly low cost. You might also consider innovatively combining the two, as in the group diary. Such a strategy allows both a variation on triangulation and a means for assessing both surface and deep levels of participants' lives.

The preceding comparisons between focus group interviews and certain more traditional strategies point out an important issue: Focus groups may be used either alone as a data-collection strategy or in combination with other techniques. In their simplest form, focus group interviews can be used as a sort of stand-alone data or what Morgan and Spanish (1984, p. 263) call *self-contained data*. This type of research is analogous to the kind of nontriangulated research you might accomplish using any single qualitative strategy.

Facilitating Focus Group Dynamics: How Focus Groups Work

Ideally, focus group procedures include a trained and practiced facilitator who asks a small group of individuals a series of open-ended questions. The moderator may use a single standard set of questions, asking each in turn, to stimulate discussion and conversation during a given session. The moderator may use the same set of questions during successive sessions. The questions may be more or less standardized depending on the needs of the research and the inclination of the investigator. In the real world, however, it is frequently inexperienced researchers who use focus group interviews and who may themselves serve as moderators. It is important, therefore, for these inexperienced researchers to prepare a *moderator's guide*.

The Moderator's Guide

The tasks of the moderator in a focus group are actually similar to those of the interviewer in face-to-face interviews. These tasks can be made more systematic (and somewhat easier for the novice) by preparing a procedural guide in advance of conducting the actual focus group. The procedures set out in the guide should eliminate some of the *fear of the unknown* that is perhaps apt to plague an inexperienced moderator of a focus group.

Preparation of the moderator's guide requires consideration of the level of language for the focus group. This may also include the language the interview will be conducted in. The guide should also provide a kind of outline or staging and the sequence of what the moderator should say and do. The moderator's guide should include:

1. Introduction and introductory activities
2. Statement of the basic rules or guidelines for the interview

3. Short question-and-answer discussions
4. Special activities or exercises
5. Guidance for dealing with sensitive issues

Introduction and Introductory Activities

As moderator, it is your job to explain to the subjects what the project is seeking and how a focus group operates. As well, you need to establish rapport with the subjects. The moderator's guide should include a basic description of the project (even though subjects may already have had the project's purpose explained in order to obtain informed consent). This can be a brief statement written out in the moderator's guide. It is also important to ask the group if they understand the project and their role in this research. Introductory activities also allow the subjects to meet you, understand what is expected of them, and become more comfortable. This can be accomplished by creating a series of activities intended to have subjects disclose a little something about themselves. For example, you might ask the group to go around the room and state their name, occupation, and one thing they think is special about themselves. Or you might ask subjects to tell about any hobbies they might enjoy. This information provides a brief period of time for subjects to learn about one another and to begin feeling more comfortable in what is otherwise a fairly unnatural and potentially disconcerting situation among strangers.

Statement of the Basic Rules or Guidelines for the Interview

Although you do not want to simply list a bunch of rigid rules of conduct, you do want to establish some ground rules around the interactions during the focus group. You need to explain that you expect an open, polite, and orderly environment where everyone in the group will be encouraged to participate. If you plan to toss questions out to the full group, to be answered by anyone, tell the group that this will be your procedure. If you intend to ask each subject a question in turn, obtain a quick answer, and then open it up for discussion by the group—then, tell them this will be how the interview will proceed. Subjects need to know what to expect. The moderator should also tell participants that everyone may have a different opinion or answer to the questions and that you want to hear all of these opinions. It is a good idea to explain the reason for any recording device and its purpose, if one is present in the room. If the session is being recorded by a hidden camera, this too should be indicated to the group as well as why the camera is not in the room. For example, you might tell the group that the camera is hidden to avoid making them feel self-conscious.

Short Question-and-Answer Discussions

Most focus groups operate with a short series of discussions, sparked by questions asked by the moderator (Krueger, 1997). These questions should be written out and listed in a similar manner to a semistructured interview schedule (see Chapter 4). You may even plan out intentional probes to be used to facilitate more information in the event that there is little discussion after asking the initial questions. Experienced moderators are likely to deviate from such a schedule, as the dynamics of the group begin to animate the focus group experience, giving it a kind of life of its own. Less experienced moderators, however, may feel more secure having a *script* of questions to ask.

Special Activities or Exercises

Although many focus groups restrict their data collection to responses from a series of questions, some, especially those undertaken with children, may include drawing or role-playing exercises so that subjects may better express their views (Wright, 1994). It may also be helpful to the researcher to have a pencil-and-paper exercise to help validate the verbal responses that children are likely to offer (Wright, 1994). The major consideration for thinking about the inclusion of various additional exercises is age and maturity of subjects.

Exercises and activities also allow the moderator to determine what subjects individually know or believe without the influence of others in the group. One useful strategy is to have the subjects fill out a brief pencil-and-paper survey that is administered before the actual question-and-answer/discussion segment of the focus group begins (to be discussed later as an *extended focus group*).

Guidance for Dealing with Sensitive Issues

As in any interviewing session, focus groups require the moderator to use sensitivity when dealing with certain subject matters. These typically include questions concerning alcohol or drug use, deviant behaviors, and certain mental health issues. In the focus group, one way to approach such sensitive issues, is to begin with a general question for discussion that deals with the subject matter. For instance, let's assume you are interested in knowing about cigarette use by Asian American teenagers. Rather than saying immediately, "Tell me about your cigarette smoking habits," you might begin with a question such as, "What do you think about cigarette smoking?" In some cases, this slightly broader question may open the door for discussion in the group about individual participants' smoking habits—but without having placed anyone on the spot. If this does not occur, the more specific question may subsequently need to be asked.

Basic Ingredients in Focus Groups

In a broader and more general sense than the specifics of a moderator's guide, it is possible to spell out some basic elements or ingredients required when conducting a focus group interview. Similar *checklists* have been suggested by Axelrod (1975), Byers and Byers (1996), Morgan (1997), Morgan and Scannell (1997), and Krueger and Casey (2000). These elements include:

1. *A clearly defined objective and/or research problem:* Is the focus group part of several other means for collecting data or is it being used as a standalone data-collection technique? Does the researcher have a clear understanding of the research problem, and the questions to be used during the focus group session(s)?

2. *The nature of the group:* What are the group's characteristics? Is the group largely homogeneous or is it heterogeneous? Is it an appropriate group for the research question(s)? If you want to know about Sioux (Native American) culture, you simply cannot ask a group of Quakers.

3. *Atmosphere/environment and rapport:* As in any research project, the facilitator must assure confidentiality of information discussed during the focus group. However, the facilitator must create rapport between himself or herself and the group as well as between group members. In other words, the researcher must make all of the group members feel comfortable talking openly in the group.

4. *An aware listening facilitator:* Facilitators, as with any interviewer, must listen to what the subjects are saying (see Chapter 4). It is important to have a schedule or agenda during the focus group; however, it should never be so inflexible that interesting topics that spontaneously arise during the group discussion are shortchanged or unnecessarily truncated. Because of the nature of group dynamics, it is possible that topics and issues not originally considered by the researcher as important surface as very important.

5. *A well-organized and prepared facilitator:* Whether the facilitator intends to work with several specific questions, or with several general topical areas, the facilitator should have a clear idea about how things will proceed. One sure way to kill a focus group discussion is to begin it without any direction or indication of what the flow of questions or topics will be. Often texts recommend that facilitators be highly trained and skilled leaders of focus groups (see, for example, Krueger, 1994). Unfortunately, this is not always practical or possible. It, therefore, becomes even more important for an inexperienced researcher serving as facilitator to demonstrate clear organization and preparedness.

6. *Structure and direction but restrained contribution to the discussion:* Although the facilitator should guide the group's discussion, he or she should avoid offering opinions and substantive comments. With any interview, the ideal product is 90 percent subjects and 10 percent researcher.

7. *Research assistance:* Many investigators use only a single researcher/facilitator during the course of a focus group. This procedure sometimes occurs because of costs or time necessities. A more idyllic situation is to have someone serve as facilitator, while someone else sits and observes the group. This second researcher is able to create field notes about the group dynamics, as well as assist in identifying voices when it comes time to transcribe the recording of the focus group interview. An even more effective record might be to videotape the focus group. Videotaping, however, is not always permissible or possible.

8. *Systematic analysis:* Whether the recording is a transcribed audiotape or a videotape of group sessions, the data must be analyzed using some systematic means. One style of analysis is analyzing the content of the statements made by subjects during the focus group (see Chapter 11). Whatever you do with the data, they should be clearly stated to ensure verifiability. This means that the analysis process should permit another researcher to arrive at similar conclusions using the same or similar documents and raw data (Krueger, 1994).

Often researchers employ a tactic called the *extended focus group*. This procedure includes a questionnaire administered to participants before the group session. The questionnaire generally includes material that will be discussed during the focus group session. Information from this questionnaire may assist both group members and the moderator. The questionnaires allow the participants to develop a commitment to a position before any group discussion begins (Sussman et al., 1991).

Information from these pregroup questionnaires may help to ensure that the moderator draws out minority opinions as well as more dominant majority ones (Wimmer & Dominick, 1987). In some ways, this is similar to the pre-jury selection questionnaire people commonly receive when called to serve on jury duty. These questionnaires elicit information that will allow the prosecuting and defense attorneys an opportunity to get to know potential jurors. When they ask questions of the jurors in a process called *voir dire,* they are guided by comments these people made in their questionnaires. Answers to their questions help the attorneys decide whom they do and do not want on the jury.

One of the most difficult tasks for a moderator is controlling dominating respondents while simultaneously encouraging passive group members.

This must be accomplished without embarrassing or completely shutting down the dominating participants. Often, like a traditional interviewer, moderators must rely on their ability to develop rapport with group members. If the moderator has been successful in developing a rapport, it may be useful in efforts to encourage the quiet members to participate.

Most researchers who use focus group techniques acknowledge that group influences can distort individual opinion. Some opinions may be more extreme and some may be less verbalized than others because of the group effects (Morgan, 1989; Sussman et al., 1991). Having some idea about how individuals thought about certain topics before the group sessions start allows the investigator to gauge this group effect. This is not to say that material obtained during the group session is false. Quite the contrary. The opinions voiced during the session, even those that contradict pregroup questionnaires, merely demonstrate the impact of group dynamics. Additional information, confirmation or refutation of beliefs, arguments, discussion, and solutions heard during the group session shape participants' thinking. What results is a collective understanding about issues discussed during the group session.

It is important, in fact, to bear in mind that data obtained from focus group interviews are not identical to individual interview data. Focus group data are *group data*. They reflect the collective notions shared and negotiated by the group. Individual interview data reflect only the views and opinions of the individual, shaped by the social process of living in a culture.

When you design a focus group interview study, your plans for participant selection must be undertaken very carefully. It should not be assumed that focus group samples necessarily are accidental or purposive. Even among marketing researchers, care is required to create samples that include subjects with necessary product user characteristics (Tynan & Dryton, 1989). For the more traditional social sciences, one should begin using standard strategies for sampling to create a sample pool. From this pool, the smaller focus groups may be formed.

For example, let us say you are interested in studying some aspect of the lives of incarcerated women. Perhaps you want to know how these women perceive their family role as mother, even though they are separated from their children (Moloney, 1997). In most states, there are few women's correctional facilities, often only one or two for the entire state. Thus, you easily can begin with a *census sample*[3] of women in prison to form the initial pool. Next, you might stratify this group into those who have children currently of juvenile status (under the age of juvenile jurisdiction) and those who do not. Using the group with children, you might now have a sample of 50 or 60 women. Assuming no rejections, you could randomly assign women in this group to five or six focus groups and conduct sessions in a fairly brief amount of time.

You can develop focus groups using other strategies to create the initial sample pool. This is particularly true if you are using focus group interviews as an additional line of action in a triangulated project. For example, Berg (1995) was interested in examining self-management programs and patient compliance among adult asthmatics. Her sampling strategy called for systematically selecting and stratifying adult asthma patients into the cells shown in Figure 5.1, each containing eight people for a total of 62 subjects.

Berg's (1995) design called for an experimental group and a control group, so she randomly assigned the subjects in each cell to one or the other. The experimental group was presented with a structured educational program regarding the use of their asthma inhaler medication. The control group was not. Using devices designed to indicate when the inhalers were used, Berg planned to determine whether the program improved patients' self-management and compliance. To this point, Berg's research amounts to a fairly standard quasi-experimental design. However, Berg's design does not provide for explanations about *why* inhalers were or were not used. She could have obtained such information with focus groups.

In this instance, Berg might have divided each of the two groups, experimental and control, into three focus groups. In these six focus group interviews, the moderator could have explored how subjects viewed their medication and why they did or did not use the inhalers as prescribed.

As illustrated earlier, samples for focus groups in the social sciences derive from a wide variety of types. Standard sampling procedures can improve the validity of group interview results. The main question that remains is, When should a focus group strategy be used?

Although this is not its primary purpose, you might consider using a version of focus group interviews to pilot an interview schedule. In this instance, you would have members of the focus group read through the instrument

Figure 5.1 Berg Sampling Strategy

	Males		Females	
	Younger Patients (under 45)	Older Patients (over 45)	Younger Patients (under 45)	Older Patients (over 45)
Serious Asthma Condition				
Moderate Asthma Condition				

under consideration. Next, the group would discuss the usual concerns researchers have about such research instruments: the level of language, comprehensibility of the questions, question order, affected wording of questions, and so forth.

As suggested throughout the examples offered in this chapter, there are numerous other occasions when a focus group could be used. This is, of course, true with many data-collection strategies. As suggested in the first chapter of this book, triangulation in qualitative research can be important to issues of validity. Whenever you can demonstrate corroboration of information you have obtained, you are on solid ground. Whether focus group techniques are used will depend on several issues. These issues have been mentioned in the preceding chapter, but they bear some reiteration.

First, you must decide whether information gathered through the focus group interview will inform the research questions. There is no point in conducting focus groups if the results are superfluous.

Second, you may want to consider aspects of time and cost effectiveness. Will focus group interviews allow you to obtain the best data for the time and money they will require?

Third, is the study population one that requires a faster data-collection strategy that might be provided by another technique? Naturally, this is related to the issue of your research questions as well as to the quality of the data. This may involve decisions about your willingness to make trade-offs between data precision and gains in data acquisition.

Last, you should consider whether using focus groups might enhance a project by adding another line of action to the study. This additional line of action may, in fact, offer either corroboration of other data or insights into areas other data fail to illuminate.

Analyzing Focus Group Data

The information collected during the course of a focus group, like that collected during the course of a face-to-face interview, is *raw data*. The researcher's job is to prepare an analytic statement based on this collected raw data. Ideally, this assessment should be thoroughly grounded in the data (Creswell, 2004; Strauss & Corbin, 1998). The first step is to transcribe the entire interview. This should be a verbatim transcription of each question asked by the moderator and each individual answer given by the focus group participants. It should include all probes asked by the moderator and various group members. It should also include any slang, dialects, or pauses offered by focus group members as they respond to the moderator and each other.

During the course of the focus group, either the moderator or a second observer working with the researcher should take copious notes. These might include various interactionary cues offered by individuals of the group (facial grimaces, head shakes, perhaps even side comments that might be lost in the transcription). These too will be useful along with the transcriptions when developing an analysis of the results of the focus group.

Taken together, the transcription and the observer notes provide a complete record of the discussion that unfolded during the focus group interview and will assist in analysis of this data. The next step is to analyze the content of the discussion to identify trends and patterns that reappear either within a single focus group or among a series of focus groups. Thus, the researcher undertakes a variation of content analysis (discussed in detail in Chapter 11), which begins by examining the text for similarly used words, themes, or answers to questions. Some system of indexing and retrieval of these terms and patterns must be used (see Chapter 11). The researcher should additionally consider the emphasis or intensity of respondents' comments (sometimes illustrated in observer notes). As well, the researcher should consider the consistency of comments and responses to probes both within a given focus group and across a series of focus groups.

There are several important rules of thumb for analyzing focus group date, which are quite different from the analysis of other textual data such as field notes or interview data:

- Avoid quantifying results or offering magnitudes; just because four of seven group members made a statement does not mean that 57 percent of the subjects agree on that statement. Such an assumption is quite meaningless and is not a finding in itself.
- Provide quotations to support your assessment of what the various trends and patterns of discussion are.
- Offer characteristics of each group member prior to offering their quoted responses in order to provide a sense of three-dimensionality to group members (e.g., a 26-year-old single Latina mother of two stated . . . ").
- Make a point, or state a specific pattern, before offering quoted materials intended to demonstrate the point or pattern.

Confidentiality and Focus Group Interviews

One final issue requires discussion: the problem of confidentiality of information obtained through the use of focus group interviews. Although it is easy to ensure that the researcher will maintain confidentiality, what can be done among the participants? Ensuring confidentiality is critical if the researcher expects to get truthful and free-flowing discussions during the course of the focus group interview. If group members feel apprehensive or inhibited by fear of somehow being exposed, they will not fully disclose their feelings and perceptions.

In marketing research situations, this issue of confidentiality may not be viewed as terribly significant. After all, who really cares if the car manufacturer learns that someone thinks its automobile is ugly or fails to perform well? What difference does it make to have some cereal company learn that someone thinks the picture on the box is childish or the taste of the product is awful? Although executives need this information to improve product quality, none of these comments is very self-disclosing.

When focus groups are used for social scientific research, however, a different kind of information is obtained. A focus group interview among rapists, for example, could reveal very sensitive pieces of information. Discussion among obese focus group members about why they eat obsessively may not be the kind of information members want to be identified with. Conversations among elementary school teachers about how they discriminate against particular ethnic groups or against girls could be very troublesome if revealed. Thus, certain procedures must be taken to ensure confidentiality.

The logical course to take is to have every member of the focus group sign a statement of confidentiality. In other forms of research, such as individual interviews, this is fairly common practice. The difference, however, is that in the individual interview, this contractual agreement is between researcher and subject. In the focus group situation, the agreement must be among *all* group members and the moderator/researcher. An example of such an agreement is offered in Figure 5.2.

Enforcement of this agreement, as with all confidentiality agreements in research, largely is one of honor rather than law. Use of this sort of document, however, does allow the participant an opportunity to think about issues of confidentiality. If a participant believes he or she will not be able to keep material confidential, this is the opportunity to withdraw. Similarly, if a group member is fearful about confidentiality, he or she can drop out of the group.

Allowing concerned or unwilling subjects to withdraw is an important ethical element in all research. It is also important for the quality of your focus group data. Having an unwilling participant in the group could prove to be very disruptive or problematic for a moderator. The discussions, topics, and solutions the group might be able to develop could be seriously compromised.

Figure 5.2   Group Agreement for Maintaining Confidentiality

This form is intended to further ensure confidentiality of data obtained during the course of the study entitled [place title of research here]. All parties involved in this research, including all focus group members, will be asked to read the following statement and sign their names indicating that they agree to comply.

I hereby affirm that I will not communicate or in any manner disclose publicly information discussed during the course of this focus group interview. I agree not to talk about material relating to this study or interview with anyone outside of my fellow focus group members and the researcher [or moderator].

Name: _____

Signature: _____

Project Director's Signature: _____

Recent Trends in Focus Groups: Online Focus Groups

In the fifth edition of *Qualitative Research Methods for the Social Sciences* (Berg, 2004), I outlined some of the recent innovations with regard to videoconferencing as an integral part of the focus group research process. The technology necessary to conduct this sort of focus group became available during the mid-1990s and quickly appeared in the marketing research industry and literature (Greenbaum, 1997, 1998). For marketing researchers, it provided a mechanism for both recording and broadcasting focus groups to remote and diverse locations at an enormous financial savings (Greenbaum, 1998). I also suggested that for the social sciences, this same technology could provide a method for securing focus group information in multiple geographic locations in both an expedient and economical manner. In other words, a researcher in Kansas could conduct a teleconference focus group with groups in New York, California, Kansas, and Ohio—all at the same time. In the current edition of the book, however, I expand on this notion of what has come to be called *online focus groups* (Clarke, 2000; Rezabek, 2000; Turney & Pocknee, 2005).

Online focus groups, like e-interviews (discussed in Chapter 4), can be conducted in one of two ways: *synchronously* or *asynchronously*. Synchronous sessions refer to sessions that are live. In other words, all participants take part at the same time. They can use a chat room or online conferencing such as CU See Me (a kind of video chat room available on the Internet). Asynchronous sessions typically use e-mail, a listserv, or mailing lists. The participants can read others' comments and contribute a comment themselves at any time, not necessarily when anyone else is participating (Adler and Zarchin, 2002; Murray, 1997; Rezabek, 2000).

As they did focus groups in general, marketing researchers have jumped into the online focus group strategy with both feet. For example, Holly Edmunds (1999, p. 23) a leading scholar in the area of marketing research, summarizes the advantages in using the Internet for market research by stating that such online focus groups (a) cut costs; (b) have potential to reach a broad geographic scope; (c) provide access to hard-to-reach participants such as business travelers and professionals who have little time during normal hours to participate; and (d) provide for a convenient and a comfortable way of participating.

On the other hand, Tom Greenbaum (2003), another leading marketing research scholar, argues against the advent of online focus groups, listing a series of problems, including the loss of the role and authority of the moderator in online focus groups; the loss of the ability to feel and experience the atmosphere that arises during the course of an in-person focus group; the inability to effectively use group dynamics as an integral part of the overall focus group process; and the loss of attentiveness on the topic being discussed by the group when undertaken online.

In the social sciences, several researchers have successfully undertaken studies using various online focus group techniques (e.g., Adler & Zarchin, 2002; Moloney, Dietrich, Strickland, & Myerburg, 2003; Turney & Pocknee, 2005). It is a safe argument that for at least for some social scientists the near future holds online focus group interviews as a likely new data-collecting strategy. However, care must be taken to select participants who can comfortably participate in an electronic medium—that is, who already have a comfort level with technology—so that they can contribute and interact in the electronic focus group freely and clearly, resulting in their best contribution. Care must also be taken that the focus group is conducted and facilitated in a professional and efficient manner with efforts made to avoid the types of losses outlined by Greenbaum (2003). Procedures must be made clear and then followed by the facilitator and participants. Hopefully, this will result in a thorough discussion of the topic(s) by all involved and important information will be revealed that can benefit the researcher.

Conclusion

The focus group interview is an innovative and evolving strategy for gathering what might otherwise be fairly difficult-to-obtain information. Recently reborn in the social sciences and revitalized in the past decade because of telecommunications and the Internet, the focus group interview promises to quickly become an integral part of data-collection technology among many qualitative researchers. It operates well as a standalone means for data collection or as an additional line of action. The limitations of focus group interviews in general, whether conducted in a traditional format or online, must be weighed against the advantages focus group interviewing may offer in a given research endeavor.

TRYING IT OUT

Suggestion 1   This suggestion is intended to allow students an opportunity to work in an unguided focus group. Divide the class into groups of approximately six or seven students. Each group begins discussing each of the following topics: how to select a course, how group members chose the college they are attending, and what types of vacations are best during spring break. Allow only 15 minutes or so for each topic. If possible, have each group tape-record its session. If recording isn't possible, have one or two members of each group take notes.

Suggestion 2   Develop a means for identifying participants for a focus group study on fear of crime among juveniles. Be certain you consider basic issues of sampling, including representation of both genders and a variety of ethnic groups, ages, and educational levels.

Suggestion 3   Create a moderator's guide for a focus group study on violence in high schools. Assume your sample will include high school students from your area.

NOTES

1. There is wide disagreement in the literature about what exactly constitutes a *small group* for focus group interviews. Some sources suggest six to nine subjects (Pramualratana, Havanon, & Knodel, 1985, p. 205); others recommend six, seven, or eight to ten group members (Bachman & Schutt, 2003, p. 243; Bogdan & Biklen, 2003, p. 101; Morgan, 1989, p. 43); still others claim that six to twelve participants may be the ideal size (Leedy & Ormrod, 2005; Lengua et al., 1992, p. 163). One thing seems certain: the more complex the research problem, the more effective it is to have a smaller size (perhaps, five to seven people) focus groups.

2. A colleague of mine, W. Timothy Austin, reminds me of an interesting point. Although most mainstream writing on focus groups similarly identifies post–World War II as a general time point of origin for the technique, this is somewhat questionable. In fact, for several hundred years, anthropologists conducted what could be described as focus group interviews when they sat around tribal campfires. However, the systematic

technique and the label *focus group* do appear to emerge in the literature shortly after World War II.

3. Census samples include all the people who fit a certain characteristic or who exist in a specific location. For instance, a nurse researcher might use such a sampling procedure to study *all* the patients being treated at a single hemodialysis center. Any potential subject who does not want to participate in the research falls into the researcher's rejection rate. Typically, this procedure is used when the total number of potential subjects is not very large.

REFERENCES

Adler, C. L., & Zarchin, Y. R. (2002). The "virtual focus group": Using the Internet to reach pregnant women on home bed rest. *Journal of Obstetric, Gynecologic, and Neonatal Nursing, 31*(4), 418–427.

Axelrod, M. (1975). 10 essentials for good qualitative research. *Marketing News 8,* 10–11.

Bachman, R., & Schutt, R. K. (2003). *The Practice of Research in Criminology and Criminal Justice* (2nd ed.). Thousand Oaks, CA: Pine Forge Press.

Bartos, R. (1986). Qualitative research: What it is and where it came from. *Journal of Advertising Research 26,* RC3–RC6.

Basch, C. E. (1987). Focus group interviews: An underutilized research technique for improving theory and practice in health education. *Health Education Quarterly 14,* 411–448.

Berg, B. (2004). *Qualitative Research Methods for the Social Sciences* (5th ed.). Boston: Allyn & Bacon.

Berg, J. (1995). *Evaluation of a self-management program for adults with asthma.* Doctoral dissertation, University of Pittsburgh.

Bogdan, R., & Knopp Bilken, S. (2003). *Qualitative Research for Education* (4th ed.). Boston: MA: Allyn and Bacon.

Byers, B., & Byers, P. Y. (March 1996). *Focus group research and juries: Literature and applications.* Paper presented at the annual meeting of the Academy of Criminal Justice Sciences, Las Vegas.

Callahan, J. T. (1983). *Upward mobility from the inside: A phenomenological study of female psychologists from working-class backgrounds.* Doctoral dissertation, Massachusetts School of Professional Psychology, Boston.

Clarke, P. (2000). The Internet as a medium for qualitative research. Paper presented at the Web 2000 Conference, Johannesburg, South Africa.

Creswell, J. W. (2004). *Educational Research* (2nd ed.). Upper Saddle River, NJ: Prentice Hall.

Denzin, N. K. (1989). *Interpretive Interactionism.* Applied Social Research Methods Series, Vol. 16. Newbury Park, CA: Sage.

Edmunds, H. (2000). *The Focus Group Research Handbook.* Thousand Oaks, CA: Sage.

Fern, E. F. (1982). The use of focus groups for idea generation: The effects of group size, acquaintanceship, and moderator on a response quality and quantity. *Journal of Marketing Research 19,* 1–13.

Grant, B. C. (1993). Focus groups versus mock trials: Which should you use? *Trial Diplomacy Journal 16,* 15–22.

Greenbaum, T. (2003). The case against Internet focus groups. *MRA Alert Newsletter* (April). Available online at: http://www.groupsplus.com/pages/case2.htm.

Greenbaum, T. (1997). *The Handbook of Focus Group Research.* Thousand Oaks, CA: Sage.

Greenbaum, T. (1998). Is your moderator ready for videoconferencing? *Focus Vision News 1*(3), 18–19.

Hagan, F. E. (2006). *Research Methods in Criminal Justice and Criminology* (7th ed.). Boston: Allyn and Bacon.

Hamel, J. (2001). The focus group method and contemporary French sociology. *Journal of Sociology 37*(4), 341–354.

Krueger, R. A. (1994). *Focus Groups: A Practical Guide for Applied Research* (2nd ed.). Thousand Oaks, CA: Sage.

Krueger, Richard A. (1997). *Developing Questions for Focus Groups.* Thousand Oaks, CA: Sage.

Krueger, R. A., & Casey, M. A. (2000). *Focus Groups* (3rd ed.). Thousand Oaks, CA: Sage.

Larson, K., Grudens-Schuck, N., and Lundy, B. (2004). Can you call it a focus group? Ames, Iowa: Iowa State University Extension. Available online at: http://www.extension.iastate.edu/pubications/PM1969A.pdf.

Leedy, P. D., & Ormrod, J. E. (2005). *Practical Research: Planning and Design* (8th ed.). Upper Saddle River, NJ: Pearson/Prentice Hall.

Lengua, L. J., Roosa, M. W., Schupak-Neuberg, E., Michaeles, M. L., Berg, C. N., & Weschler, L. F. (1992). Using focus groups to guide the development of a parenting program for difficult-to-research, high-risk families. *Family Relations 41*, 163–168.

Libresco, J. D. (1983). Focus groups: Madison Avenue meets public policy. *Public Opinion,* August/September, 51–53.

Merton, R. K. (1987). The focused interview and focus groups. *Public Opinion Quarterly 51*, 550–566.

Merton, R. K., Fiske, M., & Kendall, P. L. (1956). *The Focused Interview.* Glencoe, IL: Free Press.

Merton, R. K., & Kendall, P. L. (1946). The focused interview. *American Journal of Sociology 51*, 541–557.

Moloney, M. F., Dietrich, A. S., Strickland, O., & Myerburg, S. (2003). Using Internet discussion boards as virtual focus groups. *Advances in Nursing Science 26*(4), 274–286.

Moloney, L. (1997). *Women and children: Family perspectives among incarcerated women.* Doctoral dissertation, Indiana University of Pennsylvania, Indiana, PA.

Moran, W. T. (1986). The science of qualitative research. *Journal of Advertising Research 26*, RC16–RC19.

Morgan, D., (2002). Focus group interviewing. In J. F. Gubrum and J. A. Holstein (Eds.) *Handbook of Interview Research* (pp. 141–159). Thousand Oaks, CA: Sage.

Morgan, D. L. (1989). *Focus Groups as Qualitative Research.* Newbury Park, CA: Sage.

Morgan, D. L. (1997) *Focus Groups as Qualitative Research* (2nd ed.). Thousand Oaks, CA: Sage.

Morgan, D. L., & Scannell, A. U. (1997). *The Focus Group Guidebook.* Thousand Oaks, CA: Sage.

Morgan, D. L., & Spanish, M. T. (1984). Focus groups: A new tool for qualitative research. *Qualitative Sociology 7*, 253–271.

Murray, P. J. (1997). Using virtual focus groups in qualitative research. *Qualitative Health Research 7*(4), 542–554.

Nadilo, R. (1999). Want a quick reliable focus group? Try the Net! *Frozen Food Age 47*(10), 44–45.

Nucifora, A. (2000). Internet is revolutionizing use of focus groups. *Orlando Business Journal 17*(17), 49.

Pramualratana, A., Havanon, N., & Knodel, J. (1985). Exploring the normative basis for age at marriage in Thailand: An example from focus group research. *Journal of Marriage and the Family*, February, 203–210.

Reinharz, S. (1992). *Feminist Methods in Social Research*. New York: Oxford University Press.

Rezabek, R. J. (2000). Online focus groups: Electronic discussions for research. *Forum: Qualitative Social Research*. Vol. 1, No. 1. Available online at: http://www.qualitative-research.net/fgs-texte/1-00/1-00rezabek-e.htm.

Roth, J. (1966). Hired hand research. *The American Sociologist 1*, 190–196.

Rubin, H. J., & Rubin, I. S. (1995). *Qualitative Interviewing: The Art of Hearing Data*. Thousand Oaks, CA: Sage.

Salkind, N. J. (2003). *Exploring Research* (5th ed.). Upper Saddle River, NJ: Prentice Hall.

Schutt, R. K. (2003). *Investigating the Social World: The Process and Practice of Research* (4th ed). Thousand Oaks, CA: Pine Forge Press.

Stewart, D. W., & Shamdasani, P. M. (1990). *Focus Groups: Theory and Practice*. Newbury Park, CA: Sage.

Strauss, A. L., & Corbin, J. M. (1998). *Basics of Qualitative Research: Techniques and Procedures for Developing Grounded Theory*. Thousand Oaks, CA: Sage.

Sussman, S., Burton, D., Dent, C. W., Stacy, A. W., & Flay, B. R. (1991). Use of focus groups in developing an adolescent tobacco use cessation program: Collection norm effects. *Journal of Applied Social Psychology 21*, 1772–1782.

Taylor, S. J., & Bogdan, R. (1998). *Introduction to Qualitative Research Methods* (3rd ed.). New York: Wiley.

Turney, L., & Pocknee, C. (2005). Virtual focus groups: New frontiers in research. *International Journal of Qualitative Methods*. Vol. 4, No. 2. Available online at: http://www.ualberta.ca/~ijqm/english/engframeset.html.

Twiggs, H. F. (1994). Do-it-yourself focus groups: Big profits, modest cost. *Trial 30*(9), 42–117.

Tynan, A. C., & Dryton, J. L. (1989). Conducting focus groups: A guide for first-time users. In T. J. Hayes & C. B. Tathum (Eds.). *Focus Group Interviews: A Reader* (2nd ed., pp. 30–34). Chicago: American Marketing Association.

Whiting, R. (2001). Virtual focus groups. *Information Week*. July 30, 53.

Wimmer, R. D., & Dominick, J. R. (1987). *Mass Media Research*. Belmont, CA: Wadsworth Publishing.

Wright, P. A. (1994). Conducting focus groups with young children requires special considerations and techniques. *Technical Assistance Bulletin*. Rockville, MD: National Clearing House for Alcohol and Drug Information.

Chapter 6

Ethnographic Field Strategies

E THNOGRAPHY HAS BEEN AROUND for a very long time, particularly as practiced by cultural anthropologists; however, social scientists differ sharply on both the conceptual meaning of ethnography and its applications. Researchers frequently use the term in seemingly different ways. Spradley (1979, p. 3), for example, explains that "ethnography is the work of describing a culture. The essential core of this activity aims to understand another way of life from the native point of view." Zigarmi and Zigarmi (1980) refer to ethnographers as virtually anyone who enters the natural setting in order to conduct *field research,* a concept that itself suffers from confused understanding (see Guy, Edgley, Arafat, & Allen, 1987). Some researchers, for example, Ellen (1984) and Stoddart (1986), suggest that ethnography involves the end product of field research—namely, the written accounts of observations. Other researchers, such as Warren and Karner (2005), tend to equate ethnography with participant observation and suggest it is the written accounts of these observers. Similarly, Babbie (2004) suggests that ethnography is a detailed and accurate description of some natural setting but offers no explanations. Some early ethnographic authorities, such as Agar (1973), Johnson and colleagues (1985), Preble and Casey (1969), and Weppner (1977), describe ethnography as an extremely effective method for studying illicit drug use and users. In an attempt to differentiate this style of research from anthropological ethnography, many such drug researchers have called this form *street ethnography* or *urban ethnography.* Leininger (1985, p. 33) coined the term *ethnonursing* to describe ethnography conducted by nurses, whereas Roper and Shapira (2000) and

LoBiondo-Wood and Haber (2002) refer to this activity as *medical ethnographies*. Lofland (1996, p. 30) describes the strategy of analytic ethnography as follows:

> I use the term "analytic ethnography" to refer to research processes and products in which, to a greater or lesser degree, an investigator (a) attempts to provide generic propositional answers to questions about social life and organization; (b) strives to pursue such an attempt in a spirit of unfettered or naturalistic inquiry; (c) utilizes data based on deep familiarity with a social setting or situation that is gained by personal participation or an approximation of it; (d) develops the generic propositional analysis over the course of doing research; (e) strives to present data and analyses that are true; (f) seeks to provide data and/or analyses that are new; and (g) presents an analysis that is developed in the senses of being conceptually elaborated, descriptively detailed, and concept-data interpenetrated.

However, the various ways researchers speak about ethnography may amount to little more than terminological preferences. Agar (1986) came to this conclusion in his examination of the language differences among various ethnographers and ethnographic traditions in his book *Speaking of Ethnography.*

Nonetheless, the important point about the concept of ethnography, regardless of one's language and terminological preference, is that the practice places researchers in the midst of whatever it is they study. From this vantage, researchers can examine various phenomena as perceived by participants and represent these observations as accounts.

Wolcott (1984 [1973], 1999) captures the essence of most of these variations by defining ethnography as the science of *cultural description.* Clearly, ethnography is primarily a process that attempts to describe and interpret social expressions between people and groups. Or, as Geertz (1973) suggests, the researcher's task is to convey *thick description,* such that a wink can be distinguished from a twitch, and a parody of a wink is distinguishable from an actual wink (see Wilcox, 1988, p. 458).

Some researchers, Ellen (1984, 1987), for example, describe the ethnographic process as *subjective soaking.* According to Ellen (1984, p. 77), this occurs when the researcher "abandons the idea of absolute objectivity or scientific neutrality and attempts to merge him/herself into the culture being studied." Other subjectivist and existential approaches have given rise to the notion of fieldwork as *transition,* in which cultural elements including human ideas and perceptions are considered *opaque texts.* From this vantage, the primary objective of ethnography is to read the text. The text, however, should be considered the literal textual context of the ethnographer's notebooks, memos, and the like. This orientation toward ethnography, then, can be understood as the product of interaction between the observer and the observed (Clifford, 1980). Along similar lines, some researchers seek to understand the worldviews of native inhabitants of social environments or what may be called the *emic view*. This emic or insider's view of the world can be contrasted by the *etic view* or outsider's worldview (Creswell, 1999; LoBiondo-Wood & Haber, 2002; Tedlock, 2000).

The more traditional anthropological approach of ethnography, as represented by the works of Malinowski, Evans-Pritchard, and Boas, has been primarily concerned with this type of subjectivist translation. During the past 40 years, however, anthropological methods, like other sociological ones, have undergone considerable advancement, refinement, and change (see, e.g., Adler & Adler, 1987; Tewksbury, 2001). Ellen (1984) and Agar (1996) both point out that these changes have produced no less than a quiet revolution, resulting in a *new ethnography*.

The field of the new ethnography, as suggested in the opening paragraphs of this chapter, has experienced considerable confusion, both conceptually and methodologically. One major result of adaptation to the new ethnography has been a redefining of *ethnography* as a set of highly formal techniques designed to extract cognitive data (Ellen, 1984; Spradley, 1980; Van Maanen, 1982). Another consequence of this quiet revolution is what Spindler (1988) describes as the meteoric rise of *educational ethnography* during the past decade, particularly the past several years. As Spindler (1988, p. 1) explains: "Ethnography has become virtually a household word in professional education, and it is the rare research project today that does not have somewhere in the table of operations at least one ethnographer and somewhere in the research design some ethnographic procedures."

During the past 25 years, this new ethnography has grown popular among nursing researchers (see, for example, Leininger & McFarland, 2002; Morse & Field, 1995). Frequently, one finds this technique referred to as *ethnonursing research* (Burns & Grove, 2000; Leininger, 2002; Polit & Hungler, 1995), which means conducting a study and analysis of some local or indigenous people's viewpoints, beliefs, and practices (the emic view) about nursing care behavior and processes as mediated by cultures. For example, in a recent study by Jennifer Fenwick, Lesley Barclay, and Virginia Schmied (1999) they examined the context and nature of the interactions between health professionals and parents in two Australian level II nurseries. They found that, although the presence of mothers in the nursery was high, registered nurses remained the primary caretakers of the infants.

In the foreword to Ferrell and Hamm's (1998) recent work on ethnographies on crime and deviance, Patricia and Peter Adler characterize the evolutionary development of fieldwork as marked by an early (1920s) period of *impressionism* that emerged early in the Chicago school of urban research. Next came a period of *renaissance* (1946–1955), marked by a second generation of Chicago school researchers. This was followed by *abstract expressionism* during the 1960s and a shift of the ethnographic enterprise's sociological center to California, where focus was placed on deviant, alternative, counter-cultural, and illegal groups. Then came the *dark ages,* beginning in the late 1970s but not entirely full-blown until the 1990s. These were the years that institutional review boards (IRBs) placed strangleholds on many ethnographic research endeavors. Today, we have reached a period of *enlightenment,* a time when brave ethnographers are moving research into a new millennium. Currently, ethnography is experiencing a renewed interest and considerable healthy vigor.

The principal concern in this chapter is to examine the new ethnography as an extremely effective research strategy. Van Maanen (1982, p. 103) suggests that ethnography has become the method "that involves extensive fieldwork of various types including participant observation, formal and informal interviewing, document collecting, filming, recording, and so on." It is not, however, the intent of this chapter to diminish the significant contribution made by the more traditional (textual) orientation. In fact, a section of this chapter on ethnography as a narrative style discusses the more traditional ethnographic orientation.

One other significant aspect of ethnography is the distinction sometimes made between *micro-* and *macroethnography* (sometimes referred to as *general ethnography*). One obvious difference is the scope of a given investigation. Macroethnography attempts to describe the entire way of life of a group. In contrast, microethnography focuses on particular *incisions* at particular points in the larger setting, group, or institution. Typically, these specific points are selected because they in some manner represent salient elements in the lives of participants and in turn, in the life of the larger group or institution.

A second fundamental difference between micro- and macroethnography is that the former analytically focuses more directly on the face-to-face interactions of members of the group or institution under investigation. By examining these interactions, their implications (or as Mehan [1978] suggests, their *outcomes)* can be considered. For example, Wolcott's (1973) *The Man in the Principal's Office* was intended to offer an accurate description of the real world of one elementary school principal and, by extension, to identify the various behaviors, attitudes, and processes shared by other elementary school principals.

In spite of various differences, both micro- and macroethnography share the overarching concern for assessing everyday community life from the perspectives of participants. From detailed examinations of people and their social discourse and the various outcomes of their actions, underlying principles and concepts can be identified. As a result, neither micro- nor macroethnography is fully understandable individually without some consideration of the other. For example, it would be impossible to understand the concept of classroom management in relation to the concept of learning without some consideration of how this relates to learning environments in general (see Allen, 1986).

This chapter is divided into five sections: Accessing a Field Setting: Getting In; Becoming Invisible; Other Dangers During Ethnographic Research; Watching, Listening, and Learning; and Disengaging: Getting Out.

Accessing a Field Setting: Getting In

As Leedy and Ormrod (2005, p. 137) suggest, "The first step in an ethnographic study is to gain access to a site appropriate for answering the researcher's general research problem or question." In effect, all field investigations begin with the problem of *getting in*. This particular problem should be addressed during the design stage of the research. It involves consideration of who the subjects are and the nature of the setting.

Robert Burgess (1991b, p. 43) suggests that access is "negotiated and renegotiated throughout the research process." He further states that "access is based on sets of relationships between the researcher and the researched, established throughout a project."

Roger Vallance (2001) has a slightly different take on the matter. Vallance suggests that access should be sought through introduction and referrals. According to Vallance (p. 68):

> The essence of my contention can be summed up in the oft-quoted saying; *it is not what you know, but who(m) you know.* In a sense, this is analogous to snow-balling: using one research participant to indicate others who can be equally or more informative. . . . Instead of using contacts to widen the sample as in snow-ball sampling, the suggestion here is to use one's contacts and relationships to gain the vital, initial entry into the field, where one can engage with possible research participants.

In an ideal situation, Vallance's suggestion is probably well taken—assuming the investigator is undertaking research in an area or on a topic in which he or she knows many people actively engaged in related work or activities. However, in many instances, researchers conduct studies in areas in which they simply do not know anyone who can serve as the kind of entrance guide or core to a *snowball* sample to be rolled through the project. For example, although a number of researchers have investigated burglary, few (if any) have themselves known active burglars prior to beginning their research (see, e.g., Cromwell & Nielsen, 1999).

Hertz and Imber (1993) similarly detail the problems associated with conducting field studies in *elite settings*. As they suggest, there are very few studies of elites because elites are by their very nature difficult to penetrate. Unlike some other segments of society, elites often are visible and fairly easy to locate. Yet, because they are able to establish barriers and obstacles and because they can successfully refuse access to researchers, many elites are difficult to study.

Richard Tewksbury (2002, 2006) offers an interesting twist on an orientation originally offered by Joseph Styles (1979). Styles (p. 151) refers to an *outsider* strategy of observation, which is not fully participatory but allows the researcher to appear available to participate. Tewksbury (2002) uses this approach to gain access to a gay bathhouse (a locale where men go seeking to have sex with other men). As Tewksbury explains it, the researcher's role becomes one of a *potential participant* in various activities of the natural setting. Tewksbury (2001, p. 6) explains this potential participant role as follows:

> [It] combines aspects of complete observation, complete participation and covert observational research designs. Whereas the researcher adopting a potential participant role seeks to appear to those being researched as a "real" setting member, the "science" activities are conducted in covert manners. To anyone noticing the potential participant, the researcher is a real member of the setting being studied. To the scientific community, the potential participant is a complete observer, acting in a covert manner *inside* the research environment.

Using this strategy, Tewksbury was able to enter the bathhouse, spend several hours circulating there, and chat freely among the patrons while conducting observations of their activities, movements, interactions, and use of physical features in the facility (Tewksbury, 2002).

How might you gain access to difficult-to-reach groups? As simplistic as it may seem, the answer lies in reading the literature. While various settings and groups are *difficult* to access, most are not impossible. Ostrander (1993) says she found it rather simple to gain access to upper-class women. She further suggests that sometimes a bit of luck, taking advantage of certain relationships, considerable background work, and making the right contacts frequently ease access to restricted groups. Although researching restricted settings or groups may involve more work initially, the rewards can be quite gratifying.

It is also important during the design stage of your research to consider several other important points. For example, because most ethnographic research involves human subjects, researchers must give considerable thought to ways they can protect the subjects from harm and injury. This is especially true when dealing with restricted groups or settings. You must be mindful not to bar future researchers' access by careless protection of subjects' rights and privacy. In addition, researchers must consider how they will go about gaining permission or consent of the subjects. Of course, this itself requires a decision about whether to enter the field as an announced researcher (overtly) or as a secret researcher (covertly).

Most sources on gaining access to the field agree on one thing: Whether it is a highly accessible or a very restricted setting, decisions made during the early stages of research are critical. This is true because such decisions will lay both the conceptual and methodological foundation for the entire project. This can be likened to what Janesick (1994, pp. 210–211; 2003, pp. 46–79) describes as "choreographing the research design." In other words, just as an expressive dancer might ask, "What statement do I want to make through my dance?" an ethnographer must consider the question, "What do I want to learn from this study?"

Toward this end, the decision to enter the field overtly or covertly as an investigator is important. Each style of entrance encompasses certain problems, and regardless of the style you choose, you must address these problems.

Similarly, with either style of entrance, researchers must consider that their very presence in the study setting may taint anything that happens among other participants in that setting. As Denzin (1970, pp. 203–204) suggests: "Reactive effects of observation are the most perplexing feature of participant observation, since the presence of an observer in any setting is often a 'foreign object.' The creation of the role of participant observer inevitably introduces some degree of reactivity into the field setting."

Spindler and Spindler (1988, p. 25) similarly express their concerns about intruding by participating in the "life of the school" during their research. As a partial solution, they strive to "melt" into the classroom as much as possible. This attempt to "become invisible" will be discussed in greater detail later in this chapter.

An argument can be made for both covert and overt stances when conducting ethnographic research. For instance, a study on casual homosexual encounters such as Humphreys's *Tearoom Trade* (1975) simply could not have been undertaken if he had formally announced his identity as a researcher. Briefly, Humphreys found a public bathroom where men met for brief homosexual encounters. Standing as lookout and assumed to be a voyeur or "watch queen," Humphreys managed to learn that many of these men had wives and families. They lived heterosexual lives but occasionally had homosexual encounters. His research demonstrated rather clearly that homosexuality was not a disease, as many people had previously believed, but a lifestyle.

Similarly, in studies about people who frequent so-called adult movie theaters and book stores, the identification of an observing ethnographer might result in little information about such persons. It is also likely that such an announcement would create uncontrollable reactivity to the presence of the researcher. For example, nurses conducting ethnographic research with the intention of investigating drug theft practices of hospital staff members might create conflicts between themselves and others on the staff. Thus, a major argument for covert ethnographic research is the sensitivity of certain topics that might make it impossible to do research by other means. Naturally, in making such a case, you must additionally justify the undertaking of such research by some actual social or scientific benefit.

Scientific benefits notwithstanding, some serious ethical questions arise when covert research is conducted on human subjects. Among other concerns is the possibility that this type of research might abuse the rights and privacy of the research subjects, thereby causing them harm. For many scholars, there can be *no* justification for knowingly harming subjects.

On the other hand, entering an ethnographic study as a known researcher has several benefits. For example, in his study of medical students, Becker (1963) noted that his status as an identified researcher allowed him to ask questions of various hospital personnel more effectively. Similarly, Berg et al. (1983), in a study of adolescent involvement in alcohol, drugs, and crime, suggest that by having entered the field overtly, they succeeded in locating guides and informants (discussed in detail later). Many of these adolescents might otherwise have thought the two field ethnographers were narcs—people who are or work for the police. By having established who they were and what they were doing in the field, the two ethnographers managed to gain considerable rapport with their subjects.

Because of the ethical concerns associated with the overt/covert controversy and in light of heightened concern over falsification of research findings in scientific communities, this chapter primarily considers *getting in* as an overt activity. Issues commonly associated with determining a balance between covert and overt research techniques were more comprehensively considered in Chapter 3.

Reflectivity and Ethnography

Access and ethical concerns underscore that ethnography requires a reflective concern on the part of the researcher, or what some scholars refer to as *reflexivity* (Boyle, 1994, Hammersley & Atkinson, 1995). This reflexive characteristic implies that the researcher understands that he or she is part of the social world(s) that he or she investigates. Ethnography involves activities that fall somewhere between rigorous, dare I say, positivist approaches and more naturalistic reflections of the actual social worlds of the people being studied. Good ethnography requires that the researcher avoids simply accepting everything at face value but, instead, considers the material as raw data that may require corroboration or verification.

Ethnography, then, becomes a process of gathering systematic observations, partly through participation and partly through various types of conversational interviews (Werner & Schoepfle, 1987). Yet, it may additionally require the use of photography, computers, mapping, archival searches, and even assorted documents. Ethnographers today must do more than simply describe the populations they investigate; they must strive to understand them and, if possible, to explain their activities.

Reflexivity further implies a shift in the way we understand data and their collection. To accomplish this, the researcher must make use of an internal dialogue that repeatedly examines *what the researcher knows* and *how the researcher came to know this*. To be reflexive is to have an ongoing conversation with yourself. The reflexive ethnographer does not merely report *findings as facts* but actively constructs interpretations of experiences in the field and then questions how these interpretations actually arose (Hertz, 1997; Van Maanen, 1988). The ideal result from this process is reflexive knowledge: information that provides insights into the workings of the world *and* insights on how that knowledge came to be.

The Attitude of the Ethnographer

The researcher's frame of mind when entering a natural setting is crucial to the eventual results of a study. If you strike the wrong attitude, you might well destroy the possibility of ever learning about the observed participants and their perceptions. Matza (1969) similarly identifies researcher attitude as a crucial element in field studies. According to Matza (1969), one must enter *appreciating* the situations rather than intending to *correct* them. This sort of neutral posture allows researchers to understand what is going on around them rather than become either advocates or critics of the events they witness. In addition, appreciation does not require the interviewers to agree with or even to accept the perceptions of their subjects but merely to offer empathy.

Although many students might think it is unnecessary to suggest that ethnographers should conduct research with an appreciative attitude, in actuality it is an important recommendation.

The Researcher's Voice

Many researchers—both quantitative and qualitative alike—recommend that social science research maintain a *value neutral* position. From this perspective, social scientists are expected to study the world around them as external investigators. This means neither imposing their own views or taking any stands on social or political issues. This style of research tends to lend itself to a fairly positivist approach. During the more recent past, a number of social researchers have argued against this façade of value neutrality. Among the more vocal have been feminist researchers (Hertz, 1997; Nagy Hess-Biber, Leavy, & Yaiser, 2004; Reinhartz, 1992; Ribbens & Edwards, 1998). Feminists have worked out a research orientation that is comfortable for both the researcher and the subjects. It tends to involve strategies that listen more and talk less, that humanize the research process, and that insist that the ethnographic researcher become both involved with his or her subjects and reflexive about his or her own thoughts. Some recent researchers have also sought to encourage the writing of self-reflective or *autoethnographies*, similar in concept to more traditional autobiographies (Ellis & Bochner, 1996; Tedlock, 2003).

Objectively, social scientists should recognize that research is seldom, if ever, really value neutral. After all, the selection of a research topic typically derives from some researcher-oriented position. As previously implied in this chapter, topic selection occurs because of an interest in the subject matter, or because it is a politically advantageous area to receive grant monies, because of some inner humanistic drive toward some social problem, or because one has personal experiences or what Lofland (1996, p. 44) calls "deep familiarity" with the subject area. The fact is, research is seldom undertaken for a neutral reason. Furthermore, all humans residing in and among social groups are the product of those social groups. This means that various values, moral attitudes, and beliefs orient people in a particular manner.

For instance, a person's selection of certain terms indicates the kind of influences that a person's social groups have on him or her. During the early 1980s, I thought nothing of using the pronoun *he* consistently and exclusively in my writing. Similarly, I often used the words *policeman, chairman, postman,* and similar types of terms. By the mid-1980s, however, with the press for political correctness, my orientation changed and I began using the convention of writing *he* or *she* and using terms such as *police officer, chair,* and *postal worker.* The point here is that my basic orientations were affected, not merely my semantics. How I viewed social worlds was now different, and it is such differences that affect the possibility of value neutrality in research.

More recently, and again following from feminist researchers' lead, my writing has begun to incorporate the use of first person singular. In other words, I use the word *I.* Particularly when writing ethnographic reports, it began to be apparent that using the first person singular was more direct. Rather than saying, "The researcher began to recognize blah, blah, blah . . ." it seemed more forthright to simply say, "I began to recognize. . . ." In this manner, a researcher can take both ownership and responsibility for what is being stated. Furthermore, one's writing style becomes far less cumbersome and often eliminates passive and convoluted sentences.

Along similar lines, the use of personal biography or deep familiarity with a subject has become more common and accepted by ethnographers. One excellent example is Phil Brown's exploration of the culture of the Catskill Mountains' resorts (Brown, 1996). The "Borscht Belt," as the area is known, is where mainly metropolitan Jews fled New York and New Jersey for a summer retreat (Brown, 1996). On the other side of the coin, it was a place where young, often Jewish, college students went to work in order to earn their way through school. A number of well-known and large hotels, bungalow colonies, and camps grew up during the 1940s, and the largely Jewish resort area flourished until about the 1970s. Brown (p. 84) writes from the perspective of an observer who grew up in the Catskill culture and from the orientation of first-person deep familiarity:

> I grew up in a family of "mountain rats," a Catskill term for those who lived and worked in "the Mountains" over many years. My parents began in 1948 as owners of a small hotel, Brown's Hotel Royal, on White Lake. . . . In 1948 the chef quit at the start of the season. Unable to find a replacement, my mother, Sylvia Brown, gave herself a crash course in cooking and never left the kitchen again. After our hotel went broke two years later, she spent the rest of her working years as a chef.

Maintaining the facade of neutrality prevents a researcher from ever examining his or her own cultural assumptions (Rubin & Rubin, 1995) or personal experiences. Subjective disclosures by researchers allow the reader to better understand why a research area has been selected, how it was studied, and by whom. If a nurse studies cancer patients and explains that his or her selection of this topic resulted after a family member contracted the disease, this does not diminish the quality of the research. It does, however, offer a keener insight about who is doing the research and why. It may even provide the reader with greater understanding about why certain types of questions were investigated, while others were not.

Similarly, when a researcher reveals that he or she was tempted to, or did, intervene in the lives of his or her subjects, the reader gets a different image of both the researcher and the research. It is likely that anyone who has ever undertaken drug research among children, at the very least, has been tempted to try to convince some child that using heroin or crack cocaine is not a good thing to do. From a strictly positivist value neutral position, of course, one cannot do this. This activity is the work of social workers and not social scientists. From a softer, more humane perspective, however, it seems a reasonable activity along with the fieldwork. Having the researcher reveal that he or she did try to intervene or even the inner battle the researcher may have had resisting intervening are important pieces of information. This information allows the reader to better understand the true face of both the researcher and the study results.

Finally, presenting subjective disclosures, or giving voice to the researcher, provides insights into the world of research for the reader. Rather than merely heaping results, findings, and even analysis upon the reader, the researcher can share a small portion of the research experience.

Subjective Motivational Factors   Frequently, qualitative studies report in considerable detail the autobiographical motivations that led investigators to conduct their research as they did. These sorts of "true confessions," as Schwartz and Jacobs (1979) call them, are apparently designed to describe the initial biases, values, and theoretical orientations that eventually produced the project. As Johnson (1975) suggests, some researchers may have been motivated or inspired to conduct research in the hopes that such a project would offer positive steps toward realizing some abstract ideal (for example, advancing scientific knowledge, alleviating human misery, resolving some specific social problem, and so on).

External Motivating Factors   Conversely, Punch (1986, p. 210) suggests that the gamut of possible personal motivational factors that leads investigators to conduct research of one type or another may not result from high ideals at all. A number of features—not articulated in the researcher's confessions— may have been critically influential in the decision to study a given phenomenon or to do so in a particular manner. Certainly, the personality of the researcher may have an effect. Not all investigators are willing to associate with certain types of deviants or enter into some specialized natural settings (for example, investigating inmates in correctional institutions or drug addicts in the South Bronx).

Another simple factor, seldom discussed in detail yet perhaps responsible for much research, is geographic proximity and access opportunities. The Adlers (Adler, 1985), for example, indirectly explain that their study on drug dealers and smugglers arose almost serendipitously. After moving to California to attend graduate school and renting a condominium townhouse on the beach, they met a neighbor identified as Dave. Later, the Adlers learned that Dave was a member of a smuggling crew that imported "a ton of marijuana weekly and 40 kilos of cocaine every few months" (Adler, 1985, p. 14). The friendship that developed between Dave and the Adlers provided access to the world of high-level drug dealers and smugglers.

In a similar manner, Peshkin (1986) reports that he began his study of a fundamentalist Christian school largely as a matter of circumstance. As Peshkin (1986, p. 11) describes it:

> By means of an event which my Christian friends would call providential, and everyone else I know would call coincidental, I came to my present study. The event: a midwinter blizzard, an evening class, and a student in need of a ride home. The student was the Reverend David Householder, whose son attended a local Christian school and who assured me, when I expressed a fascination with religious schools, that he would help in every way he could to arrange for me to study his son's school.

Certainly, there is something romantic and exciting about the image of an ethnographer spending time with potentially dangerous people in interesting, albeit grimy, bars, gambling houses, various hidden erotic worlds (see, e.g., Ferrell & Hamm, 1998; Lee, 2001; Tewksbury, 1995). Ethnography can be, as Lofland and Lofland (1984) describe it, an "adventure." Yet, it is also rigorous, time-consuming, and often boring, tedious work.

Many researchers study certain settings simply because of their convenience or special ease of accessibility. Later, they endeavor to justify their choice on the basis of some grand ideal or spurious theoretical grounds (Punch, 1986). Yet what these researchers apparently fail to recognize is that everyday realities are heavily influenced by human feelings, and presentation of these feelings is legitimate!

The omission of the ethnographers' feelings for and about their research inevitably creates what Johnson (1975, p. 145) describes as "the fieldworker as an iron-willed, steel-nerved, cunning Machiavellian manipulator of the symbolic tools of everyday discourse." Including some indication of why researchers have undertaken a particular project along with the methodological procedure provides a means for making the research come alive, to become interesting to the reading audience. When research is interesting, as Lofland and Lofland (1984, p. 127) indicate, it is not only instrumental but may be expressively aesthetic. In consequence, researchers may produce what Stinchcombe (1975, p. 32) expresses as "the experience [of] a thrill at a beautiful idea."

Unfortunately, in their attempt to objectify their research efforts, many investigators ignore, omit, or conceal their feelings since such emotions are not typically considered capable of independent verification by others. Yet it is important to remember that overrationalized, highly objectified, nearly sterile methodological accounts of fieldwork efforts are not complete descriptions of the research enterprise. Mentions of researchers' personal feelings are not wholly absent from the research literature, but they are relatively rare and are frequently made anecdotally rather than with a substantive purpose in mind (Johnson, 1975).

Gaining Entry

Gaining entry, or getting in, to a research locale or setting can be fraught with difficulties, and researchers need to remain flexible concerning their tactics and strategies (Bogdan & Bilken, 2003; Shenton & Hayter, 2004; Shaffir, Stebbins, & Turowetz, 1980). Knowledge about the people being studied and familiarity with their routines and rituals facilitate entry as well as rapport once one has gained entry. Understanding a group's *argot* (specialized language), for example, may assist an investigator not only in gaining entry but also in understanding what is going on once he or she has access. In some instances, the researcher may hold some special relationship with members of a group he or she seeks entry to or may himself be a member of that group (see, e.g., Brown, 2003).

Timothy McGettigan (2001) describes his experience and expectations about gaining entry for his study of the Green Tortoise (a young adult adventure bus). McGettigan (2001, par. 3.2) explains:

> One of the unique features of the Green Tortoise is that "getting in," or what Wax (1971) refers to as "the first and most uncomfortable stage of fieldwork," is equally difficult for all. Field researchers often study well-established groups, and, prior to initiation, they can appear hopelessly inept. . . . However, on the Tortoise there was no pre-established community. Instead, all of the passengers were cast into the role of bungling outsiders.
>
> In fact, developing a cohesive in-group is one of the principal features of Tortoise journeys. Adventure travel on the Tortoise is predicated upon cramming overbooked passengers onto old, refurbished buses and taking them on long trips without precise itineraries. Because the buses are usually very crowded (e.g., there were forty-two people on this journey), passengers are forced to violate many of the niceties of conventional crowd behavior. Sean, a German man on his sixth adventure trip, noted that a common saying on the Green Tortoise is "Move your meat, lose your seat." Nevertheless, I was alarmed throughout the first few days because of how often I bumped into others and invaded their space—no matter how ill-defined.

In spite of various ethnographers' personal accounts, as a starting point it is wise, especially for the beginning researcher, to begin in the library and to locate as much information about the group as possible before attempting entry. You might also begin, as Vallance (2001) suggests, by considering your friends and social networks to see if anyone you know can offer a *referral* into the group you intend to study. But in many instances the library will be your best resource. Even when there is little literature on a specific topic, there is often considerable work on some related area.

Developing Research Bargains   Gaining entry into various settings also is affected by the kinds of arrangements or *bargains* made between researchers and subjects. Many researchers' accounts about how they gained entry to their research settings include descriptions of negotiating access with a highly visible and respected individual who held a position of rank, authority, or respect among others in the group (Calhoun, 1992; Guy et al., 1987; Haas & Shaffir, 1978; Leinen, 1993; Whyte, 1955). During recent years, there has also been an increased interest by researchers to create *research teams* that include, as members, *insiders* from the group or groups to be studied (see, for example, Jones, 1995; Tewksbury, 1997).

Gatekeepers   Gatekeepers are people or groups who are in positions to grant or deny access to a research setting (Hagan, 2006). Gatekeepers may be formal or informal watchdogs who protect the setting, people, or institutions sought as the target of research. Such individuals often hold pivotal positions in the hierarchy of the group or organization one seeks to study; although they may not be high up the hierarchical ranking, they are nonetheless in positions to stymie the researcher's ability to gain access. For example, secretaries are typically key gatekeepers in organizational settings. Secretaries can make a researcher's life easy or difficult. Yet, the social status of a secretary in most organizations is likely not as high as that of the individual for whom he or she works. Gaining access may require some sort of mediation with these individuals, and research bargains may necessarily be struck. Once a gatekeeper sees the research in a favorable light, he or she may be willing to go to bat for the researcher should obstacles arise during the course of study. Conversely, if the gatekeeper disapproves of the project or the researcher, or is somehow bypassed, he or she may become an unmovable obstacle: Angry gatekeepers may actively seek ways to block one's access or progress.

Guides and Informants   One way to handle initial relationships is to locate *guides* and *informants*. Guides are indigenous persons found among the group and in the setting to be studied. These persons must be convinced that the ethnographers are who they claim to be and that the study is worthwhile. The worth of the study must be understood and be meaningful to the guides and their group. Similarly, these guides must be convinced that no harm will befall them or other members of the group as a result of the ethnographers' presence. The reason for these assurances, of course, is so the guide can reassure others in the group that the ethnographers are safe to have around.

Sometimes persons who are willing to be guides or informants turn out to be restricted in their groups. Perhaps they are resented or disliked by others in the group. Consequently, several guides and the snowballing of guides and informants may assist ethnographers in their maneuverability while in the field. *Snowballing,* in the sense it is used here, refers to using people whom the original guide(s) introduces to the ethnographer as persons who can also vouch for the legitimacy and safety of the researcher.

The larger the ethnographers' network of reliable guides and informants, the greater their access and ability to gain further cooperation. Eventually, the need for specific guides decreases as subject networks grow in size, and the ethnographers are able to begin casual acquaintanceships by virtue of their generally accepted presence on the scene. This will be further discussed in the next section of this chapter, Becoming Invisible.

The preceding guidelines and illustrations suggest some broad considerations and tactics ethnographers may use in order to gain entry to a specific setting. Similar accounts of entry may be found throughout the literature on ethnography and field research. However, some accounts also suggest that entry is determined by the innate abilities and personalities of the ethnographers. This attitude is comparable to the notion that only certain innately gifted people can conduct effective in-depth interviews—and it is likewise inaccurate (see Chapter 4 for a comprehensive examination of this argument regarding interviewing). A more accurate description of the effects of persona may be effects from the type of role and personality an ethnographer projects. In other words, just as the characterizations and social roles played out by the interviewer affect the quality of the interview performance, so too do these activities affect the ethnographer's performance.

Naturally, indigenous ethnographers—persons who already are members of the group to be studied—possess certain strategic advantages, but as several nurses who conduct ethnography have suggested, neither their indigenous status nor special knowledge about the health care profession made conducting their research any easier (Ostrander, 1993; Peterson, 1985; Quint, 1967).

In some instances, researchers may be able to gain entry more quickly because of their indigenous status. Unfortunately, this is sometimes mistaken for an innate ability (Hoffmann, 1980). Certainly, a clumsy ethnographer, regardless of personal contacts, will produce flawed ethnographies.

Becoming Invisible

As mentioned previously, one obstacle to conducting ethnographic research is the very presence of the ethnographer in the field. Early in the history of field research, Roethlisberger and Dickenson (1939) identified a phenomenon now commonly called the *Hawthorne effect.* Briefly, the Hawthorne effect suggests that when subjects know they are subjects in a research study, they will alter their usual (routine) behavior. Fortunately, this effect is typically short-lived, and the behavior of subjects eventually returns to a more routine style. But the persistent presence of ethnographers in a social setting might certainly reactivate the Hawthorne effect in varying degrees every time someone new is introduced to the researchers. Ethnographic accounts, therefore, understandably offer readers explanations of how the ethnographers' presence was made *invisible* to the subjects.

The status as an *invisible researcher,* as Stoddart (1986) describes it, is the ability to be present in the setting, to see what's going on without being observed, and consequently, to capture the essence of the setting and participants without influencing them. Stoddart (1986, pp. 109–113) identifies six possible variations on this theme of invisible status:

1. *Disattending: Erosion of visibility by time.* When the ethnographers have been present in a domain for a long time, the inhabitants tend not to be aware of them anymore. The notice inhabitants initially took of them has eroded or worn off.

2. *Disattending: Erosion of visibility by display of no symbolic detachment.* The second variation on the theme differs slightly from the first. In this instance, a specific condition believed to facilitate ethnographer invisibility is offered—namely, the assertion that displaying no symbolic detachment from the ways of the domain promotes normalization of the ethnographers' presence. In short, ethnographers eventually just fit into the domain they are studying.

3. *Disattending: Erosion of visibility by display of symbolic attachment.* In contrast to variation 2, in which the ethnographers eventually fit in, the third variation suggests that researchers should actively work toward invisibility by displaying attachment to the domain under study. This kind of attachment typically involves participating with ordinary inhabitants in their everyday routines. By working shoulder to shoulder with inhabitants, it is asserted, the researchers' ethnographer status becomes less of a focal point for members of the study.

4. *Disattending: Erosion of visibility by personalizing the ethnographer–informant relationship.* In the fourth variation, the relationship between ethnographers and inhabitants provides the researchers with their invisible status. Simply stated, the ethnographers become invisible because their informants suspend concern over the research aspect of their identity in favor of liking the researcher as a person.

5. *Misrepresentation: Masking real research interests.* This fifth variation is based on the premise that the greatest areas of inhabitant reactivity will be in the areas the ethnographers announce to be their interest.

Thus, if the ethnographers suggest false areas of interest, the assumption is that their real interest areas will be performed as though they were not present.

6. *Misrepresentation: Masking identity as ethnographer.*   In the final variation suggested by Stoddart (1986), ethnographers do not represent themselves to the normal inhabitants as ethnographers: In other words, they conduct covert ethnography. Since the normal inhabitants of the domain under examination are not aware of the ethnographers' real activities in the setting, the ethnographers are socially invisible.

Dangers of Invisibility

From the ethnographers' perspective, it may seem ideal to obtain invisible status, but several ethical—or real—dangers exist. At least three types of dangers are inherent in conducting research invisibly. These include researcher-originated or intentional misidentification, accidental misidentification, and learning more than you want to know.

Intentional Misidentification   The first potential danger results when the ethnographers' intentional attempts to misrepresent their identity as researchers successfully isolate the subjects of a study. As Thomas's (Thomas & Swaine, 1928) frequently quoted statement expresses, "If men define situations as real, they are real to them in their consequences." In other words, when researchers misrepresent themselves and become invisible to normal inhabitants in a study domain, their assumed role as something else may be taken for real! For example, Rosenhan (1973), in a study of psychiatric hospitals, describes how he and several research associates became psychiatric patients (actually pseudopatients) by acting out various schizophrenic symptoms during intake assessments. By misrepresenting their role as researchers, Rosenhan and his associates managed to have themselves committed.

From the assumed identity of psychiatric patient, Rosenhan and his associates were able to observe and record the behavior of the hospital staff (nurses, aides, psychiatrists, and so on). After being admitted, all of the researchers discontinued their simulation of symptoms, but each had difficulty convincing doctors that they were not crazy! The length of stay in the hospitals ranged from 5 days to 52 days, with an average stay of 19 days. Eventually, each researcher was released with the discharge diagnosis of schizophrenia in remission.

Rosenhan's original purpose of demonstrating the effects of labeling in psychiatric facilities was accomplished, but this study further illustrates another point—the dangers for researchers of misidentifying themselves as other than ethnographers.

Accidental Misidentification   In contrast to intentional misidentification as researchers, ethnographers who gain invisible status may be found guilty by association. Persons outside the immediate domain under investigation may not know who the ethnographers are and simply assume they belong to the group. Although this may allow accurate assessment of many social interactions among the various participants, it is also potentially dangerous.

Particularly when investigating certain so-called deviant groups (for example, violent youth gangs, drug dealers or smugglers, car thieves) even if the ethnographers are socially invisible (as researchers) to members of this group, they may be taken as actual group members by others outside this group.

If, for example, ethnographers studying some youth gang were treated as invisible by members of this group, these interactions could be misinterpreted by members of a rival youth gang. As a result, the ethnographers' personal safety could be jeopardized in the event of a violent confrontation between the gangs. If the ethnographers are with one gang, they may be guilty of membership through association in the eyes of the rival gang.

Learning More Than You Want to Know   Another danger of researcher invisibility is learning more than you might want to know. During the course of an ethnographic study on adolescent involvement in alcohol, drugs, and crime (Berg et al., 1983), field ethnographers found that their presence was often invisible. It was common for the ethnographers to be present, for example, during criminal planning sessions. Often, the ethnographers had information concerning planned burglaries, drug deals, shoplifting sprees, car thefts, and fights several days before the event. In the case of this particular study, possession of this knowledge presented more of an ethical problem than a legal one, since the study group also possessed a Federal Certificate of Confidentiality.

Federal Certificates of Confidentiality ensure that all employees of a research study and all research documents are protected from subpoena in civil or criminal court actions. The certificate also specifies that the researchers cannot divulge confidential material. Thus, the field ethnographers could not divulge their knowledge of impending crimes without violating this agreement. Nonetheless, it was sometimes difficult for the field ethnographers to maintain their personal sense of integrity knowing in advance that certain crimes would occur and knowing also they could do nothing to stop them. One partial solution to the ethical/moral dilemma was an agreement among all of the study participants concerning special circumstances. Under certain special circumstances—that is, if information were obtained that convinced the ethnographers that someone's life or limb could be saved (for example, if a contract were placed on someone's life, or if plans were made to break someone's arm or leg)—appropriate authorities would be notified.

Certificates of Confidentiality Certificates of Confidentiality are issued by the National Institutes of Health (NIH) to protect the privacy of research subjects by ensuring that researchers and research institutes cannot be compelled to release information that could be used to identify subjects used in a given research study. Certificates of Confidentiality are issued on behalf of the researchers to their institutions or universities. Certificates of Confidentiality allow the researcher and others working on the project who have access to records and data to refuse to disclose identifying information in any civil, criminal, administrative, legislative, or other proceeding, whether at the federal, state, or local level. This translates quite literally into a protection for the interviewer from being compelled to bear witness against a subject whom the researcher may have heard or observed plan a crime.

Generally certificates are issued for a single research project and not for groups or classes of projects. In some instances, however, they can be issued to projects that may have multiple data-collection or analysis sites. The main or coordinating center (what may be called the lead institution) can apply on behalf of all the other research sites or institutions working on the project. It is the responsibility of the lead institution to ensure that all of the sites comply with the applications made on their behalf.

Application information for Certificates of Confidentiality can be found online at http://grants.nih.gov/grants/policy/coc/appl_extramural.htm. The application must be written on the university or research institute's letterhead and meet a number of human subject criteria, including assurances of informed consent, privacy, confidentiality, and having already been approved by the researcher's local institutional review board (see Chapter 3). Application for a Certificate of Confidentiality is not an assurance of being granted one.

Other Dangers During Ethnographic Research

Most novice researchers do an effective job of protecting the rights and safety of their subjects. Less common among inexperienced researchers, however, are serious concerns during the design stage of research about the investigator's own personal safety. Some research, especially ethnographic research, may be in dangerous places or among dangerous people (Williams, Dunlap, Johnson, & Hamid, 2001). Howell (1990), for example, discusses a number of crimes researchers are apt to encounter in the field (e.g., robbery, theft, rape, assault). Field investigators have encountered illness, personal injury, and even death during the course of ethnographic research.

Interestingly, the potential for personal or emotional harm to subjects is extensively covered in virtually all research methods books. The problem of personal or emotional harm to *researchers*, however, is seldom discussed (Sluka, 1990; Williams et al., 2001). Some basic elements about caution when Conducting research in general and ethnographic research in particular can be found—indirectly—in the broad methodological literature on ethnography (Adler, 1985; Adler & Adler, 1987; Broadhead & Fox, 1990; Fetterman, 1989; Johnson, 1990; Rose, 1990; Williams, Dunlap, Johnson, & Hamid, 2001; Ferrell, 2006).

Yet, contemporary ethnographers often work in settings made dangerous by violent conflict or with social groups among whom interpersonal violence is commonplace. As Lee (2001) suggests, in many cases, it is the violence itself or the social conditions and circumstances that produce this violence that actively compel attention from the social scientist. Understanding that there are potential dangers and risks to the ethnographer, therefore, is an important lesson. Knowing about these risks allows the novice researcher to determine how best to deal with them, what precautions to take, and perhaps how to avoid them.

It is possible to identify at least two distinct forms of danger that may arise during the course of ethnographic research. These include *ambient* and *situational risks*. Similar distinctions have been offered by Lee (2001), Brewer (1993), and Sluka (1990).

Ambient dangers arise when a researcher exposes himself or herself to otherwise avoidable dangers, simply by having to be in a dangerous setting or circumstance to carry out the research. Nurses who conduct research in infectious disease wards, for example, place themselves in ambient danger.

Situational danger occurs when the researcher's presence or behaviors in the setting trigger conflict, violence, or hostility from others in the setting. For instance, an ethnographer researching tavern life, who engages in alcohol consumption as a means of gaining greater acceptance by regular participants, may also evoke trouble among the regular drinkers.

Often the safety precautions you must take in research amount to little more than good common sense. For instance, you should never enter the field without telling someone where you will be and when you expect to leave the field. You must learn to be aware of your environment. What's going on around you? Is it nighttime and dark out? Is it nighttime but well lighted? Are there other people around? Being aware of your environment also means knowing your location and the locations where help can be obtained quickly (e.g., locations of telephones, police stations, personal friends).

It is important for the researcher's safety to know insiders who are ready to vouch for him or her. Often a quick word from an established insider will reassure others in a group of the researcher's sincerity or purposes.

Additionally, there are places one should avoid if possible. For example, often I send my classes out to shopping malls to practice their observational skills. The single proviso I admonish students with is: Do not conduct observations in the public bathrooms! I do this not merely because public bathrooms are designed as places for private activities (although one could argue that ethical case). I do this because public bathrooms are potentially very dangerous places for researchers. Usually, they are unmonitored and secluded from the view of others. They are sometimes frequented by thieves trying to deal stolen property or drug dealers trying to sell their wares. In other words, public bathrooms may draw a variety of undesirable and dangerous people. If you are conducting actual research on activities in public bathrooms, of course, they cannot be avoided. However, in such a situation, you are likely to take proper safety precautions. For the casual practice of observational skills, however, bathrooms are simply too risky a setting.

It is also important to note that while potential risks to researchers clearly exist, only a very small proportion of researchers has ever actually been seriously injured or killed as a direct result of research (Williams et al., 2001). Perhaps one reason for this low injury rate is that experienced researchers do recognize the potential dangers and develop plans and procedures to reduce or avoid the risks involved.

Watching, Listening, and Learning

Much ethnographic research involves entering the setting of some group and simply watching and listening attentively. Because it would be virtually impossible to observe everything or hear all that is going on at one time, ethnographers must watch and listen only to certain portions of what happens. One solution to this problem is to determine exactly what the researchers want to learn about at various points in the research.

Once the ethnographers have determined their essential aims, it should be possible to partition off the setting. This may be accomplished by bracketing certain subgroups of inhabitants of the domain and observing them during specific times, in certain locations, and during the course of particular events and/or routines. Frequently, a given partitioning snowballs into other relevant locations, subgroups, and activities. For example, during an ethnographic study of adolescents' involvement in alcohol, drugs, and crime (Carpenter et al., 1988), a central focus was how adolescents structured their leisure time.

The ethnographers spatially began by spending time with adolescents during their free periods in local junior and senior high schools. Temporally, this meant during the time before classes in the morning (approximately one hour), during their lunch periods (approximately two hours), and after school was dismissed (approximately one hour).

In addition to learning how the observed youths structured their leisure time during these free-time periods on and around school campuses, the ethnographers began to learn where, when, and how youths spent their time outside of school. New spatial partitioning began to emerge and snowball. In addition to continuing their observations of the youths at and around school campuses, the ethnographers followed various subgroups of youths in other areas of the community and during various activities (both routine and special ones).

By the conclusion of 18 months of ethnography, the field-workers had observed youths in parks, skating rinks, people's homes, school dances, video arcades, bars, movie theaters, local forests, and an assortment of other locales.

Verenne (1988) similarly writes about how youths formed cliques and made use of various spaces throughout their high school and community. Describing the availability of spaces throughout the high school, Verenne (p. 216) says:

> The adults gave the students a complex building which, surprisingly for a modern construction, offered various types of spaces that various groups could call their own. For example, there were many tables in the cafeteria, there were nearly a dozen small and only intermittently occupied offices in the library, there were the guidance office and the nurses' office. There were bathrooms, isolated stairway landings, the backstage area in the auditorium. There were hidden spots on the grounds—behind bushes, in a drainage ditch.

Regarding some of the times and ways students used various spaces, Verenne (1988, p. 216) explains:

> During the times when they were not required to be in class, the students thus continually had to make decisions about where to go or where to sit. By ordinary right they could be in only three places: the "commons" [the cafeteria was so designated when not in use for lunch], the library, or a study hall. By extraordinary right, most often by virtue of membership in some special "club," students could be found in the private offices in the back of the library, in the coordinator's office, in the room where the audiovisual equipment was kept. . . . By self-proclaimed right, students might also be found in the bathrooms for very long periods of time not solely dedicated to the satisfaction of biological functions, or on the stairway landing from which the roof could be reached.

As indicated by the preceding illustrations, often subjects group themselves in meaningful ways, which allows the ethnographer to observe them more systematically.

In some instances, the researchers can partition or restrict certain places where they watch and listen and increase observational capabilities through filming or videotaping the area. This style of observation has grown increasingly popular in educational settings. For example, in a study by Hart and Sheehan (1986), social and cognitive development among children during preschool years was investigated in relationship to play activities. To accomplish their study, Hart and Sheehan (p. 671) restricted the use of the playground to two groups of preschoolers and videotaped the children at play:

> For seven weeks from the beginning of the preschool year in the fall before the observations began, children from each of the two groups had equal access to both sides of the playground during their 30-minute outdoor play period each day. During the observational period, barricades were placed in the access routes between the two playgrounds and children from each separate class . . . were asked to stay on an assigned side.

Videotaped observations then took place over a four-week period on fair weather days while preschool activities were conducted as usual. In general, the use and versatility of videotaping during research have increased enormously as the costs of doing so have continued to fall. Other uses of videotape in research are discussed in Chapter 8.

How to Learn: What to Watch and Listen For

When inexperienced ethnographers enter the field for the first time, they are impressed by the sheer number of activities and interactions going on in the setting. The initial activities of ethnographers frequently involve getting acclimated to the setting. This involves four general aspects:

1. Taking in the physical setting
2. Developing relationships with inhabitants (locating potential guides and informants)
3. Tracking, observing, eavesdropping, and asking questions
4. Locating subgroups and stars (central characters in various subgroups)

Taking in the Physical Setting During the first few days, ethnographers usually wander around the general location they plan to use as the setting. As they walk around the area, they should begin to map the setting carefully.

This may mean literally drawing an accurate facsimile of the various physical locales in the setting (that is, the streets, the buildings, the specific rooms where inhabitants pass their time, and so on). It may mean writing detailed field notes (to be discussed later) that describe the setting. Or it may mean some combination of both mapping and detailing in field notes.

Several purposes are served by this initial task of taking in the physical setting. First, while mapping out the spatial elements of the setting, researchers can begin to think about how to cover these areas in the most efficient and effective manner (for example, the number of hours required, which days or which hours during the day or night are best, and so forth).

Second, wandering around the area allows the ethnographers to begin getting acquainted with inhabitants and vice versa. Frequently, a smile or greeting during this initial phase will pay back tenfold later during the research.

Third, often merely by walking around and watching and listening, important first impressions are drawn. The first impressions may not be entirely accurate, but they will become *points of reference* later as the researchers become more familiar and knowledgeable about the setting and its inhabitants (Guy et al., 1987).

Developing Relationships with Inhabitants   During the initial phase of research in the field, researchers typically rely heavily on *guides*. Guides may have been located before the research through friends, acquaintances, or colleagues who knew someone among the group the researchers planned on studying. Alternatively, in the event that no guides can be identified before entering the field, one or more guides simply must be located during the early period following entry (Peshkin, 1986).

Concerning this latter form of locating guides, researchers may find that having smiled and greeted several inhabitants while taking in the setting actually becomes an essential means of beginning relationships. Although it is more difficult than simply walking up and introducing themselves, ethnographers are better advised to assume a more passive role until some relationships have been established.

Another important point to impress on locals is that all information collected during the research study will be held in strict confidence. Similarly, it is critical to impress on potential guides that the researchers are who they claim to be. This may be simply accomplished by carrying a letter of introduction and photographic identification or it may require a more extensive process of having the potential guides check you out through either official channels (calling the sponsoring institution) or, in some situations, the guides' own channels!

Researchers should assure potential guides that their extensive knowledge of the people and domain will make them extremely valuable to the study. Certainly, researchers should be cautious not to become overtly insincere in their flattery. But, in truth, guides do possess certain expert knowledge and are virtually invaluable to the ethnographers for helping them gain access.

Having established a rapport with one or more guides, ethnographers can begin snowballing additional relationships with other inhabitants. The most direct way to accomplish this is to gain permission from the guides to spend some time hanging around the setting with them. As others begin to pass time in proximity, the ethnographers can ask questions of their guides about these others and may possibly obtain an introduction—including having the guides reassure newcomers of the legitimacy of the ethnographers.

Tracking, Observing, Eavesdropping, and Asking Questions Having established relationships with several guides and inhabitants, ethnographers are free to begin really learning what goes on among the inhabitants of their study domain. This is done by tracking, observing, eavesdropping, and asking questions.

Tracking literally means following the guides around during their usual daily routines and watching their activities and the other people they interact with. As researchers follow and observe, they can also eavesdrop on conversations. Although social norms typically prohibit eavesdropping, such a proscription is untenable when conducting ethnography. Bogdan (1972) similarly suggests that although eavesdropping is necessary, it is also sometimes difficult to accomplish for people who have been reared in a noneavesdropping society. Nonetheless, researchers often learn a great deal about a phenomenon or an event simply by overhearing several people discussing it.

On some occasions, during the process of eavesdropping, researchers hear terms or learn about situations that may be important but that fall on deaf ears. In other words, the ethnographers do not understand the significance of what they hear. On these occasions, ethnographers must ask questions, but, again, they should consider taking a passive role during such informal questioning. Perhaps jotting a cryptic note to ask the guide at a later time would serve better than interrupting the ongoing action with a question. Or perhaps arranging another meeting with some participant in the conversation (other than the guide) would offer a more fruitful approach. Decisions about how to pursue information will vary from situation to situation.

Locating Subgroups and Stars During the course of tracking and observing, ethnographers are able to identify certain inhabitants who tend to spend more time with one another than with others. These subgroupings may or may not represent formal groups but certainly suggest a kind of social networking.

Among these social networks, researchers can sociometrically identify individuals who appear to be more or less the central figures in a given network of inhabitants. Such central figures may be referred to as *stars*. Although ethnographers may not always need to establish a guide-type relationship with a star, it is sometimes necessary to obtain his or her goodwill.

In a manner similar to what Bogdan and Taylor (1975, pp. 30–33) describe as accessing *gatekeepers*, developing a relationship with a star may be a critical element in an ethnographic project. Even when ethnographers locate a guide and gain access to the basic setting, a star may hold the key to deeper penetration into the lives and perceptions of inhabitants of that setting. Sometimes a single gesture or word from a star will open more doors than weeks and weeks of attempts to gain access to these portals. Conversely, that same single gesture can slam doors that took months for the ethnographer to get opened. Whenever possible, it is advisable to find and gain the confidence of a star as soon as possible after entering the field.

Field Notes

The central component of ethnographic research is the *ethnographic account*. Providing such narrative accounts of what goes on in the lives of study subjects derives from having maintained complete, accurate, and detailed field notes. From the approach endorsed here, field notes should be completed immediately following every excursion into the field, as well as following any chance meeting with inhabitants outside the boundaries of the study setting (for example, at the supermarket, in a doctor's office, at a traffic light, and so on).

There are many variations about how to take field notes. Some researchers wait until they have left the field and then immediately write complete records (Bogdan, 1972). Others take abbreviated notes covertly while in the field and later translate them into complete field notes (see Festinger, Riecken, & Schacter, 1956). Burgess (1991a, p. 192) suggests that "note-taking is a personal activity that depends upon the research context, the objectives of the research, and the relationship with informants." Burgess also suggests that there are some general rules for note-taking. Among these rules are recommendations for establishing a regular time and place for writing up one's notes (including the date, time, and location of the observations) and duplicating notes for safety reasons.

Chiseri-Strater and Sunstein (2001) have devised a list of what they believe should go into all field notes. This list includes the date, time, and place of the observations; specific facts, numbers, and details of what happened at the site; sensory impressions such as sights, sounds, textures, smells, tastes; personal responses as recorded in the field notes; specific words, phrases, summaries of conversations, and insider language; questions about people or behaviors at the site for future consideration; and page numbers to keep the observations in order.

Carol Bailey (1996, pp. 80–81) claims that field notes initially consist of *mental notes,* collected while interacting in the research setting. These are then transformed into *jotted notes,* or brief reminder notes actually written down and used later to jog the researcher's memory when he or she writes more complete field notes.

There are various ways to take field notes. For example, some ethnographers carry tape recorders and periodically enter their own notes or record various conversations they witness. Other researchers carry slips of paper or index cards and simply jot notes and verbatim quotes periodically throughout the field excursion. Once out of the field, the researchers can use these notes and sketches to write full accounts. Given the advances in computers and computer software (as well as the radical cost and weight reduction in highly powerful laptop and notebook computers), many modern-day ethnographers write and store their field notes on computer disks. In addition to the advantage of compact storage, word-processing and utility programs allow ethnographers to move rapidly from one location in the notes to another to reconstruct sequences of events over time by copying and editing out extraneous elements and to produce copies of portions of the full notes at the press of a button.

From my perspective there are four distinct elements that go into creating full and detailed field notes: cryptic jottings, detailed descriptions, analytic notes, and subjective reflections.

Cryptic Jottings   Cryptic jottings are taken while still in the field. These may include brief statements (a sentence or less), sketches (line drawings), short notes (a paragraph or so), and odd or unusual terms or phrases heard while in the field that might serve as a memory trigger later when writing full field notes.

Detailed Descriptions   Detailed descriptions are undertaken once you have exited the field. Detailed descriptions are the heart of any narrative field notes. They should include as much texture, sensation, color, and minutia as your memory permits. Conversations should be replicated as near to verbatim as memory permits (the cryptic jotting can help a great deal with this). Details should include how people appeared, what they said, what they did, and even if they had any noticeable imperfections (speech impediments, scars, tattoos, etc.).

Analytic Notes   Analytic notes, sometimes referred to as *observer comments,* are ideas that occur to you as you write up the full field notes. These may be linkages between people in the study, theories that might serve to explain something happening in the field, or simply a judgmental observation about a participant (e.g., "The guy looked like a thug"). To make sure these are kept separate from the actual narrative, it is important to encapsulate these in brackets clearly labeled *Observer Comments*, or simply O.C. (e.g., [O.C.]).

Subjective Reflections   Subjective reflections are a self-reflexive opportunity for you as the researcher to make personal observations and comments about feelings that you might have developed as a result of having observed some scary or personally rewarding event in the field. These may include statements about how angry something made you or how surprised you were when you learned some piece of information. Like *observer comments*, these remarks should be encapsulated in brackets, labeled *Subjective Reflections*, or S.R. (e.g., [S.R.]).

Several additional elements to include in field notes are the time and duration of the field excursion and a consistent alteration of names and places. Concerning the former, in addition to indicating the time researchers enter and exit the field, it is important to make note of the time at which conversations, events, or activities occurred throughout the field session. These temporal sequencing marks allow ethnographers to recreate more systematically the field session. With regard to the latter issue of altering the names of people and places, the point is to protect the identities of inhabitants. Toward this end, it is advisable for ethnographers to maintain a continuous list of pseudonyms assigned to every person and location recorded in their field notes. This will assist both confidentiality and systematic retrieval of data during later analysis phases of the research.

Finally, even the opinions, preconceived notions, and general feelings about certain observed situations are also legitimate entries in field notes. However, these ethnographer-originated entries should always be bracketed and identified so that they are not mistaken as actual observations or perceptions the inhabitants themselves made.

Erosion of Memory   Individuals vary in the extent and degree of accuracy with which they can remember—in detail—events and conversations witnessed during a field excursion. Through repetition, concentration, and sincere effort, the researchers' ability to retain even minute elements, such as facial grimaces, tongue clicks, and even belt-buckle ornaments, begins to increase greatly. In addition, carefully concentrating on remembering elements of observed situations assists ethnographers in maintaining their role as researchers.

Clues and Strategies for Recalling Data   Although precise reproduction of every nuance of behavior, conversation, and event during a field excursion is impossible, highly accurate, detailed field notes can be produced. Novice ethnographers are frequently quite amazed to learn just how much material they can recall (over a short period of time) even without any specific training.

Some field researchers use various systems of mnemonics as memory aids. Mnemonics are devices—sometimes verbal, sometimes spatial, and sometimes physical—that aid in recall. Based on the idea that people more easily remember information if it is attached to a spatial, personal, or otherwise meaningful image, mnemonics relies on associations between the material to be memorized and a construct that makes it memorable.

Many people, for example, use the following common mnemonic device to remember how many days are in each month of the year:

Thirty days hath September,

April, June, and November;

All the rest have thirty-one

Excepting February alone:

Which hath but twenty-eight, in fine,

Till leap year gives it twenty-nine.

Mnemonics may also take the form of acronyms (words formed out of the initial letters of other words). For example, many of us recall from our elementary school days learning the name ROY G. BIV as a mnemonic device for remembering the color spectrum (red, orange, yellow, green, blue, indigo, and violet).

Some ethnographic researchers develop various mnemonic devices in order to remember how people looked, the description of settings, and so forth. These various devices serve as memory triggers to help the researcher recall nuances of his or her observations when he or she sits down to draft full field notes.

According to Bogdan and Taylor (1975), many field observers use the analogy of a *switch* to describe their procedure for remembering people, conversations, and details of a setting. These individuals suggest that they can literally turn on and turn off the intense concentration necessary for good-quality recall.

Of course, as they gain experience, ethnographers tend to develop their own cryptic note-taking styles for use in the field. Nonetheless, several general suggestions can be offered to novice ethnographers to facilitate their recollection of events that occur during a field session. Some suggestions have been implied or mentioned previously in this chapter and are summarized here for the sake of convenience.

1. *Record key words and key phrases while in the field.* It would be ill advised to try to stop the participants in a conversation and attempt to write down their every word. It would also be distracting to pull out a tape recorder

and place it between the participants in a natural conversation. On the other hand, it may be possible during the course of their conversation to abstract certain key terms or sentences and jot these down. Whether researchers write these phrases on a napkin, an index card, or a scrap of brown paper bag is unimportant. What is important is that these phrases are taken down. It is also advisable to indicate the time the conversation occurred. Interestingly, later, in the privacy of their offices, ethnographers can usually reconstruct almost the entire conversation simply by rereading these cryptic key terms and sentences. Researchers typically will have a certain amount of memory erosion, but because of the memory-triggering effects of the key words and phrases, this erosion should be lessened.

2. *Make notes about the sequence of events.* From one perspective, activities occurring during a field session are beyond the control of the ethnographers and are consequently unstructured. However, if ethnographers gain a certain perspective, it is possible to apply a kind of pseudostructure: identifying a sequence of events. As researchers jot brief, cryptic notes, they should indicate their observed sequence of events: what occurred before the noted action, what was observed, and what occurred following this noted event. Researchers frequently find it useful, when sorting through their scraps of in-field notes, to lay them out in sequence. By rethinking the field session, following the sequence in which it actually occurred, researchers are able to recall the details and substance of even very long conversations.

3. *Limit the time you remain in the setting.* Field-note writing operates at approximately a 4:1 ratio with the time in the field. If researchers spend two hours in the field, it may require as long as eight full hours to write comprehensive field notes. Particularly for novice ethnographers, whose skill at recall may not be fully developed, only very short (15–30 minute) intervals in the field should be attempted at first. Although it is sometimes tempting to remain in the field for hours and hours, researchers must remember that in doing so, they reduce the likelihood of producing high-quality, detailed field notes.

On occasion, of course, ethnographers may be willing to forgo comprehensive notes in order to gain entry to some special event or ceremony. On these occasions, researchers actually turn off their intentional field concentration until the special event occurs. This, too, should be mentioned in the notes in order to account for the two or three hours during which nothing has been annotated in the field notes.

4. *Write the full notes immediately after exiting the field.* Although this may seem obvious, it still needs to be mentioned. As previously indicated, erosion of memory begins immediately and progresses rapidly. The longer researchers wait to translate their cryptic notes to full notes, the greater the

likelihood of contamination from erosion. It is advisable to schedule field sessions in such a manner that full notes can be written immediately after exiting the field. Even the interruption for a meal could be sufficient to flaw the full notes.

5. *Get your notes written before sharing them with others.* Ethnographic research is often very exciting. Ethnographers frequently observe some event or conversation that so excites them that they simply need to share it with someone (often a colleague). The basic rule of thumb here is to refrain from talking; write it up and talk about it later. Besides possibly forgetting important details from a time lag before writing up notes, researchers may also accidentally embellish events. Although this embellishment may be completely unintentional, it can still flaw and contaminate otherwise important data.

What Complete Notes Should Look Like   Both in order to increase the systematic structure of later data retrieval and in order to ensure comprehensive detail without loss of quality, field-note pages should be standardized as much as possible. This means that every sheet of field notes should contain certain consistent elements: the time the ethnographer entered and exited the field; the date of the field session; a brief, descriptive topic label that captures the essence of the field session; and a page number.

As an illustration, consider the following field-note excerpt, which represents approximately two or three minutes in the field setting:

June 15, 2002, Longlane Beach
Time In: 10:00 A.M.
Time Out: 11:00 A.M.
TIME: 10:00 A.M. [O.C.: I arrived at the beach and found parking. It was slightly overcast out and gray—June gloom—as many locals called it.] I exited my car and walked toward the pier. There were many empty stalls near the pier and only a few cars pulling in. I walked up a set of cement steps to the wooden pier. The pier stretched for about a quarter of a mile into the ocean and was about 20 feet wide. At the end of the pier was a fast-food restaurant called Jaspers. I could see several people standing at the end of the pier fishing.

There were no people standing along the railings toward my end of the pier, but a tall, very slim man in his early forties had just exited the public bathrooms located at the base of the pier, about 12 feet from where I stood. He walked swiftly toward and then past me. He was wearing a bright orange tank top and black narrow Speedo trunks. His hair was graying and thin; his face was long and narrow and was punctuated by a huge, gray mustache that flowed into double-turned handlebars at each end. Around his waist he wore a fanny-pack that bounced as he moved toward Jaspers at the end of the pier. On his feet the man wore water socks with a Nike swoosh on the side.

I walked toward Jaspers and was about a halfway there when I noticed a woman walking toward me (away from Jaspers). The woman, in her late twenties or early thirties, held the hand of a small boy who was screaming, "I want ice cream! I want ice cream!" Streams of tears were running down the little boy's checks. The boy was about three or four years old and wearing a pair of swim trunks with the Big Dog logo on it, no shirt and barefoot. The woman wore a blue cover-up (like a sarong). Her blonde hair was pulled back and held with a wooden clip. Her face was almost hidden by an oversized pair of black sunglasses. On her feet she wore black flip-flops.

As illustrated in the preceding field-note excerpt, considerable detail about the setting and the people moving around in this setting is included. As well, the notes begin with an example of how an observer comment might be included. After reading the ethnographer's full field notes, it should be possible for a person to visualize exactly what the ethnographer saw and heard during the field session.

Having concluded their field sessions (the data-gathering phase of the project) the ethnographers will have presumably amassed hundreds or even thousands of pages of field notes. These field notes will take up considerable space and an even longer time to read. Organizing large quantities of such notes is very time consuming and both physically and mentally exhausting. It is desirable, then, to amass these notes in some systematic fashion and perhaps even to reduce their bulk for analytic purposes (Becker, Gordon, & LeBailly, 1984).

To accomplish the dual task of keeping large quantities of field notes and reproducing them in reduced form, many researchers rely on computers. An additional advantage to using computers, beyond storage and reproduction, is their ability to allow textual material to be retrieved in an efficient and speedy manner. There are several ways one can make use of computers when developing field notes. The most obvious is to use any commercial word-processing program. Word-processing programs are designed to handle, store, and retrieve textual material or, in this case, data. Alternately, one might choose one of the commercial programs designed for qualitative data storage and analysis (see, for example, Dennis, 1984; Tallerico, 1991). These programs provide a structure into which novice researchers can pour their field notes. As well, they provide a method by which to efficiently create a duplicate set or a data-reduced set of field notes.

You must be cautious when reducing qualitative data such as field notes. If you reduce too much, details and nuance of the data may be lost, impairing if not ruining the analysis. As well, some studies will require greater amounts of detail than others (Becker, Gordon, & LeBailly, 1984). In these cases, field notes will need to be kept closer to their original form. In most cases, however, various aspects of field notes may be redundant. For example, descriptions of the same individuals, locations, and settings need not be reproduced in full every time they arise. Researchers may find it better to briefly summarize such material or cite it only once. Similarly, many researchers find it more effective for analytical purposes to create a set of summarized field notes that is keyed or cross-indexed to its original lengthier versions. Thus, two or three pages of notes may be reproduced to perhaps a half page of summary. Since the full notes are cross-indexed to this summary, the researcher can fairly easily retrieve these lengthier versions during analysis.

Computers and Ethnography

At one time—in fact, as recently as the last edition of this book—the basic recommendation with regard to computers and ethnography was that using computers was a convenient way to write, store, and even access written field notes. But, as a number of writers have been pointing out during the past several years, *there are a lot more interesting things for ethnographers to do with computers than just write up field notes!* (See, for example, Coffey, Atkinson, & Holbrook, 1996; Dicks & Mason, 1998; Mason & Dicks, 1999; Weaver & Atkinson, 1994). With new types of computing media provided by the Web, CD-ROMs, high-speed DSL, and other sorts of broadband connections, a new world has opened to ethnographers. It may be as Mason and Dicks (1999) suggest that *hypermedia ethnography* is the new frontier.

This new hypermedia ethnography can permit ethnographers to include the full gamut of what Spradely (1979) terms the *ethnographic record:* photographs, music, field notes, interview data, and so forth. The new computer technologies allow the ethnographer to bridge the gaps that exist between audio, visual, and written documentation of field events. Hypermedia potentially allows the ethnographer to produce more richly textured and at the same time more accessible (in the broadest sense of this term) narrative reports, complete with an assortment of links among data, analysis, and interpretative and supportive texts that might comment on the analysis (Gibbs, Friese, & Mangabeira, 2002).

Although qualitative researchers have been slower than their quantitative counterparts to take advantage of the new technological benefits afforded by computers and the Internet, as suggested here and in Chapter 4, qualitative researchers are now seemingly making up for lost time. But before anyone can run off too quickly and post ethnographies on the Web with all sorts of interesting links, the researcher needs to analyze the data.

Analyzing Ethnographic Data

Analysis of data is not an exact science. With some types of data (particularly survey questionnaire data), there are many different ways to make sense of the information once the data are collected, organized, and coded. However, when dealing with ethnographic data, researchers must make somewhat narrower choices. For example, even though it is certainly possible to test hypotheses using ethnographic data, the process differs somewhat from research that uses survey data. Ethnographic research can potentially demonstrate the plausibility of a hypothesis, but it cannot actually prove its validity. Using reductionistic procedures to cull numbers from the ethnographic data is not really in keeping with the ethnographic process. Thus, two effective ways remain to analyze ethnographic research while preserving the rich textual detail of the data: inductive content analysis and ethnographic narrative accounts.

Systematic analysis of ethnographic data typically begins by reading the field notes—whether one wants to produce ethnographic accounts or a content analysis of the data. The purposes of this initial reading of the notes are to reinforce any hypotheses or themes developed during the data-collection phase and to generate new hypotheses and themes previously unrealized—in short, to ground themes and hypotheses to the data (Glaser & Strauss, 1967). During this initial coding, researchers undertake what is called *open coding* (explained comprehensively in Chapter 11). Briefly, open coding allows researchers to identify and even extract themes, topics, or issues in a systematic manner.

Next, ethnographers should begin to notice and systematically create records of patterns in the conversations and activities of people depicted in the notes. This *coding* process is discussed more completely in Chapter 11.

At this juncture, the researchers must decide whether to undertake a comprehensive content analysis or to rely on lengthy textual accounts to document themes and patterns observed in the data. Although both procedures are certainly similar, there is at least one important difference, which concerns whether, conceptually, ethnography is viewed strictly as a means for collecting data or as both the means and the product of the ethnographic process (Stoddart, 1986). In the first instance, researchers may easily accomplish a comprehensive content analysis, but if the second conceptual stance is taken, the researchers must demonstrate topics and patterns by presenting appropriate (and often lengthy) narrative textual accounts from the field notes.

As with all analytic strategies, strengths and weaknesses are associated with each approach. The most important problem commonly associated with qualitative data of any type is the question of confidence in the accuracy of suggested patterns. In the case of content analysis, researchers might manage to convince their audience by suggesting the magnitude (frequency) of a given theme or pattern (see Chapter 11). In the case of ethnographic narratives, researchers must rely on the pattern being sufficiently clear in itself (as presented in the field notes) to convince an audience of its accuracy (Stoddart, 1986).

Burns (1980) illustrates how one effectively uses ethnographic narrative accounts in his "Getting Rowdy with the Boys." Burns offers a detailed examination of the drinking behavior of a single group of young working-class males. His procedure involves describing the sequence of events and interactions experienced by these young men during one evening in several different drinking environments. As Burns indicates, his analysis of the ethnographic narrative account offered may be termed *thick description* (Geertz, 1973). This type of analysis is directed toward drawing out a complete picture of the observed events, the actors involved, the rules associated with certain activities, and the social contexts in which these elements arise. Burns (1980) accomplishes this by first presenting the narration (chiefly the detailed field notes of his ethnographic experience during the observed evening). Next, Burns steps out of the field and, in his role as a social scientist, analyzes the narrative contents, highlighting apparent structural components of situations, meanings suggested by actors and events, and patterns that emerge during the course of the narrative. To some extent, this lengthier narrative technique is justified in the following passage from Festinger et al. (1956, p. 252):

> Our material is largely qualitative rather than quantitative, and even simple tabulations of what we observed would be difficult. Owing to the complete novelty and unpredictability of the movement, as well as the pressure of time, we could not develop standard categories of events, actions, statements, feelings, and the like, and certainly could not subject the members of the group to any standardized interview, in order to compare indices before and after disconfirmation.

In a similar manner, Humphreys (1970, p. 22) states:

> My concern in this study has been with the description of a specific style of deviant behavior and of the population who engage in that activity. Beyond such systematic, descriptive analysis, I have tried to offer, in the light of deviance theory, some explanation as to why, and how these people participate in the particular form of behavior described [namely, casual homosexual encounters].

Other Analysis Strategies: Typologies, Sociograms, and Metaphors

Data analysis is an interesting and creative part of the research process. Ethnographic data lend themselves to several different methods of interpretation and analysis beyond strict content analysis techniques. Some of these techniques include *typologies*, *sociograms*, and *metaphors*. Each of these is briefly discussed next.

Typologies

A *typology* is a systematic method for classifying similar events, actions, objects, people, or places, into discrete groupings. For example, McSkimming and Berg (1996) did a study of gambling and gaming in rural American taverns. After more than six months of observations in the field, they found four major types of tavern patrons:

1. *Regular drinking patrons.* These individuals regularly sat at the bar and chatted among themselves as they consumed several alcoholic beverages. They were highly in-group oriented and would not speak with outsiders (transient patrons).
2. *Regular gaming patrons.* These individuals sporadically consumed alcoholic beverages but primarily socialized with others involved mostly in playing darts or billiards.
3. *Regular gambling patrons.* These individuals sporadically consumed alcoholic beverages and involved themselves in darts and/or billiards. A primary distinction between these and gaming patrons was that gambling patrons regularly placed wagers (of cash, drinks, or other valuable items) against the outcome of a dart or billiard game.
4. *Transient patrons.* These individuals drifted into and out of the tavern scene, sometimes returning for a second or occasionally a third visit but not with any sort of regular pattern of attendance. Transient patrons were excluded from conversations among regular drinking patrons but were permitted to game and gamble occasionally with others.

McSkimming and Berg's (1996) typology permitted them to see various distinctions between the various people who frequented the tavern. For example, regular drinkers were more interested in *maintaining* friendships with one another and discussing family activities than with establishing new friendships or light social banter. Such observations permitted McSkimming and Berg to better understand some of the social roles and interaction patterns they observed among people moving through the social world of the tavern.

Not all typologies are textually based. Again, owing to changes in technology and a growing emphasis in visual ethnography or photoethnography (Pink, 2001; Schwartz & Jacobs, 1997), some typologies are photographically based. For example, in a recent study by Kephart and Berg (2002) the researchers examined 452 photographs of graffiti created by gangs in a city in southern California. After carefully examining each photo for patterns of similarity or dissimilarity, they sorted the pictures into five groups: (1) Publicity Graffiti (spreading the gang's name); (2) Roll Call Graffiti (listing the names of the members of the gang); (3) Territorial Graffiti (the name of the gang in specific locations identifying turf); (4) Threatening Graffiti (specific threats toward other gangs or individuals); and (5) Sympathetic Graffiti (condolences to gang members and their families upon deaths).

Typically, researchers follow a basic three-step guideline for developing typologies. First, they assess the collected material and then seek out mutually exclusive categories. Second, researchers make sure that all of the elements being classified have been accounted for (an exhaustive grouping of elements). Third, researchers examine the categories and their contents and make theoretically meaningful appraisals. The use of mutually exclusive categories assures that every element being considered appears only in a single category. But, to be exhaustive, every element needs to be placed into one or another of these categories. A theoretically meaningful appraisal does not necessarily mean that you link your observations to lofty theories such as Durkheim's theory of *anomie*. Rather, it simply means that there is an attempt to attach some social meaning to the way things fall into categories in your typology.

Although typologies may seem like oversimplification of social life, this is actually their beauty. They permit the researcher to present data in an organized and simple fashion, allowing the reader to better understand the explanations offered as interpretation and analysis of the typology scheme. A major goal of typologies, then, is to provide additional understanding of the material collected during the course of the research.

Sociograms

Sociograms are part of a larger group of techniques known as *sociometry*. These procedures allow the researcher to make assessments about the degree of affinity or disdain that members of a group have toward one another. Thus, they allow you to consider friendship patterns, social networks, work relationships, and social distance in general. Sociometry can be described as a means of assessing group relational structures such as hierarchies, friendship networks, and cliques. Sociograms, then, are graphic displays of how well people get along with one another based on responses to a sociometric test. A sociometric test typically includes three basic characteristics:

1. A specific number of choices are used (varying with the size of the group).
2. A specific number of choices are allowed (varying according to the functions and/or activities of the groups tested).
3. Different levels of preference are assigned to each choice.

Positive Peer Nominations   The early users of sociometric tests typically employed a *peer nomination* version of this test. In this procedure, the group members were asked to name three or more peers whom they liked the most, or whom they best liked working with, or who were their best friends (depending on the kind of group). A group member's score was then computed as the number of nominations he or she received from other members of the group. This version of the sociometric test is called *positive peer nominations*. As users of sociometric tests refined these procedures, adaptations naturally arose.

Negative Peer Nominations   One such adaptation to peer nominations initially was introduced by Dunnington (1957) and again by Moore and Updergraff (1964). This adaptation involved a request for negative nominations. In other words, in addition to asking for three especially liked peers, a second request was made that members identify the three peers least liked (or least desirable to work with). This strategy was used to identify two groups of peers—namely, a *popular group* (high frequency of positive nominations) and a disliked or *rejected group* (high frequency of negative nominations). Subsequent research in which juveniles are identified as members of these groups indicates that rejected children often are more aggressive and likely to engage in antisocial behavior (Dodge, Cole, & Brakke, 1982; Hartup, Glazer, & Charlesworth, 1967). This suggests significant utility for those interested in studying delinquents, youth movements, school cliques, and even gang structures.

Peer Rating Procedures   Another adaptation that has come into common use is the *peer rating procedure*, a sociometric test similar in many ways to the nomination procedure. Group members respond to the usual sociometric questions (Who do you like to work with? Be with? etc.) for every other member of the group. Each group member is given a list containing the names of all group members and asked to rate every other member using a five-point Likert-like scale. The scale for these five points is typically a graduated series of statements that moves from expressions of favor to expressions of disfavor for members of the group. An example of this sort of scale is shown in Figure 6.1. As in traditional Likert scales, you assess the mean rating score for each person. A mean rating in the low range indicates that the group member is not well liked by others in the group. A mean rating in the high range indicates that the group member is well liked. As Jennings (1948) warned, however, identification of this sociometric pattern *is not* the completion of the research but only the beginning. The use of mathematics to locate sociometric stars, then, should not be overemphasized. It is a convenient tool but not the substantive result of research.

Once you have identified the social relations and social structures that exist, you still must examine the incumbents of positions in this structure. Assisted by the sociometric information, you are better equipped to locate appropriate guides, informants, and gatekeepers of the group. Thus, you might begin an investigation with a sociometric survey and then pursue the research through other ethnographic field techniques, interviews, or even unobtrusive measures. Sociometric choice tests, then, provide yet another line of action you can use in a triangulated research design.

Mapping and the Creation of Sociograms   Another way you can create sociograms is to do them in the field. In this case, you use direct observations of individuals and objects as they are arranged in the setting. Essentially, this involves the creation of social/environmental maps and, from these, sociograms.

This strategy of sociometric mapping depends on a fairly stable setting, and as such, it is not always applicable. Often, this type of sociometric mapping is used in social psychological applications of organizational research. For example, how executives place themselves around a board meeting table may be mapped and may delineate power and informal influence structures. By knowing this information, a researcher (or executive) can interrupt or weaken the amount of influence emanating from certain segments of the members. For instance, by placing himself or herself or a nonmember of some informal influence clique among several actual members, he or she can affect the ability of those members to wield influence and authority during a board meeting.

Similarly, knowledge about sociometric body language and even furniture placement can influence interactions. For example, when you enter someone's office, how is it arranged? Is there a chair near the desk, inviting you to sit near the desk's occupant? Or is the chair far from the desk, perhaps across the room, requiring a guest to physically move it to be near the desk's occupant? Usually, when you move furniture in another person's office, you must first ask permission. Thus, tacitly, you hold a subordinate role in the

Figure 6.1   A Sample Sociometric Assessment

(Question/Choices)
Directions: On a separate sheet, write the name of everyone in your group or organization. Read the following paragraphs and place their corresponding numbers in front of every name for which they apply. You may use the number 1 only once, and please place only a single number by each name. By your own name, please place a zero.

My Very Best Friend
1. I would like to have this person as one of my very best friends. I would like to spend a great deal of time with this person. I think I could tell some of my problems and concerns to this person, and I would do everything I could to help this person with his or her problems and concerns. I will give a number 1 to my very best friend.

My Other Friend(s)
2. I would enjoy working and doing things with this person. I would invite this person to a party in my home, and I would enjoy going places with this person and our other friends. I would like to talk and do a variety of things with this person and to be with this person often. I want this person to be one of my friends. I will give a number 2 to every person who is my friend.

I Do Not Know This Person
3. I do not know this person very well. Maybe I would like this person if I got to know him or her; maybe I would not. I do not know whether I would like to spend time or work with this person. I will place a number 3 in front of the name of every person I do not know very well.

I Do Not Care for This Person
4. I will greet this person when I see him or her around school or in a store, but I do not enjoy being around this person. I might spend some time with this person–if I had nothing to do, or I had a social obligation to attend where this person also was in attendance. I do not care for this person very much. I will place a number 4 in front of the name of every person I do not care for very much.

I Dislike This Person
5. I speak to this person only when it is necessary. I do not like to work or spend time with this person. I avoid serving on the same groups or committees with this person. I will place a number 5 in front of the name of every person I do not like.

relationship. Alternately, you might choose to stand while the other party sits. This, of course, immediately shifts the power structure to the seated occupant of the office because he or she is able to leave you standing or suggest you pull up a chair. This situation is also somewhat reminiscent of school days, when you were called before the school's principal where you stood, at the foot of the desk, being scolded.

The arrangement of people and objects in a setting may have an impact on interactions and relationships. This, in turn, can be a useful tool in research. This type of applied sociometric strategy frequently begins with a *mapping* of the setting. This sort of mapping is also useful in other types of institutional investigations. For example, it could prove useful in a study of how inmates use environmental space in a prison or a study of the effect of environmental design on inmates. Alternatively, it might prove fruitful in an examination of how children use and perhaps territorially divide playground space. It might even be useful in a study of a game arcade located in some mall or in similar studies of leisure-time activities in amusement parks. Again, sociometric strategies are extremely flexible. They are limited only by your imagination.

To describe how you might develop the sort of sociometric maps just discussed, let us assume an investigator wants to study some group of youths in a particular neighborhood. One way to begin this task is to create a drawing or *map* of the setting. All the stable physical elements observed in the setting (for example, access ways, trees and shrubs, buildings, stores, street lamps, public telephones, and so forth) should be included in this map. The map might be duplicated a number of times so that every time the researcher enters the field, he or she can work on a fresh map.

While in the field, the researcher can add symbols to represent individual gang members, dyads (groups of two), triads (groups of three), gender, leadership roles, and so forth. Over time, and by assessing the successive annotated maps and actual field notes, the researcher will be able to identify the stars and any satellite cliques that constitute the groups under study. Stars will become apparent *over time* when you use observation to create a sociogram. Typically, you find only one or two stars in a given group. Even when you locate several stars, typically one will demonstrate himself or herself to hold some degree of influence over the others.

Satellite cliques are sometimes mistaken as representing a star and his or her followers. In fact, satellite cliques usually contain several members influenced by what appears to be a single individual. However, this individual frequently is himself or herself influenced by a more centralized star.

Sociometric maps also can assist the investigator in understanding how a group uses its environmental space and maintains territorial control over areas, the locus of control in various power and influence arrangements, and the social space (proximity) between different members and nonmembers of the group(s).

Metaphors

Another analytic strategy is to use metaphors (Bailey, 1996; Richardson, 1994). *Metaphors* are comparisons such as "the skinhead's scalp was like velvet, smooth and soft to the touch." Identifying a metaphor that fits some aspect of your setting or your study population can help you see things in a different way. Begin by asking, "What does this situation or circumstance seem to be?" "What else is it like?" "What does it remind me of?" Trying to come up with an appropriate metaphor is a good exercise for reflecting on the material and data you have already collected and begun to interpret and analyze. It also will require you to consider these data from different conceptual angles than you might otherwise have used.

For example, you might consider the way police arrest suspects, only to have the courts let them go (on bail, for example) as *revolving door* justice. Or you might consider the way nurses give reports as an informational *swap-meet*. Metaphors provide an avenue to see important elements of social support, interaction, networking, relationships, and a variety of other socially significant factors, and allow the researcher to represent action when theorizing about various explanations or relationships.

Disengaging: Getting Out

Although it is certainly possible to maintain complete professional distance when distributing questionnaires to anonymous subjects, it is not as easy during ethnography. Because relationships are virtually the stock and trade of a good ethnographer, care must be taken when leaving the field.

Exiting any field setting involves at least two separate operations: first, the physical removal of the researchers from the research setting and, second, emotional disengagement from the relationships developed during the field experience. In some situations *getting out* is described as a kind of mechanical operation, devoid of any (personal) emotional attachments on the part of the ethnographer. Concern is sometimes shown, and efforts made, to avoid distressing a research community. However, negative repercussions can occur in the forms of possible effects on the group(s) as a whole or with the possible reception future field investigators might expect (Chadwick et al., 1984; Shaffir et al., 1980).

Even when the emotions of field relationships are mentioned, they frequently are described exclusively as concern over the perspective of the inhabitant of the natural setting. For example, Shaffir, Stebbins, and Turowetz (1980, p. 259) state:

> Personal commitments to those we study often accompany our research activity. Subjects often expect us to continue to live up to such commitments permanently. On completing the research, however, our commitment subsides and is often quickly overshadowed by other considerations shaping our day-to-day lives. When our subjects become aware of our diminished interest in their lives and situations, they may come to feel cheated—manipulated and duped.

The point is not to underplay the possible emotional harm a callous investigator might cause a research group, but it should be noted that relationships are two-way streets. Subjects make personal emotional commitments, and so, too, do many researchers—even without actually bonding. Often, when researchers leave the field, they have developed some deep feelings for their subjects. These feelings may not always be positive but are nonetheless psychologically affecting.

Ethnographers can certainly absent themselves from the field and simply dismiss the subjects from their minds, but it is likely that the ethnographers will continue to hold at least some proprietary interest in the welfare of the subjects. For example, during the course of conducting the research discussed in Carpenter and colleagues (1988), the ethnographers commonly spoke about "their" kids with almost parental concern or, on occasion, with almost parental pride in certain accomplishments.

A strong commitment and attachment developed between many of the youthful subjects and the ethnographers. When it came time to leave the field, the ethnographers informally continued to keep an eye on many of the subjects for over a year. This essentially amounted to asking about specific kids when they accidentally ran into mutual acquaintances or getting involved in the lives of these special kids when their paths crossed by chance (for instance, in a supermarket or shopping mall). Other field investigators have indicated similar prolonged interest in research subjects, even many years after physically leaving the setting. Letkemann (1980, p. 300), for instance, indicates that even 10 years after exiting the field, and more than 800 miles away from the site, he continued to stay informed about the welfare of his subjects.

Because of the uniqueness of every field situation, there are different nuances to exiting. Ethnographers, however, must always be mindful that the time will come to leave—at least physically. Toward this end, researchers must prepare both the community members and themselves for the exit. Perhaps a quick exit will work in some cases (Festinger et al., 1956; Rains, 1971), whereas a more gradual drifting off may be required in other circumstances (Glaser & Strauss, 1967). Unfortunately, these research-related decisions are not easily made.

TRYING IT OUT

As with all research methods, researchers must practice, stumble, and even sometimes fail to accomplish the research project in order to appreciate how ethnographic strategies operate. Several suggestions for brief microethnographic projects follow. As with the practice of interviewing strategies (see Chapter 4), these suggestions are intended as exercises, not actual research projects in themselves.

Suggestion 1 Position yourself in a public location where many people congregate. Shopping malls, bus terminals, and airports are good examples of the sorts of places I mean. Next, simply sit and watch and listen. Construct field notes of the observations and what you heard (do not engage in any conversations or interviews). Repeat this activity for several days. Be certain that you write up full notes after you have left the field each day. Bear in mind that the time you spend in the field geometrically increases when you write up your full notes. Initially, spend no more than 15 or 20 minutes at a time in the field.

Suggestion 2 Go to your school's library or cafeteria every day at the same time for about a week. Each day, sketch a simple map (a sociogram) of the room. Include any tables, chairs, devices, and people you see each day. At the end of the week, compare the drawings, to see if any changes can be detected.

REFERENCES

Adler, P. A. (1985). *Wheeling and Dealing*. New York: Columbia University Press.
Adler, P. A., & Adler, P. (1987). *Membership Roles in Field Research*. Newbury Park, CA: Sage.
Agar, M. H. (1973). *Ripping and Running: A Formal Ethnography of Urban Heroin Addicts*. New York: Seminar Press.
Agar, M. H. (1986). *Speaking of Ethnography*. Beverly Hills, CA: Sage.
Agar, M. H. (1996). *The Professional Stranger* (2nd ed). San Diego, CA: Academic Press.
Allen, J. D. (1986). Classroom management: Students' perspectives, goals, and strategies. *American Educational Research Journal 23*(3), 437–459.
Babbie, E. (2004) *The Practice of Social Research* (10th ed.). Belmont, CA: Wadsworth.
Bailey, C. A. (1996). *A Guide to Field Research*. Thousand Oaks, CA: Pine Forge Press.
Becker, H. S. (1963). *Outsiders: Studies in the Sociology of Deviance*. New York: Free Press.

Becker, H. S., Gordon, A. C., & LeBailly, R. K. (1984). Field work with the computers: Criteria for assessing systems. *Qualitative Sociology* 7(1–2), 16–33.

Berg, B. L., & Doerner, W. G. (November 1987). *Volunteer police officers: An unexamined aspect of police personnel.* Paper presented at the annual meeting of the American Society of Criminology, Montreal, PQ.

Berg, B. L., Ksander, M., Loughlin, J., & Johnson, B. (1983, August). *Cliques and groups: Adolescents' affective ties and criminal activities.* Paper presented at the annual meeting of the Society for the Study of Social Problems, Detroit.

Bogdan, R. (1972). *Participant Observation in Organizational Settings.* Syracuse, NY: Syracuse University Press.

Bogdan, R., & Taylor, S. (1975). *Introduction to Qualitative Research Methods.* New York: Wiley.

Boyle, J. S. (1994). Styles of ethnography. In Janice M. Morse (Ed.), *Critical Issues in Qualitative Research Methods* (pp. 159–185). Thousand Oaks, CA: Sage.

Brewer, J. D. (1993). Sensitivity as a problem in field research: A study of routine policing in Northern Ireland. In C. M. Renzetti & R. M. Lee (Eds.), *Researching Sensitive Topics.* Newbury Park, CA: Sage.

Brown, P. (1996). Catskill culture: The rise and fall of a Jewish resort area seen through personal narrative and ethnography. *Journal of Contemporary Ethnography* 25(1), 83–119.

Broadhead, R. S., & Fox, K. J. (1990). Takin' it to the streets: AIDS outreach as ethnography. *Journal of Contemporary Ethnography 19*, 322–348.

Burgess, R. G. (1991a). Keeping field notes. In R. G. Burgess (Ed.), *Field Research: A Sourcebook and Field Manual.* New York: Routledge.

Burgess, R. G. (1991b). Sponsors, gatekeepers, members, and friends: Access in educational settings. In W. B. Shaffir & R. A. Stebbins (Eds.), *Experiencing Fieldwork: An Inside View of Qualitative Research.* Newbury Park, CA: Sage.

Burns, N., & Grove, S. K. (2000). *The Practice of Nursing Research: Conduct, Critique and Utilization* (2nd ed.). Philadelphia: W. B. Saunders.

Burns, T. F. (1980). Getting rowdy with the boys. *Journal of Drug Issues 80*(1), 273–286.

Calhoun, T. C. (1992). Male street hustling: Introduction processes and stigma containment. *Sociological Spectrum 12*, 35–52.

Carpenter, C., Glassner, B., Johnson, B., & Loughlin, J. (1988). *Kids, Drugs, and Crime.* Lexington, MA: Lexington Books.

Chadwick, B. A., Bahr, H. M., & Albrecht, S. L. (1984). *Social Science Research Methods.* Englewood Cliffs, NJ: Prentice Hall.

Chiseri-Strater, E., & Sunstein, B. S. (2001). *Fieldworking: Reading and Writing Research* (2nd ed.). New York: St. Martin's Press.

Clifford, J. (1980). Fieldwork, reciprocity and the making of ethnographic texts: The examples of Maurice Leenhardt. *Man 15,* 518–532.

Coffey, A., Atkinson, P., & Holbrook, B. (1996). Qualitative data analysis: Technologies and representations. *Sociological Research Online 1*(1). Available online at www.socresonline.org.uk/socresonline/1/1/4.html

Creswell, J. W. (1999). *Qualitative Inquiry and Research Design: Choosing Among Five Traditions.* Thousand Oaks, CA: Sage.

Cromwell, P., & Nielsen, A. L. (1999). *In Their Own Words: Criminals on Crime.* Los Angeles: Roxbury Publishing.

Dennis, D. L. (1984). Word crunching: An annotated bibliography on computers and qualitative data analysis. *Qualitative Sociology* 7(1/2), 148–156.

Denzin, N. K. (1970). *Sociological Methods: A Sourcebook*. Chicago: Aldine.

Dicks, B., & Mason, B. (1998). Hypermedia and ethnography: Reflections on the construction of a research approach. *Sociological Research Online 3*(3). Available online at www.socresonline.org.uk/socresonline/3/3/3.html

Dodge, K. A., Cole, J. D., & Brakke, N. P. (1982). Behavioral patterns of socially rejected and neglected adolescents: The roles of social approach and aggression. *Journal of Abnormal Child Psychology 10*, 389–410.

Dunnington, M. J. (1957). Behavioral differences of sociometric status groups in a nursery school. *Child Development 28*, 103–111.

Ellen, R. F. (1984). *Ethnographic Research*. New York: Academic Press.

Ellen, R. F. (1987). *Ethnographic Research* (2nd ed.). New York: Academic Press.

Fenwick, J., Barclay, L., & Schmied, V. (June 1999). Activities and interactions in level II nurseries: A report of an ethnographic study. *Journal of Perinatal & Neonatal Nursing 13*(1), 53.

Ferrell, J., (2006). Criminological verstehen: Inside the immediacy of crime. In J. M. Miller & R. Tewksbury (Eds.), *Research Methods: A Qualitative Reader*. Upper Saddle River, NJ: Pearson/Prentice Hall.

Ferrell, J., & Hamm, M. S. (1998). *Ethnography at the Edge: Crime, Deviance, and Field Research*. Boston: Northeastern University Press.

Festinger, L., Riecken, H. W., & Schacter, S. (1956). *When Prophecy Fails*. New York: Harper and Bros.

Fetterman, D. M. (1989). *Ethnography: Step by Step*. Newbury Park, CA: Sage.

Geertz, C. (1973). Thick description: Toward an interpretive theory of culture. In C. Geertz (Ed.), *The Interpretation of Culture*. New York: Basic Books.

Gibbs, G. R., Friese, S., & Mangabeira, W. C. (May 2002). The use of technology in qualitative research. Introduction to issue *3*(2) of *Forum Qualitative Social Research*. Available online at www.qualitative-research.net/fqs/fqs-eng.htm

Glaser, B. G., & Strauss, A. (1967). *The Discovery of Grounded Theory: Strategies for Qualitative Research*. Chicago: Aldine.

Guy, R. F., Edgley, C. E., Arafat, I., & Allen, D. E. (1987). *Social Research Methods*. Boston: Allyn and Bacon.

Haas, J., & Shaffir, W. (August 1978). *Do new ways of professional socialization make a difference? A study of professional socialization*. Paper presented at the Ninth World Congress of Sociology, Uppsala, Sweden.

Hagan, F. E. (2006). *Research Methods in Criminal Justice and Criminology* (7th ed.). Boston: Allyn and Bacon.

Hammersley, M., & Atkinson, P. (1995). *Ethnography: Principles in Practice* (2nd ed.). New York: Routledge.

Hart, C. H., & Sheehan, R. (1986). Preschoolers' play behavior in outdoor environments: Effects of traditional and contemporary playgrounds. *American Educational Research Journal 23*(4), 668–678.

Hartup, W. W., Glazer, J. A., & Charlesworth, R. (1967). Peer reinforcement and sociometric status. *Child Development 38*, 1017–1024.

Hertz, R. (1997). Introduction: Reflexivity and voice. *Reflexivity and Voice*. Thousand Oaks, CA: Sage.

Hertz, R., & Imber, J. B. (1993). Fieldwork in elite settings (Introduction). *Journal of Contemporary Ethnography 22*(1), 3–6.

Hoffmann, J. E. (1980). Problems of access in the study of social elites and boards of directors. In W. Shaffir, R. Stebbins, & A. Turowetz (Eds.), *Fieldwork Experience.* New York: St. Martin's Press.

Howell, N. (1990). *Surviving Fieldwork: A Report of the Advisory Panel on Health and Safety in Fieldwork.* Washington, DC: American Anthropological Association.

Humphreys, L. (1970). *Tearoom Trade.* Chicago: Aldine.

Humphreys, L. (1975). *Tearoom Trade: Impersonal Sex in Public Places* (Enl. ed.). Chicago: Aldine.

Janesick, V. J. (2003) The choreography of qualitative research design. In N. K. Denzin & Y. S. Lincoln (Eds.), *Strategies of Qualitative Inquiry* (2nd ed.; pp. 46–79). Thousand Oaks, CA: Sage.

Janesick, V. J. (1994). The dance of qualitative research design. In N. K. Denzin & Y. S. Lincoln (Eds.), *Handbook of Qualitative Research.* Thousand Oaks, CA: Sage.

Jennings, H. H. (1948). *Sociometry in Group Relations.* Washington, DC: American Council on Education.

Johnson, B., Goldstein, P. J., Preble, E., Schmeidler, J., Lipton, D. S., Spunt, B., & Miller, T. (1985). *Taking Care of Business.* Lexington, MA: Lexington Books.

Johnson, J. C. (1990). *Selecting Ethnographic Informants.* Newbury Park, CA: Sage.

Johnson, J. M. (1975). *Doing Field Research.* New York: Free Press.

Jones, R. (1995). Prison as a hidden social world. *Journal of Contemporary Criminal Justice 11,* 106–118.

Kephart, T., & Berg, B. L. (2002). *Gang graffiti analysis: A methodological model for data collection.* Paper presented at the annual meeting of the Academy of Criminal Justice Sciences, March 2002, Anaheim, CA.

Lee, R. M. (2001). *Dangerous Fieldwork.* Thousand Oaks, CA: Sage.

Leedy, P. D. & J. E. Omrod (2005). *Practical Research: Planning and Design.* Upper Saddle River, NJ: Pearson/Prentice Hall.

Leinen, S. (1993). *Gay Cops.* New Brunswick, NJ: Rutgers University Press.

Leininger, M. (Ed.) (1985). *Qualitative Research Methods in Nursing.* Orlando, FL: Grune & Straton.

Leininger, M., & McFarlane, M. (2002). *Transcultural Nursing: Concepts, Theories, Research and Practice* (3rd ed.). New York: McGraw-Hill.

Letkemann, P. (1980). Crime as work: Leaving the field. In W. Shaffir, R. Stebbins, & A. Turowetz (Eds.), *Field Work Experience.* New York: St. Martin's Press.

Lincoln, Y. S., & Guba, E. G. (1985). *Naturalistic Inquiry.* Beverly Hills, CA: Sage.

LoBiondo-Wood, G., & Haber, J. (2002). *Nursing Research: Methods, Critical Appraisal and Utilization* (5th ed.). St. Louis, MO: Mosby.

Lofland, J. (1996). Analytic ethnography: Features, failings, and futures. *Journal of Contemporary Ethnography 24*(1), 30–67.

Lofland, J., & Lofland, L. H. (1984). *Analyzing Social Settings: A Guide to Qualitative Observation and Analysis.* Belmont, CA: Wadsworth Publishing.

Mason, B., & Dicks, B. (1996). The digital ethnographer. *Cybersociology,* 6. Available online at www. socio.demon.co.uk/magazine/6/dicksmason.html

Matza, D. (1969). *Becoming Deviant.* Englewood Cliffs, NJ: Prentice Hall.

McGettigan, T. (2001). Field research for boneheads: From naivete to insight on the Green Tortoise. *Sociological Research Online 6*(2). Available online at www.socresonline.org. uk/6/2/mcgettigan.html

McSkimming, M. J., & Berg, B. L. (March 1996). Methodological strategies for a rural study of tavern gambling and gaming, presented at the annual meeting of the Academy of Criminal Justice Sciences, Las Vegas, NV.

Mehan, H. (1978). Structuring school structure. *Harvard Educational Review 48*(1), 32–64.

Miller, J. M., & Tewksbury, R. (2006). *Research Methods: A Qualitative Reader.* Upper Saddle River, NJ: Pearson/Prentice Hall.

Moore, S. G., & Updergraff, R. (1964). Sociometric status of preschool children related to age, sex, nurturance giving, and dependence. *Child Development 35*, 519–524.

Morse, M. M., & Field, P. A. (1995). *Qualitative Research Methods for Health Professionals.* Thousand Oaks, CA: Sage.

Nagy Hesse-Biber, S., Leavy, P., & Yaiser, M. L. (2004). Feminist approaches to research as a process: Reconceptulatizing epistemology, methodology, and method. In *Feminist Perspectives on Social Research* (pp. 3–26). New York: Oxford University Press.

Ostrander, S. A. (1993). Surely you're not in this just to be helpful: Access, rapport, and interviews in three studies of elites. *Journal of Contemporary Ethnography 22*(1), 7–27.

Peshkin, A. (1986). *God's Choice: The Total World of a Fundamentalist Christian School.* Chicago: University of Chicago Press.

Peterson, B. H. (1985). A qualitative clinical account and analysis of a care situation. In M. M. Leininger (Ed.), *Qualitative Research Methods in Nursing.* Orlando, FL: Grune & Stratton.

Pink, S. (2001). *Doing Visual Ethnography.* Thousand Oaks, CA: Sage.

Polit, D. F., & Hungler, B. (1995). *Nursing Research: Principles and Methods.* Philadelphia: Lippincott.

Preble, E., & Casey, J. J. (1969). Taking care of business: The heroin user's life on the street. *International Journal of Addiction 4*, 1–24.

Punch, M. (1986). *The Politics and Ethics of Field Work.* Newbury Park, CA: Sage.

Quint, J. C. (1967). *The Nurse and the Dying Patient.* New York: Macmillan.

Rains, P. (1971). *Becoming an Unwed Mother.* Chicago: Aldine.

Reinharz, S. (1992). *Feminist Methods in Social Research.* New York: Oxford University Press.

Ribbens, J., & Edwards, R. (1998). *Feminist Dilemmas in Qualitative Research.* Thousand Oaks, CA: Sage.

Roper, J., & Shapira, J. (2000). *Ethnography in Nursing Research.* Thousand Oaks, CA: Sage.

Rose, D. (1990). *Living the Ethnographic Life.* Newbury Park, CA: Sage.

Rosenhan, D. L. (1973). On being sane in insane places. *Science 179*(19), 250–258.

Rubin, H. J., & Rubin, I. S. (1995). *Qualitative Interviewing: The Art of Hearing Data.* Thousand Oaks, CA: Sage.

Schwartz, H., & Jacobs, J. (1979). *Qualitative Sociology: A Method to the Madness.* New York: Free Press.

Schwartz, H., & Jacobs, J. (1997). *Qualitative Sociology: A Method to the Madness.* New York: The Free Press.

Shaffir, W. B., Stebbins, R. A., & Turowetz, A. (1980). *Fieldwork Experience: Qualitative Approaches to Social Research.* New York: St. Martin's Press.

Shenton, A. K. & Hayter, S. (2004). Strategies for gaining access to organizations and informants in qualitative studies. *Education for Information 22*(3–4), 223–231.

Sluka, J. A. (1990). Participant observation in violent social contexts. *Human Organization 49*(2), 114–126.

Spindler, G. (1988). *Doing the Ethnography of Schooling.* Prospect Heights, IL: Waveland Press.

Spindler, G., & Spindler, L. (1988). Roger Harker and Schonhausen: From familiar to strange and back again. In G. Spindler (Ed.), *Doing the Ethnography of Schooling.* Prospect Heights, IL: Waveland Press.

Spradley, J. P. (1979). *The Ethnographic Interview.* New York: Holt, Rinehart & Winston.

Spradley, J. P. (1980). *Participant Observation.* New York: Holt, Rinehart & Winston.

Stinchcombe, A. C. (1975). Merton's theory of social structure. In L. Coser (Ed.), *The Idea of Social Structure.* New York: Harcourt Brace Jovanovich.

Stoddart, K. (1986). The presentation of everyday life. *Urban Life 15*(1), 103–121.

Styles, J. (1979). Outsider/insider: Researching gay baths. *Urban Life 8*(2), 135–152.

Tallerico, M. (1991). Application of qualitative analysis software: A view from the field. *Qualitative Sociology 14*(3), 275–285.

Tedlock, B. (2003). Ethnography and ethnographic representation. In N. K. Denzin & Y. S. Lincoln (Eds.) *Strategies of Qualitative Inquiry* (2nd ed., pp. 165–213). Thousand Oaks, CA: Sage.

Tedlock, B. (2000). Ethnography and ethnographic representation. In N. K. Denzin & Y. S. Lincoln (Eds.), *Handbook of Qualitative Research* (2nd ed.). Thousand Oaks, CA: Sage.

Tewksbury, R. (1995). Cruising for sex in public places: The structure and language of men's hidden, erotic worlds. *Deviant Behavior: An Interdisciplinary Journal 17,* 1–19.

Tewksbury, R. (1997). Assumed and presumed identities: Problems of self-presentation in field research. *Sociological Spectrum 17,* 127–155.

Tewksbury, R. (2001). Acting like an insider: Studying hidden environments as a potential participant. In J. M. Miller & R. Tewksbury (Eds.), *Extreme Methods: Innovative Approaches to Social Science Research,* (pp. 4–12).

Tewksbury, R. (2002). Bathhouse intercourse: Structural and behavioral aspects of an erotic oasis. *Deviant Behavior: An Interdisciplinary Journal 23,* 75–112.

Tewksbury, R. (2006). Acting like an insider: Studying hidden environments as a potential partizipant. In J. Mitchell Miller & Rizhard Tewksbury (Eds.) *Research Methods* (pp. 3–12). Upper Saddle River, NJ: Pearson/Prentice Hall.

Thomas, W. I., & Swaine, D. (1928). *The Child in America.* New York: Knopf.

Vallance, R. J. (2001). Gaining access: Introducing referred approval. *Issues in Educational Research 11,* 65–73.

Van Maanen, J. (1982). Fieldwork on the beat. In J. Van Maanen, J. Dabbs, Jr., & R. R. Faulkner (Eds.), *Varieties of Qualitative Research.* Beverly Hills, CA: Sage.

Van Maanen, J. (1988). *Tales of the Field: On Writing Ethnography.* Chicago: University of Chicago Press.

Verenne, H. (1988). Jocks and freaks: The symbolic structure of the expression of social interaction among American senior high school students. In G. Spindler (Ed.), *Doing the Ethnography of Schooling.* Prospect Heights, IL: Waveland Press.

Warren, C. A. B., & Karner, T. X. (2005). *Discovering Qualitative Methods: Field Research, Interviews, and Analysis.* Los Angeles, CA: Roxbury.

Wax, R. H. (1971). *Doing Fieldwork: Warnings and Advice.* Chicago: University of Chicago Press.

Weppner, R. S. (1977). *Street Ethnography.* Beverly Hills, CA: Sage.

Werner, O., & Schoepfle, G. M. (1987). *Systematic Fieldwork: Foundations of Ethnography and Interviewing,* Vol. 1. Newbury Park, CA: Sage.

Whyte, W. F. (1955). *Street Corner Society.* Chicago: University of Chicago Press.

Wilcox, K. (1988). Ethnography as a methodology and its applications to the study of schooling: A review. In G. Spindler (Ed.), *Doing the Ethnography of Schooling.* Prospect Heights, IL: Waveland Press.

Williams, T., Dunlap, E., Johnson, B. D., & Hamid, A. (2001). Personal safety in dangerous places. In J. M. Miller & R. Tewksbury (Eds.), *Extreme Methods: Innovative Approaches to Social Science Research* (pp. 216–238). Boston: Allyn and Bacon.

Wolcott, H. F. (1973). *The Man in the Principal's Office: An Ethnography* (Reprint, 1984). Prospect Heights, IL: Waveland Press.

Wolcott, H. F. (1999). *Ethnography: A Way of Seeing.* Walnut Creek, CA: Sage.

Zigarmi, D., & Zigarmi, P. (1980). The psychological stresses of ethnographic research. *Education and Urban Society 12*(3), 291–322.

Chapter 7

Action Research

L ET'S SAY YOU HAVE been called to assist a neighborhood walk-in clinic that is interested in conducting an evaluation of its service-delivery system. The actual problems are not known so careful initial assessment on your part will be necessary. You are aware that understanding the clients' situations, needs, and responsibilities will emerge slowly during the course of the project. Time, however, is limited, so identifying some time-efficient research methods is essential. As well, the health professionals running the clinic inform you that it is critical that you include client-based perspectives in your study.

About now, you are probably thinking back to your studies on research methods and perhaps to earlier chapters in this book. What type of a research design will permit you to examine a variety of yet undetermined situational and conditionally based issues? At this point, you really don't have much more than a general idea about the research. As Chapter 2 indicates, design is an excellent place to begin, but how do you proceed? A trip to the library to consult pertinent literature is helpful for general and background information, but the literature will not provide much insight about specific conditions and situations facing the clients at the walk-in clinic you have been asked to evaluate. There may be an answer, however, to this dilemma: *action research.*

For the past several decades, the practice of *action research* has been a fairly common mode of investigation in educational research, especially among researchers interested in classroom teaching practices and teacher education (see, e.g., Brown, 1988; Bray, Lee, Smith, & Yorks, 2000; Brown & Doling, 1998; Burnaford, Fischer, & Hobson, 2001; Calhoun, 1994; Freire, 1972a, 1972b; Kemmis & McTaggart, 1988; Stringer, 2004). Many sources credit Kurt Lewin (1890–1947) with coining the term *action research* in about 1934 (Mills, 2000). According to Lewin, action research is a process that "gives credence to the development of powers of reflective thought, discussion, decision and action by ordinary people participating in collective research on 'private troubles' that they have in common" (Adelman, 1993, p. 8). Today action research represents a viable, practical strategy for social studies requiring systematic, organized, and reflective investigations (Stringer, 1999, 2004). In its present use, action research is one of the few research approaches that embraces principles of participation, reflections, empowerment, and emancipation of people and groups interested in improving their social situation or condition.

Action research, sometimes called *participatory action research* (PAR), is a research framework that evolved from a number of different intellectual traditions. It can be defined as a kind of collective self-reflective enquiry undertaken by participants in social relationship with one another in order to improve some condition or situation with which they are involved. Thus, it is a highly collaborative, reflective, experiential, and participatory mode of research in which all individuals involved in the study, researcher and subjects alike, are deliberate and contributing actors in the research enterprise (Gabel, 1995; Stringer & Dwyer, 2005; Wadsworth, 1998).

The origins of action research are not entirely clear. Holter and Schwartz-Barcott (1993) state that action research originated in the field of psychology with Kurt Lewin (1946). Yet, it has also been traced to anthropological- and sociological-based community research by investigators such as William Goodenough (1963), Elton Mayo (1933), and William Foote Whyte (1943, 1991). Action research can also be found in feminist literature (see, e.g., Burman, 2004; Reid, 2000, 2004; Reinharz, 1992) and in the literature on educational change and teaching practices (e.g., Anderson, 2004; Anderson, Herr, & Nihlen, 1994; Kemmis & McTaggart, 1988). PAR has also become a more common methodological framework employed in nursing research studies (e.g., Holter & Schwartz-Barcott, 1993; Jenkins et al., 2005; Seymour-Rolls & Hughes, 1998).

Action research has a wide range of applications in classrooms, schools, hospitals, justice agencies, and community contexts. The commonalities that draws these disciplines together in the conducting of action research are

- A highly rigorous, yet reflective or interpretive, approach to empirical research
- The active engagement of individuals traditionally known as subjects as participants and contributors in the research enterprise
- The integration of some practical outcomes related to the actual lives of participants in this research project
- A spiraling of steps, each of which is composed of some type of planning, action, and evaluation

Stated slightly differently, action research can be understood as a means or model for enacting local, action-oriented approaches of investigation and applying small-scale theorizing to specific problems in particular situations (Reason, 1994; Stringer, 1999). Put another way, action research is a method of research in which creating a positive social change is the predominant force driving the investigator and the research.

Drawing on various traditions from which action research originates, a number of assumptions or values can be outlined. These include the following:

- The democratization of knowledge production and use
- Ethical fairness in the benefits of the knowledge generation process
- An ecological stance toward society and nature
- Appreciation of the capacity of humans to reflect, learn, and change
- A commitment to nonviolent social change.

Action research targets mainly two primary tasks. First, it is intended to uncover or produce information and knowledge that will be directly useful to a group of people (through research, education, and sociopolitical action). Second, it is meant to *enlighten* and *empower* the average person in the group, motivating each one to take up and use the information gathered in the research (Fals-Borda & Rahman, 1991; Reason, 1994).

The Basics of Action Research

Action research is a collaborative approach to research that provides people with the means to take systematic action in an effort to resolve specific problems. This approach endorses consensual, democratic, and participatory strategies to encourage people to examine reflectively their problems or particular issues affecting them or their community. Furthermore, it encourages people to formulate accounts and explanations of their situation and to develop plans that may resolve these problems.

Action research focuses on methods and techniques of investigation that take into account the study population's history, culture, interactive activities, and emotional lives. Although action research makes use of many traditional data-gathering strategies, its orientation and purpose are slightly different. It does not use, for instance, elaborate and complex routines originating exclusively from the perspective of the researcher; instead, action research collaborates with the very people it seeks to study. The language and content of action research also differ from other approaches—especially those that utilize

Figure 7.1 The Action Research Spiral Process

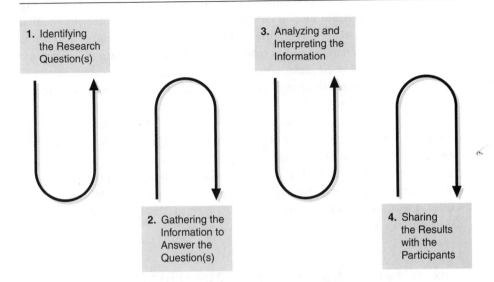

1. Identifying the Research Question(s)

2. Gathering the Information to Answer the Question(s)

3. Analyzing and Interpreting the Information

4. Sharing the Results with the Participants

complex, sophisticated, difficult-to-understand statistical techniques. Language and content with this approach are easy to understand by both professional researchers and lay people alike.

The basic action research procedural routine involves four stages: (1) identifying the research question(s), (2) gathering the information to answer the question(s), (3) analyzing and interpreting the information, and (4) sharing the results with the participants. Similar to the way I described the general research process in Chapter 2, action research follows a kind of spiraling progression rather than the more traditional linear one (see Figure 7.1).

Kemmis and McTaggart (1988) also describe the action research process as a spiral of activity: plan, act, observe, and reflect. Other formulations of action research suggest a somewhat varied grouping of activities, but the process they delineate is similar—typically, a spiral, or what Stringer and Dwyer (2005, p. 5) label "a research helix." For example, Stringer (1999) and Stringer and Dwyer's (2005) discussion on spirals lists *look, think, and act.* In effect, different sources seeking to describe the action research procedure all seem to describe essentially the same set of activities, simply in different ways and in different sequences. One could reasonably argue that all research requires action. After all, research itself is a type of action, and most research produces some sort of consequence (even apathy). With many types of research, the consequence is some sort of change or modification with the way something is done or understood. If our approach is metaphysical, the very act of asking questions and actively seeking answers can be viewed as a kind of intervention into a situation or problem and will inevitably bring about changes in those individuals involved. Whether these individuals then choose to continue along the same paths as they had before the research was conducted or to change their course means the new situation will either be different from before or remain essentially the same. In either event, the decision to change or not to change constitutes action or, more precisely, action or inaction.

In action research, investigators are aware of the inevitable effect of intervention and the subsequent potential for change. Most action research, then, consciously seeks to study something in order to change or improve it. This may be a situation uncovered by the researcher or brought to the attention of the investigator by some interested or involved party. Let's consider the four stages described in the current discussion of the action research process.

Identifying the Research Question(s)

The first stage of the action research process involves the researcher assisting the people in the research population—who may be called the *stakeholders*—to examine their situation and to recognize their problems. Alternatively, the researcher may identify a problem and bring it to the attention of the stakeholders. It is important for the action research investigator to recognize that the issues to be studied are considered important by the stakeholder and are not simply of interest to the researchers. This means that the task of the investigator is to assist individuals in the stakeholding group to jointly formulate research question(s), and as the research questions are created, to assist in formulating questions that are actually answerable. To some extent, this notion relates to the size of the problem at hand, but it also has to do with the type of information that may be available to the researcher. For example, the study may involve a community health workshop where many of the participants are drug addicts. Although considerable information may be available concerning drug addiction, treatment programs, and even direct information from participants, in this study it may not be possible to extend findings from gathered information beyond this particular community health workshop.

A good way to develop answerable relevant questions is to brainstorm or perhaps conduct focus groups with stakeholders (see Chapter 5). In these meetings, the investigator can ask: "What are the kinds of problems or issues you face?" With a little bit of digging, the investigator should be able to uncover relevant problems for study.

Gathering the Information to Answer the Question(s)

Any information the investigator gathers can potentially be used to answer the questions or solve the problems that have been identified. How one goes about gathering these data is essentially a matter of the investigator's choice and largely depends on limitations set by the stakeholders or the nature of the problem and setting. Thus, as in any standard methodological approach (see Chapter 2) the investigator is guided by the research question. Some problems will direct the investigator toward conducting interviews with relevant parties. Other problems may require various types of ethnographic or observational data. Still other studies may seem to be best addressed with archival data. Naturally, some investigators may choose to triangulate their studies in an effort to strengthen their findings and potentially enrich the eventual analysis and understandings.

Analyzing and Interpreting the Information

At this stage of the research process, participants need to focus on analyzing and interpreting the information that has been gathered. Data analysis, from the action research perspective, involves examination of the data in relation to potential resolutions to the questions or problems identified during the first stage of the research process.

The actual task of analysis will depend on the data-gathering method or methods used in stage 2 of this research process. The overall effort will be to create descriptive accounts based on the information captured by various data-collection technologies. Following are two alternative sets of general procedures investigators may consider to assist stakeholders in formulating descriptive accounts of the problems and issues that confront them. Readers should recognize similarities to processes for analyzing and understanding interviews, ethnography, and other forms of qualitative techniques described earlier in this text.

Procedures for Using Interview and Ethnographic Data

The process for recording responses in Chapter 3 outlines interviewing; Chapter 4, focus groups; and Chapter 5, ethnographic research. These same techniques may also be used in an action research framework. Hence, responses to questions (from interviews) and statements from field notes (ethnography) should be recorded and then placed in summary charts or on tally sheets showing the textual context as well as summaries of the materials. In most cases, analysis involves creating categories or themes and then sorting answers to questions or statements from the fieldwork into these categories. The data are sorted into piles that share some broader characteristic (the theme or category name). After accomplishing this, you can then write a summary that captures the essence of each broader categorical characteristic. This material will be used to create descriptive accounts of the stakeholders (discussed later).

Guiding Questions of Analysis: Why, What, How, Who, Where, When?

There are a number of questions one can pose to the data at a meeting with participants that will provide a guiding procedure for analyzing this material. The first question, *why*, establishes a general focus for the investigator and stakeholders, reminding everyone what the purpose of the study originally was. The remaining questions—*what, how, who, where,* and *when*—enable participants to identify associated influences (Stringer, 1999). The intent is not to create categories or themes but rather to better understand the data in context of the setting or situation. *What* and *how* questions help to establish the problems and issues: What is going on that bothers people? How do these problems or issues intrude on the lives of the people or the group? *Who, where,* and *when* questions focus on specific actors, events, and activities that relate to the problem or issues at hand. The purpose here is not for participants to make quality judgments about these elements; rather, it is to assess the data and clarify information that has been gathered. This process is likely to draw out more than a mere explanation of already gathered information. It is likely to provide further history and context to the material (in a manner similar to a focus group interview). Additionally, this process provides a means for participants to reflect on things that they have themselves discussed (captured in the data) or that other participants have mentioned.

Descriptive Accounts and Reports

There are two major concerns in developing descriptive accounts and creating reports of these accounts. First, it is critical that accounts reflect the perceptions of *all* stakeholders in the study population. If accounts exclude portions of the group, the resulting analysis may provide inadequate basis for viable action. Accounts, then, need to be created collaboratively (Stringer, 1999). Second, except in situations in which the stakeholders amount to only a very few people, all of them usually cannot be included in all steps of the process all of the time. In such situations, the investigator needs to make every effort to regularly keep all stakeholders informed of various activities and provide opportunities for people to read various accounts as they develop (not simply after the project is complete). In this way, these individuals can also be afforded the opportunity to provide their own input by way of feedback to what they have read.

Sharing the Results with the Participants

One of the operative principles of action research is to inform and empower people to work collectively to produce some beneficial change. This necessarily includes both informal and formal meetings with the investigator at every stage of the research process. Stringer (1999, p. 81) suggests a number of activities that an investigator can use in order to maximize participation by many of the participants, especially when these participants may include large numbers of diverse stakeholders:

- *Focus groups* in which people with similar interests or agendas discuss particular issues
- *In-group forums* in which people from single-interest or stakeholder groups discuss particular issues
- *Informal meetings* that form spontaneously in response to particular circumstances or issues
- *Agency, institution,* or *departmental meetings* that provide personnel with opportunities to discuss common interests or agendas
- *Community group meetings* in which community members meet to explore interests or agendas

It is also important that when the study is over, the stakeholders still need to know what the results are. This can be accomplished in a wide variety of ways. Traditionalists are likely to think about providing some form of a report to each participant in the study. However, this may still make the information inaccessible to some participants. As Denzin (1997) suggests, there is a growing need (perhaps demand) for methods of reporting that represent people's lived experience in clear, everyday language. Traditional methods of presenting participants with paper copies of technical reports tend to include stiff or stilted scientific jargon that is meaningless to the average lay person.

Current technology provides a means for communicating with a large number of people in an interesting, engaging, and accessible manner. For example, information may be placed on a project Web site and its address provided to those participants interested in using the Internet. Others may be more interested in seeing material presented via some form of presentation placed on a videotape (e.g., a verbal presentation of a report, a dramatic presentation or some type of role-played reenactment of situations uncovered in the research, etc.).

The Action Researcher's Role

The formally trained researcher stands with and alongside the community or group under study, not outside as an objective observer or external consultant. The researcher contributes expertise when needed as a participant in the process. The researcher collaborates with local practitioners as well as stakeholders in the group or community. Other participants contribute their physical and/or intellectual resources to the research process. The researcher is a partner with the study population; thus, this type of research is considerably more value-laden than other more traditional research roles and endeavors.

The approach a researcher takes when conducting action research, therefore, must be more holistic, encompassing a broad combination of technological, social, economic, and political aspects of relationships and interactions between the researcher and the stakeholders in the project.

Types of Action Research

Several sources outline three distinct types of action research. For example, Grundy (1988, p. 353) discusses three modes of action research: technical, practical, and emancipating. Holter and Schwartz-Barcott (1993, p. 301) discuss three types of action research—that of a technical collaborative approach, a mutual collaborative approach, and an enhancement approach. McKernan (1991, pp. 16–27) also lists three types of action research: the scientific-technical view of problem solving, the practical-deliberate action research mode, and a critical emancipating action research.

If we collapse these generally similar categories, we derive something like *a technical/scientific/collaborative mode, a practical/mutual collaborative/deliberate mode,* and *an emancipating/enhancing/critical mode.*

Technical/Scientific/Collaborative Mode

Janet Masters (1998) outlines early advocates of action research such as Lippitt and Radke in 1946, Lewin in 1947, Corey in 1953, and Taba and Noel in 1957 as having advocated a fairly rigorous scientific method of problem solving. From this approach, the primary goal was to test a particular intervention based on a prespecified theoretical framework. The relationship in this mode of action research was between the research and a practitioner. For example, a relationship might arise between a researcher and a clinical psychologist working with a family support group of some type. The researcher serves as a collaborator and a facilitator for the practitioner, whereas the practitioner brings information from the researcher to his or her clients (Holter & Schwartz-Barcott, 1993, p. 301). In effect, the researcher will work with the clinical psychologist, who in turn will act as a kind of liaison between the researcher and his or her clients throughout the research process. The communication flow within this type of research is primarily between the facilitator (practitioner) and the group, so that the researcher's ideas may be communicated to the group (Grundy, 1998). In other words, the researcher identifies a problem after collaborating with the practitioner and then provides information to this practitioner who facilitates its implementation with the group.

A Practical/Mutual Collaborative/Deliberate Mode

In this mode of action research, the researcher and the practitioner come together and collaboratively identify potential problems and issues, their underlying causes, and possible interventions (Holter & Schwartz-Barcott, 1993, p. 301). The research problem is defined only after the researcher and practitioner have assessed the situation and reach a mutual understanding. This sort of "practical action research," as Grundy (1988, p. 357) describes it, seeks to improve practice-and-service delivery of the practitioner through application of the "personal wisdom of the participants." The communication flow in this mode of action research starts with the researcher and facilitator working collaboratively and then flows from the practitioner (facilitator) to the group of stakeholders.

This design of action research creates a more flexible approach than the *technical/scientific/collaborative mode* in that it embraces a greater concern for empowering and emancipating stakeholders working with the practitioner. The gain in flexibility and effects of emancipating participants does, however, reduce some degree of measurement precision and control over interpretations, interactive communications, and detailed descriptions (McKernan 1991). These are not seen, however, as the primary goals in this mode of action research. Rather, "the goal of practical action researchers is understanding practice and solving immediate problems" (McKernan, 1991, p. 20).

Practitioners involved in such mutual collaborative approaches to action research tend to reflect on their own practice styles, incorporate new information developed by the research, and implement interventions that may effect lasting changes in the groups with whom they participate. Unfortunately, the changes that result in such projects tend to be associated with the change agents (those facilitators working in the research); consequently, the interventions may cease to be used when these individuals leave the system.

Emancipating/Enhancing/Critical Science Mode

This third mode of action research "promotes emancipatory praxis in the participating practitioners; that is, it promotes a critical consciousness which exhibits itself in political as well as practical action to promote change" (Grundy, 1987, p. 154). There are actually two distinct goals in this approach to action research. The first goal is an attempt to increase the closeness between the day-to-day problems encountered by practitioners in specific settings and the theories used to explain and resolve the problem; in other words, an attempt to bring together theory and book knowledge with real-world situations, issues, and experiences.

The second goal is to assist practitioners in lifting their veil of clouded understandings and help them to better understand fundamental problems by raising their collective consciousness (Holter & Schwartz-Barcott, 1993). This is accomplished by developing a social critique, wherein the consideration of theory and practice comes together. Development of this sort of social criticism has three parts: theory, enlightenment, and action (see Grundy, 1988). The generation of action-oriented policy, then, may be seen as following from this mode of action research and this tri-part notion of theory, enlightenment, and action. It is actually the coming together of theory and enlightenment that provides the emancipation and empowerment to the participants, which then leads to action and change.

In addition to these three general categories, Eileen Ferrance (2000) argues that within the area of school-based action research, the following particular types can be delineated:

- An individual teacher investigating a problem in his or her classroom.
- A collaborative action research study with two or more teachers interested in addressing a classroom or a department's issue (either a shared problem or one specific to a particular class or category of classes (e.g., biology classes).

- A schoolwide research focus on issues relevant and common to an entire school.
- A districtwide research that requires a focus on issues that may be organizational, community, or performance based or may involve processes involving teacher and or administrative decisions.

While these may be considered *types* of educational action research, they might also be seen as methodological foci, or organizational strategies in school-based educational action research studies.

Photovoice and Action Research

During the past several decades, the use of photographs in ethnographic research has begun to move toward a greater action research orientation. That is to say that before the 1990s, qualitative investigators used photographs more or less traditionally to either serve as data in themselves (see, e.g., Dowdall & Gorden, 1989; Jackson, 1977; Musello, 1980) or simply to illustrate and/or document the ethnographic record (see Spradley, 1979). The current trend among some action researchers is to use photographs as a means to enable the investigator to gain perceptual access to the world from the viewpoint of individuals who have not traditionally held control over the means of imaging the world. This technique is called photovoice (Clark & Zimmer, 2001; Wang, Cash, & Powers, 2000; Wang & Redwood-Jones, 2001).

Photovoice researchers literally give their subjects a camera and ask them to photograph certain aspects of their lives. Often this is undertaken in addition to more traditional elements of observation and field note-taking or photos taken by the investigator. For example, as part of a larger investigation, Clark and Zimmer (2001) gave disposable cameras to women in their study at three-month intervals and asked them to record events or situations these women felt were relevant to their children's health in general. This activity resulted in 1,018 mother-generated photographs. These were added to photographs taken by both researchers and their assistants during home visits to these women (an additional 943 photographs). In effect, the photovoice method puts cameras in the hands of folks in the community so that they can document what they see in their community from the ground up. In turn, these photos are discussed among participants and then brought to the attention of community leaders or appropriate policymakers.

In another recent study conducted by Caroline Wang and her associates (2004), 41 youths and adults (including a number of political leaders of the community) were given cameras and asked to photographically document their community's assets and concerns, and then to critically discuss these images with policymakers of that community. The project provided these youths an opportunity to express their concerns about violence in their neighborhood and provided policymakers with an opportunity to hear concerns and consider ways to provide funding for local violence-prevention programs.

The Goals in Photovoice

There are essentially three major goals when using photovoice as an action research strategy:

1. Empowering and enabling people to reflect their personal and community concerns.
2. To encourage a dialogue and to transfer knowledge and information about personal and community issues through discussions about photographs among participants.
3. To access the perception of those not in control of various problem issues and share this information with those who are in control (policy makers, politicians, health professionals, educators, etc.).

Central to action research is the notion of it being participatory. As an action research strategy, then, photovoice is also necessarily participatory. Photovoice allows participants to define themselves, their families, their work, and anything else that can be focused through the viewfinder of a camera. Because these photographs are then discussed with others, they provide a means by which others can share the meanings participants attach to the people, scenes, objects, and situations captured in the photographs.

According to Wang (2000), study members themselves guide each step of the research process so that their voice can be fully expressed. After the photographs have been taken, the method has three stages: selecting photographs, contextualizing stories, and codifying issues.

Selecting Photographs   The participants will need to identify which of the photographs they believe most accurately reflect their concerns and issues or which photographs best depict their view about the world around them. As in other action research strategies, this can be accomplished in small or large groups.

Contextualizing Stories   In this stage, the participants share stories about their photographs. In more traditional research terms, they *offer accounts* about the photographs, why they were taken, what the image means to the individual, and what they intended the photograph to depict. Sharing stories is a key element in this technique because it quite literally offers the *voice* element to the photographs. In the absence of this stage, photographs do not provide the inner perceptions of their creators (the participants who took the photographs).

Codifying   Like any other coding stage, this one identifies the central issues, themes, or theories that emerge during the course of contextualizing and discussing the photographs in the various groups. During this stage, participants may earmark certain concerns that they want to target for action or prioritize issues for action.

Photovoice provides a means for involving people in both sharing and defining issues, problems, and concerns. As an action research technique, it allows the investigator to gain insights as well as to inform relevant policy makers or other change agents. It is a means by which participants can reflect, both individually and together, on their own concerns, made visible in photographs and given voice through discussions and accounts.

Action Research: A Reiteration

In an effort to better summarize the various activities, procedures, and data-collecting strategies available to researchers through use of an action research framework, I offer Figure 7.2, which is loosely adapted from John Creswell's (2004) "Taxonomy of Action Research Data Collection Techniques."

Note that this figure continues to follow the overall structure suggested earlier in this chapter of *identifying a research question, gathering information to answer the question,* and *analyzing and interpreting the information.* Also note that the various modes of *enquiry* are not intended as absolutes nor intended to be read across the figure. Rather, they should be considered as similar to lines of action, as described in Chapter 2 in the discussion on *triangulation.* Hence, one can mix and match, so to speak, various elements shown in this figure in order to structure an action research framework for a study.

Figure 7.2 A Taxonomy of the Action Research Framework

Experience (through collaboration, observation, and sharing) →	Enquiry (methods of asking questions by researchers and/ or stakeholders) →	Examining (reviewing and making use of collected information)
Meet with Shareholders (individually or town meeting)	Discuss issues	Review Relevant Literature (scholarly and specific document related to the stake holders)
Participant Observation (Actively involved participation)	Interviews (informal or arranged semistructured)	Analysis of Interview transcripts
Collaborative Observation (actively involved participant with other stakeholders)	Focus groups	Assessment of focus group transcripts
	Photovoice	Discussion of Photographs (possible public display)
Accessed Observation (passive observer, working with stakeholders)	Archival (use of available records)	Review of Archived Documents
		Presentation of results to stakeholders

TRYING IT OUT

1. Divide the class into two separate groups. Designate one of the students in each group as *researcher.* Next, see if you can identify problems and issues facing each group of students. Remember, this may involve several meetings of the group (small town meetings) led by the *researcher* of each group. Once each group has devised a list of concerns and issues (the action focus), have the *researcher* report this to one large town meeting of the entire class. How similar were the concerns listed by each group?

2. Divide the class into three groups. Have each group identify a concern or interest of the entire group that exists on campus. Now have students take photographs that depict their group's concern or interest. The groups will need to meet separately to discuss their photographs and share their meanings. Finally, have the groups exhibit their photographs. The exhibition may be accomplished by hanging the photographs in a hall, using the

classroom walls, launching them onto the Web, and so on. Be sure some narratives have been included with the photographs.

REFERENCES

Adelman, C. (1993). Kurt Lewin and the origins of action research. *Educational Action Research 1*(1), 7–25.

Anderson, J. P. (2004). *A Short Guide to Action Research.* Boston: Allyn and Bacon.

Anderson, G. L., Herr, K., & Nihlen, A. S. (1994). *Studying Your Own School.* Thousand Oaks, CA: Corwin Press.

Bray, J. I., Smith, L., & Yorks, L. (2000). *Collaborative Inquiry in Practice: Action Reflection, and Making Meaning.* Thousand Oaks, CA: Sage.

Brown, A., & Dowling, P. (1998). *Doing Research/Reading Research. A Mode of Interrogation for Education.* London: Falmer.

Brown, L. (1988). *Group Self-Evaluation: Learning for Improvement.* School Improvement Plan. Secretariat, Education Department of Victoria Canada.

Burman, E. (2004). Organizing for change? Group-analytic perspectives on a feminist action research project. *Group Analysis 37*(1), 91–108.

Burnaford, G. E., Fischer, J., & Hobson, D. (2001). *Teachers Doing Research: The Power of Action Through Inquiry* (2nd ed.). Mahwah, NJ: Eribaum.

Calhoun, E. (1994). *How to Use Action Research in the Self-Renewing School.* Alexandria, VA: Association for Supervision and Curriculum Development.

Clark, L., & Zimmer, L. (2001). What we learned from a photographic component in a study of Latino children's health. *Field Methods 13*(4), 303–328.

Creswell, J. W. (2004). *Educational Research* (2nd ed.). Upper Saddle River, NJ: Prentice Hall.

Denzin, N. (1997). *Interpretative Ethnography.* Thousand Oaks, CA: Sage.

Dowdall, G. W., & Golden, J. (1989). Photographs as data: An analysis of images from a mental hospital. *Qualitative Sociology 12*(2), 183–213.

Fals-Borda, O., & Rahman, M. A. (Eds.). (1991). *Action and Knowledge: Breaking the Monopoly with Participatory Action Research.* New York: Intermediate Technology/ Apex.

Ferrance, E. (2000). *Action Research.* Providence, RI: Northeastern and Island Regional Educational Laboratory at Brown University.

Freire, P. (1972a). *Cultural Action for Freedom.* Middlesex, England: Harmmondsworth, Penguin.

Freire, P. (1972b). *Pedagogy of the Oppressed.* Middlesex, England: Harmmondsworth, Penguin.

Gabel, D. (1995). Presidential address. National Association for Research in Science Teaching (NARST), San Francisco.

Goodenough, W. (1963). *Cooperation in Change: An Anthropological Approach to Community Development.* New York: Russell Sage.

Grundy, S. (1987). *Curriculum: Product or Praxis.* London, England: The Falmer Press.

Grundy, S. (1988). Three modes of action research. In S. Kemmis & R. McTaggert (Eds.), *The Action Research Reader* (3rd ed.). Geelong, Australia: Deakin University Press.

Holter, I. M., & Schwartz-Barcott, D. (1993). Action research: What is it? How has it been used and how can it be used in nursing? *Journal of Advanced Nursing 128,* 298–304.

Hughes, I., & Seymour-Rolls, K. (2000). Participatory action research: Getting the job done. *Action Research E-Reports,* 4. Available online at http://www.fhs.usyd.edu.au/arow/arer/004.htm.

Jackson, B. (1977). *Killing Time: Life in the Arkansas Penitentiary.* Ithaca, NY: Cornell University Press.

Jenkins, E., Jones J., Keen, D., Kinsella, F., Owen, T., Pritchard, D., & Rees, S. (2005). Our story about making a difference in nursing practice through action research. *Educational Action Research. 13*(1), 259–274.

Kemmis, S., & McTaggart, R. (1988) *The Action Research Planner* (3rd ed.). Geelong, Australia: Deakin University Press.

Lewin, K. (1946). Action research and minority problems. *Journal of Social Issues 2,* 34–46.

Masters, J. (1998). The history of action research. In I. Hughes and B. Dicks (Eds.), *Action Research Electronic Reader.* Available online at www.scu.edu.au/schools/gcm/ar/arr/arow/default.html

Mayo, E. (1933). *The Human Problems of an Industrial Civilization.* New York: Macmillan.

McKernan, J. (1991). *Curriculum Action Research. A Handbook of Methods and Resources for the Reflective Practitioner.* London: Kogan Publishers.

Mills, G. E. (2000). *Action Research: A Guide for the Teacher Researcher.* Upper Saddle River, NJ: Prentice Hall.

Musello, C. (1980). Studying the home mode: An exploration of family photography and visual communications. *Studies in Visual Communication 6*(1), 23–42.

Reason, P. (1994). Three approaches to participative inquiry. In N. K. Denzin & Y. S. Lincoln (Eds.), *Handbook of Qualitative Research* (pp. 324–339). Thousand Oaks, CA: Sage.

Reid, C. (2004). Advancing women's social justice agendas: A feminist action research framework *International Journal of Qualitative Methods 3*(3). Available online at http://www.ualberta.ca/~backissues/33/html/reid.html.

Reid. C. (2000). Seduction and enlightenment in feminist action research. *Feminist Qualitative Research 28*(1–2), 169–189.

Reinharz, S. (1992). *Feminist Methods in Social Research.* New York: Oxford University Press.

Seymour-Rolls, K., & Hughes, I. (1998). Participatory action research: Getting the job done. In I. Hughes & B. Dicks (Eds.), *Action Research Electronic Reader.* Available online at www.scu.edu.au/schools/gcm/ar/arr/arow/default.html

Spradley, J. P. (1979). *The Ethnographic Interview.* New York: Holt, Rinehart & Winston.

Stringer, E. (2004). *Action Research in Education.* Upper Saddle River, NJ: Pearson/Merrill/Prentice Hall.

Stringer, E. T. (1999). *Action Research* (2nd ed.). Thousand Oaks, CA: Sage.

Stringer, E., & Dwyer, R. (2005). *Action Research in Human Services.* Upper Saddle River, NJ: Pearson/Merrill/Prentice Hall.

Wadsworth, Y. (1998). What is participatory action research? *Action Research International,* Paper 2. Available online at www.scu.edu.au/schools/gcm/ar/ari/p-ywadsworth98.html

Wang, C. (2000). *Strength to Be: Community Visions and Voices.* Ann Arbor, MI: University of Michigan Press.

Wang, C., Cash, J. L., & Powers, L. S. (2000). Who knows the streets as well as the homeless? Promoting personal and community action through photovoice. *Health Promotion Practice 1*(1), 81–89.

Wang, C., & Redwood-Jones, Y. A. (2001). Photovoice ethics. *Health Education and Behavior 28*(5), 560–572.

Whyte, W. F. (1943). *Street Corner Society.* Chicago: University of Chicago Press.

Whyte, W. F. (Ed.). (1991). *Participatory Action Research.* Newbury Park, CA: Sage.

Chapter 8

Unobtrusive Measures in Research

I N THE PRECEDING FOUR chapters, research procedures that require an intrusion into the lives of subjects have been discussed. Researcher reactivity—the response of subjects to the presence of an intruding investigator—has been considered as it applies to interviewers and ethnographers. In each case, suggestions have been offered concerning how to make positive use of the reactivity or to neutralize it. In this chapter unobtrusive (nonintruding) research strategies will be examined.

Although such intrusive techniques as direct observation frequently find their way into most conventional research methods books, unobtrusive strategies less regularly do. In fact, when research methods books do mention unobtrusive procedures, they typically define terms (e.g., Frankfort-Nachmias & Nachmias, 2000), give only a brief elaboration on the work of Webb and colleagues (1981), or confuse unobtrusive measures with general content analysis strategies of analysis (Babbie, 2001). Even comprehensive compendiums of qualitative strategies and techniques omit the topic of unobtrusive measures and nonreactive techniques (see, for example, Denzin & Lincoln, 1994; 1998). However, unobtrusive measures actually make up a particularly interesting and innovative strategy for collecting and assessing data. In some instances, unobtrusive indicators provide access to aspects of social settings and their inhabitants that are simply unreachable through any other means.

To some extent, all the unobtrusive strategies amount to examining and assessing human traces. What people do, how they behave and structure their daily lives, and even how humans are affected by certain ideological stances can all be observed in traces people either intentionally or inadvertently leave behind. The more unusual types of unobtrusive studies are sometimes briefly highlighted in textbook descriptions of unobtrusive measures—just before dismissing these techniques in favor of measures regarded as more legitimate.

For instance, it is fairly common to hear how an investigator estimated the popularity of different radio stations in Chicago by having automobile mechanics record the position of the radio dial in all the cars they serviced (Z-Frank, 1962). Sawyer (1961, cited in Webb, Campbell, Schwartz, Sechrest, & Grove, 1981) examined liquor sales in Wellesley, Massachusetts, a so-called dry town (i.e., no liquor stores were permitted). To obtain an estimate of liquor sales, Sawyer studied the trash from Wellesley homes—specifically, the number of discarded liquor bottles found at the Wellesley trash dump. Not very long following this study, the *science of garbology* began to arise with what has come to be known as the University of Arizona's Garbage Project, which originated in 1973 (Rathje & Murphy, 2001). This study, developed by anthropologists at the University of Arizona, and still ongoing today, sought to understand the relationship between mental, behavioral, and material realities that made up human consumption and disposal, including examination of diet and nutrition, recycling, waste disposal techniques, and food waste and food recovery. In short, garbology provides a kind of mirror on the society it investigates—especially if one follows the old adage *you are what you eat* (Lepisto, 2005).

In some instances, almost absurd situations have been ascribed to findings culled form unobtrusive data. For example, Jelenko (1980) describes a rock on the campus of Wright State University that was regularly painted by students. He determined the accretion of paint each time the rock was painted and calculated that in 7,778 years the rock would have grown (from the layers of paint) to a size that would encroach on the gymnasium located 182 meters away.

During the past 30 years in law enforcement, an area commonly known as *crime analysis* has evolved. Crime analysis involves the study of criminal incidents, and identification of crime patterns, crime trends, and criminal problems. Crime analysis is accomplished by a variety of diverse and unobtrusive techniques. For instance, during the 1980s, the Florida Department of Law Enforcement (FDLE) officers regularly read local newspapers from across the state, looking for articles about fraudulent bank checks, car thefts, certain congames commonly associated with gypsies, and other patterns of criminal behavior. As these patterns developed in the various cities' newspaper stories, they charted the cities and the crimes on a map of Florida. In this manner, they could see if there were any migrating patterns from one Florida city to the next and could predict the onslaught of certain crimes in particular areas in advance. When a pattern was identified, they contacted local law enforcement officials to warn them of the impending criminal activities. Today, these same kinds of activities are handled by inputing information to a computer program generically referred to as a geographic information system (GIS), or GIS mapping.

Regardless of whether this information is the consequence of hand-culled articles from newspapers or records of local crime incidents collected and entered into a GIS mapping program, the important fact is that these activities are actually an application of the utility of unobtrusive research strategies. Crime analysis, like the previous illustrations of unobtrusive data-collection strategies, demonstrates that information can be culled from various traces and records created or left by humans (whether intended or inadvertent).

Many types of unobtrusive data provide avenues for the study of subjects that might otherwise be very difficult or impossible to investigate. Helen Bramley (2002), for example, examined "Diana," Princess of Wales, as a contemporary goddess by examining the historical descriptions of goddesses of the past. Robert Pullen and his associates (2000) studied cheating by examining 100 discarded cheat sheets from a variety of disciplines discovered on and off campus. From the cheat sheets examined, the researchers assessed the location where the sheets had been discarded, the nature of their content, their physical size, and several other factors. Stan Weber (1999) used several literature sources to develop an assessment of the orientation and etiologies of citizen militia in the United States, an interesting contemporary phenomenon that might not otherwise have been successfully researched. And Brian Payne (1998) conducted a kind of meta-analysis of studies on health care crimes, using existing literature and research studies on Medicare and Medicaid frauds as his data source.

In this chapter, several broad categories of unobtrusive strategies are examined in detail. This approach is not meant to suggest that the various unobtrusive techniques are necessarily ordered in this manner. It is intended, rather, to simplify presentation by simultaneously discussing similar techniques under like headings. The categories will be considered under the headings Archival Strategies and Physical Erosion and Accretion.

Archival Strategies

As Denzin (1978, p. 219) remarks, archival records can be divided into public archival records and private archival records. In the case of the former, *records* are viewed as prepared for the expressed purpose of examination by others. Although access to public archives may be restricted to certain groups (for example, certain law enforcement records, credit histories, school records, and so on), they are typically prepared for some audience. As a result, public archival records tend to be written in more or less standardized form and arranged in the archive systematically (for instance, alphabetically, chronologically, or numerically indexed).

In contrast to these public orientations and formal structures, private archival records typically are intended for personal (private) audiences. Except for published versions of a diary or personal memoirs (which in effect become parts of the public archival system), private archival records reach extremely small—if any—audiences.

Public Archives

Traditionally, the term *archive* brings to mind some form of library. Libraries are, indeed, archives; but so too are graveyard tombstones, hospital admittance records, police incident reports, computer-accessed bulletin boards, motor vehicle registries, newspaper morgues, movie rental stores, and even credit companies' billing records. As Webb and his colleagues (1981, 2000) suggest, virtually any *running record* provides a kind of archive.

In addition to providing large quantities of inexpensive data, archival material is virtually nonreactive to the presence of investigators. Many researchers find archival data attractive because public archives use more or less standard formats and filing systems, which makes locating pieces of data and creating research filing systems for analysis easier (see Loftland, Snow, Anderson, & Lofland, 2006).

Naturally, as in any research process, serious errors are possible when using archival data. If this possibility is recognized, however, and controlled through data triangulation, for example, errors need not seriously distort results (Webb et al., 2000).

Modifying and modernizing the four broad categories suggested by Webb and his colleagues (1966, 1981, 2000) results in a three-category scheme. This scheme identifies varieties of public archival data as commercial media accounts, actuarial records, and official documentary records.

Commercial Media Accounts   Commercial media accounts represent any written, drawn, or recorded (video or audio) materials produced for general or mass consumption. This may include such items as newspapers, books, magazines, television program transcripts, videotapes and DVDs, drawn comics, maps, and so forth.

When Johannes Gutenberg developed the moveable type printing press, he could not have foreseen the advances in the technology of writing and publishing that are now commonplace. Today, with the assistance of microchips, microprocessors, flatbed scanners, CD burners, flash drives, and laser printers, the only limitation on writing, storage, and printing are time and inclination. Similarly, with technological developments in video and digital cameras, and the equipment used to view these recordings, very high-tech equipment is available and affordable, opening new worlds of running records to both official agencies and private citizens.

One excellent illustration of the use of television program transcripts as a type of public archival record is Molotch and Boden's (1985) examination of the congressional Watergate hearings of 1973. In their effort to examine the way people invoke routine conversational procedures to gain power, Molotch and Boden created transcriptions from videotapes of the hearings. By examining the conversational exchanges between relevant parties during the hearings, Molotch and Boden (1985) manage to develop a blow-by-blow account of domination in the making.

In a similar vein, following the O. J. Simpson trial, Frank Schmalleger (1996) offered a commentary on the exchanges between the defense and prosecution based on court transcripts he downloaded from the Internet.

Molotch and Boden (1985) are primarily concerned with the audio portion of the videotapes. Schmalleger (1996) is similarly interested only in the written transcript of verbal exchanges. Other researchers, however, have concentrated on visual renderings, such as still photographs. Jackson (1977), for example, used photographs to depict the prison experience in his *Killing Time: Life in the Arkansas Penitentiary*. Another example of the use of still photographs is Goffman's (1979) examination of gender in advertisements. Goffman's research suggests that gender displays, like other social rituals, reflect vital features of social structure—both negative and counterbalancing positive ones.

As another illustration, Gottschalk (1995) used photographs as an intricate element in his ethnographic exploration of the "Strip" in Las Vegas. Gottschalk's use of photos evokes an emotional content about the Strip not actually possible in words alone. Their inclusion, then, significantly heightens the written account of his ethnography.

Actuarial Records   *Actuarial records* also tend to be produced for special or limited audiences but are typically available to the public under certain circumstances. These items include birth and death records; records of marriages and divorces; application information held by insurance and credit companies; title, land, and deed information; and similar demographic or residential types of records.

Private industry has long used actuarial information as data. Insurance companies, for example, establish their price structures according to life expectancy as mediated by such factors as whether the applicant smokes, drinks liquor, sky dives (or engages in other life-threatening activities), works in a dangerous occupation, and so forth. Similarly, social scientists may use certain actuarial data to assess various social phenomena and/or problems. Although each of these preceding categories of public archival data may certainly be separated conceptually, it should be obvious that considerable overlap may occur.

Although archival information is a rich source of primary data, albeit underused, such data frequently contain several innate flaws as well. For example, missing elements in an official government document may represent attempts to hide the very information of interest to the investigators, or missing portions of some official document may have merely resulted from the carelessness of the last person who looked at the document and lost a page.

It is sometimes difficult to determine possible effects from editorial bias and control over what gets published and what does not. Bradley, Boles, and Jones (1979) expressly mention this element as one of two weaknesses in their study of cartoons in men's magazines in relation to the changing nature of male sexual mores and prostitution. In addition, they indicate as a second weakness their inability to measure precisely audience reaction merely by examining cartoons that appeared in *Esquire* and *Playboy* over a 40-year period.

When dealing with aggregate statistical data, missing values or nonresponses to particular questions can be accounted for. In some instances, data sets can be purchased and cleaned of any such missing pieces of information. Unfortunately, when using archival data, it may sometimes be impossible to determine, let alone account for, what or why pieces of data are missing. This again suggests the need to incorporate multiple measures and techniques in order to reduce potential errors, but it should not prevent or discourage the use of archival data.

Formal actuarial records (for instance, birth, death, and marriage records) are used frequently as data in social science research. Aggregate data such as aptitude test scores, age, income, number of divorces, smoker or nonsmoker, gender, occupation, and the like are the lifeblood of many governmental agencies (as well as certain private companies). Sharon DeBartolo Carmack (2002) points out that there are a number of places one can locate interesting information about records of death. For example, death certificates, which can frequently be located in coroner's records or in local county courthouses (as public information) can provide fascinating information about the cause of death of an individual. Similarly, family Bibles can provide a host of information on births, marriages, and deaths and can serve as fodder for a number of interesting studies about families, genealogy, traits, and personality characteristics.

Among the more interesting variations on unobtrusive actuarial data are those described by Warner (1959). As part of his classic five-volume series on

"Yankee City" (the other volumes include Warner & Low, 1947; Warner & Lunt, 1941, 1942; Warner & Srole, 1945), Warner offered *The Living and the Dead: A Study of the Symbolic Life of Americans.*

In his study, Warner (1959) used official cemetery documents to establish a history of the dead and added interviewing, observation, and examination of eroded traces as elements in his description of graveyards. From his data, Warner was able to suggest various apparent social structures present in grave-yards that resembled those present in the social composition of Yankee City (Newburyport, Massachusetts). For instance, the size of headstones typically was larger for men than for women, plots were laid out so that the father of a family would be placed in the center, and so forth.

Webb and his colleagues (1981, p. 93) point out that tombstones them-selves can be interesting sources of data. They also mention the possible analy-sis of different cultures by, for example, considering the relative size of the headstones of men as compared to women (1981).

In fact, tombstones often reveal several other interesting things. For example, most tombstones contain birth and death dates, and many include social role information (for example, "beloved son and father," "loving wife and sister"). In some cases, the cause of death may even be mentioned (for instance, "The plague took him, God rest his soul" or "Killed by Indians"). In consequence, tombstones cease to be merely grave markers and become viable actuarial records. Examination of information in a given cemetery can reveal waves of illness, natural catastrophes, relative social status and prestige, ethnic stratification, and many other potentially meaningful facts.

More recently, Dean Eastman, a history teacher at Beverly High School in Beverly, Massachusetts, has been using tombstone data in her class on "Primary History through the History of Beverly," and then "Tiptoeing through the Tombstones." These courses allow her students to analyze infor-mation on the tombstones as they evolved through Puritan New England. These gravestone symbols include death heads, cherubs, urns and willow branches, inscriptions, borders, and various styles popular in New England circa 1620–1820 (Eastman, 2002).

Official Documentary Records   Schools, social agencies, hospitals, retail establishments, and other organizations have reputations for creating an abun-dance of written records, files, and communications (Bogdan & Biklen, 1992). Many people regard this mountain of paper—or electronic records—as something other than official documents. In fact, *official documentary records* are originally produced for some special limited audiences, even if they eventu-ally find their way into the public domain. These records may include official court transcripts, police reports, census information, financial records, crime statistics, political speech transcripts, internally generated government agency reports, school records, bills of lading, sales records, and similar documents. Official documents may also include less obvious, and sometimes less openly available, forms of communications such as interoffice memos, printed e-mail messages, minutes from meetings, organizational newsletters, and so forth. These materials often convey important and useful information that a researcher can effectively use as data.

Official documentary records may offer particularly interesting sources of data. Blee (1987), for example, bases her investigation of gender ideology and the role of women in the early Ku Klux Klan on a content analysis of official documentary records. As Blee (p. 76) describes it, "The analysis of the WKKK [Women's Ku Klux Klan] uses speeches and articles by the imperial commander of the women's klan, leaflets and recruiting material and internal organizational documents such as descriptions of ceremonies, rituals and robes and banners, membership application forms and the WKKK constitution and laws."

Naturally, not all research questions can be answered through the use of archival data, or at least not archival data alone. Some studies, however, are so well suited to archival data that attempts to examine phenomena in another manner might not prove as fruitful. For example, Poole and Regoli (1981) were interested in assessing professional prestige associated with criminology and criminal justice journals. In order to assess this, they counted the number of citations for various journals (in the *Index of Social Science Citations*) and ranked each cited journal from most to least citations. The operative assumption was that the journals with the greatest frequency of citation reflected the subjective preference of professionals working in the field. In consequence, those journals that enjoyed the most frequent reference in scholarly works possessed the greatest amount of prestige.

In a similar fashion, Thomas and Bronick (1984) examined the professional prestige of graduate criminology and criminal justice programs by ranking each on the basis of volume of publication citations per faculty member during a single year (1979–1980). Thomas and Bronick examined both the total number of citations of faculty in each department studied and the number of citations per each experience year of faculty members in each department. By assessing both the quantity of publications and publication weight (by considering proportions of publications in prestigious journals) Thomas and Bronick managed to rank the graduate programs.

Although most archival data can be managed unobtrusively, researchers must sometimes be cautious regarding certain ethical concerns. For example, since some archives include certain identifiers such as names and addresses, their use requires that researchers take steps to ensure confidentiality. For instance, police complaint records typically are open to the public (with the exception of certain criminal complaints involving minors) and contain much identifying information. Similarly, during the recent past, a growing number of newspapers have begun publishing police blotter sections. These typically indicate the names, addresses, occupations, charges, and frequently the case dispositions of crimes committed during the day or evening preceding the published account. Certainly these types of data could prove valuable in a variety of studies. But care is necessary if you are to avoid identifying the individuals depicted in these press accounts or crime reports.

A simple removal of certain particularly sensitive identifiers (for example, names and addresses) and aggregation of the data according to some nonidentifying factor might be sufficient. For instance, in a study of crime in relation to geographic-environmental factors that was mapped by C. Ray Jefferys, particulars of identity were unnecessary. Using official criminal reports occurring in Atlanta during 1985 and 1986, Jefferys annotated a map of the city and identified high-risk locations for particular categories of crime.

Social scientists have traditionally used a variety of official types of reports and records. Several governmental agencies exist literally in order to generate, assess, and disseminate research information. In many cases, in addition to straightforward statistical analysis, detailed reports and monographs are made available. Furthermore, and because of the technological advances in audio- and videotaping devices, it is becoming increasingly possible to obtain verbatim accounts of governmental hearings, congressional sessions, and similar events.

Burstein and Freudenberg (1978), for example, were interested in how public opinion influenced legislative votes. Although legislators certainly possess the right to vote their consciences even against the general wishes of their constituents, they do not usually do so. Burstein and Freudenberg examined 91 bills and motions, concerning the issue of the Vietnam War, submitted both before and after the 1970 invasion of Cambodia. These bills were compared against public opinion poll information that had been conducted throughout the war years and ranged from opinions against the war from the beginning to those opinions that approved of and supported the ways the president handled the situation.

Stated simply, Burstein and Freudenberg (1978) found that before the 1970 invasion of Cambodia, public opinion had an influence on some of the dovish (antiwar) legislators but that hawkish (prowar) legislators were generally unaffected. Similarly, funding the Vietnam War, although not a particularly important dimension in affecting vote outcomes before 1970, did become relevant in votes after the 1970 invasion. The explanation offered by Burstein and Freudenberg suggests that while the financial costs of Vietnam were bearable before the invasion of Cambodia, these costs became insupportable after the invasion.

Today, in addition to voting records, the behavior of Congress and state legislatures can be unobtrusively assessed through other traces. Because of technological innovations and increased permissiveness on the part of state and federal legislators (perhaps in response to the secretiveness that surrounded Watergate) many congressional and state legislature debates and votes are televised.

Videotape can now capture the kind of joke-making at one another's expense that is rather common in state legislature committee meetings, as well as the various symbolic gestures and ceremonial rituals that typically occur but have gone unrecorded for years. Analysis of these types of interactions may reveal some interesting and telling things about how both politics and votes actually operate.

For example, Masters and Sullivan, professors at Dartmouth College, have examined meanings encoded in the facial grimaces and symbolic gestures of politicians during speeches. In order to study the various clucks, furrowed brows, smiles, head tilts, hand motions, and so forth, Masters and Sullivan examined videotapes of speeches made by political leaders (Masters & Sullivan, 1988).

The use of videotape in a variety of settings is becoming one of the most useful and complete running records available to archival researchers. Examination of videotape records, to quote Bell Telephone, "is almost like being there." Many law enforcement agencies, for example, now routinely videotape persons as they are tested for driving while intoxicated, or when conducting crime scene investigations, and maintain these taped records for prolonged periods of time (Berg, 1999).

Educational researchers have long recognized the utility of videotaping in classroom- and playground-based studies; the videotapes frequently provide access for other investigators who may use these videotapes as a source of secondary data for analysis (Stigler, Gonzales, Kawanaka, Knoll, & Serrano, 1999).

Albrecht (1985) described the uses of videotape and film—for defining social problems (including uncovering secrets about situations), creating records of behavior, testing the representative nature of these records, constructing hypotheses, and building grounded theory.

As noted in Chapter 6, many ethnographies of schooling have been compiled by using videotaping strategies. For example, Erickson and Mohatt (1988) describe their efforts to uncover cultural organizations of participation structure in classrooms. They videotaped both first-grade teachers and their students across a one-year period. In order to capture the students and their teachers in usual interaction routines, each hour-long tape cassette was photographed with a minimum of camera editing. In other words, the camera operator did not pan the room or zoom in and out for close-ups. Rather, wide-angle shots of the classroom and its participants were utilized. The result was an effective collection of data that gave a microethnographic look at how interactions between teachers and students differ when the two groups belong to different cultural groups (in this case, Native American and non–Native American).

Certainly videotapes should prove to be important and useful as audiovisual transcripts of official proceedings, capturing emergent and/or serendipitous acts in various social settings, and creating behavioral records. In fact, in 1987, the *American Behavioral Scientist* devoted an entire issue to the use of videocassette recorders (VCRs) in research. But other video-related official documents may prove equally useful—in particular, the receipt records from sales and rentals of commercial video programs. For example, the issue of whether watching violence on television is related to committing violence in society is a long-standing question. In 1969, the National Commission on the Causes and Prevention of Violence (Eisenhower, 1969, p. 5) concluded: "Violence on television encourages violent forms of behavior, and fosters moral and social values about violence in daily life which are unacceptable in civilized society."

Since 1969, a number of studies have similarly concluded that watching violent television programs encourages violent behavior (see Comstock, 1977; Eron, 1980; Phillips, 1983). Yet the debate over whether watching violence on television encourages violent behavior continues. Central issues in this debate include the question of whether people who became aggressive after viewing violent programs might already have been aggressive; whether the violence depicted on the program was or was not rewarded and/or justified (that is, was it the good guys or the bad guys who were violent?), and whether the viewer was watching a real-life violent event (e.g., hockey, boxing, football) or a fictionalized one.

Many researchers regard the link between media violence and violent behavior as well established. Other researchers claim that this link remains unsubstantiated. Jeffrey Johnson and his associates (2002) recently reported on a 17-year study of a community sample of 707 individuals. The researchers found that there was a significant association between the amount of time spent watching television during adolescence and early adulthood and the likelihood of subsequent aggressive acts against others. For example, the researchers found that 14-year-old boys who were allowed to watch three hours or more of television a day were about twice as likely as those who watched less than an hour of television a day to commit a crime by the time they reached early adulthood.

Although television certainly offers an inexpensive education in a variety of violent techniques, so too can video rental stores. Since videotape rental stores have sprouted up across the nation faster than weeds grow in a vegetable garden, they may offer an efficient measure of popular film genre choices. Whether their records amount to boxes of sales receipts or, more than likely, microcomputer disks, comprehensive records of the titles that are rented or sold and the frequency of rentals or sales are potentially available.

By identifying and tabulating the rental rate of certain movies that depict a range and variety of violence, researchers may be able to discover which dimensions of violence appear to be the most popular (e.g., vigilante behavior, retaliation, national reprisals, sporting events, and so on).

In addition, since sales slips are keyed to membership's identification numbers (so that store owners can keep tabs on their wares), it may be possible to gain demographic information on who rents what by checking membership application records (another official document record). Estimates of which films are rented how frequently and by whom may allow greater understanding of Eron's (1980) notion that watching violence may encourage desensitization, role-modeling, and approval of violence in others.

Webb and his colleagues (1981) may have been correct at the time when they suggested that videotaped records were disorganized and not widely accessible, but times have changed. The past several years have seen tremendous growth in the use of visual and auditory media and equipment—both analog and, more recently, digital—by official agencies, researchers, and private citizens. In addition to an increased number of sales and rental suppliers, most urban libraries now offer fairly sizable collections of videotapes and DVD movies and documentaries. Even children's books and games are produced in video formats of one type or another. Supermarkets and convenience stores carry huge selections of videos and DVDs. Large movie rental chains have cropped up across the nation, and where you do not find one, you are likely to find a mom-and-pop movie rental store. The array of possible uses for and access to video and digital film data have simply grown too large to be overlooked or ignored by researchers.

Although video technology might have us looking toward moving pictorial representation of life, still photography also possesses considerable research value. Analysis of photographs, or *visual ethnography,* as it is sometimes referred to (Pink, 2001; Schwartz, 1989), offers yet another interesting avenue for unobtrusive research. The use of photographs as data requires a theory of how pictures should be used by both picture makers and viewers. Photos can be used either as data in themselves (Dowdall & Golden, 1989) or to assist in the conduct of interviews as illustrative devices (Musello, 1980; Wagner, 1979). In the former case, photos provide a sense of what existed, perhaps years in the past, as well as a viewpoint—namely, that of the photographer. As Chapter 7 illustrated, one can also give *voice* to photographs by allowing their creators to share meanings that they associate with these pictures (see Chapter 7, Photovoice and Action Research).

As the technique of photovoice demonstrates, photographs can mean different things to different people. They also may intentionally reflect the photographer's viewpoint and not the viewer's. Thus, many researchers—outside the context of photovoice—consider photographs somewhat ambiguous. Rather than seeing this ambiguity as a disadvantage, however, visual ethnographers see it as a negotiation of meanings by viewers. These researchers believe that photos can be presented to people and discussed within the comfortable context of a family viewing of pictures. By doing this, visual ethnographers suggest that they can identify a verbal context for delineating what should be seen in a photo and what significance can be attached to various images (Musello, 1980; Pink, 2001; Schwartz, 1989).

In effect, what arises in some cases is a kind of *photo-interview* (Schwartz, 1989). In this situation, interviews actually center on or around a discussion of photographs. When interviews are held in comfortable locales, such as subjects' homes or lounges, the interaction is quite relaxed. Although more intrusive than actual unobtrusive measures, such photo-interviews create the familiar context of friends looking at and chatting about family photos.

Similarly, audio recordings as data also have a wide variety of applications. Audiotapes of natural conversations are typically used by conversational analysts as the sole source of data (Schwartz & Jacobs, 1979; Ten Halve, 2000).

As Chapter 9 more fully details, oral histories are often recorded or transcribed, creating excellent data for present or future unobtrusive researchers. This form of *history-telling* (Portelli, 1992), creating records of oral histories, also suggests some intrusion into the lives of subjects. However, oral historians and historiographers (discussed in Chapter 9) often create and archive documents that later researchers can use as unobtrusive data.

Other Types of Official Documentary Sources of Data   Webb and colleagues (1981, pp. 108ff) suggest that researchers have used a variety of interesting official documents as unobtrusive data. Among these are weather report data in relation to bad moods (Persinger, 1975); emotional well-being and altruism (Cunningham, 1979); seasonal effects on panhandlers (Cialdini et al., 1975); and climate in relation to sexual activity (Smolensky, 1980).

Along similar lines, Freedman (1979) indicated that the self-admittance patient census in a New York state psychiatric facility located in Syracuse increased significantly following the first freeze (late November or early December). Conversely, Freedman suggested a like number of discharges occurred suddenly around late March and April (after which they tapered off) as the weather grew warmer. Freedman's explanation was that street people checked themselves into the facility to avoid the severely cold winter weather of Syracuse.

Private Archives: Solicited and Unsolicited Documents

Thus far, the discussion has centered on running records prepared primarily for mass public consumption. Other types of archival records, however, are created for smaller, more specific audiences than the public in general. These private archival records include autobiographies (memoirs), diaries and letters, home movies and videos, and artistic and creative artifacts (drawings, sketches). In some cases, these documents occur naturally and are discovered by the investigators (unsolicited documents); in other situations, documents may be requested by investigators (solicited documents). An example of an unsolicited private record might be an existing house log, for instance, of a delinquency group home, which could be used to investigate staff and client relationships in order to determine misbehavior patterns. An example of a solicited document, on the other hand, would be a daily work journal kept by nurses in an intensive care unit at the request of researchers for the purpose of assessing staff and task effectiveness.

Private records are particularly useful for creating case studies or life histories. Typically, owing to the personal nature of private documents, the subjects' own definitions of the situation emerge in their private records, along with the ways they make sense of their daily living routines. Precisely, these bits of self-disclosure allow researchers to draw out complete pictures of the subjects' perceptions of their life experiences.

Perhaps the most widely accepted form of personal document is the autobiography. In their discussions of autobiographies, Bogdan and Taylor (1975), Denzin (1978), Webb et al. (1981), and Taylor and Bogdan (1998), each draw extensively from Allport's (1942) monograph entitled *The Use of Personal Documents in Psychological Science*. Allport distinguishes among three types of autobiography: comprehensive autobiographies, topical autobiographies, and edited autobiographies.

Comprehensive Autobiography   Inexperienced researchers are usually most familiar with the comprehensive autobiography. This category of autobiography spans the life of the individual from his or her earliest recall to the time of the writing of the work and includes descriptions of life experiences, personal insights, and anecdotal reminiscences (Smith, 1994; Taylor & Bogdan, 1998).

Topical Autobiography In contrast to the rounded and complete description of experiences offered in comprehensive autobiographies, a *topical autobiography* offers a fragmented picture of life. Denzin (1978, p. 221) suggests that Sutherland's (1937) treatment of "Chic Conwell," who was a professional thief, illustrates this type of autobiographical style. The topical autobiography is an "excision from the life of the subject. As such it invites comparison with other kinds of lives" (Denzin, 1978, p. 221). Other examples of this sort of excision are Bogdan's (1974) examination of "Jane Fry," a prostitute, and Rettig, Torres, and Garrett's (1977) examination of "Manny," a criminal drug addict.

Edited Autobiography In the case of edited autobiographies, researchers serve as editors and commentators, eliminating any repetition in descriptions, making lengthy discourses short and crisp, and highlighting and amplifying selected segments of the material while deleting other segments. Regarding the issue of which segments should be edited and which retained as intended by the author, Allport (1942, p. 78) offers a broad guideline and suggests that all unique styles of speech (for example, slang, colloquialism, street jargon, and the like) remain unedited. Researchers should only edit for the sake of clarity— eliminating repetition; shortening long, convoluted explanations; and so forth. An example of such an edited life history can be found in the writing of Jane Ribbens (1998) who describes the nature of motherhood from an autobiographical perspective.

The intimacy afforded by diaries and personal journals, although conceptually recognized by Allport (1942) and Denzin (1978), remains an underutilized element in research. In diaries, individuals are free to express their feelings, opinions, and understandings fully. In contrast, published autobiographies must maintain the readers' interest or perhaps distort reality in order to project the author's desired public image.

Kevin Courtright (1994) suggests there are several important advantages to using the *diary method*. First, it provides a defense against memory decay as respondents are typically asked to record their events either as they happen or shortly thereafter. Second, respondents who are asked to keep diaries act both as *performers* and *informants*. Thus, diaries are able to provide information about the writer (as performer) and of others who interact with the respondent/writer (as observer). As informant, the respondent is able to reflect on his or her own performance and that of those with whom he or she has interacted. The respondent can further articulate explanations of purpose, allocate praise or blame, and even act as a critic. Finally, the diary method provides an opportunity for the subject to reflectively recreate the events, since the diary is written and maintained by the subject him or herself (Courtright, 1994).

Reinharz (1992) has discussed the use of autobiography by feminist social researchers. Reinharz suggests that some feminist researchers have written full autobiographies (e.g., Hewlett, 1986; Oakley, 1984; Riley, 1988). However, a greater number of feminist researchers have offered self-disclosures in either prefaces or postscripts to their published research. These explanations or expositions of personal and professional lives can provide subject matter similar to more traditional autobiographical data.

The use of autobiography continues to meet resistance in some academic circles and has even been called "self-indulgent" (Mykhalovskiy, 1996). In defense of the strategy of autobiography, Mykhalovskiy (1996, p. 134) has written, "The abstract, disembodied voice of traditional academic discourse [is] a fiction, accomplished through writing and other practices which remove evidence of a text's author, as part of concealing the condition of its production." But, all in all, autobiography, whether offered as a full and lengthy unfolding of one's life or as snippets of disclosure in prefaces and appendices, can be extremely useful. This information offers more than simply a single individual's subjective view on matters. An autobiography can reflect the social contours of a given time, the prevailing or competing ideological orientations of a group, or the self-reflections about one's activities in various roles. In short, autobiographies offer a solid measure of data for the research process.

During the past decade, a new type of diary has evolved, the online journal, sometimes called a *weblog* or simply a *blog* (Berger, 2004; Taylor, 2002; Thottam, 2002). Blogs vary in their content from fairly traditional diary entries—the woes and joys of the writer—to descriptions and criticisms of books, movies, and life events. In addition, many link the reader to other bloggers, informational Web pages, photographs, search engines, and various other locations on the Web. Blogs today are not just simple Web pages; rather, they are often sophisticated pages with multiple frames, links, audio elements, streaming video, and considerable interconnectivity. Yet, blogs are actually fairly simple to construct, and most end users begin with a template or shell that is frequently provided by the blog site. The simplicity of blogging is made clear at www.blogger.com, which walks the reader through a series of steps to establish his or her own blog. Other locations that provide access to blogging and bloggers include www.dairyland.com, www.pitas.com, www.diary-x.com, and www.theblogspot.com. Perhaps the most fascinating thing about blogs is their potential as research data. Like any unsolicited documents, they provide insights into their creators' perceptions on a wide assortment of subjects and interest areas (Branscum, 2001). There are even lists of blog communities such as Globe of Blogs, located at http://globeofblogs.com/?x=webrings.

One could even employ blogs as a means for intentionally soliciting journal or diary data that could be easily accessed by the researcher from any computer with a Web connection. The logic of using such a solicited journal document is not uncommon in educational research and assessment research in which instructors may ask students to maintain journals during the course of the semester (see, e.g., Lockhart, 2002).

Another distinct form of intimate private record is the *letter*. In contrast to the autobiography or diary, the letter is not simply a chronicle of past experiences. Letters are designed to communicate something to some other person. As a result, they are geared toward a *dual audience*—namely, the writer and the recipient (Denzin, 1978). The topic of the letter and the social roles and personal relationships of both the writer and receiver must, therefore, be considered.

The classic example of letters as a source of research data, of course, is Thomas and Znaniecki's (1927) *The Polish Peasant*. In their study, Thomas and Znaniecki learned of an extensive correspondence among recent Polish immigrants in America and their friends and relatives remaining in Poland. As part of their pool of data, Thomas and Znaniecki solicited copies of letters written to Poland as well as those received by Polish immigrants from their homeland. A small fee was offered for each letter submitted. Typically, however, they received only one side of a given letter exchange. In spite of limitations, Thomas and Zaniecki managed to uncover a variety of social values and cultural strains associated with the transition from Poland to America.

Suicide has been studied using letters as a viable data source (Garfinkel, 1967; Jacobs, 1967; Salib, Cawley, & Healy, 2002). In one study, Jacobs examined 112 suicide notes and found that notes could be categorized into six groups, the largest of which was what Jacobs (1967, p. 67) termed *first form notes*. From the content of these suicide notes, Jacobs deduced that the authors were involved in long-standing and complex problems. Unable to solve these problems, they found no rational alternative other than taking their own lives. In order to justify this final act, the individuals begged indulgence and forgiveness from the survivors.

In another study, by Salib, Cawley, and Healy (2002), the researchers investigated suicide notes in 125 older people whose deaths were ruled suicides by a coroner over a period of 10 years. The goal of the study was to see whether there was a difference between older victims of suicide who left notes and those who did not. All of the data was from deceased people aged 60 and over whose deaths were ruled suicides. The study found that many older people may be isolated and have no one with whom to communicate, while others may no longer have the ability to express themselves. Interestingly, the investigators could not identify consistent parameters to differentiate between those who left notes and those who did not; nonetheless, the lack of specific findings does not mean that absence of a suicide note necessarily indicates a less serious attempt (Salib, Cawley, & Healy, 2002).

A Last Remark about Archival Records

Throughout the preceding review of various archival studies, a variety of research topics were related to archival materials. The purpose of this was to suggest the versatility and range of knowledge that can be served by archival research.

An attempt was also made to indicate both the enormous quantity of information and the technological innovations available in connection to archival data. Collections of both privately and publicly held videotaped materials are certainly among the most striking and exciting of recent additions to viable archival sources.

However, researchers should be cautious in the use of archival data. Although an extraordinarily useful source of data for some research questions, archives may be the wrong source of data for some other questions. It is particularly important to use multiple procedures (triangulation) when working with archival data in order to reduce possible sources of error (missing data and so on).

Physical Erosion and Accretion: Human Traces as Data Sources

As implied in the section title, what follows is an examination of various physical traces. Quite literally, traces are physical items left behind by humans, often as the result of some unconscious or unintentional activity, that tell us something about these individuals. Because these traces have been left behind without the producers' knowledge of their potential usefulness to social scientists, these pieces of research information are *nonreactively produced*. Two distinct categories of traces are *erosion measures* (indicators of wearing down or away) and *accretion measures* (indicators of accumulation or buildup).

Erosion Measures

Physical evidence is often the key to solving criminal cases. Similarly, physical evidence is frequently the key to resolving social scientific questions in research. *Erosion measures* include several types of evidence indicating that varying degrees of selective wear or use have occurred on some object or material. In most cases, erosion measures are used with other techniques in order to corroborate one another.

An example of an erosion measure would be using replacement records in order to determine which of a series of high school French language tapes was most frequently used. The hypothesis would be that the tape that required the greatest amount of repair or replacement was the one most frequently used.

Unfortunately, several other explanations exist for why a particular tape frequently needs repair. In other words, there can be alternative hypotheses to explain this erosion. Thus, caution is once again advised when using erosion measures.

In spite of their obvious limitations as data sources, erosion measures do contribute interestingly to social scientific research. Perhaps the most widely quoted illustration of how erosion measures operate involves a study at the Chicago Museum of Science and Industry cited by Webb and colleagues (1981, p. 7):

> A committee was formed to set up a psychological exhibit at Chicago's Museum of Science and Industry. The committee learned that the vinyl tiles around the exhibit containing live, hatching chicks had to be replaced every six weeks or so; tiles in other areas of the museum went for years without replacement. A comparative study of the rate of tile replacement around the various museum exhibits could give a rough ordering of the popularity of the exhibits.

Webb and his colleagues (1981) additionally note that beyond the erosion measure, unobtrusive observations (covert observers) indicated that people stood in front of the chick display longer than they stood near any other exhibit. Additional evidence may be necessary to determine whether the wear shown on tiles near the chick exhibit resulted from many different people walking by or smaller numbers of people standing and shuffling their feet over prolonged periods of time. Nonetheless, the illustration does indicate the particularly interesting kinds of information provided by augmenting data sources with erosion measures. This case further illustrates how multiple measures may be used to corroborate one another.

Another example of an erosion measure cited by Webb and colleagues (1981) involves the examination of wear on library books as an index of their popularity. A variation on this book-wear index might be the examination of textbooks being sold back to a bookstore in order to determine if any signs of use are apparent. For example, if the spine of the book has been broken, it might indicate that the student had actually opened and turned the pages. You might likewise consider whether page corners have been turned down or sections of text highlighted.

Accretion Measures

In contrast to the selective searching out of materials suggested in erosion measures, *accretion measures* represent deposits over time. These trace elements are laid down naturally, without intrusion from researchers.

As an illustration of accretion measures, consider the findings in Siu's (cited in Burgess & Bogue, 1964) study of Chinese laundrymen. Siu found that calendars with nude female figures were common in certain laundry shops. The study showed that such calendars were more frequently hung in shops run by younger men who were labeled sexual deviants by others. Perhaps more significant, Siu suggested that displays of these calendars were due to the Chinese laundrymen's view that it was legitimate to associate with prostitutes. Siu explained that hanging calendars with nudes merely served to reinforce this general belief pattern.

Although accretion measures may seem more immediately related to the example of paint deposits described in the beginning of this chapter, that is but one form of accretion. As illustrated in the Siu study, the deposit of almost any object or material by humans can be an accretion. In fact, as illustrated by the work of Rathje (1979), even garbage may contain important clues to social culture.

Another illustration of accretion is the examination by Kephart and Berg (2002a, 2002b) of gang graffiti collected from various locations throughout a single city in Southern California. Kephart and Berg were able to establish a typology of symbolic messages concealed in the various renderings of gang graffiti and to distinguish between certain categories of messages and mere graffiti *tags* (names and/or initials of individual artists left on walls, poles, and curbs). Because the researchers could actually link specific instances of graffiti with their artists, local law enforcement was able to identify these vandals and obtain reparations to cover the cost of the graffiti's removal.

Some Final Remarks about Physical Traces

There are several advantages to erosion and accretion measures. Certainly, it should be clear that they are themselves rather inconspicuous and unaffected by researchers who locate and observe them. In consequence, the trace data are largely free of any reactive measurement effects. However, interpreting these physical traces and affixing meaning is problematic and may severely bias the results. Thus, researchers must always remember to obtain corroboration. Similarly, any single trace of physical evidence may have strong *population restrictions* (Webb et al., 1981, p. 32). It is not likely, for example, that a complete description of some group can be accomplished on the merits of some worn spot on a tile or a smudge on some wall. Similarly, physical traces may be selectively found only at certain times and in only certain places. Denzin (1978, p. 260) offers the following example:

> Chinese laundrymen may no longer display calendars with nude women, or they may only make such displays when their wives are not living with them. In this respect it would be inappropriate to draw conclusions about their relationship to sexual ideology without data on the temporal and spatial dimensions.

Certainly, for example, Chinese laundrymen today, to the extent that they still exist, are likely to be considerably different from their counterparts in the 1920s when Siu made his study [actually his dissertation].

In conclusion, physical traces, although terribly interesting and useful in many ways, are only one of several possible strategies that should be used in concert.

TRYING IT OUT

Researchers can practice using unobtrusive measures in a variety of ways. Some of the unobtrusive data more readily accessible for students/researchers are those offered in the headlines of daily newspapers, the covers of magazines, the commercials on television, the titles of movies they view on their videocassette players, and so forth.

Suggestion 1   Locate an old cemetery in your community (the older the better). Now, using headstones and grave markers as your primary data, develop an assessment of the symbols used on the gravestones and markers. You might want to take photographs or draw facsimiles of various symbols illustrated on the gravestones and markers. These may include religious symbols (crosses, stars, and so on), decorative elements (urns, leaves, angels, and so on), epitaphs (for example, "here lies John Brown, a good father, brother and husband," and so on). Take note of the dates on the headstones and grave markers—in what year did they start being flat metal markers rather than standing stone gravestones? Is there any indication of military status? After compiling your data, write a brief report explaining what you found.

Suggestion 2   Have the class locate blog membership lists from any blog community list (you can try DiaryLand.com or Weblogs.com). Systematically locate the profile or self-description of 50 blog members and record all demographic information (e.g., gender, age, marital status, educational level, or whatever other information they provide). Examine your results and assess whether there are certain categories of people, based on your sampling, that are involved in blogging.

Suggestion 3   A final practice suggestion involves obtaining permission from a campus organization or group to review the minutes of meetings for the past several years. Using these data, identify possible patterns such as cliques of members who seem to make similar motions, voting records, who holds positions of leadership, and so forth. It may be best to use a group or organization that you belong to (a fraternity, sorority, or political group).

REFERENCES

Albrecht, G. L. (1985). Videotape safaris: Entering the field with a camera. *Qualitative Sociology 8*(4), 325–344.

Allport, G. (1942). *The Use of Personal Documents in Psychological Science.* New York: Social Science Council.

American Behavioral Scientist 30(5). (1987). Special issue on the VCR age.

Babbie, E. (2001). *The Practice of Social Research.* Belmont, CA: Wadsworth.

Berg, B. L. (1999). *Policing in Modern Society.* Boston: Butterworth Heinemann.

Berger, P. (2004). Are you blogging yet? *Information Searcher 14*(2), 1–2.

Blee, K. (1987). Gender ideology and the role of women in the 1920s Klan movement. *Sociological Spectrum 7*, 73–97.

Bogdan, R. (1974). *Being Different: The Autobiography of Jane Fry.* New York: Wiley.

Bogdan, R., & Biklen, S. K. (1992). *Qualitative Research for Education* (2nd ed.). Boston: Allyn and Bacon.

Bogdan, R., & Taylor, S. (1975). *Introduction to Qualitative Research Methods.* New York: Wiley.

Bradley, D. S., Boles, J., & Jones, C. (1979). From mistress to hooker. *Qualitative Sociology 2*(2), 42–62.

Bramley, H. (2002). Diana, Princess of Wales: The contemporary goddess. *Sociological Research Online 7*(1). Available online at www.socreasonline.org.uk/7/1/bramley.html

Branscum, D. (March 5, 2001). Who's blogging now? More and more Internet users are sharing their lives in public online journals called Weblogs that can be strangely addictive. *Newsweek, 62.*

Burgess, E. W., & Bogue, D. (Eds.), (1964). *Contributions to Urban Sociology.* Chicago: University of Chicago Press.

Burstein P., & Freudenberg, W. R. (1978). Changing public policy: The impact of opinion, antiwar demonstrations, and war costs on Senate voting in Vietnam War motions. *American Journal of Sociology 84*, 99–122.

Cialdini, R. B., Vincent, E. J., Lewis, S. K., Catalan, T., Wheeler, D., & Darby, B. L. (1975). Reciprocal concession procedure for inducing compliance: The door-in-the-face technique. *Journal of Personality and Social Psychology 34*, 206–215.

Comstock, G. S. (1977). Types of portrayal and aggressive behavior. *Journal of Communication 27*, 189–198.

Cooke, M. (1998). Little examined elements in the welfare reform debate: The diminished male and the decreased value of education in the labor market. *Free Inquiry in Creative Sociology 26*(1), 31–41.

Courtright, K. E. (March 1994). An overview of the use and potential advantages of the diary method. Paper presented at the annual meeting of the Academy of Criminal Justice Sciences, Boston, Massachusetts.

Cunningham, M. R. (1979). Weather, mood and helping behavior. Quasi experiments with the sunshine Samaritan. *Journal of Social Psychology 37*, 1947–1956.

DeBartolo Carmack, S. (2002). *Your Guide to Cemetery Research.* Cincinnati, OH: Betterway Books.

Denzin, N. K. (1978). *The Research Act.* New York: McGraw-Hill.

Denzin, N. K., & Lincoln, Y. S. (Eds.). (1994). *Handbook of Qualitative Research.* Thousand Oaks, CA: Sage.

Denzin, N. K., & Lincoln, Y. S. (Eds.). (1998). *Strategies of Qualitative Inquiry* (Handbook of Research Paperback Edition, Vol. 2). Thousand Oaks, CA: Sage.

Dowdall, G. W., & Golden, J. (1989). Photographs as data: An analysis of images from a mental hospital. *Qualitative Sociology 12*(2), 183–213.

Eastman, D. (2002). Tiptoeing through the tombstones. *Common-Place. The Interactive Journal of Early American Life 2*(2). Available online at www.common-place.org/vol-02/no-02/school/

Eckberg, D. L. (1984). Job-related letters as bureaucratic propaganda. *Qualitative Sociology 7*(4), 340–351

Eisenhower, M. (1969). *Commission Statement on Violence in Television Entertainment Programs.* National Commission on the Causes and Prevention of Violence. Washington, DC: U.S. Government Printing Office.

Erickson, F., & Mohatt, G. (1988). Cultural organization of participation structures in two classrooms of Indian students. In G. Spindler (Ed.), *Doing the Ethnography of Schooling.* Prospect Heights, IL: Waveland Press.

Eron, L. D. (1980). Prescriptions for reduction of aggression. *American Psychologist 35,* 244–252.

Frankfort-Nachmias, C., & Nachmias, D. (2000). *Research Methods in the Social Sciences* (6th ed.). New York: St. Martin's Press.

Freedman, J. (1979). Lecture notes from a course on clinical sociology. Syracuse University, Syracuse, NY.

Garfinkel, H. (1967). *Studies in Ethnomethodology.* Englewood Cliffs, NJ: Prentice Hall.

Glassner, B., & Hertz, R. (Eds.). (1999). *Qualitative Sociology as Everyday Life.* Thousand Oaks, CA: Sage

Goffman, E. (1979). *Gender Advertisements.* New York: Harper and Row.

Gottschalk, S. (1995). Ethnographic fragments in postmodern spaces. *Journal of Contemporary Ethnography 24*(2), 195–228.

Hewlett, S. A. (1986). *Lesser Life: The Myths of Women's Lives in America.* New York: Morrow.

Jackson, B. (1977). *Killing Time: Life in the Arkansas Penitentiary.* Ithaca, NY: Cornell University Press.

Jacobs, J. (1967). A phenomenological study of suicide notes. *Social Problems 15,* 60–72.

Jelenko, C., III (1980). The rock syndrome: A newly discovered environmental hazard. *Journal of Irreproducible Results 26,* 14.

Johnson, J. G., Cohen, P., Smailey, E. M., Kasen, S., & Brook, J. S. (2002). Television viewing and aggressive behavior during adolescence and adulthood. *Science 297,* 2468–2471.

Kephart, T., & Berg, B. (2002a). "The Use of Photographs as Data in a Study of Gang Graffiti: A Research Note." Presented at the annual meeting of the Academy of Criminal Justice Sciences, Anaheim, CA, March.

Kephart, T., & Berg, B. (2002b). Gang graffiti analysis: A methodological model for data collection. Presented at the Annual Meeting of the Western Criminal Justice Society, San Diego, CA., February.

Lepisto, C. (2005). The garbage project *Treehugger.* April 24, Available online at http://www.treehugger.com/files/2005/04/the_garbage_pro.php.

Lockhart, M. (2002). The use of student journals to increase faculty and learner inquiry and reflection. *Academic Exchange Quarterly 6*(1), 6–15.

Lofland, J., Snow, D. A., Anderson, L., & Lofland, L. H. (2006). *Analysing Social Settings: A Guide to Qualitative Observation and Analysis* (4th ed.). Belmont, CA: Wadsworth.

Masters, R., & Sullivan, D. (1988). Happy warriors: Leaders' facial displays, viewers' emotions and political support. *American Journal of Political Science 32*(2), 345–368.

Molotch, H., & Boden, D. (1985). Talking social structure: Discourse domination and the Watergate hearing. *American Sociological Review 50*(3), 273–287.

Musello, C. (1980). Studying the home mode: An exploration of family photography and visual communications. *Studies in Visual Communication 6*(1), 23–42.

Mykhalovskiy, E. (1996). Reconsidering table talk: Critical thoughts on the relationship between sociology, autobiography, and self-indulgence. *Qualitative Sociology 19*(1), 131–151.

Oakley, Ann. (1984). *Taking It Like a Woman*. New York: Random House.

Payne, B. (1998). Conceptualizing the impact of health care crimes on the poor. *Free Inquiry in Creative Sociology 26*(2), 159–167.

Persinger, M. S. (1975). Lag response in mood reports to changes in the weather matrix. *International Journal of Biometeorology 19,* 108–114.

Phillips, D. P. (1983). The impact of mass media violence on U.S. homicides. *American Sociological Review 48,* 560–568.

Pink, S. (2001). *Doing Visual Ethnography: Images, Media and Representation in Research.* Thousand Oaks, CA: Sage.

Poole, E. D., & Regoli, R. M. (1981). Periodical prestige in criminology and criminal justice: A comment. *Criminology 19,* 470–498.

Portelli, A. (1992). History-telling and time: An example from Kentucky. *Oral History Review 20*(1/2), 51–66.

Pullen, R., Ortloff, V., Casey, S., & Payne, J. (2000). Analysis of academic misconduct using unobtrusive research: A study of discarded cheat sheets. *College Student Journal 34*(4), 616–625.

Rattie, W. L., & Murphy, C. (2001). *Rubbish: The Archaeology of Garbage.* Tucson, AZ: University of Arizona Press.

Rathje, R. H. (1979). Trace measures. In L. Sechrest (Ed.), *Unobtrusive Measurement Today.* San Francisco: Jossey-Bass.

Reinharz, S. (1992). *Feminist Methods in Social Research.* New York: Oxford University Press.

Rettig, R. P., Torres, M. J., & Garrett, G. R. (1977). *Manny: A Criminal Addict's Story.* Boston: Houghton Mifflin.

Ribbens, J. (1998). Hearing my feeling voice? An autobiographical discussion of motherhood. In J. Ribbens & R. Edwards (Eds.), *Feminist Dilemmas in Qualitative Research.* Thousand Oaks, CA: Sage.

Riley, M. W. (Ed.). (1988). *Sociological Lives.* Newbury Park, CA: Sage.

Salib, E., Cawley, S., & Healy, R. (2002). The significance of suicide notes in older adults. *Aging and Mental Health 6,* 186–190.

Sawyer, H. G. *The meaning of numbers.* Paper presented at the annual meeting of the American Association of Advertising Agencies, 1961. Cited in Eugene J. Webb, Donald T. Campbell, Richard D. Schwartz, Lee Sechrest, and Janet Belew Grove, *Nonreactive Measures in the Social Sciences.* Boston: Houghton Mifflin, 1981.

Schmalleger, F. (1996). *The Trial of the Century: People of the State of California vs. Orenthal James Simpson.* Englewood Cliffs, NJ: Prentice Hall.

Schwartz, D. (1989). Visual ethnography: Using photography in qualitative research. *Qualitative Sociology 12*(2), 119–154.

Schwartz, H., & Jacobs, J. (1979). *Qualitative Sociology: A Method to the Madness.* New York: Free Press.

Smith, L. M. (1994). Biographical Method. In N. K. Denzin & Y. S. Lincoln (Eds.), *Handbook of Qualitative Research.* Thousand Oaks, CA: Sage.

Smolensky, M. (1980). To everything there is a season. *Science News 18,* 150–151.

Stigler, J. W., Gonzales, P., Kawanaka, T., Knoll, S., & Serrano, A. (1999). *Third International Mathematics and Science Study.* Washington, DC: National Center for Education Statistics.

Sutherland, E. H. (1956). *The Professional Thief.* Phoenix, 1937. (Reprint.) Chicago: University of Chicago Press.

Taylor, C. (February 11, 2002). Psst, wanna see my blog? Impromptu online journals are popping up all over the Web. If I can figure out how to build one, you can too. *Time 159*(6), 68.

Taylor, S. J., & Bogdan, R. (1998). *Introduction to Qualitative Research Methods* (3rd ed.). New York: Wiley.

Ten Halve, P. (2000). *Doing Conversational Analysis.* Thousand Oaks, CA: Sage.

Thomas, C., & Bronick, M. J. (1984). The quality of doctoral programs in deviance criminology and criminal justice: An empirical assessment. *Journal of Criminal Justice 12*(1), 21–37.

Thomas, W. I., & Znaniecki, F. (1927). *The Polish Peasant.* New York: Knopf.

Thottam, J. (January–February 2002). Dotcom diaries: Online journals called blogs show you the lives—and links—of fascinating strangers. *On 7*(1), 24–33.

Wagner, J. (1979). *Images of Information: Still Photography in the Social Sciences.* Beverly Hills, CA: Sage.

Warner, L. W. (1959). *The Living and the Dead: A Study of the Symbolic Life of Americans.* New Haven: Yale University Press.

Warner, L. W., & Low, J. O. (1947). *The Social System of the Modern Community. The Strike: A Social Analysis.* New Haven: Yale University Press.

Warner, L. W., & Lunt, P. S. (1941). *The Social Life of a Modern Community.* New Haven: Yale University Press.

Warner, L. W., & Lunt, P. S. (1942). *The Status System of a Modern Community.* New Haven: Yale University Press.

Warner, L. W., & Srole, L. (1945). *The Social Systems of American Ethnic Groups.* New Haven: Yale University Press.

Webb, E, Cambell, D. T., Schwartz, R. D., & Sechrest, L., (2000). *Unobtrusive Measures* (rev. ed.) Thousand Oaks, CA: Sage.

Webb, E., Campbell, D. T., Schwartz, R. D., & Sechrest, L. (1966). *Unobtrusive Measures: Nonreactive Research in the Social Sciences.* Chicago: Rand McNally.

Webb, E., Campbell, D. T., Schwartz, R. D., Sechrest, L., & Grove, J. B. (1981). *Nonreactive Measures in the Social Sciences.* Boston: Houghton Mifflin.

Weber, S. C. (1999). Origins, orientations and etiologies of the U.S. citizen militia movement, 1982–1997. *Free Inquiry in Creative Sociology 27*(1), 57–66.

Z-Frank stresses radio to build big Chevy dealership. (1962). *Advertising Age 33,* 83.

Chapter 9

Historiography and Oral Traditions

What is Historical Research?

What exactly is meant by historical research, or what some call *historical event research* (Bachman & Schutt, 2003)? The obvious answer to this question is that historical research, or *historiography*, is an examination of elements of history. Unfortunately, this answer begs the next question: What is history? Often, in common parlance, the term *history* is used synonymously with the word *past* and refers conceptually to events of long ago (McDowell, 2002). From a social science perspective, history is an account of some past event or series of events. Historiography, then, is a method for discovering, from records and accounts, what happened during some past period, but it is not simply fact-centered; rather, historiography seeks to offer theoretical explanations for various historical events (Johnson & Christensen, 2003).

You can open textbooks from many disciplines and locate *time lines,* lists or drawings of time-ordered events shown in chronological sequence. This chronology of historical events allows the presenter to describe interesting or important past events, people, developments, and the like. It is a classification system some might call *historical.* Furthermore, it provides the reader with a sense of which things or events came before others. It is not, however, historiography. Historical time lines can be quite illuminating and do have their place. They are, however, passive and somewhat lackluster and lifeless. Historiography, on the other hand, attempts to fashion a descriptive written account of the past. Such a narrative account is flowing, revealing, vibrant, and alive!

Historiography involves far more than the mere retelling of facts from the past. It is more than linking together tired old pieces of information found in diaries, letters, or other documents, important as such an activity might be. Historical research is at once descriptive, factual, and fluid (Matejski, 1986). Historical research is not merely creative nostalgia. In fact, it is important to distinguish nostalgia from historical research.

Nostalgia, or the retelling of comfortable past pleasantries, events, or situations, lacks research rigor. In contrast to nostalgia, *historical research* attempts to systematically recapture the complex nuances, the people, meanings, events, and even ideas of the past that have influenced and shaped the present (Hamilton, 1993; Leedy, 1999; McDowell, 2002). In nursing research, as Burns and Grove (2004) note, historical research provides a means for history of a profession to be transmitted to those entering the profession. Historical analysis of social knowledge, traditions, and conditions can increase appreciation and understanding of contemporary issues of health, race relations, crime and corrections, education, business trends, and an infinite array of social, political, and spiritual realms. Lusk (1997a) summarized the importance of historical research for nurses when she studied nursing's claim to professional status by examining classifications of American nurses as professional and nonprofessional from 1919 to 1930 (see also LoBiondo-Wood & Haber, 2002; Lusk, 1997b).

Notter (1972), Lusk (1997b), and Neuman (2003) all concur that historical research extends beyond a mere collection of incidents, facts, dates, or figures. It is the study of the relationships among issues that have influenced the past, continue to influence the present, and will certainly affect the future (Glass, 1989). Ironically, it is only during recent history that standard social science research methods books have begun looking seriously at historical research. Many methods texts omit any consideration of this methodology (e.g., Bogdan & Biklen, 1992; Fitzgerald & Cox, 2002; Gilgun, Daly, & Handel, 1992; Taylor & Bogdan, 1998). In some cases, history is mentioned only in terms of its possible threat to internal validity (Frankfort-Nachmias & Nachmias, 2000; Rosnow & Rosenthal, 2002; Shaughnessy & Zechmeister, 1999) or its effect on construct validity (Taylor, 1994). In other texts, the use of historical research is used synonymously with comparative analysis (see, for example, Babbie, 2001, 2002). Sarnecky (1990), however, suggests that an increased interest in historiography has been evident during recent years, which he attributes to the move away from a traditional focus on abject positivism and toward a broader perspective that is more generally supportive of knowledge offered by historical research.

Historical research, then, involves a process that examines events or combinations of events in order to uncover accounts of what happened in the past. Historical research allows contemporary researchers to "slip the bonds of their own time" (Hamilton, 1993, p. 43) and descend into the past. This provides access to a broader understanding of human behavior and thoughts than would be possible if we were trapped in the static isolation of our own time.

Such tragic isolation is illustrated in H. G. Wells' classic, *The Time Machine* (published in 1895). When the protagonist arrives in the distant future, a near utopia seems to exist. Yet the people of the future millennia have been actually raised as the slaves and food of a group of mutant creatures. When the protagonist tries to learn how such a situation could have developed, no one can tell him. They have no sense of their history. How things had come to be as they are and how things might be changed were concepts lost on these people. They were oblivious to their past, living in the isolation of a single time period—the present.

Most American students are never formally introduced to historical methods of research and analysis. Instead, there seems to be an assumption that one can become expert at historical research through some tacit process, that merely by taking a history course or two, one can automatically gain the ability to perform historical research (Leedy, 1999; Salkind, 2003). This is, of course, not accurate. There is a simple reason one cannot learn how to do historical research and analysis in typical history courses: Such courses present the end product of the research, not the process by which it was uncovered. Hence, many people confuse the study of history with the method of historical research.

Nonetheless, understanding the historical nature of phenomena, events, people, agencies, and even institutions is important. In many ways, it may be as important as understanding the items themselves. One cannot fully evaluate or appreciate advances made in knowledge, policy, science, or technology without some understanding of the circumstances within which these developments occurred (Salkind, 2003). There is a parallel with dating. When you go out on a first date, there is usually considerable small talk between yourself and your date. Each person attempts to get to know the other. Small talk often centers on questions about your background and the other person's. Where were you born, raised, and educated? What do you like to do in your spare time, and do you have hobbies? What are your favorite foods, colors, and television shows? Do you or your date have brothers or sisters, and how well do you each get along with your parents? All of this information goes into the process of getting to know each other and into decisions about whether to go home early, kiss on the first date, or even continue the relationship. Could you make the decision to continue a relationship and perhaps even to marry without knowing about the other person's background? It is unlikely, and so it is with historical research. Knowledge of the past provides necessary information to be used in the present in order to determine how things may be in the future. What, then, does historical research involve?

The major impetus in historical research, as with other data-collection strategies, is the collection of information and the *interpretation* or analysis of the data. Specifically, historical research is conducted for one or more reasons: to uncover the unknown; to answer questions; to seek implications or relationships of events from the past and their connections with the present; to assess past activities and accomplishments of individuals, agencies, or institutions; and to aid generally in our understanding of human culture.

As with the example of getting to know your date, a basic assumption underlying historical research is that you can learn about the present from the past. You must use care, however, and avoid imposition of modern thoughts or understanding when considering information about the past (Marshall & Rossman, 1999). Researchers must seek to understand both literal and latent meanings of documents and other historical sources within their historical time frames. Definitions and connotations for terms change over time. A hundred years ago, the word *nurse* conjured up images of handmaidens and subservient clinical helpers to physicians. Today, however, one envisions nurses as health professionals—members of a team that includes physicians.

This is likewise true regarding different cultures and cultural terms and meanings. You must be careful not to impose your own cultural judgments on other cultures' meanings. For example, in Israel today, the common word for *nurse* in Hebrew actually translates to *sister*. It is likely this corresponds more to the connotation in early American history of the subservient handmaiden. Yet it would not be appropriate, as it would not be in other research strategies, to make judgmental statements about the term's connotation.

Passing judgment about the rightness or wrongness of earlier connotations or meanings within other cultures literally misses the point of historical research. What should be of interest and importance to the historiographer is the progression from the older image to the newer one. In the case of different cultures, the historical research is interested in comparisons, not judgments. For example, the historical researcher might be interested in the impact of changed images on modern practices. You might consider how the meaning of *nurse* affects patient care, other health professionals, and medical institutions in general.

Also, historical research provides a window to understanding today various symbols used in the past. Elman (1996), for example, examines the use of pink and black triangles by the Nazis to designate gay men and women, respectively. Elman's (1996, p. 3) discussion indicates that the "pink triangles symbolized the femaleness of this group of detainees whose masculinity was diminished within the context of Nazi heterosexism." Lesbians were classified as asocials who were made to wear black turned-down triangles. These asocials were especially despised because the color of their triangle was viewed as an insult to the black uniform of the elite black-uniformed SS (*Schutzstaffel*).

Life Histories and Historiography

Like the confusion between the concepts of history and historiography, there is sometimes a confusion between life histories and historiography. Researchers taking life histories, as a variation on traditional depth interviewing strategies, are sometimes confronted with problems similar to those faced by historiographers. This is because researchers involved in life histories often move beyond the limits of the depth interview and seek external corroborating pieces of evidence. This may be called *construction of a life history* and involves depth interviewing as merely a single line of action. This may also cause confusion because in the construction of a life history, the researcher may find it necessary to assess the motives of authors of crucial documents. This action is quite similar to how historiographers attempt to make such assessments. For example, the comments made in a diary or a suicide note must be assessed in order to ensure who the author is or was and what his or her motive might have been.

These concerns, however, are really issues that lie at the heart of any form of document analysis. As historical methods unfold throughout the remainder of this chapter, readers will also see similarities with previous descriptions of archival unobtrusive strategies.

From the perspective presented in this book, depth interview life histories or constructed documentary-based life histories are merely elements potentially useful as data in the larger historiographic analysis. Thus, any strategies that attempt to collect information from the past and to weave these pieces of information into a meaningful set of explanations fit my perspective on historical research. The reconstruction of the past from such information or data falls under the label *historiography* (Denzin, 1978). Let us further consider the types and sources of data used in historiographies.

What Are the Sources of Data of Historical Researchers?

The sources of data used by historiographers parallel those of many other social scientists: confidential reports, public records, government documents, newspaper editorials and stories, essays, songs, poetry, folklore, films, photos, artifacts, and even interviews or questionnaires. The historiographer classifies these various data as either *primary sources* or *secondary sources*.

- *Primary Sources.* These sources involve the oral or written testimony of eyewitnesses. They are original artifacts, documents, and items related to the direct outcome of an event or an experience (Salkind,

2003). They may include documents, photographs, recordings, diaries, journals, life histories, drawings, mementos, or other relics.

- *Secondary Sources.* Secondary sources involve the oral or written testimony of people not immediately present at the time of a given event. They are documents written or objects created by others that relate to a specific research question or area of research interest. These elements represent secondhand or hearsay accounts of someone, some event, or some development. Secondary sources may include textbooks, encyclopedias, oral histories of individuals or a group, journal articles, newspaper stories, and even obituary notices (Brink & Wood, 1989; Leedy & Ormrod, 2005). They may also include information that refers not to a specific subject but to a class of people (Denzin, 1978). These may involve court records of delinquents, lab information about asthmatic patients, reading scores of an entire grade level at an elementary school, and other aggregated information about some group.

Doing Historiography: Tracing Written History as Data

You begin historical research just as you begin any research project. This was described in detail in Chapter 2 but bears some reiteration here. You begin with an idea or a topic. This may be organized as a research problem, a question, a series of questions, or a hypothesis or series of hypotheses.

Next, you seek basic background information through a literature review. As you create this literature review, your topic and questions may be altered or refined and become clearer and better delineated. As you refine the research focus, you also begin to consider where and what you will use as sources of historical data. You might outline this procedure as follows:

1. Identify an idea, topic, or research question.
2. Conduct a background literature review.
3. Refine the research idea and questions.
4. Determine that historiography will be the data-collection process.
5. Identify and locate primary and secondary data sources.
6. Confirm the authenticity and accuracy of source materials.
7. Analyze the data and develop a narrative exposition of the findings.

As described in Chapter 2, you often begin with a broad idea or question for research. Initially, it may reflect an area of research more than it does a specific research statement: for instance, "women in law enforcement." You then need to begin seeking basic background information about this broad topic, just as you would with any other research problem. As you read the literature, you might begin to refine the topic and realize that how women are treated in police work has changed over time.

For example, you might notice that in 1845, when the first woman was hired by the New York City police department, she was hired as a *matron* (Berg, 1999; Feinman 1986). You might also notice that during the nineteenth century, matrons seemed to fit a social worker role more than they did a law enforcement one. That is, their primary responsibilities were to assist victims of crime, runaways, prostitutes, and children (Feinman, 1986; Hamilton, 1924). Moreover, this general social work orientation carried through until late into the 1960s (Berg, 1999; Berg & Budnick, 1986; Talney, 1969). You might now refine the original research focus to examine the changing role of policewomen. You might also begin to consider historiography as an appropriate way to examine this research problem. Next, you will need to locate sources of data regarding the topic. These will be sorted into primary and secondary classifications. Looking over the various books and journal articles you have already amassed during this preliminary literature review is a good first step. Certainly, many of these documents will fit into the secondary source classification. However, by examining the reference sections in these documents, you might also locate leads to or actual primary data references. These may include references to autobiographies written by people during the period of interest or newspaper stories reporting interviews with people of the time. These may also include references to diaries, letters, notes, or personal journals. They may even include the court transcripts of some hearing or the minutes of some agency's meeting.

In other words, you begin to seek primary sources that contain the descriptions of a witness to the time or to the event now the focus of the research. You may be able to obtain these documents directly from a library or similar archive, or you may need to contact agencies or organizations. You may even need to contact individuals directly who are still alive and can bear witness to some situation or aspect of interest to the research.

For many, locating and gathering primary data is considered the actual data-collection component of historical research (Glass, 1989). Historical researchers must make serious efforts to locate as much source material related to the original event as possible. These may be memos, diary entries, witnesses' accounts—all of which serve to establish a cohesive understanding of the situation. This will eventually result in insights into the meaning of the event or situation. Metaphorically, this becomes a drawing together of the pieces of a puzzle to form a complete picture.

However, it also is important to recognize that often secondary sources provide both access to primary ones and details not always immediately apparent in the primary sources. Many different pieces of information—both primary and secondary—will be necessary before the researcher can adequately fit them all together into a cogent exposition.

For example, Victoria Time (1999) examined the exposition of criminological theory as elaborated through the characterizations of William Shakespeare. To demonstrate her argument, that Shakespeare was in fact reflecting various contemporary criminological positions, Time (1999) presents various noted criminological theorists of that time and their theories (primary data). Then she explores the various characters in Shakespeare's plays and demonstrates how these characters display or project these theoretical propositions (potentially a type of primary data—as Shakespeare's work—or secondary data as demonstrating the theoretical works of various theorists).

Primary source materials are subject to two kinds of evaluations or criticisms: First, you must determine whether a document or artifact is authentic, which is sometimes referred to as *external criticism* or *validity*. Second, you must determine the accuracy of meaning in the material, which is called *internal criticism* and is related to the document's reliability.

External Criticism

External criticism is primarily concerned with the question of veracity or genuineness of the source material. Was a document or artifact actually created by the author? Wilson (1989, p. 137) suggests that "documents cannot be taken to reflect the truth unless they are really what they appear to be rather than forgeries or frauds." In short, is it a valid piece of primary data? Counterfeit documents are not uncommon. Throughout history there have been numerous hoaxes perpetrated on the literary, historical, scientific, and social science communities. For example, there have been many literary forgeries. Major George de Luna Byron claimed to be the natural son of George Gordon, Lord Byron, and a Spanish countess. He successfully produced and sold many forgeries of works alleged to have been written by Shelley, Keats, and others—including his alleged father, Byron (*Encyclopaedia Britannica*, 1987, p. 136).

More commonly known is the Thomas Chatterton–Rowley manuscripts incident. In this case, poems written by Thomas Chatterton (1752–1835) were passed off by the young writer as the works of a medieval cleric. Controversy over these poems caused a scholarly feud that lasted for many years. In fact, it has been said that this controversy actually led to the Gothic revival in literature (*Encyclopaedia Britannica*, 1987, p. 136).

An even more bizarre incident occurred in the early 1980s, when two men passed off 60 volumes alleged to be the diaries of Adolf Hitler. They sold them to the German magazine *Stern* for a sum amounting to nearly $3 million.

Almost three years later, *Stern* discovered that these diaries were complete phonies, and the magazine sued the sellers. The forgers were forced to return their ill-gotten money and were sentenced to prison ("Hitler Diaries," 1985; "Two Charged," 1984).

In 1993, George Jammal appeared on national television claiming to have obtained a piece of the original Noah's Ark (Jaroff, 1993). Jammal claimed to have obtained the chunk of ark during a 1984 search for the ark on Mount Ararat in Turkey. He explained that he and a friend known only as Vladimir had "crawled through a hole in the ice into a wooden structure. [They] got very excited when [they] saw part of the room was made into pens, like places where you keep animals" (Jaroff, 1993, p. 51). Unfortunately, Vladimir was allegedly killed, and all photographic evidence was lost on the journey. But Jammal had managed to return safely with a piece of the ark.

The television network made no effort to verify Jammal's story. After the story was aired, however, network executives learned that Jammal was an actor who had been telling this and other versions of the ark story for years (Jaroff, 1993). There never was a Vladimir, and the piece of ark is nothing more than a piece of ordinary pine Jammal soaked in fruit juices and baked in his oven (Jaroff, 1993).

Hollywood has rediscovered and is likely to encourage a resurgence of hoaxes involving crop circles. In 2002, Disney's Touchstone Pictures released the movie *Signs* starring Mel Gibson. The movie tells the story of a Pennsylvania pastor, played by Gibson, who turns to farming as a way to escape his theological doubt after the death of his wife in a car accident. The pastor is thrown into the media spotlight when 500-foot crop circles begin appearing in his fields. And it is these crop circles, in reality, that have been the subject of considerable research, debate—oh, yes—and hoaxes (Karr, 2002).

Crop circles are geometric patterns of matted-down grain stalks that originally gained media attention in the 1970s when wheat crops in England were found to have these huge patterns form allegedly overnight. They evolved into world-famous phenomenon during the 1980s and 1990s complete with controversy, pseudoscience, and credulous crop circle investigators known better as *cereologists* or *croppies* who argued that these patterns were formed by either extraterrestrials or *plasma vortices* (a spinning mass of air that has accumulated a significant fraction of electrically charged material).

Cereologists argued that hoaxers could not be responsible for crop circles because the grain stalks found in crop circles were bent and not broken and because there were never any footprints found leading to or away from the patterns. Scientific investigators have countered these arguments by explaining that, from mid-May to August, wheat is naturally green and pliable, so it could easily have been bent and not broken. Furthermore, the ruts left by tractor tires and tramlines that divide wheat fields into closely spaced parallel rows could easily provide access routes for hoaxers who would leave no footprints.

On September 10, 1991, the ABC-TV morning news program *Good Morning, America* aired a special segment featuring two men, Doug Bower and Dave Chorley, who claimed responsibility for many of the crop circles that had been appearing across the English countryside since the mid-1970s—including the first few crop circles ever discovered. Using "two wooden boards, a piece of string and a bizarre sighting device attached to a baseball cap" (Fischer & Nickell, 1992), the two men demonstrated how they had created their crop circles, forming one themselves right in front of the television cameras. According to Doug and Dave, as they liked to be called, this was a process that they had performed nearly every weekend during the wheat growing season between 1975 or so and 1991 (Nickell, 1996). Perhaps even more interesting was the fact that many of these hoaxed crop circles were declared by cereologists as impossible to have been the products of hoaxes.

Frauds, hoaxes, and forgeries are not uncommon, and this can be particularly problematic for the naïve or novice researcher. It is very important, therefore, that researchers carefully evaluate their sources. You must ensure that the document or artifact is genuine. This is true for credibility of both the research and the historical researcher. Being duped can jeopardize your ability to be taken seriously during later research investigations. Authenticating documents and objects, of course, is a study in itself. Therefore, researchers should not hesitate to seek the assistance of others more proficient than themselves when attempting to authenticate source material. This may mean calling on handwriting experts, scientists for carbon dating, linguists knowledgeable in writing dialects or period styles, and other specialists.

When undertaking an external criticism of some document, the following questions should be asked:

- Who wrote the source (primary or secondary)?
- What is the authenticity, authority, bias/interest, and intelligibility of the source?
- What was the view of the event or phenomenon when the document was written?
- What or who was the intended audience?
- What sources were privileged or ignored in the narrative?
- What evidence is offered or compiled?
- In what historical context was the document itself written?

Internal Criticism

The question, Is this material genuine? is separate from the question, What does this document mean? Important collateral questions include: What was the author trying to say? Why did the author write the document? and even, What inferences or impressions can be taken from the contents of the document? (Leedy & Ormrod, 2001).

For example, what exactly did Mary Hamilton (1924, p. 183) mean when in reference to police matrons, she wrote, "The policewoman has been likened to the mother. Hers is the strong arm of the law as it is expressed in a woman's guiding hand"? Was she endorsing the role of matron as nurturing social worker? Or was she suggesting that because women possess the capacity to be nurturers, they can also provide strong abilities as law enforcers? This example is a bit unfair since the quote is taken somewhat out of the context of Hamilton's writings. However, it should serve to illustrate the sometimes difficult task faced by historical researchers when they attempt to consider the internal validity of documents.

Another example of this task of assessing internal meaning might be assessing the meaning of propaganda offered on various hate-mongering Web sites. Questioning the content's accuracy is certainly one level of internal criticism the researcher might undertake. But another example might involve questioning what the content of statements conveys in terms of intent. Is the material intended to simply spew racial or religious disgust and hate? Or is the material intended to attract supporters, gain notoriety, or do something else? When you are making these kinds of internal meaning criticisms, the actual task becomes questioning exactly what the words mean.

To assess this deeper level of meaning required in an internal criticism, the following sorts of questions are helpful:

- What was the author trying to say?
- What was the author's motive for making the statement or creating the document?
- What inferences are offered in the statement by the author?
- Is the author's statement accurate?
- Was the sentiment of the author similar or contrary to one of the time period?
- Was the statement or document supposed to provide moral lessons?

These issues of external and internal criticism are very important for ascertaining the quality of the data and, in turn, the depth of the interpretation or analysis. Rigorous evaluations of the external and internal value of the data ensure valid and reliable information and viable historical analysis.

These external and internal evaluations also tend to separate historical research from most other forms of archival unobtrusive measures. Traditional archival methods also use secondary source material, such as medical history files, court records, or even arrest reports. However, these are treated as primary data sources and are seldom checked by external or internal evaluations. Instead, there is the tacit assumption of authenticity and accuracy and, therefore, validity and reliability of the data.

During the analysis phase of historical research, data are interpreted. The researcher will review the materials he or she has been so carefully collecting and evaluating. Data will be sorted and categorized into various topical themes (more fully described in Chapter 11). This *content analysis* strategy will allow the researcher to identify patterns within and between sources. Additional sources may be required in order to further explain these patterns as they arise. Any research questions that are proposed will be explained, supported, or refuted only insofar as the data can successfully argue such positions. If the data are faulty, so too will the analysis be weak and unconvincing.

The analysis and synthesis of the data allow the researcher to return to the original literature review and compare commentaries with the researcher's own observations. Thus, the analysis in historical research is deeply grounded in both the data and the background literature of the study. Exposition involves writing a narrative account of the resulting patterns, connections, and insights uncovered during the process of the research. These may extend well into the external and internal criticism you made of the data, as well as the patterns identified through content analysis.

Historiographers view history as a field of human action and action as the result of individual and collective reasoning (Roberts, 1996). This reasoning is understood as mediated through various circumstances and impacted by a variety of social, political, economic, ideological, and cultural influences. The actual task of historical researchers, then, is to reconstruct the reasons for past actions. They accomplish this by identifying evidence of past human thinking, which are established as valid and meaningful data. These, in turn, are interpreted with regard to how and why decisions and actions have occurred.

What Are Oral Histories?

From the historiographic approach offered in this chapter, historical documentary evidence is taken to include both written and oral sources. As suggested earlier, the term *written document* may include personal documents such as letters, journals, blog entries, diaries, poems, autobiographies, and even plays. However, novice researchers should be aware that historical researchers use a wide variety of data sources and combine numerous method-ologies. Perhaps because of the varied historiographic lines of action one might use when undertaking oral histories, Bogdan and Bilken (2003) catego-rize this strategy as a *case history* (discussed in Chapter 10).

The written sources of documentary evidence can indeed be varied. Even when examining the history of some local event, person, or phenomenon, a researcher will likely encounter a wide range of written documents. Whether the study focuses on a local event, an individual, or some larger phenomenon, the documents available to a researcher will influence his or her perspective. As Samuel (1975, p. xiii) has commented, "It is remarkable how much history has been written from the vantage point of those who have had the charge of run-ning—or attempting to run—other people's lives, and how little from the real life experience of people themselves." As a result, claims Samuel (1975), researchers often obtain only one perspective on the past—the perspective represented in official or residual documents of leaders, administrators, or other dignitaries.

Examples of selecting oral history as a strategy to overcome these deficien-cies are found in the works of Studs Terkel (2005, 2004, 2000, 1997). Terkel, who may be regarded as America's leading proponent of oral histories with ordinary people, has spent a lifetime interviewing a wide range of Americans, musing on fundamental questions about their lives, hopes, and dreams. In his various books, Terkel has discussed life with hard-hat construction workers, rock singers, death row inmates, and even Paul Tibbets, the pilot of the plane that dropped the bomb on Hiroshima.

Many historiographers realize that oral histories allow researchers to escape the deficiencies of residual and official presentations in documentary records (Samuel, 1991). This is especially true when researchers construct original oral histories and are capable of reconstructing moderately recent his-tories—those that are part of a link to a given living memory. This provides access to the past for, perhaps, as long 100 years.

But this research strategy required locating a population of individuals who possessed firsthand information on the subject area that the researcher desired to investigate. Thus, one of the major stumbling blocks for these researchers was proximity. Even if the researcher could not always locate indi-viduals with whom to create original oral histories, there were a number of archives that housed existing oral histories on a number of topics. However, a number of archives of oral histories across the country (and the globe), were not widely accessible; you had to travel to use these oral histories. In addition, in some cases, only copies (at the researcher's expense) of transcribed versions of certain oral histories were available.

Today, thanks to the Internet, there are literally hundred of oral history archives that provide online audio versions of many of their oral histories, as well as written transcripts that are immediately available for downloading or printing. Contemporary oral history archives offer material on a wide assortment of subjects. You can find material online on everything from jazz musicians to women in American history. One can even find an interview with Studs Terkel, the man who has literally interviewed America (Albin, 1999). There are numerous culturally related archives and an assortment of political and religious ones. The potential reach of oral histories today has expanded far beyond the possibilities of even ten years ago.

Oral histories certainly can provide considerable background and social texture to research. However, given the growing number and accessibility of these documents, they also provide an increased understanding and *lifeline* between the present and the past. Oral histories are extremely dynamic.

Written documents sometimes may dictate the structure of a research project. In other words, the inherent limitations of the documents are imposed on the research. If these documents have filtered through official agencies or organizations, they may reflect only front-stage information. Facts critical for understanding research questions or hypotheses may have been combed out of the written documents (see Chapter 8 on archival data). However, the real-life experiences and memories of people cannot so easily be omitted, edited, erased, shredded, or swept away.

Oral histories also offer access to the ordinary, unreported interests and tribulations of everyday life along with the better documented occurrence of floods, earthquakes, and other natural disasters (Burgess, 1991; Ritchie, 1995; Terkel, 2005; Tonkin, 1995; Yow, 2005). Oral histories allow researchers to investigate ordinary people as well as documents (e.g., Blythe, 1973; Harkell, 1978; Newby, 1977; Patai & Gluck, 1991; Terkel, 2000, 1997).

Single oral histories as well as series oral histories have been transcribed and published as both analyzed and unanalyzed documents (Reinharz, 1992). Collections of these published oral histories have been accumulated and stored in archives that are now easily accessible via the Internet. Often, these archived oral histories are biographical in nature or may share the autobiographical impressions of an individual regarding some segment of his or her life. For example, the Columbus (Ohio) Jewish Historical Society has a Web site (www.gcis.net/cjhs/oral.htm) (1999) that contains audio recordings of interviews with an assortment of elderly people from Columbus, Ohio, who tell of early life in the city.

Other sites offer narratives by people who had been born into slavery (*Born in Slavery: Slave Narratives from the Federal Writer's Project, 1936–1938*, located online at http://memory.loc.gov/ammem/snhtml/ snhome.html) or interviews with the entire small town of Kellytown in Charlottesville, Virginia, whose roots go back to the 1800s (see *Oral Histories of Kellytown*, located online at http://monticello.avenue.gen.va.us/Community/Neighborhoods/Kellytown/ History). In addition, many archives have Web sites that provide access to abstracts of oral histories and permit investigators to make their arrangements to use these audio and transcribed oral histories (for example, the University of Kentucky Oral History Program Web site located at www.uky.edu/Libraries/ Special/oral_history/FindAid.htm and the Hogan Jazz Archive, housed at Tulane University in New Orleans, located at www.tulane.edu/~1miller/ OralHistoryIntroduction.html).

Biography has always been an important aspect of social science research. This is because biographies draw people and groups out of obscurity; they repair damaged historical records and they give powerless people a voice. The use of oral histories and biographical data has also been popular among women in feminist literature (Hertz, 1997; Patai & Gluck, 1991; Reinharz, 1992; Ribbens & Edwards, 1998). For example, Griffith (1984, p. xix) details the usefulness of biographical data in understanding the women's movement in the United States:

> Initial efforts to record the lives of eminent American women were made in the 1890s, as the first generation of college-educated women sought to identify women of achievement in an earlier era. [These women] established archives for research and wrote biographies of colonial and contemporary women, like Abigail Adams and Susan B. Anthony. Organizations like the Daughters of the American Revolution related their members to the past that provided proud models of accomplishment. The second surge of biographies came with the renaissance of women's history in the late 1960s.

As suggested by Griffith's (1984), first-person accounts such as oral histories and biographies are necessary if a researcher is to understand the subjectivity of a social group that has been "muted, excised from history, [and] invisible in the official records of their culture" (Long, 1987, p. 5).

The historical method can be used to access information otherwise simply unavailable to researchers. It provides a means for answering questions and offering solutions that might otherwise go unmentioned and unnoticed. Using a historical method to answer questions or examine problems in one area also facilitates answers to questions and problems in other areas. For example, examination of correctional officers historiographically will necessarily draw in consideration of social reforms, role development, institutional development, questions about education, and numerous other areas. The strength of historical research rests on its applicability to diverse areas and the enormity of information and knowledge it can uncover.

TRYING IT OUT

Suggestion 1   In the library or in a local newspaper's morgue, locate the obituaries of 10 public figures (famous actors, political figures, etc.). Next, locate at least one newspaper story about their deaths.

Suggestion 2   Obtain an oral history from an elderly person in your family. Have him or her tell you about his or her life as a child, an adolescent, an adult, and now as an older adult. You might want to consult Chapter 4 before you begin. Record the oral history on audio- or videotape.

Suggestion 3   Create a brief historiography of your major department, college, or university. You should include both achieved documents (old college catalogs are a good place to start and are likely to be found in the library) and oral histories (talk with some of the older school administrators or faculty).

REFERENCES

Albin, K. (1999). Studs Terkel: An interview with the man who interviews America. Available online at www.grandtime.com/studs.html
Babbie, E. (2001). *The Practice of Social Research* (9th ed.). Belmont, CA: Wadsworth.
Babbie, E. (2002). *The Basics of Social Research* (2nd ed.). Belmont, CA: Wadsworth.
Bachman, R., & Schutt, R. K., (2003). *The Practice of Research in Criminology and Criminal Justice* (2nd ed.). Thousand Oaks, CA: Pine Forge Press.
Berg, B. L. (1999). *Policing Modern Society.* Boston: Butterworth/Heinemann.
Berg, B. L., & Budnick, K. J. (1986). Defeminization of women in law enforcement: A new twist in the traditional police personality. *Journal of Police Science and Administration 14,* 314–319.
Blythe, R. (1973). *Akenfield: Portrait of an English Village.* New York: Dell.
Bogdan, R., & Kopp-Bilken, S. (2003). *Research for Education* (4th ed.). Boston, MA: Allyn and Bacon.
Bogdan, R., & Biklen, S. K. (1992). *Qualitative Research for Education* (2nd ed.). Boston: Allyn and Bacon.
Brink, P. J., & Wood, M. J. (1989). *Advanced Design in Nursing Research.* Newbury Park, CA: Sage.
Burgess, R. G. (1991). Personal documents, oral sources and life histories. In R. G. Burgess (Ed.), *Field Research: A Sourcebook and Field Manual* (pp. 131–135). New York: Routledge.
Burns, N., & Grove, S. K., (2004). *The Practice of Nursing Research* (5th ed.). Philadelphia: Elsevie.
Burns, N., & Grove, S. K. (1993). *The Practice of Nursing Research* (2nd ed.). Philadelphia: W. B. Saunders.
Denzin, N. K. (1978). *The Research Act.* Chicago: Aldine.

Elman, R. A. (1996). Triangles and tribulations: The politics of Nazi symbols. *Journal of Homosexuality 30*(3), 1–11.

Encyclopaedia Britannica (Vol. 14, pp. 135–138). (1987). Chicago: University of Chicago Press.

Feinman, C. (1986). *Women in the Criminal Justice System.* New York: Praeger.

Fischer, J. F., & Nickell, J. (1992). The crop circle phenomenon: An investigative report. *Skeptical Inquirer 16*(2), 136–149.

Fitzgerald, J. D., & Cox, S. M. (2002). *Research Methods and Statistics in Criminal Justice* (3rd ed.). Belmont CA: Wadsworth.

Frankfort-Nachmias, C., & Nachmias, D. (1996). *Research Methods in the Social Sciences* (5th ed.). New York: St. Martin's Press.

Frankfort-Nachmias, C., & Nachmias, D. (2000). *Research Methods in the Social Sciences: With GSS Data Disk.* New York: WH Freeman.

Gilgun, J. F., Daly, K., & Handel, G. (Eds.). (1992). *Qualitative Methods in Family Research.* Newbury Park, CA: Sage.

Glass, L. (1989). Historical research. In P. J. Brink & M. J. Wood (Eds.), *Advanced Design in Nursing Research.* Newbury Park, CA: Sage.

Griffith, E. (1984). *In Her Own Right: The Life of Elizabeth Cady Stanton.* New York: Oxford University Press.

Hamilton, D. B. (1993). The idea of history and the history of ideas. *Image: Journal of Nursing Scholarship 25*, 45–48.

Hamilton, M. (1924). *The Policewoman: Her Service and Ideas.* New York: Arno Press and the New York Times (Reprinted 1971).

Harkell, G. (1978). The migration of mining families to the Kent coalfield between the wars. *Oral History 6*, 98–113.

Hertz, R. (1997). *Reflexivity and Voice.* Thousand Oaks, CA: Sage.

Hitler diaries trial stirs judge to disbelief and ire. (1985, January 6). *New York Times,* p. A14.

Jaroff, L. (1993, July 5). Phony *ark*aeology: In a pseudo documentary, CBS falls victim to a hoaxer. *Time,* 51.

Johnson, B., & Christensen, L. B. (2003). *Educational Research: Quantitative, Qualitative, and Mixed Approaches, Research Edition* (2nd ed.). Boston: Allyn and Bacon.

Karr, B. (2002). Hollywood fertilizes profits with crop circles. *Skeptical Briefs Newsletter.* Committee for the Scientific Investigation of Claims of the Paranormal, Amherst, NY. Available online at www.csicop.org/list/listarchive/msg00350.html.

Leedy, P. D. (1999). *Practical Research: Planning and Design* (6th ed.). Englewood Cliffs, NJ: Prentice Hall.

Leedy, P. D., & Ormrod, J. E. (2001). *Practical Research* (7th ed.). Upper Saddle River, NJ: Merrill/ Prentice Hall.

Leedy, P., & Ormrod, J. E (2005). *Practical Research: Planning and Design* (8th ed.). Upper Saddle River, NJ: Saddlebrook: Prentice Hall.

LoBiondo-Wood, G., & Haber, J. (2002). *Nursing Research: Methods, Critical Appraisal and Utilization.* St. Louis, MO: Mosby.

Long, J. (1987). *Telling women's lives: The new sociobiography.* Paper presented at the annual meeting of the American Sociological Association, Chicago.

Lusk, B. (1997a). Professional classification of American nurses, 1910–1930. *Western Journal of Nursing Research 7*, 448–467.

Lusk, B. (1997b). Historical methodology for nursing research. *Image, Journal of Nursing Scholarship 29*(4), 355–359.

Marshall, C., & Rossman, G. B. (1999). *Designing Qualitative Research* (3rd ed.). Thousand Oaks, CA: Sage.

Martell, L. K. (2001). Maternity care during the post–World War II baby boom: The experience of general duty nurses. In Roberta J. Peteva (Ed.), *A Cross Section of Nursing Research*. Los Angeles: Pyrczak Publishing.

Matejski, M. (1986). Historical research: The method. In P. Munhall & C. J. Oiler (Eds.), *Nursing Research: A Qualitative Perspective* (pp. 175–193). Norwalk, CT: Appleton-Century-Crofts.

McDowell, W. H.(2002). *Historical Research: A Guide for Writers of Dissertations, Theses, Articles, and Books*. Boston: Longman.

Neuman, W. L. (2003). Social Research Methods: Qualitative and Quantitative Approaches. Boston: Allyn & Bacon.

Newby, H. (1977). *The Deferential Worker*. London: Allen Lane.

Nickell, J. (1996). Lenengood's crop-circle plant research. Committee for the Scientific Investigation of Claims of the Paranormal, Amherst, NY. Available online at www.csicop.org/sb/9606/crop_circle.html

Notter, L. (1972). The case for historical research in nursing. *Nursing Research 21*, 483.

Patai, D., & Gluck, S. B. (1991). *Women's Worlds: The Feminist Practice of Oral History*. New York: Routledge.

Reinharz, S. (1992). *Feminist Methods in Social Research*. New York: Oxford University Press.

Ribbens, J., & Edwards, R. (1998). *Feminist Dilemmas in Qualitative Research*. Thousand Oaks, CA: Sage.

Ritchie, D. A. (1995). *Doing Oral History* (Twayne's Oral History, No. 15). Toronto, Canada: Twayne Publishing.

Roberts, G. (1996). Narrative history as a way of life. *Journal of Contemporary History 31*, 221–228.

Rosnow, R. L., & Rosenthal, R. (2002). *Beginning Behavioral Research*. Upper Saddle River, NJ: Prentice Hall.

Salkind, N. J. (2003). *Exploring Research* (5th ed.). Upper Saddle River, NJ: Prentice Hall.

Salkind, N. J. (1996). *Exploring Research* (4th ed.). Englewood Cliffs, NJ: Prentice Hall.

Samuel, R. (1975). *Village Life and Labour*. London: Routledge and Kegan Paul.

Samuel, R. (1991). Local history and oral history. In R. G. Burgess (Ed.), *Field Research: A Sourcebook and Field Manual* (pp. 136–145). New York: Routledge.

Sarnecky, M. T. (1990). Historiography: A legitimate research methodology for nursing. *Advances in Nursing Science 12*(4), 1–10.

Shaughnessy, J. J., & Zechmeister, E. B. (1999). *Research Methods in Psychology* (4th ed.). New York: McGraw-Hill.

Talney, R. (1969). Women in law enforcement: An expanded role. *Police 14*, 49–51.

Taylor, R. B. (1994). *Research Methods in Criminal Justice*. New York: McGraw-Hill.

Taylor, S. J., & Bogdan, R. (1998). *Introduction to Qualitative Research Methods* (3rd ed.). New York: John Wiley & Sons.

Terkel, S. (2005). *American Dreams: Lost and Found*. New York: The New Press.

Terkel, S. (2004). *Hope Dies Last*. New York: The New Press.

Terkel, S. (2000). *Hard Times*. New York: The New Press.

Terkel, S. (1997). *Working*. New York: The New Press.

Time, V. M. (1999). *Shakespeare's Criminals: Criminology, Fiction, and Drama*. Westport, CT: Greenwood.

Tonkin, E. (1995). *Narrating Our Pasts: The Social Construction of Oral History.* Cambridge, England: Cambridge University Press.

Two charged in Hamburg in "Hitler diary" fraud. (1984, March 23). *New York Times,* p. A4.

Wells, H. G. (1895). *The Time Machine* (Rev. ed., 1977). Edited by F. D. McConnell. New York: Oxford University Press.

Wilson, H. S. (1989). *Nursing Research* (2nd ed.). Reading, MA: Addison-Wesley.

Yow, V. R. (2005). *Recording Oral History: A Guide for the Humanities and Social Sciences* (2nd ed.). New York: Rowman & Littlefield.

Chapter 10

Case Studies

The Nature of Case Studies

The case study method is defined and understood in various ways. Some sources define the case study method as an attempt to systematically investigate an event or a set of related events with the specific aim of describing and explaining this phenomenon (see, e.g., Bromley, 1990). Bogdan and Biklen (2003, p. 54) define case study as "a detailed examination of one setting, or a single subject, a single depository of documents, or one particular event (see also Gomm, Hammersley, & Foster, 2000; Yin, 2003). Hagan (2006, p. 240) simply defines the case study method as "in-depth, qualitative studies of one or a few illustrative cases." Previous editions of my own book (see Berg, 2004) define case study as a method involving systematically gathering enough information about a particular person, social setting, event, or group to permit the researcher to effectively understand how the subject operates or functions. Taken together, these various definitions suggest that case study is an approach capable of examining simple or complex phenomenon, with units of analysis varying from single individuals to large corporations and businesses; it entails using a variety of lines of action in its data-gathering segments, and can meaningfully make use of and contribute to the application of theory (Yin, 2003).

Given the scope of the method, case studies can be rather pointed in their focus or approach a broad view of life and society. For example, an investigator may confine his or her examination to a single aspect of an individual's life such as studying a medical student's actions and behaviors in medical school. Or the investigator might attempt to assess the social life of an individual and his or her entire background, experiences, roles, and motivations that affect his or her behavior in society. Extremely rich, detailed, and in-depth information characterize the type of information gathered in a case study. In contrast, the often extensive large-scale survey research data may seem somewhat superficial in nature (Champion, 2006).

Many qualitative investigators use the case study approach as a guide to their research. By concentrating on a single phenomenon, individual, community, or institution, the researcher aims to uncover the manifest interaction of significant factors characteristic of this phenomenon, individual, community, or institution. But, in addition, the researcher is able to capture various nuances, patterns, and more latent elements that other research approaches might overlook. The case study method tends to focus on holistic description and explanation; and, as a general statement, any phenomenon can be studied by case study methods (Gall, Borg, & Gall, 1995; 1998).

The case study method is not a new style of data gathering and analytic technique. The fields of medicine and psychology, for example, by their very nature, require physicians and psychologists to examine patients case by case. Case studies are commonly used in business, information systems, and law curricula to help students bridge the gap between foundational studies and practice. The use of diaries and biographies, a popular method among some feminist and other social scientists, approaches the case study method, as does ethnobiography (Hesse-Biber & Yaiser, 2004; Reinharz, 1992). In education, case studies abound and include studies of unique people and programs as well as special programming (Herreid, 2005; McLeod, 1994; Stake, 1995). In fact, case studies by certain social scientists represent classical research efforts in sociology and criminology. Consider, for example, Edward Sutherland's (1937) *The Professional Thief;* Clifford R. Shaw's (1930) *The Jack Roller;* Robert Bogdan's (1974) lengthy life history/autobiography, *Being Different: The Autobiography of Jane Fry;* and Rettig, Torres, and Garrett's (1977) *Manny: A Criminal Addict's Story.*

Theory and Case Studies

Yin (2003) indicates that there has been a revived interest in the role of theory and case studies. Interestingly, a cursory review of the literature suggests that a vigorous renewal of this interest appears to occur in the areas of business, marketing, and information systems, as well as in the social sciences (see, e.g., Alexander & Bennett, 2005; Fernandez, 2005; Woodside & Wilson, 2003). Typically, although not exclusively, case study methods are found in the literature associated with theory building rather than theory testing (Dyer & Wilkins, 1991, Woodside & Wilson, 2004), but some sources suggest the utility of case study strategies in theory testing or in combining both theory development and testing (Alexander & Bennett, 2005; Woodside & Wilson, 2003).

How does the case study method inform theory? Case studies can provide a kind of deep understanding of phenomenon, events, people, or organizations, similar to Geertz's (1973) notion of "thick description." In essence, case studies open the door to the "sensemaking" processes created and used by individuals involved in the phenomenon, event, group, or organization under study (Weick, 1995). Sensemaking is the manner by which people, groups, and organizations make sense of stimuli with which they are confronted how they frame what they see and hear, how they perceive and interpret this information, and how they interpret their own actions and go about solving problems and interacting with others.

Yin (2003, pp. 4–5) tends to endorse a theory-before-research model (see Chapter 2) and indicates that theory development prior to the collection of case study data can be important for the following reasons:

- It can assist selecting the cases to be studied and whether to use a single-case or multiple-case design.
- It helps the researcher specify what is being explored when undertaking exploratory case studies.
- It aids in defining a complete and appropriate description when undertaking descriptive case studies.
- It can stimulate rival theories when undertaking explanatory cases studies.
- It can support generalizations the researcher may seek to make to other cases.

Others, however, argue that case studies can be used to generate theory (grounded theory) and follow a pattern similar to theory after research (see Chapter 2). Fernandez (2005, p. 47), cites Eisenhardt (1989, pp. 546–547), for instance, arguing that using case data to build grounded theory has three major strengths:

1. Theory building from case studies is likely to produce theory; this is so because "creative insight often arises from juxtaposition of contradictory or paradoxical evidence" (p. 546). The process of reconciling these accounts using the constant comparative method forces the analyst to a new gestalt, unfreezing thinking and producing "theory with less research bias then theory built from incremental studies or armchair, axiomatic deduction" (p. 546).
2. The emergent theory "is likely to be testable with constructs that can be readily measured and hypotheses that can be proven false" (p. 547). Because of the close connection between theory and data,

it is likely that the theory can be further tested and expanded by subsequent studies.

3. The "resultant theory is likely to be empirically valid" (p. 547). This is so because a level of validation is performed implicitly by constant comparison, questioning the data from the start of the process. "This closeness can lead to an intimate sense of things ... that often produces theory which closely mirrors reality" (p. 547).

In other words, theory can be uncovered and informed as a consequence of the data collection and interpretations of this data made throughout the development of the case study—hence, a grounded theory case study. What might this process look like? The researcher would start with some sort of research idea, then develop a plan—including whether to use a single- or multiple-case approach—identify the location of the study (in what group or organization), determine how access is to be obtained, and consider what data-collection strategies to use. Once access is obtained, data must be collected; as the data is collected, the researcher constantly considers what is being unearthed, making comparisons between information (data) collected and assessments with other researchers (to assure unbiased interpretations and analysis) and the literature. The investigator then must reflect on the information collected and the problem(s) initially addressed to deliberate over what the findings mean and what their implications may be. Finally, the researcher can offer some theoretical implications for whatever problems or issues were being explored, described, or explained in the study. Figure 10.1 offers a visualization of this model of developing grounded theory through the case study method.

The Individual Case Study

As in any other research situation, one must determine how broad an area of social life will be covered. In most research this decision is largely dictated by the research question and the nature of the research problem under investigation. When examining an individual case study, a similar type of assessment must be undertaken. In some instances, a single lengthy interview may yield sufficient information to produce answers to the research question(s). In other circumstances, several interviews may be necessary, and these may require supplementation by field notes during direct observation, copies of journal or diary entries from the subject, or other forms of documentation.

Several reasons may make it necessary for a broader, more sweeping investigation. First, the research may itself focus on a broad area such as the subject's relationships in a particular group, necessitating that the group

Figure 10.1 Developing Grounded Theory Through the Case Study Method

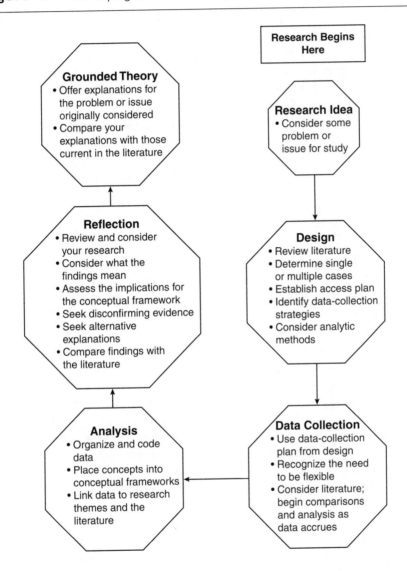

also be examined. It would be unwise, for example, to examine various aspects of changes in the quality of life of hemodialysis patients without also examining how family members perceive changes occurring in the family group itself.

A second reason for broadening a case study is the realization that all the aspects of an individual's social life are interconnected and often one of them cannot be adequately understood without consideration of the others.

The Use of Interview Data

The particular focus of a study might be a woman's adjustment to becoming "the boss" in some predominantly male corporate organization. In order to fully understand this adjustment, it would be helpful to learn how she adjusts to changes in other situations, perhaps adjustments in her home or among friends or in social organizations. These may be accomplished using various standard techniques of interviewing to collect data.

Of these areas of additional study, perhaps the most generally rewarding to the subject is found to be her home and family background. The physical aspects of the home—its size, its neatness or disorder, its furnishings, indications of intellectual, athletic, or aesthetic interests such as books, pictures, records, sporting equipment, and the like—can all be of value in this case study. Even evidence of social support from family members should be observed and included in the research. Obviously, to understand the subject's adjustments to the work role, the researcher must observe the subject in the work site and speak with various coworkers. It should be likewise obvious that to understand the subject's role in her family, several visits to the home will be necessary. Also it may be fruitful to speak with (interview) various family members (husband, children, or other relatives in the home) who can provide various pieces of background information and insights.

Unless an individual is exceptionally isolated, he or she is likely to have some role in the neighborhood community. Some people enjoy an elevated position of respect and position in their business, social, or political life. Others may hold no particularly high level of respect but function as participants in various activities. Still others may actually be social outcasts. This type of information could be very useful for understanding how a woman business executive adjusts to her new position in the company. Visits to neighbors, various social organizations to which the subject may be a member, conversations with local tradespersons, and the subject's clergy person all may supply useful information.

Yin (1998) identifies five researcher skills associated with conducting good case studies. To a large extent, these are similar and an extension to three skills offered by Merriam (2001). The first is an *inquiring mind* and the willingness to ask questions before, during, and after data are collected, as well as to constantly challenge oneself about why something appears to have happened or be happening. The second is the ability of the investigator to *listen*, to include *observation* and *sensing* in general, and to assimilate large amounts of new information without bias. Third is *adaptability* and *flexibility* to handle unanticipated events and to change data-collection strategies if they do not seem to be functioning effectively and to use alternative sources of data that may be more fruitful. Fourth is a thorough *understanding of the issues* being studied in order not merely to record data but to interpret and react to these data once collected. The researcher must be able to determine, for example, if different sources of data are adequate or if additional sources are required. The fifth quality is *unbiased interpretation of the data*. Yin suggests that a good test for bias is the degree to which the researcher is open to contradictory findings. He recommends reporting preliminary findings to colleagues, who may offer alternative explanations that would require further investigation. This notion is similar to a researcher taking an intellectual risk by providing sufficient information for others to replicate the research and potentially to find contradictory results.

Throughout the preceding paragraphs, the chief suggestions for information (data) gathering has been the use of interviews and observation. As implied earlier, however, it is often also useful to supplement this information with various documentary sources. You should, therefore, be familiar with the possible use of records concerning the life course of the subject. These may include birth, marriage, divorce, property ownership, and educational records of the subject. They may additionally include an assortment of other more or less official documents such as police actions, court records, evaluations of work records, and so forth. All of these official documents are potentially valuable sources of information in a case study.

The Use of Personal Documents

The general use of personal documents is discussed in Chapter 8 of this book. As suggested there, personal documents involve any written record created by the subject that concerned his or her experiences. The common types of documents classified under this label include autobiographies, diaries and journals, letters, and memos written by a subject in a research investigation. In addition, and given the extent to which people today use photographic and video equipment, these items may also serve as categories of personal documents.

Autobiographical documents include a considerable variety of written material. They may be published or unpublished documents, cover an entire life span, or focus on only a specific period in a subject's life or even a single event. Even a written confession to a crime may be seen by some researchers as a type of autobiographical document.

Diaries and journals also may arise in a number of varieties. A diary may be kept with no purpose in mind beyond the writer's personal desire to maintain a record of daily events. It may be maintained in order to provide some therapeutic release; or as a kind of log and chronological listing of daily events during new experiences such as an internship. Or a diary or journal may be created at the specific request of a researcher as a contribution to some study. In the latter case, one may consider the material in a solicited document (see Chapter 8).

Letters provide an intriguing view into the life of the author. Typically, letters are not created by the writer with the intention of having them used by a researcher. As a result, they frequently reflect the inner worlds of the writer. They may record the writer's views, values, attitudes, and beliefs about a wide variety of subjects. Or they may describe the writer's deepest thoughts about some specific event or situation about which they report. Historians have long seen the value of letters to document events during past time periods. Letters written by military figures and politicians, for example, may allow researchers to better understand how and why certain battles have been fought. Letters written by criminals such as serial killers and bombers provide insight into how the culprit thinks and potential explanations for their actions. Letters are simply replete with potentially useful information.

For example, Elizabeth Roberson (1998) explored the letters of Eli Landers, a young Confederate soldier (see also Wasta & Lott, 2002). Landers wrote letters from the battlefield to his mother and sister that express his emotional views of the war, his personal losses, as well as specific details about the Civil War.

The use of memoranda has become commonplace in virtually all work settings. Memos may contain strictly work-related information or casual insider jokes and communications. They may reflect the tone and atmosphere of a work setting as well as the potential level of anxiety, stress, and morale of the writer. Moreover, they may even show the research aspects of the workplace culture or work folkways. Also, they may contain information relevant to understanding the general organizational communications network used in the setting, the leadership hierarchy, various roles present in the setting, and other structural elements.

Photographic and video equipment has become so inexpensive that many people now regularly record their lives and the lives of their family members in this manner. It becomes important, therefore, for researchers to consider how these items may illustrate various aspects of the subject's life and relationships. This may involve stepping back and examining the entire photograph in terms of what it shows in general; it may include an examination of the expressions of people shown in the picture; it could involve consideration of where the picture or video was taken or recorded such as on a vacation, in the home, or at a party; or it may involve determination of the reason the photograph or video was created—as a simple family record to commemorate some situation, to have as a keepsake, to document some event or situation, and so forth.

The literal value of personal documents as research data is frequently underestimated in contemporary research texts and courses. Although such documents are certainly extremely subjective in their nature, these data should not be viewed as a negative or in this case even as some sort of limitation or shortcoming. It is the very fact that these documents do reflect the subjective views and perceptions of their creators that makes them useful as data in a case study. It is precisely through this subjectivity that these documents provide information and insight about the subject that might not be captured through some other more pedestrian data-collection technique.

Intrinsic, Instrumental, and Collective Case Studies

Stake (1994, 1995) suggests that researchers have different purposes for studying cases. He suggests that case studies can be classified into three different types: *intrinsic, instrumental,* and *collective.*

Intrinsic case studies are undertaken when a researcher wants to better understand a particular case. It is not undertaken primarily because it represents other cases or because it illustrates some particular trait, characteristic, or problem. Rather, it is because of its uniqueness or ordinariness that a case becomes interesting (Creswell, 1998; Stake, 1994, 2000). The role of the researcher is not to understand or test abstract theory or to develop new or grounded theoretical explanations; instead, the intention is to better understand intrinsic aspects of the particular child, patient, criminal, group, organization, or whatever the case may be.

Instrumental case studies provide insights into an issue or refine a theoretical explanation, making it more generalizable (Creswell, 2002; Stake, 1994). In these situations, the case actually becomes of secondary importance. It serves only a supportive role, a background against which the actual research interests will play out. Instrumental case studies often are investigated in depth, and all aspects and activities are detailed but not simply to elaborate the case per se. Instead, the intention is to help the researcher better understand some external theoretical question, issue, or problem. Instrumental case studies may or may not be viewed as typical of other cases. However, the choice of a particular case for study is made because the investigator believes that his or her understanding about some other research interest will be advanced.

Stake (1994, 2000) also points out that because researchers often have multiple interests, there is no solid line drawn between intrinsic and instrumental studies. In fact, a kind of "zone of combined purpose separates them" (Stake, 1994, p. 237).

Collective case studies (Stake 1994, 2000) are also known as multiple-case studies, cross-case studies, comparative case studies, and contrasting case studies (Merriam, 2001). Thus, collective case studies involve extensive study of several instrumental cases, intended to allow better understanding, insight, or perhaps improved ability to theorize about a broader context. Yin (2003) argues that multiple cases may be selected in order to try replicating insights found in individual cases or to represent contrasting situations. Regardless of one's purpose, Yin (2003, p. 46) indicates that multiple-case studies are frequently "considered more compelling, and the overall study is therefore regarded as more robust."

Case Study Design Types

There are several appropriate designs for case studies according to Yin (1994, 2003) and Winston (1997): exploratory, explanatory, and descriptive. These three approaches consist of either single- or multiple-case studies in which the cases studied are actual replications, not sampled cases. Each approach is discussed next.

Exploratory Case Studies

When conducting exploratory case studies, fieldwork and data collection may be undertaken before defining a research question. This type of study may be seen as a prelude to a large social scientific study. Nonetheless, the study must have some type of organizational framework that has been designed prior to beginning the research. The sort of exploratory study may be useful as a pilot study, for example, when planning a larger, more comprehensive investigation.

Explanatory Case Studies

Explanatory case studies are useful when conducting causal studies. Particularly in complex studies of organizations or communities, one might desire to employ multivariate cases to examine a plurality of influences. This might be accomplished using a pattern-matching technique suggested by Yin and Moore (1988). *Pattern-matching* is a situation in which several pieces of information from the same case may be related to some theoretical proposition.

Descriptive Case Studies

Descriptive case explorations require that the investigator present a descriptive theory, which establishes the overall framework for the investigator to follow throughout the study. What is implied by this approach is the formation and identification of a viable theoretical orientation before enunciating research questions. The investigator must also determine before beginning the research exactly what the unit of analysis in the study will be.

In creating formal designs for case-study investigations, Yin (1994, p. 20) recommends five component elements:

- Study questions
- Study propositions (if any are being used) or theoretical framework
- Identification of the unit(s) of analysis
- The logical linking of the data to the propositions (or theory)
- The criteria for interpreting the findings

A study's *questions* are generally directed toward *how* and *why* considerations, and their articulation and definition are the first task of the researcher. Sometimes, the study's *propositions* derive from these how and why questions and assist in developing a theoretical focus. Not all studies will have propositions. An exploratory study, rather than having propositions, may have a stated purpose or criteria that will provide guidance and a kind of operating framework for the case study to follow. The *unit of analysis* defines what the case study is focusing on (what the case is), such as an individual, a group, an organization, a city, and so forth. *Linkages between the data and the propositions* (or theory) and the *criteria for interpreting the findings,* according to Yin (1994), typically are the least developed aspects of case studies.

Jason Jensen and Robert Rodgers (2001, pp. 237–239) offer a typology of types of case studies:

1. *Snapshot case studies.* Detailed, objective studies of one research entity at one point in time. Hypothesis testing by comparing patterns across subentities (e.g., comparing departments within the case study agency).
2. *Longitudinal case studies.* Quantitative and/or qualitative studies of one research entity at multiple time points.
3. *Pre–post case studies.* Studies of one research entity at two time points separated by a critical event. A critical event is one that on the basis of a theory under study would be expected to impact case observations significantly.

4. *Patchwork case studies.* A set of multiple case studies of the same research entity, using snapshot, longitudinal, and/or pre–post designs. This multi-design approach is intended to provide a more holistic view of the dynamics of the research subject.

5. *Comparative case studies.* A set of multiple case studies of multiple research entities for the purpose of cross-unit comparison. Both qualitative and quantitative comparisons are generally made.

Unfortunately, researchers do not always have good theories to work with in a given situation, particularly when exploring cutting-edge issues. In these situations, a logic model, or what Patton (2001) calls a "theory of action," may be developed. This *theory of action* will define how the researcher expects an intervention, event, or process to take a case from one situation to the next. In effect, this theory of action will define the issues to be examined during the analysis, thereby providing linkages among the research question(s), propositions, and analytic criteria.

The Scientific Benefit of Case Studies

The scientific benefit of the case study method lies in its ability to open the way for discoveries (Shaughnessy & Zechmeister, 1999). It can easily serve as the breeding ground for insights and even hypotheses that may be pursued in subsequent studies. However, whenever one considers the scientific value of case studies, two points should be addressed. First, does this procedure involve too many subjective decisions made by the investigator to offer genuinely objective results? Second, does this method offer information that can be seen as useful beyond the individual case? In other words, can findings be generalized? Let us consider each of these questions separately.

Objectivity and the Case Method

Objectivity is a somewhat elusive term. For some researchers it involves the creation of analytic strategies in an almost sterile environment. Often, qualitative research of any type is viewed as suspect when questions of objectivity are asked. However, objectivity is actually closely linked with reproducibility (replication). The question is not simply whether or not an individual researcher has made some subjective decision regarding how the researcher should progress or how the study is designed. These types of considerations are regularly undertaken by all who undertake social scientific research—whether quantitatively or qualitatively oriented.

When a quantitative methodologist identifies which level of statistical acceptability he or she will use for some statistical measure, it is often a subjective decision. For example, let's say the researcher sets the level at .05. Does that alter the findings when it is statistically significant at the .05 level, but not at the .001 level? Thus, objectivity apparently lies someplace other than in the kinds of decisions made by a researcher regarding various aspects of the research strategy.

For many researchers, objectivity rests on the ability of an investigator to articulate what the procedures are so that others can repeat the research if they so choose. It also has the effect of placing the researcher's professional ego on the line. It is akin to saying, "Here is how I did my research, and here are my results. If any reader has questions or challenges, go out and repeat the study to see what you find." From this perspective, case studies, like any other research procedure, require that the investigator clearly articulate what areas have been investigated and through what means. If someone has doubts about the findings, he or she is free to replicate the research with a similar case subject.

If the investigator's findings and analysis were correct, subsequent research will corroborate this. If the research produced from a case study is faulty, in error, or inaccurate, this too will be shown by subsequent research. As in any scientific research, findings from a single study are seldom accepted immediately without question and additional research investigations. In this light, case methods are as objective as any other data-collection and analysis strategies used by social scientists.

Generalizability

The second concern addresses the question of generalizability. For many, the question is not even necessary to ask. This is because there is clearly a scientific value to gain from investigating some single category of individual, group, or event simply to gain an understanding of that individual, group, or event. For those with a more positivist orientation who have concern about generalizing to similar types of individuals, groups, or events, case methods are still useful and to some extent generalizable.

When case studies are properly undertaken, they should not only fit the specific individual, group, or event studied but also generally provide understanding about similar individuals, groups, and events. This is not to say that an explanation for why one gang member is involved in drug dealing immediately informs us about why *all* drug-dealing gang members are also involved in this activity. It does, however, suggest an explanation for why some other gang members are likely to be involved in these behaviors. The logic behind this has to do with the fact that few human behaviors are unique, idiosyncratic, and spontaneous. In fact, if this were the case, the attempt to undertake any type of survey research on an aggregate group would be useless. In short, if we accept the notion that human behavior is predictable—a necessary assumption for all behavior science research—then it is a simple jump to accept that case studies have scientific value. "It is the task of the researcher to determine what it is he or she is studying; that is, of what is this a case?" (Bogdan & Biklen, 1992, p. 66).

Case Studies of Organizations

Case studies of organizations may be defined as the systematic gathering of enough information about a particular organization to allow the investigator insight into the life of that organization. This type of study might be fairly general in its scope, offering approximately equal weight to every aspect of the organization. For instance, you might conduct an organizational case study on a police department. During this investigation you may examine subunits such as the juvenile division, traffic division, criminal investigations, homicide, and so forth. The results will be a thorough understanding about how the agency operates and how each subunit fits together and serves the overall objectives of the organization. For instance, Barbara French and Jerry Stewart (2001) examined how contemporary law enforcement agencies engage in new organizational practices that focus on empowering line officers, encouraging teamwork, and creating an atmosphere conducive for participative management.

On the other hand, you may specialize, during an organizational case study, by placing particular emphasis on a specific area or situation occurring in the organization. For example, Susan Slick (2002) explored how a learning community operated among a cohort of graduate students in education attending a special pilot master's degree program at the University of Wisconsin–Stevens Point campus. This learning community fostered group goals and values for working and learning collaboratively.

There are a number of reasons that a particular organization may be selected for a case study. For example, a researcher may undertake a case study of an organization to illustrate the way certain administrative systems operate in certain types of organizations. Or the researcher may be interested in accessing how decisions are made in certain types of organizations or even how communications networks operate. In fact, the case method is an extremely useful technique for researching relationships, behaviors, attitudes, motivations, and stressors in organizational settings.

Case Studies of Communities

A *community* can be defined as some geographically delineated unit within a larger society. Such a community is small enough to permit considerable cultural (or subcultural) homogeneity, diffuse interactions and relationships between members, and to produce a social identification by its members. The literal application of this term *community* is somewhat fluid. However, it does not actually include an entire nation, a state, or even a large city. It would, however, include a particular neighborhood within a city such as a Chinatown, a Little Italy, or the Jewish section, or even an enclave of Amish farmers all residing within a four- or five-mile radius.

A case study of a community may, however, address a larger entity by placing its focus on a smaller unit of analysis, perhaps a group or social institution such as the Catholic church. Linkogle (1998), for example, undertook a study of the role of popular religion in social transformation in Nicaragua from 1979 to 1998. He examined some general issues around popular religion in Latin America and its relationship to the practice and pronouncements of the Catholic church. Linkogle's primary focus was how popular religious practices may impact and shape gender and political and religious identities.

Case studies of communities can be defined as the systematic gathering of enough information about a particular community to provide the investigator with understanding and awareness of what things go on in that community; why and how these things occur; who among the community members take part in these activities and behaviors, and what social forces may bind together members of this community. As with other variations of case studies, community case studies may be very general in their focus, offering approximately equal weight in all of the various aspects of community life. Or community case studies may specifically focus on some particular aspect of the community or even some phenomenon that occurs within that community. For example, you may consider a community in general, such as examining an Amish farming community. In such an investigation, you may be interested in the various daily routines of members as well as their social interactions. You might consider any political ideologies that predominate among members of the community and how these affect behaviors among both insiders and outsiders, and so forth. On the other hand, you may be interested in a particular phenomenon occurring within the Amish community. For instance, you may be interested in how social control mechanisms operate in the community. Will the community handle an errant youth who may have shoplifted some petty item such as a magazine, or will the outside, non-Amish community's laws apply? Of course, if you investigate the latter phenomenon, to remain a community case study, this exploration would have to be undertaken against the backdrop of the life of the community. Although there are other styles of research that might explore a particular question in isolation from the background of the community, these would not be accurately called case studies.

Robert and Helen Lynd's study of Middletown, first published in 1929, stands as a classic example of how community case studies operate. This research was among the earliest systematic studies of an American community where the purpose was primarily to develop a scientific understanding of community life.

Data Collection for Community Case Studies

The various data-collection strategies used in community case studies are, for the most part, those already discussed in this chapter. However, in addition, community case studies frequently make use of maps. These may include existing maps used for various human ecological purposes, as well as maps created by the researcher in order to indicate physical and social proximity of items and events occurring in the community.

Human ecological concerns have long been important foci in community case studies. Human ecology is concerned with the interrelationships among people in their spatial setting and physical environment. An ecological focus might consider how various physical environmental elements shape the lives of people in a community or the life of the community itself. Do rivers block a community's expansion? Are railroad tracks or major highways located close enough to encourage industry in a community? Has a coal mine played out and closed down, sending hundreds of community members to unemployment, and so forth? Maps are frequently the basic tool necessary for a consideration of such ecological concerns in a community case study.

Community Groups and Interests

In a manner similar to how one might break down a community into its constituent physical parts, its human members too can be divided into groups. These groups may be classified in a number of different ways. For example, there may be different ethnic groups all residing in the same community. Although some ethnic groups are sufficiently large enough and homogeneously located to constitute a community in themselves, this is not always the case. In many communities several distinct ethnic groups reside in both physical and social proximity but manage to retain their own individual ethnic identity. In some cases, the ethnic groups may retain certain of their distinctive ethnic features but merge or assimilate into their surrounding social life.

In such a case, one would need to consider this ethnic group both as a thing apart from the community, as well as an element of the larger community.

The study of any group in a community begins much as you would begin any research study, namely, in the library (see Chapter 2). The logical place to begin considering community groups is in published sources. In addition, community case studies may include an examination of census data, local histories, newspaper accounts of group activities and events, any official records of various organizations related to the group or community, and so on. As with other variations of case studies, interviews may provide useful information or even historical explanations for various groups or the presence of certain conditions in the community. Researchers even use fairly traditional strategies of observation to learn about groups in a community. Observations may include consideration of the types of homes and housing in the community, places used for leisure or amusement, schools and religious institutions in the community, and so forth.

Interest groups are another way you might divide up the inhabitants of a community. In this case, you may include street gangs, various social clubs or organizations in the community (Boy and Girl Scouts, YMCAs, Little Leagues, Bowling Leagues, and so forth), lodges and fraternal organizations, political clubs, business associations, and the like. Membership in many of these interest groups is rather ephemeral and transient. Even the more stable of interest groups are likely to lack the continuity of ethnic or religious groups. Direct observation of these interest groups, along with interviews with members, is probably the best general method for studying these kinds of groups.

Social classes may also be viewed as a type of grouping that allows the researcher to divide up a community. Although you might argue about what division labels to actually use as categories of class, some categorical labeling schema can be conceived. In keeping with the community case study mode, you could consider how members of each social class operate in the community and how these categories fit together to form the entire community.

In essence, there are numerous ways of grouping together people of a community for the purpose of systematically exploring life in that community. Community case studies are large-scale undertakings. They may be time-consuming and expensive if they are to be comprehensive. The community is a sufficiently large segment of society that it permits a wide and diverse array of social phenomena to occur and to be observed. Although not as popular in recent years as they were during the 1930s and 1960s, especially in areas of urban sociology and urban ecology, community case studies continue to offer an important and valuable means to understanding communities and community members.

TRYING IT OUT

Suggestion 1 Using available archival information located in your school's library and various administrative offices, conduct an organizational case study of your college or university. This will involve using at least some historical tracings (see Chapter 9).

Suggestion 2 Select an adult relative and conduct a modified case study. For this project, examine only the roles and behaviors of the individual during some aspect of his or her life. This may be during school activities, work life, home life, and so forth. Limit the time on this project to one week of data collection. Remember, this is simply practice, not actual research.

REFERENCES

Alexander, G. L., & Bennett, A. (2005). *Case Studies and Theory Development in the Social Sciences.* Cambridge, MA: MIT Press.

Berg, B. (2004). *Qualitative Research Methods for the Social Sciences* (5th ed.). Boston: Allyn and Bacon.

Bogdan, R. C., & Biklen, S. K. (2003). *Qualitative Research for Education* (4th ed.). Boston: Allyn and Bacon.

Bogdan, R. (1974). *Being Different: The Autobiography of Jane Fry.* New York: Wiley.

Bogdan, R., & Biklen, S. K. (1992). *Qualitative Research for Education.* Boston: Allyn and Bacon.

Bromley, D. B. (1990). Academic contributions to psychological counseling: A philosophy of science for the study of individual cases. *Counseling Psychology Quarterly 3*(3), 299–307.

Champion D. J. (2006). *Research Methods for Criminal Justice and Criminology* (3rd ed.). Upper Saddle River, NJ: Pearson/Prentice Hall.

Champion, D. J. (1993). *Research Methods for Criminal Justice and Criminology.* Englewood Cliffs, NJ: Prentice Hall.

Creswell, J. W. (2002). *Educational Research: Planning, Conducting, and Evaluating Quantitative and Qualitative Research.* Upper Saddle River, NJ: Merrill Prentice Hall.

Creswell, J. W. (1998). *Qualitative Inquiry and Research Design: Choosing Among Five Traditions.* Thousands Oaks, CA: Sage.

Eisenhardt, K. (1989). Building theories from case study research. *Academy of Management Review 14*(4), 532–550.

Fernandez, W. (2005). The grounded theory method and case study data in IS research: Issues and design. In D. N. Hart & S. D. Gregor (Eds.), *Information Systems Foundations: Constructing and Criticising.* Canberra, Australlia: The Australian National University E Press, pp. 43–60.

French, B., & Stewart, J. (2001). Organizational development in a law enforcement environment. *The FBI Law Enforcement Bulletin 70*(9), 14.

Gall, M. G., Borg, W. R., & Gall, J. P. (1995). *Educational Research and Introduction.* New York: Longman Publishing Group.

Gall, M. G., Borg, W. R., & Gall, J. P. (1998). *Applying Educational Research*. New York: Longman Publishing Group.

Geertz, C. (1973). *The Interpretation of Culture*. New York: Basic Books.

Gomm, R., Hammersley, M., & Foster, P. (Eds.) (2000). *Case Study Method*. Thousand Oaks, CA: Sage.

Hagan, F. E. (2002). *Research Methods in Criminal Justice and Criminology*. Boston: Allyn and Bacon.

Hamel, J., Dufour, S., & Fortin, D. (1993). *Case Study Method*. Thousand Oaks, CA: Sage.

Hesse-Biber, S. N., & Yaiser, M. L. (2004). *Feminist Perspectives on Social Research*. New York: Oxford University Press.

Jensen, J. L., & Rodgers, R. (2001). Cumulating the intellectual gold of case study research. *Public Administration Review 61*(2), 236–246.

Linkogle, S. (1998). The revolution and the Virgin Mary: Popular religion and social change in Nicaragua. *Sociological Research Online 3*(2). Available online at www.socresonline.org.uk/socresonline/3/2/8.html

Lynd, R. S., & Lynd, H. M. (1929). *Middletown*. New York: Harcourt, Brace.

McLeod, B. (1994). *Language and Learning: Educating Linguistically Diverse Students*. Albany, NY: SUNY Press.

Merriam, S. B. (2001). *Qualitative Research and Case Study Applications in Education*. San Francisco: Jossey-Bass.

Patton, M. Q. (2001). *Utilization-Focused Evaluation: The New Century Text* (4th ed.). Thousand Oaks, CA: Sage.

Reinharz, S. (1992). *Feminist Methods in Social Research*. New York: Oxford University Press.

Rettig, R. P., Torres, M. J., & Garrett, G. R. (1977). *Manny: A Criminal Addict's Story*. Boston: Houghton Mifflin.

Roberson, E. W. (1998). *Weep Not for Me Dear Mother: The Letters of Eli Landers*. New York: Pelican.

Shaughnessy, J. J., & Zechmeister, E. B. (1999). *Research Methods in Psychology* (4th ed.). New York: McGraw-Hill.

Shaw, C. R. (1930). *The Jack Roller*. Chicago: University of Chicago Press.

Slick, S. (2002). Teachers are enthusiastic participants in a learning community. *The Clearing House 75*(4), 198–202.

Stake, R. E. (2000). Case studies. In N. K. Denzin & Y. S. Lincoln (Eds.), *Handbook of Qualitative Research* (2nd ed., pp. 435–454). Thousand Oaks, CA: Sage.

Stake, R. E. (1994). Case studies. In N. K. Denzin & Y. S. Lincoln (Eds.), *Handbook of Qualitative Research*. Thousand Oaks, CA: Sage.

Stake, R. E. (1995). *The Art of Case Study Research*. Thousand Oaks, CA: Sage.

Sutherland, E. H. (1937). *The Professional Thief*. Chicago: University of Chicago Press.

Wasta, S., & Lott, C. (2002). Eli Landers: Letters of a Confederate soldier. *Social Education 66*(2), 122–130.

Weick, K. E. (1995). *Sensemaking in Organizations*. Thousand Oaks, CA: Sage.

Winston, T. (July 1997). An introduction to case study. *The Qualitative Report 3*(2). Available online at www.nova.edu/ssss/QR/QR3-2/tellis1.html.

Yin, R. K. (2002). *Case Study Research, Design and Methods* (3rd ed.). Newbury Park, CA: Sage.

Yin, R. K. (2003). *Case Study Research* (3rd ed.). Thousand Oaks, CA: Sage.

Yin, R. K. (1994). *Case Study Research: Design and Methods* (2nd ed.). Beverly Hills, CA: Sage.

Yin, R. K. (1998). The abridged version of case study research: Design and method. In L. Bickman & D. J. Rog, *Handbook of Applied Social Research Methods*. Thousand Oaks, CA: Sage.

Yin, R., & Moore, G. (1988). The use of advanced technologies in special education. *Journal of Learning Disabilities 20*(1), 60.

Woodside, A. G., & Wilson, E. J. (2004). Case study research methods for theory building. *Journal of Business & Industrial Marketing 18*(6/7), 493–508.

Chapter 11

An Introduction to Content Analysis

T HROUGHOUT THE PRECEDING CHAPTERS, techniques and strategies for collecting and organizing data have been discussed. With a partial exception for Chapters 4, 6, and perhaps 7, in which limited analytic procedures are mentioned, analysis of data has not yet been extensively discussed. In this chapter the task of analysis is considered at length.

The instructions in this chapter are intended to assist novice researchers in their attempt to learn the methodological technique(s) for standard content analysis. The chapter begins with a brief explanation of what content analysis is in an effort to orient the fledgling researchers. Next, the chapter offers a brief discussion on analysis approaches in qualitative research. Following this, some general discussion on concerns and debates regarding content analysis are presented. Then a number of procedures for analyzing content analysis are examined. These include consideration of what to count and what to analyze, the nature of *levels and units of analysis,* and how to effectively employ *coding frames.* In the next section, the strengths and weaknesses of content analysis as an analytic technique are discussed, and *analytic induction* is examined in relation to content analysis procedures. Finally, this chapter addresses *word crunching,* the use of computers in qualitative research.

What Is Content Analysis?

Content analysis is a careful, detailed, systematic examination and interpretation of a particular body of material in an effort to identify patterns, themes, biases, and meanings (Leedy & Ormrod, 2005; Neuendorf, 2002). Typically, content analysis is performed on various forms of human communications; this may include various permutations of written documents, photographs, motion pictures or videotape, and audiotapes. For example, Edward Armstrong (2001) used content analysis to assess the portrayal of violence against women in Gangsta rap music lyrics. Armstrong examined lyrics of 490 songs produced between 1987 and 1993. Armstrong concluded that Gangsta rap music continues to teach, promote, and glamorize violence and misogyny and needs serious attention in order to deglamorize violent and misogynist behaviors among youthful followers of this genre of music.

Content analysis has been used by a wide variety of disciplines, including sociology, criminology, psychology, education, business, journalism, art, and political science. Regardless of where it is used, content analysis is chiefly a *coding operation* and *data interpreting process* (Bogdan & Bilken, 2003; Maxfield & Babbie, 2006; Morse & Richards, 2002).

Analysis of Qualitative Data

There are a number of procedures used by qualitative researchers to analyze their data. Miles and Huberman (1994) identify three major approaches to qualitative data analysis: interpretative approaches, social anthropological approaches, and collaborative social research approaches.

Interpretative Approaches

This orientation allows researchers to treat social action and human activity as *text*. In other words, human action can be seen as a collection of symbols expressing layers of meaning. Interviews and observational data, then, can be transcribed into written text for analysis. How one interprets such a text depends in part on the theoretical orientation taken by the researcher. Thus, a researcher with a phenomenological bent will resist condensing data or framing data by various sorting or coding operations. A phenomenologically oriented researcher might, instead, attempt to uncover or capture the *telos* (essence) of an account. This approach provides a means for discovering the practical understandings of meanings and actions. Researchers with a more general interpretative orientation (dramaturgists, symbolic interactionists, etc.) are likely to organize or reduce data in order to uncover patterns of human activity, action, and meaning.

Social Anthropological Approaches

Researchers following this orientation often have conducted various sorts of field or case study activities to gather data. In order to accomplish data collection, they have necessarily spent considerable time in a given community, or with a given assortment of individuals in the field. They have participated, indirectly or directly, with many of the individuals residing in or interacting with the study population. This provides the researcher with a special perspective on the material collected during the research, as well as a special understanding of the participants and how these individuals interpret their social worlds.

Analysis of this sort of data can be accomplished by setting information down in field notes and then applying the interpretative style of treating this information as text. However, frequently this analytic process requires the analysis of multiple sources of data such as diaries, observations, interviews, photographs, and artifacts. Determining what material to include or exclude, how to order the presentation of substantiating materials, and what to report first or last are analytic choices the researcher must make.

Researchers employing the social anthropological approach usually are interested in the behavioral regularities of everyday life, language and language use, rituals and ceremonies, and relationships. The analytic task, then, is to identify and explain the ways people use or operate in a particular setting; how they come to understand things; account for, take action, and generally manage their day-to-day life. Many researchers using this approach begin with a conceptual or theoretical frame, then move into the field in order to test or refine this conceptualization.

Collaborative Social Research Approaches

Researchers operating in this research mode work with their subjects in a given setting in order to accomplish some sort of change or action (see Chapter 7 on action research). The analysis of data gathered in such collaborative studies is accomplished with the participation of the subjects who are seen by the researcher as *stakeholders* in the situation in need of change or action. Data are collected and then reflexively considered both as feedback to craft action and as information to understand a situation, resolve a problem, or to satisfy some sort of field experiment. The actual analytic strategies applied in this effort may be similar to the interpretative and social anthropology approaches.

Given these diverse yet overlapping approaches, you can see certain facets of research that recur during any style of qualitative analysis. Following is a fairly standard set of analytic activities arranged in a general order of sequence:

- Data are collected and made into text (e.g., field notes, transcripts).
- Codes are analytically developed or inductively identified in the data and affixed to sets of notes or transcript pages.
- Codes are transformed into categorical labels or themes.
- Materials are sorted by these categories, identifying similar phrases, patterns, relationships, and commonalties or disparities.
- Sorted materials are examined to isolate meaningful patterns and processes.
- Identified patterns are considered in light of previous research and theories, and a small set of generalizations is established.

During the remainder of this chapter, these features will be discussed and considered in relationship to content analysis. The next section will consider the nature of content analysis as a technique.

Content Analysis as a Technique

In content analysis, researchers examine artifacts of social communication. Typically, these are written documents or transcriptions of recorded verbal communications. Broadly defined, however, content analysis is "any technique for making inferences by systematically and *objectively* identifying special characteristics of messages" (Holsti, 1968, p. 608). From this perspective, photographs, videotape, or any items that can be made into text are amenable to content analysis. In this chapter, objective analysis of messages conveyed in the data being analyzed is accomplished by means of explicit rules called *criteria of selection*, which must be formally established before the actual analysis of data.

The criteria of selection used in any given content analysis must be sufficiently exhaustive to account for each variation of message content and must be rigidly and consistently applied so that other researchers or readers, looking at the same messages, would obtain the same or comparable results. This may be considered a kind of reliability of the measures and a validation of eventual findings (Selltiz, Jahoda, Deutsch, & Cook, 1967). The categories that emerge in the course of developing these criteria should reflect all relevant aspects of the messages and retain, as much as possible, the exact wording used in the statements. They should not be merely arbitrary or superficial applications of irrelevant categories. Holsti (1968, p. 598) explains this type of content analysis procedure: "The inclusion or exclusion of content is done according to consistently applied criteria of selection; this requirement eliminates analysis in which only material supporting the investigator's hypotheses are examined."

Content Analysis: Quantitative or Qualitative?

One of the leading debates among users of content analysis is whether analysis should be quantitative or qualitative. Berelson (1952), for example, suggests that content analysis is "objective, systematic, and quantitative." Similarly, Silverman (1993, p. 59) dismisses content analysis from his discussion of qualitative data analysis "because it is a quantitative method." Selltiz et al. (1959, p. 336), however, state that concerns over quantification in content analysis tend to emphasize "the procedures of analysis," rather than the "character of the data available." Selltiz et al. suggest also that heavy quantitative content analysis results in a somewhat arbitrary limitation in the field by excluding all accounts of communications that are not in the form of numbers as well as those that may lose meaning if reduced to a numeric form (definitions, symbols, detailed explanations, photographs, and so forth). Other proponents of content analysis, notably Smith (1975), suggest that some blend of both quantitative and qualitative analysis should be used. Smith (1975, p. 218) explains that he has taken this position "because qualitative analysis deals with the forms and antecedent-consequent patterns of form, while quantitative analysis deals with duration and frequency of form."

Abrahamson (1983, p. 286) suggests that "content analysis can be fruitfully employed to examine virtually any type of communication." As a consequence, content analysis may focus on either quantitative or qualitative aspects of communication messages.

Some authors of methods books have written about the procedure of *narrative analysis* as distinguishable from the procedure of content analysis (see, for example, Manning & Cullum-Swan, 1994; Silverman, 1993). In narrative analysis, the investigator typically begins with a set of principles and seeks to exhaust the meaning of the text using specified rules and principles but maintains a qualitative textual approach (Boje, 1991; Heise, 1992; Manning & Cullum-Swan, 1994; Silverman, 1993). In contrast to this allegedly more textual approach, content analysis is suggested to be limited to counts of textual elements. Thus, the implication is that content analysis is more reductionistic and ostensively a more positivistic approach. I argue here that content analysis can be effective in qualitative analysis—that "counts" of textual elements merely provide a means for identifying, organizing, indexing, and retrieving data. Analysis of the data, once organized according to certain content elements, should involve consideration of the literal words in the text being analyzed, including the manner in which these words are offered. In effect, the researcher should undertake what Bogdan and Bilken (2003) call data interpretations, which involves developing ideas about the information found in the various categories, patterns that are emerging, and meanings that seem to be conveyed. In turn, this analysis should be related to the literature and broader concerns and to the original research questions. In this manner, the analysis provides the researcher a means by which to learn about how subjects or the authors of textual materials view their social worlds and how these views fit into the larger frame of how the social sciences view these issues and interpretations.

From this perspective, content analysis is not a reductionistic, positivistic approach. Rather, it is a passport to listening to the words of the text and understanding better the perspective(s) of the producer of these words.

This chapter strives for a blend of qualitative and quantitative analysis: the descriptions of quantitative analysis show how researchers can create a series of tally sheets to determine specific frequencies of relevant categories. The references to qualitative analysis show how researchers can examine ideological mind-sets, themes, topics, symbols, and similar phenomena, while grounding such examinations to the data.

Manifest Versus Latent Content Analysis

Another controversy concerning the use of content analysis is whether the analysis should be limited to *manifest content* (those elements that are physically present and countable) or extended to more *latent content*. In the latter case, the analysis is extended to an interpretive reading of the symbolism underlying the physical data. For example, an entire speech may be assessed for how radical it was, or a novel could be considered in terms of how violent the entire text was. Stated in different words, manifest content is comparable to the *surface structure* present in the message, and latent content is the *deep structural* meaning conveyed by the message.

Holsti (1969, p. 598) has tried to resolve this debate: "It is true that only the manifest attributes of text may be coded, but this limitation is already implied by the requirement of objectivity. Inferences about latent meanings of messages are therefore permitted but . . . they require corroboration by independent evidence." One reasonable interpretation of this passage, and of a similar statement made by Berelson (1952, p. 488ff), suggests that although there are some dangers in directly inferring from latent symbolism, it is nonetheless possible to use it (see also Merton, 1968, pp. 366–370, on the use of content analysis in examining propaganda). To accomplish this sort of "deciphering" (Heilman, 1976) of latent symbolic meaning, researchers must first incorporate independent corroborative techniques. For example, researchers may include agreement between independent coders concerning latent content or some noncontent analytic source (Krippendorff, 2003; Neuendorf, 2001). Finally, and especially when latent symbolism may be discussed, researchers should offer detailed excerpts from relevant statements (messages) that document the researchers' interpretations. A safe rule of thumb to follow is the inclusion of at least three independent examples for each interpretation.

Blending Manifest and Latent Content Analysis Strategies

Perhaps the best resolution of this dilemma about whether to use manifest or latent content is to use both whenever possible. In this case, a given unit of content would receive the same attention from both methods—to the extent that coding procedures (discussed presently) for both the manifest and latent content are reasonably valid and reliable (Babbie, 2002). By reporting the frequency with which a given concept appears in text, researchers suggest the magnitude of this observation. It is more convincing for their arguments when researchers demonstrate the appearance of a claimed observation in some large proportion of the material under study (e.g., 20 percent, 30 percent, 40 percent).

Researchers must bear in mind, however, that these descriptive statistics—namely, proportions and frequency distributions—do not necessarily reflect the nature of the data or variables. If the theme "positive attitude toward shoplifting," appears 50 times in one subject's interview transcript and 25 times in another subject's, this would not be justification for the researchers to claim that the first subject is twice as likely to shoplift as the second subject. In short, researchers must be cautious not to take or claim magnitudes as findings in themselves. The magnitude for certain observations is presented to demonstrate more fully the overall analysis.

Communication Components

According to Holsti (1969) and Carney (1972), communications have three major components: the message, the sender, and the audience (see also Littlejohn & Foss, 2004). The message should be analyzed in terms of explicit themes, relative emphasis on various topics, amount of space or time devoted to certain topics, and numerous other dimensions. Occasionally, messages are analyzed for information about the sender of the communication.

Strauss (1990) similarly differentiates between what he calls *in vivo codes* and *sociological constructs*. In vivo codes are the literal terms used by individuals under investigation, in effect, the terms used by the various actors themselves.

These in vivo codes then represent the behavioral processes, which will explain to the researcher how the basic problem of the actors is resolved or processed. In contrast, sociological constructs are formulated by the analyst (analytic constructions). Terms and categories, such as *professional attitude, family oriented, obsessive workaholic,* and *educationally minded,* might represent examples of sociological constructs. These constructs, of course, need not derive exclusively from sociology and may come from the fields of education, nursing, psychology, and the like. Strauss (1990) explains that these constructs tend to be based on a combination of things, including the researcher's scholarly knowledge of the substantive field under study. The result of using constructs is the addition of certain social scientific meanings that might otherwise be missed in the analysis. Thus, sociological constructs add breadth and depth to observations by reaching beyond local meanings and understandings to broader social scientific ones.

What to Count: Levels and Units of Analysis

When using a content analysis strategy to assess written documents, researchers must first decide at what level they plan to sample and what units of analysis will be counted. Sampling may occur at any or all of the following levels: words, phrases, sentences, paragraphs, sections, chapters, books, writers, ideological stance, subject topic, or similar elements relevant to the context. When examining other forms of messages, researchers may use any of the preceding levels or may sample at other conceptual levels more appropriate to the specific message. For example, when examining television programs for violent content, researchers might use segments between commercials as the level of analysis, or they might choose to use the entire television program (excluding commercials) as the level (see, e.g., Fields, 1988).

Category Development: Building Grounded Theory

Strauss (1987) describes the considerable misconception surrounding the development of grounded theory. The term *misconception,* as Strauss (1987, p. 55) points out, seems more appropriate than *criticism.* Misconception implies an inaccurate reading of material pertaining to building grounded theory. On the other hand, criticism connotes more of a challenge to or detraction from the benefits of this process. Central to misconception are the notions that grounded theory is an entirely inductive process, that it does not verify findings, and that it somehow molds the data to the theory rather than the reverse.

Strauss (1987, p. 55), in a lengthy note, singles out Miles and Huberman (1983) as illustrating several instrumental misconceptions (brackets in original text contain Strauss's responses):

> In Miles and Huberman (1983, p. 57) there is also a misunderstanding about grounded theory technology. The material in my book, written before their publication appeared, runs directly counter to some of their remarks, that: the grounded theory approach has a lot going for it. Data get well molded to the codes that represent them, and we get more of a code-in-use flavor than the generic code-for-many-uses generated by prefabricated start lists.... The tradeoff here is that earlier segments may have different codes than later ones. [They may, in part, of course.] Or to avoid this everything may have to be recorded once a more empirically sculpted scheme emerges. [No.] This means more overall coding time, and longer uncertainty about the coherence of the coding frame. [Probably, but deliberate, in part].

In addition, Miles and Huberman (1983, pp. 63–64) promote the worrisome notion that coding is not an enjoyable task, which suggests that other aspects of the research enterprise are more fun. This text as well as Strauss (1987) strongly disagree. Coding and other fundamental procedures associated with grounded theory development are certainly hard work and must be taken seriously, but just as many people enjoy finishing a complicated jigsaw puzzle, many researchers find great satisfaction in coding and analysis. As researchers move through the coding process and begin to see the puzzle pieces come together to form a more complete picture, the process can be downright thrilling. Time consuming, tiring, and even laborious as the process is, it is seldom boring!

The categories researchers use in a content analysis can be determined inductively, deductively, or by some combination of both (Strauss, 1987). Abrahamson (1983, p. 286) indicates that an inductive approach begins with the researchers "immersing" themselves in the documents (that is, the various messages) in order to identify the dimensions or *themes* that seem meaningful to the producers of each message. In a deductive approach, researchers use some categorical scheme suggested by a theoretical perspective, and the documents provide a means for assessing the hypothesis. In many circumstances, the relationship between a theoretical perspective and certain messages involves both inductive and deductive approaches. However, in order to present the perceptions of others (the producers of messages) in the most forthright manner, a greater reliance on induction is necessary. Nevertheless, as will be shown, induction should not be undertaken to the exclusion of deduction.

The development of inductive categories allows researchers to link or *ground* these categories to the data from which they derive. Certainly, it is reasonable to suggest that insights and general questions about research derive from previous experience with the study phenomena. This may represent personal experience, scholarly experience (having read about it), or previous research undertaken to examine the matter. Researchers, similarly, draw on these experiences in order to propose tentative comparisons that assist in creating various deductions. Experience, thus, underpins both inductive and deductive reasoning.

From this interplay of experience, induction, and deduction, Glaser and Strauss formulate their description of grounded theory. According to Glaser and Strauss (1967, pp. 2–3):

> To generate theory . . . we suggest as the best approach an initial, systematic discovery of the theory from the data of social research. Then one can be relatively sure that the theory will fit the work. And since categories are discovered by examination of the data, laymen involved in the area to which the theory applies will usually be able to understand it, while sociologists who work in other areas will recognize an understandable theory linked with the data of a given area.

What to Count

Seven major elements in written messages can be counted in content analysis: words or terms, themes, characters, paragraphs, items, concepts, and semantics (Berelson, 1952; Berg, 1983; Merton, 1968; Selltiz et al., 1959).

Words   The *word* is the smallest element or unit used in content analysis. Its use generally results in a frequency distribution of specified words or terms.

Themes   The *theme* is a more useful unit to count. In its simplest form, a theme is a simple sentence, a string of words with a subject and a predicate. Because themes may be located in a variety of places in most written documents, it becomes necessary to specify (in advance) which places will be searched. For example, researchers might use only the primary theme in a given paragraph location or alternatively might count every theme in a given text under analysis.

Characters   In some studies, *characters* (persons) are significant to the analysis. In such cases, you count the number of times a specific person or persons are mentioned rather than the number of words or themes.

Paragraphs   The *paragraph* is infrequently used as the basic unit in content analysis chiefly because of the difficulties that have resulted in attempting to code and classify the various and often numerous thoughts stated and implied in a single paragraph.

Items   An *item* represents the whole unit of the sender's message—that is, an item may be an entire book, a letter, speech, diary, newspaper, or even an in-depth interview.

Concepts   The use of *concepts* as units to count is a more sophisticated type of word counting than previously mentioned. Concepts involve words grouped together into conceptual clusters (ideas) that constitute, in some instances, variables in a typical research hypothesis (Sanders & Pinhey, 1959, p. 191). For instance, a conceptual cluster may form around the idea of deviance. Words such as *crime, delinquency, kiting,* and *fraud* might cluster around the conceptual idea of deviance (Babbie, 2001). To some extent, the use of a concept as the unit of analysis leads toward more latent than manifest content.

Semantics   In the type of content analysis known as *semantics,* researchers are interested not only in the number and type of words used but also in how affected the word(s) may be—in other words, how strong or weak a word (or words) may be in relation to the overall sentiment of the sentence (Sanders & Pinhey, 1959).

Combinations of Elements

In many instances, research requires the use of a combination of several content analytic elements. For example, in my study (Berg, 1983) to identify subjective definitions for Jewish affiliational categories (Orthodox, Conservative, Reform, and Nonpracticing), I used a combination of both item and paragraph elements as a content unit. In order to accomplish a content analysis of these definitions (as items), I lifted every respondent's definitions of each affiliational category verbatim from an interview transcript. Each set of definitions was additionally annotated with the transcript number from which it had been taken. Next, each definition (as items) was separated into its component definitional paragraph for each affiliational category. An example of this definitional paragraphing follows (Berg, 1983, p. 76):

Interview #60: Orthodox

Well, I guess, Orthodox keep kosher in [the] home and away from home. Observe the Sabbath, and, you know . . . , actually if somebody did [those] and considered themselves an Orthodox Jew, to me that would be enough. I would say that they were Orthodox.

Interview #60: Conservative

Conservative, I guess, is the fellow who doesn't want to say he's Reform because it's objectionable to him. But he's a long way from being Orthodox.

Interview #60: Reform

Reform is just somebody that, they say they are Jewish because they don't want to lose their identity. But actually I want to be considered a Reform, 'cause I say I'm Jewish, but I wouldn't want to be associated as a Jew if I didn't actually observe any of the laws.

Interview #60: Nonpracticing

Well, a Nonpracticing is the guy who would have no temple affiliation, no affiliation with being Jewish at all, except that he considers himself a Jew. I guess he practices in no way, except to himself.

Units and Categories

Content analysis involves the interaction of two processes: specification of the content characteristics (basic content elements) being examined and application of explicit rules for identifying and recording these characteristics. The *categories* into which you code content items vary according to the nature of the research and the particularities of the data (that is, whether they are detailed responses to open-ended questions, newspaper columns, letters, television transcripts, and so on).

As with all research methods, conceptualization and operationalization necessarily involve an interaction between theoretical concerns and empirical observations. For instance, if researchers wanted to examine newspaper orientations toward changes in a state's seat-belt law (as a potential barometer of public opinion), they might read newspaper articles and editorials. As they read each article, the researchers could ask themselves which ones were in favor of and which ones were opposed to changes in the law. Were the articles' positions more clearly indicated by their manifest content or by some undertone? Was the decision to label one article pro or con based on the use of certain terms, on presentation of specific study findings, or because of statements offered by particular characters (e.g., celebrities, political figures)? The answers to these questions allow the researchers to develop inductive categories in which to slot various units of content.

As previously mentioned, researchers need not limit their procedures to induction alone. Both inductive and deductive reasoning may provide fruitful findings. If, for example, investigators are attempting to test hypothetical propositions, their theoretical orientation should suggest empirical indicators of concepts (deductive reasoning). If they have begun with specific empirical observations, they should attempt to develop explanations grounded in the data (grounded theory) and apply these theories to other empirical observations (inductive reasoning).

There are no easy ways to describe specific tactics for developing categories or to suggest how to go about defining (operationalizing) these tactics. To paraphrase Schatzman and Strauss's (1973, p. 12) remark about methodological choices in general, the categorizing tactics worked out—some in advance, some developed later—should be consistent not only with the questions asked and the methodological requirements of science but also with a relation to the properties of the phenomena under investigation. Stated succinctly, categories must be grounded in the data from which they emerge (Denzin, 1978; Glaser & Strauss, 1967). The development of categories in any content analysis must derive from inductive reference (to be discussed in detail later) concerning patterns that emerge from the data.

For example, in a study evaluating the effectiveness of a Florida-based delinquency diversion program, I (Berg, 1986) identified several thematic categories from information provided on intake sheets. By setting up a tally sheet, I managed to use the criminal offenses declared by arresting officers in their general statements to identify two distinct classes of crime, in spite of arresting officers' use of similar-sounding terms. In one class of crime, several similar terms were used to describe what amounted to the same type of crime. In a second class of crime, officers more consistently referred to the same type of crime by a consistent term. Specifically, I found that the words *shoplifting, petty theft,* and *retail theft* each referred to essentially the same category of crime involving the stealing of some type of store *merchandise,* usually not exceeding $3.50 in value. Somewhat surprisingly, the semantically similar term *petty larceny* was used to describe the taking of cash whether it was from a retail establishment, a domicile, or an auto. Thus, the data indicated a subtle perceptual distinction made by the officers reporting juvenile crimes.

Dabney (1993) examined how practicing nurses perceived other nurses who worked while impaired by alcohol or drugs. He developed several thematic categories based on previous studies found in the literature. He was also able to inductively identify several classes of drug diversion described by subjects during the course of interviews. For instance, many subjects referred to *stockpiled drugs* that nurses commonly used for themselves. These drugs included an assortment of pain killers and mild sedatives stored in a box, a drawer, or some similar container on the unit or floor. These stockpiled drugs accumulated when patients died or were transferred to another hospital unit and this information did not immediately reach the hospital pharmacy.

Classes and Categories

Three major procedures are used to identify and develop classes and categories in a standard content analysis and to discuss findings in research that use content analysis: common classes, special classes, and theoretical classes.

Common Classes   The first are the *common classes* of a culture in general. These classes are used by virtually anyone in society to distinguish between and among persons, things, and events (for example, age, gender, mother, father, teacher, and so on). These common classes, as categories, provide for lay people a means of designation in the course of everyday thinking and communicating and to engender meaning in their social interactions (see Duncan, 1962; Schatzman & Strauss, 1973; Strauss, 1959). These common classes are essential in assessing whether certain demographic characteristics are related to patterns that may arise during a given data analysis.

Special Classes   *Special classes* are those labels used by members of certain areas (communities) to distinguish among the things, persons, and events within their limited province (Schatzman & Strauss, 1973). These special classes can be likened to jargonized terms used commonly in certain professions but not by lay people. Alternatively, these special classes may be described as *out-group* versus *in-group* classifications. In the case of the out-group, the reference is to labels conventionally used by the greater (host) community or society; as for the in-group, the reference is to conventional terms and labels used among some specified group or that may emerge as theoretical classes.

Theoretical Classes   The *theoretical classes* are those that emerge in the course of analyzing the data (Schatzman & Strauss, 1973). In most content analysis, these theoretical classes provide an overarching pattern (a key linkage) that occurs throughout the analysis. Nomenclature that identifies these theoretical classes generally borrows from that used in special classes and, together with analytically constructed labels, accounts for novelty and innovations.

According to Schatzman and Strauss (1973), these theoretical classes are special sources of classification because their specific substance is grounded in the data. Because these theoretical classes are not immediately knowable or available to observers until they spend considerable time going over the ways respondents (or messages) in a sample identify themselves and others, it is necessary to retain the special classes throughout much of the analysis.

The next problem to address is how to identify various classes and categories in the data set, which leads to a discussion of open coding.

Open Coding

Inexperienced researchers, although they may intellectually understand the process described so far, usually become lost at about this point in the actual process of coding. Some of the major obstacles that cause anguish include the so-called true or intended meaning of the sentence and a desire to know the real motivation behind a subject's clearly identifiable lie. If the researchers can get beyond such concerns, the coding can continue. For the most part, these concerns are actually irrelevant to the coding process, particularly with regard to *open coding*, the central purpose of which is to open inquiry widely. Although interpretations, questions, and even possible answers may seem to emerge as researchers code, it is important to hold these as tentative at best. Contradictions to such early conclusions may emerge during the coding of the very next document. The most thorough analysis of the various concepts and categories will best be accomplished after all the material has been coded. The solution to the novice investigators' anguish, then, as suggested by Strauss (1987, p. 28) is to "believe everything and believe nothing" while undertaking open coding.

Strauss (1987, p. 30) suggests four basic guidelines when conducting open coding: (1) ask the data a specific and consistent set of questions, (2) analyze the data minutely, (3) frequently interrupt the coding to write a theoretical note, and (4) never assume the analytic relevance of any traditional variable such as age, sex, social class, and so forth until the data show it to be relevant. A detailed discussion of each of these guidelines follows.

1. *Ask the data a specific and consistent set of questions.* The most general question researchers must keep in mind is, What study are these data pertinent to? In other words, what was the original objective of the research study? This is not to suggest that the data must be molded to that study. Rather, the original purpose of a study may not be accomplished and an alternative or unanticipated goal may be identified in the data. For example, in Pearson's (1987) evaluation of a New Jersey intensive problem supervision program, the original aim was to demonstrate cost-effectiveness. Although objective indicators failed to support

the cost-effectiveness of the experimental program, several indirect indicators suggested that the program nonetheless was fairly successful. These other measures involved repeated reports from relatives of probationers about changes in attitudes demonstrated by the program participants. For instance, the wife of one participant reported that her husband had begun to send child-support payments in full and on time. Parents of another program participant reported that their child had begun to show personal responsibility by doing household chores around the home—something the individual had previously never undertaken.

Thus, Pearson (1987) points to an unanticipated benefit from the program. This illustration demonstrates the need both to keep the original study aim in mind and to remain open to multiple or unanticipated results that emerge from the data.

2. *Analyze the data minutely.* Strauss (1987; 1990) cautions that researchers should remember that they are conducting an initial coding procedure. As such, it is important to analyze data minutely. Students in qualitative research should remind themselves that in the beginning, more is better. Coding is much like the traditional funnel used by many educators to demonstrate how to write papers. You begin with a wide opening, a broad statement; narrow the statement throughout the body by offering substantial backing; and finally, at the small end of the funnel, present a refined, tightly stated conclusion. In the case of coding, the wide end represents inclusion of many categories, incidents, interactions, and the like. These are coded minutely during open coding. Later, this effort ensures extensive theoretical coverage that will be thoroughly grounded. At a later time, more systematic coding can be accomplished, building from the numerous elements that emerge during this phase of open coding.

The question that arises, of course, is when to stop this open coding process and move on to the speedier, more systematic coding phase. Typically, as researchers minutely code, they eventually saturate the document with repetitious codes. As this occurs and the repetition allows the researchers to move more rapidly through the documents, it is usually safe to conclude that the time has come to move on.

3. *Frequently interrupt the coding to write a theoretical note.* This third guideline suggested by Strauss (1987) directs researchers closer to grounded theory. Often, in the course of coding, a comment in the document triggers ideas. Researchers should take a moment to jot down a note about these ideas, which may well prove useful later. If they fail to do so, they are very likely to forget the idea. In many instances, researchers find it useful to keep a record of where in each document similar comments, concepts, or categories seem to convey the same elements that originally triggered the theory or hypothesis. For example,

during the coding process of a study on adolescents' involvement with alcohol, crime, and drugs, interview transcripts revealed youths speaking about drugs and criminal activities as if they were almost partitioned categories (Carpenter Glassner, Johnson, & Loughlin, 1988). Notes scribbled during coding later led to theories on drug-crime event sequences and the nexus of drug-crime events.

4. *Never assume the analytic relevance of any traditional variable such as age, sex, social class, and so on until the data show it to be relevant.* As Strauss (1987, p. 32) indicates, even these more mundane variables must "earn their way into the grounded theory." This assumes that these variables are necessarily contributing to some condition, but it does not mean you are prohibited from intentionally using certain variables deductively. The first guideline— What study are these data pertinent to?—is germane to the coding process. Consequently, if researchers are interested in gender differences, naturally, they begin by assuming that gender might be analytically relevant, but if the data fail to support this assumption, the researchers must accept this result.

It is also important to bear in mind that there is no single best way to code data. Morse and Richards (2002) point out that there are actually many ways of coding, and coding is undertaken in qualitative research for a variety of purposes. Morse and Richards (p. 112) distinguish between three types of coding, each of which contributes differently to the overall process of analysis. The first type of coding they discuss involves the storage of information and is called *descriptive coding*. The second type is coding used to gather material by *topic*. The third is coding used when the goal is the development of concepts, which Morris and Richards (p. 112) call *analytic coding*.

Bogdan and Bilkin (2003, pp. 161–168) offer a virtual typology of code terms, including *setting/context codes, definition of the situation codes, process codes, activity codes, event codes, strategy codes, relationship and social structural codes, narrative codes,* and *methods codes*. Regardless of what terms are used to classify coding categories or how many are included in the analysis process, coding is a necessary aspect to organizing data and interpreting what the data says. Furthermore, the more organized and systematic the coding schemes, the easier it is to allow the data to *talk to you* and inform you about various research-related questions you might have. It is also important to note that qualitative analysis is not something that you begin after you completely finish collecting all the data (Warren & Karner, 2005). Rather, analysis starts as the data begins to indicate the necessary categories and codes to use and as these elements begin to form patterns and conceptual realities each time the researcher reads and rereads a transcript, undertakes another day of fieldwork, or reviews some document.

Coding Frames

Content analysis is accomplished through the use of *coding frames*. The coding frames are used to organize the data and identify findings after open coding has been completed. The first coding frame is often a multileveled process that requires several successive sortings of all cases under examination. Investigators begin with a general sorting of cases into some specified special class. In many ways, this first frame is similar to what Strauss (1987, p. 32) describes as axial coding. According to Strauss (1987) *axial coding* occurs after open coding is completed and consists of intensive coding around one category. The first sorting approximates Strauss's description of axial coding. An example may better illustrate this process.

I (Berg, 1983) began my first sorting by separating all cases into Jewish affiliational categories declared by respondents during an initial telephone contact. Subjects' responses came after being asked in a screening question: "With which of the following do you most closely associate yourself: Reform, Orthodox, Conservative, or Nonpracticing?" (Subjects were consistently asked this question using the preceding affiliational ordering in an attempt to guard against certain acquiescent response sets.)

This procedure separated my sample (cases) into four groupings bearing the conventional affiliational titles listed previously. After completing this sorting, I carefully read the responses to the identical question asked in the course of each respondent's in-depth interview. Subsequently, each affiliational grouping was subdivided into three groups using the following criteria of selection:

1. The first subdivision in each category consisted of all cases in which respondents' answers to the interview version of the question, "With which of the following . . ." (1) were consistent with the response given during the telephone screening and (2) were offered with no qualification or exception.

2. The second subdivision in each category consisted of cases in which respondents qualified their responses with a simple modifier (usually a single adjective), but were otherwise consistent with the response offered on the telephone screening question (for example, "I am a *modern* Orthodox Jew.").

3. The third subdivision consisted of all cases in which the respondents offered detailed explanations for their affiliational declarations that were also consistent with their telephone screening response. For example, one male respondent explained that just as his father had switched from being an Orthodox to a Conservative affiliate, so too

did he make a switch from being a Conservative to a Reform affiliate. His declaration of *Reform,* however, was consistent with what he had originally declared during the telephone screening.

4. The fourth subdivision consisted of all cases in which the respondents contradicted their original telephone screening question response or indicated that they simply could not determine where they fit in terms of the four conventional affiliational categories.

Using the preceding criteria, I sorted my cases into the indicated subdivisions. Following this, and using a sorting process similar to the preceding one, I again subdivided each newly created subgroup to produce a typological scheme containing 16 distinct categories, the overarching or key linkage in every case being the subjective declaration of each respondent (at two distinct iterations of the same question).

Having sorted and organized my data, I was ready to interpret the patterns apparent from both the organizational scheme and the details offered in response to interview questions. At this juncture in my analysis, relevant theoretical perspectives were introduced in order to tie the analysis both to established theory and to my own emerging grounded theory (Glaser & Strauss, 1967; Strauss & Corbin, 1998). These theoretical considerations and sociological constructs led me to analyze several other detailed responses to interview questions. These other questions concerned respondents' involvement in and knowledge of religious symbols and ceremonies. In order to preserve the key linkages throughout the entire analysis process, each subsequent analysis of responses was performed against the newly created typological scheme of subjective identification labels (the 16-category scheme mentioned previously).

Berg and his associates (2004) offer another example of this axial coding or sorting process in their examination of descriptions of sexual risk taking provided by Latino men who have sex with other men. Codes were created using the constructs (analytic categories) shaped by certain questions asked during the course of the interview process. In addition, specific, data-grounded themes were also used to sort the responses to various questions.

Strauss (1990) similarly outlines the coding process. According to Strauss (1990), the analyst begins with a procedure he calls *open coding.* This procedure is described as an unrestricted coding of the data. With open coding, you carefully and minutely read the document line by line and word by word to determine the concepts and categories that fit the data. These concepts, once uncovered, are entirely tentative. As you continue working with and thinking about the data, questions and even some plausible answers also begin to emerge. These questions should lead you to other issues and further questions concerning various conditions, strategies, interactions, and consequences of the data.

A Few More Words on Analytic Induction

As Robinson (1951) suggests, "Since Znaniecki stated it in 1934, the method of analytic induction has come into important use." The use of analytic induction, however, also has involved a number of refinements—including several variations on its style and purpose. For example, Sutherland and Cressey (1966) refined the method and suggest that it be used in the study of causes of crime. Even before Sutherland (1950), Lindesmith (1947) had discovered the usefulness of an analytic inductive strategy in a study of opiate users. Lindesmith (1952, p. 492) describes analytic induction as follows:

> The principle which governs the selection of cases to test a theory is that the chances of discovering a decisive negative case should be maximized. The investigator who has a working hypothesis concerning the data becomes aware of certain areas of critical importance. If his theory is false or inadequate, he knows that its weakness will be more clearly and quickly exposed if he proceeds to the investigation of those critical areas. This involves going out of one's way to look for negative evidence.

Adding further refinements to the method, Glaser and Strauss suggest that analytic induction should combine analysis of data after the coding process with analysis of data while integrating theory. In short, analysis of data is grounded to established theory and is also capable of developing theory. Glaser and Strauss (1967, p. 102) describe their refinements as follows:

> We wish to suggest a third approach to the analysis of qualitative data—one that combines, by an analytic procedure of constant comparison, the explicit coding procedures of the first approach [analysis of data after coding] and the style of theory development of the second [the integration of data and theory]. The purpose of the constant comparative method of joint coding and analysis is to generate theory more systematically than allowed by the second approach, by using explicit coding and analytic procedures. While more systematic than the second approach, this method does not adhere completely to the first, which hinders the development of theory because it is designed for provisional testing and not discovering hypotheses.

Glaser and Strauss (1967) suggest that such a joint coding and analysis of data is a more honest way to present findings and analysis. Similarly, Merton (1968, pp. 147–148) discusses the "logical fallacy underlying post factum explanations" and hypothesis testing. Merton states:

> It is often the case in empirical social research that data are collected and only then subjected to interpretative comment. . . . Such post factum explanations designed to "explain" observations, differ in logical function from speciously similar procedures where the observational materials are utilized in order to derive fresh hypotheses to be confirmed by new observations.

A disarming characteristic of the procedure is that the explanations are indeed consistent with the given set of observations. This is scarcely surprising, in as much as only those post factum hypotheses are selected which do accord with these observations. . . . The method of post factum explanation does not lend itself to nullifiability.

Researchers should make extensive use of Glaser and Strauss's (1967) style of analytic induction and, perhaps more directly, of Strauss's (1987) rearticulation of their position. According to Strauss (1987, p. 12):

Because of our earlier writing in Discovery (1967) where we attacked speculative theory—quite ungrounded in bodies of data—many people mistakenly refer to grounded theory as "inductive theory" in order to contrast it with say, the theories of Parson or Blau. But as we have indicated, all three aspects of inquiry (induction, deduction, and verification) are absolutely essential. . . . In fact, it is important to understand that various kinds of experience are central to all these modes of activity—induction, deduction, and verification—that enter into inquiry.

Throughout the analysis, researchers should incorporate all appropriate modes of inquiry. Thus, both logically derived hypotheses and those that have "serendipitously" (Merton, 1968) arisen from the data may find their way into the research.

Interrogative Hypothesis Testing

In order to verify and assess the applicability of a given hypothesis, researchers should use a style of *negative case* testing suggested by Robinson (1951), Lindesmith (1952), Manheim and Simon (1977), Denzin (1978, 1989), and during more recent years, Morse and Richards (2002) and Warren and Karner (2005). The process of negative case testing involves the investigator intentionally seeking negative or unique cases until the data are saturated and built into an emerging pattern; at that point, the investigator looks for confirmation of a developing theory or a specific hypothesis. This testing process involves the following steps:

1. Make a rough hypothesis based on an observation from the data.
2. Conduct a thorough search of all cases to locate negative cases (that is, cases that do not fit the hypothesized relationship).
3. If a negative case is located, either discard or reformulate the hypothesis to account for the negative case or exclude the negative case.
4. Examine all relevant cases from the sample before determining whether "practical certainty" (Denzin, 1978) in this recommended analysis style is attained.

For example, based on a reading of responses to the open-ended question, "With which of the following do you most closely associate yourself: Conservative, Orthodox, Reform, or Nonpracticing?" I (Berg, 1983) hypothesized that certain groups of persons offered instrumentally oriented answers (that is, oriented to achievement and goals) while other groups offered expressively oriented answers (that is, sentimental, feeling oriented, and symbolic). I further hypothesized that these styles of responses could be linked to particular categories relevant to the analysis of differential involvement with religious activities and subjective affiliational identification. However, after carefully reexamining each case, with these hypotheses in mind, I found many negative cases. At each negative juncture, I attempted to reformulate the hypotheses to account for the cases that did not fit. Unfortunately, I soon realized that my hypotheses had become artificial and meaningless. Consequently, I soon abandoned them. None of the successive formulations were constructed de novo but were based on some aspect of the preceding hypothetical relationship (see Denzin, 1978, pp. 193–194; Lindesmith, 1947, pp. 9–10).

Howard S. Becker (1998) has offered a similar approach, which he calls the *null hypothesis trick*. Becker suggests that the researcher should initially assume that the data reveal no patterns or relationships. Then the researcher should tease out various conditions under which the observed pattern might develop. Esterberg (2002, p. 175) also offers an explanation of this null hypothesis trick, suggesting that you state a relationship in your research as not existing and then seek "clear evidence, based on examples from the data, that there is one." Again, effectively this so-called null hypothesis trick is paramount to interrogative hypothesis testing.

It may be argued that the search for negative cases sometimes neglects contradictory evidence (that is, when a case both affirms and in some way denies a hypothetical relationship) or distorts the original hypothetical relationship (that is, when the observers read into the data whatever relationship they have hypothesized—a variation on post factum hypothesizing). To accomplish content analysis in the style recommended here, researchers must use several safeguards against these potential flaws in analysis. First, whenever numbers of cases allow, examples that illustrate a point should be lifted at random from among the relevant grouped cases. Second, every assertion made in the analysis should be documented with no fewer than three examples. Third, analytic interpretations should be examined carefully by an independent reader (someone other than the actual researchers) to ensure that their claims and assertions are not derived from a misreading of the data and that they have been documented adequately. Finally, whenever inconsistencies in patterns do emerge, these too should be discussed in order to explain whether they have invalidated overall patterns. Failure to mention these inconsistencies in pattern is a less than forthright presentation of the data and analysis.

In effect, the use of the foregoing safeguards avoids what Glaser and Strauss (1967, p. 5) describe as *exampling*. According to Glaser and Strauss, exampling is finding examples for "dreamed-up, speculative, or logically deducted theory after the idea occurred," rather than allowing the patterns to emerge from the data. For instance, in the course of analyzing responses to the question, "How do you celebrate Chanukkah, if at all?" during an early analysis of the data, I (Berg, 1983) suggested that gift giving was emphasized to a greater extent by some affiliational groups than by others. However, when this section was read by an independent reader, the reader noticed that several negative cases had been presented in evidence of this assertion. What I had originally missed was that the more traditional affiliational group members had described their style of gift giving in the midst of a number of traditional (religious) rituals. On the other hand, many of the nonpracticing affiliational group members had described gift giving as being in competition with an observance of Christmas and, thus, actually fused their observance of Chanukkah with an observance of Christmas.

Stages in the Content Analysis Process

As a means of recapitulation of what has been described in this chapter as the content analysis process, consider the model offered in Figure 11.1. In the first stage of content analysis you begin with the research question. Specifically, what are you interested in finding an explanation for? Next, many researchers move to developing a number of sociological constructs or analytic categories by sorting the themes or category labels of the various chunks of data (generally segments of text from field notes, interview transcripts, or whatever textual data are being analyzed). These analytic categories arise from reading the literature, links to the research question, or even directly from interview questions (in the case of depth interviews).

After establishing the analytic categories, the next step is to read through the data. Although you need not read through all transcripts or every page of field notes, you should read through a fairly hefty amount of the data. As you do, you can begin to jot down what seem to be on the surface relevant themes and category labels for sorting the data. You are also likely to notice that some of the analytic categories you have already identified (or similar versions of them) emerge. As you conduct this segment of the analysis, it is important to keep in mind that the categories should have some relationship with the research question and should not simply be random words that seem to occur with some regular frequency.

Figure 11.1 Stage Model of Qualitative Content Analysis

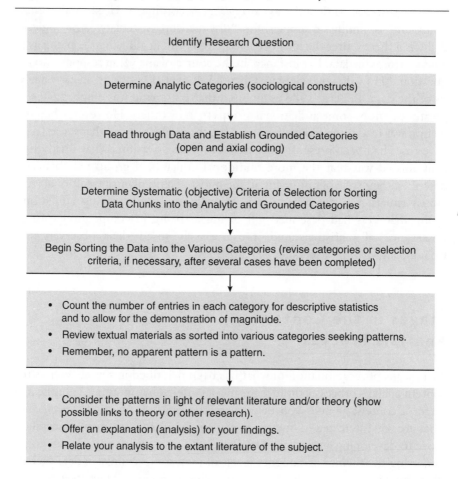

After establishing the analytic and grounded categories, you need to establish objective criteria for selection. The idea here is to offer some explicit definition or coding rules for each category (either analytic or grounded). This criterion might simply be the specific statement of a particular phrase or word, or it might include several inferential levels. For example, you might sort data chunks into a category provided the subject (or field notes) has described a particular event, such as a holiday, or a type of event or activity. In the Berg and colleagues (2004) study, for example, one analytic category they used was labeled *sexual risks*. Anytime the subject mentioned behaviors that represented a sexual risk, that information was sorted into this category. This included descriptions of unprotected sex or having sex with a partner who was a stranger, as well as having multiple sexual partners.

Once the criteria for selection for various categories have been accomplished, the next stage is to sort the data accordingly. This can be accomplished in a number of ways. At one time most researchers created tally sheets with the specific categories listed at the top of each sheet. Then the data were read and each time a segment or data chunk fit the criteria, its location was recorded (e.g., case number 5, page 22, line 54). Or, alternatively, some researchers literally cut the text, labeled it (with its case and page location), and cast it (physically) into a box labeled with the appropriate category. Today, researchers can employ a variety of electronic means to undertake this same sorting and casting process, including the more systematic use of textual computer programs that permit creation of the categories (both analytic and grounded ones) and then seek and locate text that has been specified.

After sorting or locating data chunks, I recommend taking a surface look at the data by counting the number of items of data chunks that have been cast into each category. Although not really a finding in itself, having a larger number of chunks of data from many cases in a particular category does suggest to the researcher where to look for patterns. As well, if many of these items say similar things that establish a pattern, then you are able to offer the reader some idea of how strong the pattern is by describing its magnitude (the proportion of the sample that made similar comments or statements). A common rule of thumb is that a minimum of three occurrences of something can be considered a pattern. The rationale for this as follows: once is an accident, twice is a coincidence, and three times moves beyond mere chance to a pattern.

Once thematic (categorical) patterns have been identified, they still need to be explained. Inexperienced researchers often see this segment of the analysis process as the most challenging. Once again you must consult the literature and consider your pattern findings in light of previous research and existing theory. Do your findings confirm previous similar research? Do they contradict previous studies? How can you explain these differences or similarities? As you begin to consider answers to these sorts of questions, you should also begin to see that you are conducting analysis.

Strengths and Weaknesses of the Content Analysis Process

Perhaps the most important advantage of content analysis is that it can be virtually unobtrusive (Webb et al., 1981, 2004). Content analysis, although useful when analyzing depth interview data, may also be used nonreactively: no one needs to be interviewed, no one needs to fill out lengthy questionnaires, no one must enter a laboratory. Rather, newspaper accounts, public addresses, libraries, archives, television shows, movies, and similar sources allow researchers to conduct analytic studies.

An additional advantage is that content analysis is cost effective (Babbie, 2004). Generally, the materials necessary for conducting content analysis are easily and inexpensively accessible. One college student working alone can effectively undertake a content analysis study, whereas undertaking a national survey, for instance, might require enormous staff, time, and expense.

A further advantage to content analysis is that it provides a means by which to study a process that occurs over long periods of time that may reflect trends in a society (Babbie, 2004). As examples, you might study the portrayal of women in the media from 1800 to 1993 or you might focus on changing images of women in the media from 1982 to 1992. For instance, McBroom (1992) recently examined women in the clergy as depicted in the *Christian Century* between 1984 and 1987. McBroom (1992, p. 208) reports:

> 1984 was a year when the issue of women's ordination gained support in the news media, as indicated by the number of positive references, especially articles, during the year. . . . The next year, 1985, was a year of transition, as few references were recorded for that year. The data for the years 1986 and 1987 indicate a growing negative response to the issue of the ordination of women, especially in the negative news reports.
>
> The data . . . indicate that, in general, conditions and opportunities for women in the clergy in the United States deteriorated rather than improved during these years.

Thus, using content analysis, McBroom (1992) was able to examine data during individual years as well as over the span of all years under study.

The single serious weakness of content analysis may be in locating unobtrusive messages relevant to the particular research questions. In other words, content analysis is limited to examining already recorded messages. Although these messages may be oral, written, graphic or videotaped, they must be recorded in some manner in order to be analyzed.

Of course, when you undertake content analysis as an analysis tool rather than as a complete research strategy, such a weakness is minimal. For example, if researchers use content analysis to analyze interview data or responses to open-ended questions (on written questionnaires), this weakness is virtually nonexistent.

Another limitation (although some might call it a weakness) of content analysis is that it is ineffective for testing causal relationships between variables. Researchers and their audiences must resist the temptation to infer such relationships. This is particularly true when researchers forthrightly present the proportion or frequency with which a theme or pattern is observed. This kind of information is appropriate to indicate the magnitude of certain responses; however, it is not appropriate to attach cause to these presentations.

As with any analytic method, the advantages of content analysis must be weighed against the disadvantages and against alternative research strategies. Although content analysis may be appropriate for some research problems and designs, it is not appropriate in every research situation. It is a particularly beneficial procedure for assessing events or processes in social groups when public records exist. It is likewise helpful in many types of exploratory or descriptive studies. But if you are interested in conducting experimental or causal research, content analysis is virtually useless.

Computers and Qualitative Analysis

It has now been 40 years since General Inquirer, the first software program designed to assist in the analysis of textual data, became public (Stone, Dunphy, Smith, & Ogilvie, 1966; Tesch, 1991). Of course, when General Inquirer came out, affordable personal computers did not exist. To use the original form of General Inquirer, one needed access to a large mainframe computer and sufficient time to read and digest its book-length instructions. This program largely operated on the basis of counting and numerous calculations. Yet, it did work exclusively with textual data (Tesch, 1991). A version of General Inquirer is still available today for the modern personal computer and qualitative researcher via an online server and weblog (see Philip Stone's Weblog at http://blogs.law.harvard.edu/inquirer).

Most experienced (and even many novice) qualitative researchers are aware today that a number of computer programs for qualitative data exist—even if they do not use them. An entire area of research and discussion known as *Computer Assisted Qualitative Data Analysis* or CAQDA has evolved during the past two decades (Alpi, 2004; Dohan & Sanchez-Janowski, 1998; La Pelle, 2004; Lewins & Silver, 2005). Throughout the 1980s, many academic journals published articles directing considerable attention toward commercially available software designed specifically for qualitative analysis (Conrad & Reinharz, 1984; Drass, 1980; Gerson, 1984; Heise, 1981; Jacobs, 1987; Seidel, 1984).

In 1987, Brent, Scott, and Spencer reported that 77 percent of the qualitative researchers they surveyed on computer use said they used computers in their research. In 1991, Tesch reported that over 3,000 people had purchased a single dedicated qualitative analysis software package called The Ethnograph (Tesch, 1991). In a 1991 survey of qualitative researchers by Miles and Huberman (1994), three quarters of respondents reported using computer software for data entry, coding, searching and retrieval, display, and concept building. Miles and Huberman also found that satisfaction with computer software was mixed among these researchers.

It would be impossible to estimate how many qualitative researchers today use either such dedicated software packages or word processing programs in their analysis.

To be sure, the potential for using computers in qualitative research for analytic purposes or, as Dennis (1984) calls it, *word crunching*, is enormous. Some researchers have adapted commercial software packages to their personal qualitative sorting or data management needs. For example, Lotus 1-2-3 and similar spreadsheets can be applied to a wide assortment of tasks common in content analysis. You can, for instance, create fields to contain shorthand versions of themes, classes, or categories and corresponding fields to indicate tallies of these categorical containers. After you sort textual data into these fields, calculations of the magnitude (how many times a theme has been placed in a given thematic category) can be automatically determined. La Pelle (2004) argues that it is possible to use various components of word-processing programs to simulate many of the functions of dedicated qualitative data analysis software packages (see also Dabney, 1993; Norman, 1989).

Weitzman and Miles (1995) produced a sourcebook on computer software for qualitative data analysis. In this book they review 24 different programs that might be helpful to qualitative researchers. And Dohan and Sanchez-Jankowski (1998) similarly reviewed more than 20 programs. But as Weitzman and Miles (1995, p. 10) so aptly state, "There is no computer program that will ['analyze' your data . . . Computers don't analyze data; people do." Weitzman and Miles (1995) also explain that choosing the right software package depends not only on the nature of your data—interview transcripts, field notes, or other documents—but also on how you desire to approach and analyze these data. In other words, what exactly do you want to accomplish with the analysis?

In addition, Weitzman and Miles (1995) suggest that choosing a software program to assist in qualitative analysis depends on what I will call a computer comfort level. If a researcher is new to computers or not very comfortable using them, it is probably better to begin with a simple word-processing program. This will provide an opportunity for the novice to learn about and explore the computer operating system and become more comfortable with creating files, moving text and, in general, more confident about computers. If, on the other hand, the researcher is fairly well acquainted with computers and computer operating systems, he or she might want to explore one or another of a number of more dynamic database management programs.

Morse and Richards (2002, p. 80) point out that software intended for qualitative research allows researchers the versatility of not only storing materials but also storing "ideas, concepts, issues, questions, models, and theories. Researchers can relate the various materials by coding relevant sections of text, by linking them, or by writing about them."

Weitzman and Miles (1995) as well as Gibbs, Friese, and Mangabeira (2002) outline approximately six general types of functions available in software programs used in CAQDA. In many cases, multiple functions are available in a given program. These functions include word processing, text retrievers, textbase managers, code-and-retrieve programs, code-based theory builders, and conceptual network builders.

Word Processors

Word processors allow you to create text-based files and to effectively find, move, reproduce, and retrieve sections of the text in each file. These provide a means for transcribing interviews or audio portions of video, writing up or editing field notes, coding text for indexing and retrieval purposes, and even writing up findings in reports.

Text Retrievers

Software packages such as Metamorph, Orbis, Sonar, Professional, The Text Collector, WordCruncher, or ZyINDEX are dedicated text search programs (Weitzman and Miles, 1995). These programs specialize in locating every instance of a specified word, phrase, or character string. As well, these programs are able to locate combinations of these items in one of several files.

Textbase Managers

Although similar in basic function to text retrievers, textbase managers provide a greater capacity for organizing, sorting, and making subsets of the textual data. Several examples of these programs include askSam, Folio VIEWS, Tabletop, and MAX. Some of these programs are intended to manage fairly structured text organized into records or specific case files and fields or specified areas in a given case. Other programs are capable of dealing with more free-flowing forms of text and, in some cases, even certain quantitative information.

Code-and-Retrieve Programs

Code-and-retrieve programs, according to Weitzman and Miles (1995), are often developed by qualitative researchers rather than commercial software developers. These programs are intended to assist the researcher in dividing text into segments or chunks, attach codes, and find and display these coded sections. These programs tend to fill in for the kind of cutting, pasting, and sorting of hard copy data qualitative researchers once used. HyperQual2, Kwalitan, QUALPRO, Martin, and The Ethnograph are all examples of code-and-retrieve types of programs.

Code-Based Theory Builders

These types of programs are also frequently developed by researchers. Usually, these programs include the capacity to code and retrieve and also offer special features that assist you in developing theoretical connections between coded concepts. As a result, higher-order classifications and connections can be formulated. Weitzman and Miles (1995) list AQUAD, ATLAS.ti, Hyper-RESEARCH, NUD.IST, and QCA as examples.

Conceptual Network Builders

Programs designed for conceptual network building are intended to assist the researcher in building and testing theory. These programs provide the capacity to create graphic networks. Variables are displayed as nodes (usually rectangles or ellipses) linked to other nodes by lines or arrows representing relationships. These networks represent various types of semantic networks that evolve from the data set and the concepts used by the researcher. Examples of these programs include ATLAS.ti (which is also a code-based theory builder), MECA, and SemNet.

Ann Lewins and Christina Silver (2005, p. 5), have created a checklist of questions to assist researchers in determining what sort of CAQDA package might work best for them:

- What kind(s) and amounts of data do you have, and how do you want to handle it?
- What is your preferred style of working?
- What is your theoretical approach to analysis, and how well developed is it at the outset?
- Do you have a well-defined methodology?
- Do you want a simple-to-use software that will mainly help you to manage your thinking and *thematic* coding?
- Are you more concerned with the language and the terminology used in the data, the comparison and occurrence of words and phrases across cases or between different variables?
- Do you want both thematic and quantitative content information from the data?

- Do you want a multiplicity of tools (not quite so simple) enabling many ways of handling and interrogating data?
- How much time do you have to learn the software?
- How much analysis time has been built into the project?
- Are you working individually on the project or as part of a team?
- Is this one phase of a larger project—do you already have quantitative data?
- Is there a package—and peer support—already available at your institution or place of work?

A review of the preceding list suggests many nuances that one might otherwise overlook when considering whether or not to use a CAQDA package; and although new computer packages and applications for qualitative research are introduced nearly daily, computer use in qualitative research remains in its infancy. For some researchers, it makes no difference whether they use a dedicated qualitative analysis program or apply some utility or word-processing program to the task. This is because, clearly, qualitative researchers have not yet adequately figured out how best to use computers in their research work.

In part, this may be because none of the tasks currently accomplished by computers and used in qualitative research really move beyond data organization and management. Any computer program or adaptation still requires that the researcher think through the analytic and theoretical relationships between original conceptualizations and eventual empirical evidence. Quantitative application of computers, which is enormously fast, largely makes hand calculation obsolete. Computers make it easy for researchers to take hundreds of thousands of cases and quickly determine a vast number of statistical aspects of the data set. Yet even quantitative computer programs cannot by themselves (at least not yet) extrapolate on or beyond the statistical manipulations made on the data.

In the case of qualitative analysis, this problem of extrapolation is made even more difficult. Analysis of data is often intertwined in the presentation of findings and the explanation of results. Creating an apparatus that can simultaneously present the findings and describe their analytic importance would require perfection of artificial computer intelligence—a step into the future at least several decades away.

As a result, the use of computers by qualitative researchers remains, for now, an attempt to locate "chunks of technology" (Gerson, 1984) that are available, affordable, and seem to work for the present. It is important, however, to remember that computers are intended to reduce the amount of overall time a researcher spends in the data organization and analysis phase of research. If you spend enormous amounts of time trying to locate, learn how to use, and enter data into a computer program, this process may defeat the original time-saving purpose of computers. Nonetheless, the use of computers in qualitative research can significantly assist novice researchers. This is because programs such as The Ethnograph provide clear directions on how to begin organizing data into a usable structure. As you become more experienced and adept at both data analysis and computer operations, you may feel more confident and try other computer applications or adaptations.

Qualitative Research at the Speed of Light

Many areas in quantitative research have been able to quickly adapt to the advances made in computer technology by creating faster and more advanced statistical analytic packages. Qualitative research, however, may seem to have lagged behind. In part, this may be because the natures of textual, visual, and auditor analyses simply have not lent themselves neatly to any computer program. Partly, however, this may only be the outward appearance of matters, because qualitative research can actually embrace a wider element of the contemporary computer age because of its interest in textual, visual, and auditor analyses. Specifically, I refer to the huge amount of information that is available to explore through the Internet. As suggested elsewhere in this book (see in Chapter 5 the section on historiography), changes in information available on the Web during the recent past have been enormous. It is likely that such changes will continue to increase with geometric progression.

In the summer of 2000, as I sat writing the revision that was the fourth edition to this book, I predicted the following:

> I can easily forecast that with the advances in satellite technology and wireless communications, qualitative researchers will soon (perhaps by the 5th edition of this book) be able to upload and download from the Internet a wide variety of different types of qualitatively relevant data for analysis from any location in the world. (Berg, 2001, p. 264)

To a large measure, I believe that my predictions have come true. Most mid-priced contemporary laptop computers today come equipped with or have the option for being equipped with wireless communications. As suggested in Chapters 7 and 9, there are a number of computer links for those researchers interested in action research or oral histories. As well, there is a growing number of electronic journals and numerous sites for other general literature sources, global communications, and even Web storage areas. For example, try surfing over to Howard S. Becker's Web site (www.soc.ucsb.edu/faculty/hbecker) and you will have an opportunity to read a variety of Howie's works—even some of which, as he describes them, have been published in obscure places.

Other truths predicted in the fourth and reiterated in the fifth editions of this book also hold for today—namely, that there continues to be little advancement in computer programs for qualitative *analysis* per se. The programs that Nigel Fielding (1993) and Beth Rogers (1996) wrote about, and those that Ann Lewins and Christina Silver (2005) continue to describe, generally remain available—but little has been done with them to improve their capabilities beyond chiefly data management and retrieval programs—in spite of so-called *artificial intelligence* components available in some programs. Yet, the vast space of the Internet has provided for qualitative researchers new realms and opportunities both for researching subjects of study and providing access to new opportunities.

Following is a list of just a few Internet sites that might allow interested readers to begin their journey into the vast space that is the Internet to locate the qualitative research areas of the Web.

1. Qualpage, a resource listing for qualitative researchers: www.ualberta. ca/~jrnorris/qual.html
2. The Qualitative Research Page, a listing of relevant topics and resources: www.oit.pdx.edu/~kerlinb/qualresearch
3. The Qualitative Report, an online journal that also provides an alpha-betized listing of helpful qualitative research Web sites on a variety of interesting topics: www.nova.edu/ssss/QR/Web.html
4. The Institute of Sociology, Friedrich Schiller University, lists various links to information on computer text analysis packages: www.intext. de/textanae.htm
5. The Social Science Information Gateway provides a listing of resources for qualitative analysis including sites for information regarding computer-based text analysis: sosig.esrc.bris.ac.uk/about_us
6. ATLAS.ti, a software site designed for qualitative text, audio and video data: www.atlasti.de
7. CAQDAS Network, a general listing of computer-assisted qualitative analysis Web sites: caqdas.soc.surrey.ac.uk/website.htm

TRYING IT OUT

Suggestion 1 Select a topic of interest to you, such as crime, medical advances, ecology, technology, or another broad concern. Next, using your school library's collection of the *New York Times*, locate 10 consecutive weeks of the Sunday Week in Review section. Now see if you can locate articles with headlines that relate to your topic of interest. If you accomplish these tasks, you have actually conducted a rudimentary form of thematic content analysis. Your topic served as the theme and the newspaper story headlines as your units of analysis.

Suggestion 2   Without writing their names on the paper, have everyone in your class write a response to the following question: If you could change one thing in the world today, what would it be?

Ask each classmate to write his or her gender and age at the bottom of the response, but remind them not to write their names. Have each person make enough photocopies to distribute one copy to every person in the class. Now everyone has a set of data to work with.

Next, go through the responses and see if you can locate any patterns of similarity or difference. Sort the responses into groups according to the patterns or themes that emerge as you read through the responses. Try to make the following assessments:

1. How many times have students identified the same (or very similar) things they would change if they could?
2. What proportion of the class used identical words to describe what they would change?
3. Are patterns any different if you first sort them according to gender?
4. Are patterns any different if you first sort them into the following age groupings: *young* (under 20 years old), *older* (21–25 years old), *oldest* (over 25 years old)?

REFERENCES

Abrahamson, M. (1983). *Social Research Methods.* Englewood Cliffs, NJ: Prentice Hall.

Alpi, K. M. (2004). An introduction to computer assisted qualitative data analysis software. *Hypothesis* 18(1), 9–10.

Armstrong, E. G. (2001). Gangsta misogyny: A content analysis of the portrayals of violence against women in rap music, 1987–193. *Journal of Criminal Justice and Popular Culture* 8(2), 96–126.

Babbie, E. (2002). *The Basics of Social Research* (2nd ed.). Belmont, CA: Wadsworth.

Babbie, E. (2001). *The Practice of Social Research* (9th ed.). Belmont, CA: Wadsworth.

Babbie, E. (2004). *The Practice of Social Research* (10th ed.). Belmont, CA: Wadsworth.

Becker, H. S. (1998). *Tricks of the Trade: How to Think About Your Research While You're Doing It.* Chicago: University of Chicago Press.

Berelson, B. (1952). *Content Analysis in Communications Research.* Glencoe, IL: Free Press.

Berg, B. L. (1983). *Jewish identity: Subjective declarations or objective life styles.* Doctoral dissertation, Syracuse University, Syracuse, NY.

Berg, B. L. (1986). Arbitrary arbitration: Diverting juveniles into the justice system. *Juvenile and Family Court Journal 37*(5), 31–42.

Berg, B. L. (2001). *Qualitative Research Methods for the Social Sciences.* Boston: Allyn and Bacon.

Berg, B., Sañudo, F., Hovell, M., Sipan, C., Kelley, N., & Blumberg, E. (2004). The use of indigenous interviewers in a study of Latino men who have sex with men: A research note. *Sexuality and Culture 8*(1), 87–103.

Bogdan, R. C., & Biklen, S. K. (2003). *Qualitative Research for Education* (4th ed.). Boston: Allyn and Bacon.

Boje, D. (1991). The story telling organization: A study of story performance in an office supply firm. *Administrative Science Quarterly 36*, 106–126.

Carney, T. F. (1972). *Content Analysis.* Winnipeg: University of Manitoba Press.

Carpenter, C., Glassner, B., Johnson, B., & Loughlin, J. (1988). *Kids, Drugs, and Crime.* Lexington, MA: Lexington Books.

Conrad, P., & Reinharz, S. (Eds.). (1984). Computers and qualitative data. *Qualitative Sociology 7*(1/2).

Dabney, D. A. (1993). *Impaired nursing: Nurses' attitudes and perceptions about drug use and drug theft.* Master's thesis, Indiana University of Pennsylvania, Indiana, PA.

Dennis, D. L. (1984). Word crunching: An annotated bibliography on computers and qualitative data analysis. *Qualitative Sociology 7*(1/2), 148–156.

Denzin, N. K. (1989). *The Research Act* (3rd ed.). Englewood Cliffs, NJ: Prentice Hall.

Denzin, N. K. (1978). *The Research Act.* New York: McGraw-Hill.

Drass, K. A. (1980). The analysis of qualitative data: A computer program. *Urban Life 9*, 322–353.

Dohan, D., & Sanchez-Jankowski, M. (1998). Using computers to analyze ethnographic field data: Theoretical and practical considerations. *Annual Review of Sociology 24*, 477–491.

Duncan, H. D. (1962). *Communication and Social Order.* New York: Bedminster Press.

Esterberg, K. G. (2002). *Qualitative Methods in Social Research.* Boston: McGraw Hill.

Fielding, N. (1993). Analyzing qualitative data by computer. *Social Research UPDATE Issue 1*(1). Department of Sociology, University of Surrey, England. Available online at www. Soc.Surrey.ac.uk/sru/srul.html

Fields, E. E. (1988). Qualitative content analysis of television news: Systematic techniques. *Qualitative Sociology 11*(3), 183–193.

Gerson, E. M. (1984). Qualitative research and the computer. *Qualitative Sociology 17*(1/2), 61–74.

Gibbs, G. R., Friese, S., & Mangabeira, W. C. (2002). The use of technology in qualitative research. Introduction to Issue *3*(2) of *FQS. Forum Qualitative Sozialforschung/Forum: Qualitative Social Research 3*(2). Available online at www.qualitative-research.net/fqs/fqs-eng.htm

Glaser, B., & Strauss, A. (1967). *The Discovery of Grounded Theory: Strategies for Qualitative Research.* Chicago: Aldine.

Heilman, S. (1976). *Synagogue Life: A Study in Symbolic Interaction.* Englewood Cliffs, NJ: Prentice Hall.

Heise, D. R. (Ed.). (1981). Microcomputers and social research. *Special Issue of Sociological Methods and Research.*

Heise, D. (1992). *Ethnography* (2nd ed.). Chapel Hill: University of North Carolina Press.

Holsti, O. R. (1968). Content analysis. In G. Lindzey & E. Aaronson (Eds.), *The Handbook of Social Psychology.* Reading, MA: Addison-Wesley.

Holsti, O. R. (1969). *Content Analysis for the Social Sciences and Humanities*. Reading, MA: Addison-Wesley.

Jacobs, E. (1987). Qualitative research traditions: A review. *Review of Educational Research 57*(1), 1–50.

Krippendroff, K. (2003). *Content Analysis: An Introduction to Its Methodology*. Thousand Oaks, CA: Sage.

LaPelle, N. (2004). Simplifying qualitative data analysis using general purpose software tools. *Field Methods 16*(1), 85–108.

Leedy, P. D., & Ormrod, J. E. (2005). *Practical Research: Planning and Design* (8th ed.). Upper Saddle River, NJ: Pearson/Merrill/Prentice Hall.

Lewins, A., & Silver, C. (2005). Choosing a CAQDAS package. Available online at http://cagdas.soc.surrey.ac.uk/ChoosingCAQDASV2Lewins&SilverJun05.pdf.

Lindesmith, A. R. (1947). *Opiate Addiction*. Bloomington: Indiana University Press.

Lindesmith, A. R. (1952). Comment on W. S. Robinson's the logical structure of analytic induction. *American Sociological Review 17*, 492–493.

Littlejohn, S. W., & Foss, K. A. (2004). *Theories of Human Communication*. Belmont, CA: Wadsworth.

Manheim, H. L., & Simon, B. A. (1977). *Sociological Research*. Homewood, IL: Dorsey Press.

Manning, P. K., & Cullum-Swan, B. (1994). Narrative, content, and semiotic analysis. In N. K. Denzin & Y. S. Lincoln (Eds.), *Handbook of Qualitative Research*. Thousand Oaks, CA: Sage.

Maxfield, M. G., & Babbie, E. (2006). *Basics of Research Methods for Criminal Justice and Criminology*. Belmont, CA: Thompson/Wadsworth.

McBroom, J. R. (1992). Women in the clergy: A content analysis of the *Christian Century*, 1984–1987. *Free Inquiry in Creative Sociology 20*(2), 205–209.

Merton, R. K. (1968). *Social Theory and Social Structure*. New York: Free Press.

Miles, M. B., & Huberman, M. A. (1983). *Qualitative Data Analysis*. Beverly Hills, CA: Sage.

Miles, M. B., & Huberman, M. A. (1994). *Qualitative Analysis: An Expanded Sourcebook* (2nd ed.). Thousand Oaks, CA: Sage.

Morse, J. M., & Richards, L. (2002). *Read Me First: For a User's Guide to Qualitative Methods*. Thousand Oaks, CA: Sage.

Neuendorf, K. A. (2002). *The Content Analysis Guidebook*. Thousand Oaks, CA: Sage.

Norman, E. (1989). How to use word processing software to conduct content analysis. *Computers in Nursing 7*, 127–128.

Pearson, F. (1987). Taking quality into account: Assessing the benefits and costs of New Jersey's intensive supervision program. In B. R. McCarthy (Ed.), *Intermediate Punishment*. Monsey, NY: Willow Tree Press.

Robinson, W. S. (1951). The logical structure of analytic induction. *American Sociological Review 16*, 812–818.

Rodgers, B. (1996). Computational qualitative data analysis software programs. University of Wisconsin, Milwaukee, School of Nursing. Available online at www.uwm.edu/~brodg/software.htm

Sanders, W., & Pinhey, T. K. (1959). *The Conduct of Social Research*. New York: Holt, Rinehart & Winston.

Schatzman, L., & Strauss, A. (1973). *Field Research: Strategies for a Natural Sociology*. Englewood Cliffs, NJ: Prentice Hall.

Seidel, J. (1984). The Ethnograph. *Qualitative Sociology 7*(1/2), 110–125.

Selltiz, C., Jahoda, M., Deutsch, M., & Cook, S. W. (1959). *Research Methods in Social Relations*. New York: Holt, Rinehart & Winston.

Selltiz C., Jahoda, Deutsch, M., & Cook, S. W. (1967). *Research Methods in Social Relations* (2nd ed.). New York: Holt, Rinehart & Winston.

Silverman, D. (1993). *Interpreting Qualitative Data*. Thousand Oaks, CA: Sage.

Smith, H. W. (1975). *Strategies of Social Research*. Englewood Cliffs, NJ: Prentice Hall.

Stone, P. J., Dunphy, D. C., Smith, M. S., & Ogilvie, D. M. (1966). *The General Inquirer: A Computer Approach to Content Analysis*. Cambridge, MA: MIT Press.

Strauss, A. L. (1959). *Mirrors and Masks*. Glencoe, IL: Free Press.

Strauss, A. L. (1987). *Qualitative Analysis for Social Scientists*. New York: Cambridge University Press.

Strauss, A. L. (1990). *Qualitative Analysis for Social Scientists* (2nd ed.). New York: Cambridge University Press.

Strauss, A. L., & Corbin, J. M. (1998). *Basics of Qualitative Research: Techniques and Procedures for Developing Grounded Theory*. Thousand Oaks, CA: Sage.

Sutherland, E. H. (1950). *Principles of Criminology* (2nd ed.). Philadelphia: J. B. Lippincott.

Sutherland, E. H., & Cressey, D. (1966). *Principles of Criminology* (7th ed.). New York: J. B. Lippincott.

Tesch, R. (1991). Introduction. *Qualitative Sociology 14*(3), 225–243.

Warren, C., & Karner, T. (2005). *Discovering Qualitative Methods*. Los Angeles: Roxbury.

Webb, E. J., Campbell, D. T., Schwartz, R. D., & Sechrest, L. (2004). *Unobtrusive Measures* (rev. ed.). Thousand Oaks. CA: Sage.

Webb, E. J., Campbell, D. T., Schwartz, R. D., Sechrest, L., & Grove, J. B. (1981). *Nonreactive Measures in the Social Sciences*. Boston: Houghton Mifflin.

Weitzman, E. A., & Miles, M. B. (1995). *Computer Programs for Qualitative Data Analysis*. Thousand Oaks, CA: Sage.

Chapter 12

Writing Research Papers: Sorting the Noodles from the Soup

NINETEEN YEARS AGO, MY children Alex and Kate, who were then nearly four and nearly six, respectively, sat around the kitchen table eating alphabet soup for lunch. Kate was stirring her soup with great care and deliberation. She managed to capture several letters on her spoon, carefully spilled off the liquid, and spelled out her name. "Look, Daddy, I wrote my name with my noodles! K-A-T-I-E." Alex, seeing the attention his sister received, pulled his dripping spoon from the soup and, spilling much of it onto the floor, proudly held it up and exclaimed, "Me too!" Unfortunately, his letters spelled out "XCYU," a unique spelling of Alex, or simply a failure to sort the noodles from the soup in a fashion that made his noodles mean something to others.

Qualitative research similarly can result either in improved social scientific understanding or in meaningless gibberish. This chapter is designed to enable inexperienced researchers to offer up their noodles for inspection by others in an understandable and meaningful fashion—in other words, to write up the research so that it will be disseminated in an understandable form and to appropriate audiences. Before actually getting to the mechanics of writing up research papers, I believe it is important to write a few lines on the perils of plagiarism.

Plagiarism: What It Is, Why It's Bad, and How to Avoid It

Ironically, depending upon the *source*, you are likely to find a range of meanings and definitions for the term *plagiarism*. Regardless of these variations, at their root these definitions share the notion that plagiarism involves passing off the ideas and words of others as your own without clearly acknowledging the actual source of those ideas and words. Importantly, in academe as in the real world of the social sciences, journalism, the arts, the pure sciences, and virtually everywhere else, plagiarism is considered very bad regardless of whether it is done intentionally or unintentionally.

The label of plagiarism can describe any of the following actions:

- Turning in someone else's written work as your own (regardless of whether you have their permission to do so).
- Purchasing a written work from a professional *paper mill*, your sorority or fraternity, the smart kid in class, or any other source, and passing it off as your own work.
- Copying sentences, paragraphs, or whole pages from a textbook, Web site, or other written source without indicating the actual source of this material.
- Copying sentences, paragraphs, or whole pages from a textbook, Web site, or other written source without including proper quotation marks, page references, or indentation (in the case of longer excerpts)—even when proper citation of the actual source is offered.
- Paraphrasing sentences, paragraphs, or whole pages but failing to provide proper citation of the original source.
- False paraphrasing (changing one or two words) in sentences, paragraphs, or whole pages and failing to provide proper citation of the original source.

Why Plagiarism Occurs

It is likely that much of the plagiarism that occurs in colleges and universities, and perhaps even among some novice researchers, is what I classify as innocent or just *stupid* plagiarism; still, some is intentional and undertaken for a variety of reasons. Some of the more common intentional reasons for plagiarism include, "I was running out of time, and the source said exactly what I wanted to say." "The source said it so much better than I possibly could have." "It was a stupid assignment, and I have more important things to do with my time." "Everybody else was doing it."

Innocent or plain stupid plagiarism, the heading for which I believe the bulk of college- and university-based plagiarism can fall under, involves errors in citation because the students simply do not understand that their actions constitute plagiarism—they are kind of stupid in this regard. By the way, authorities are typically no less sympathetic to stupid plagiaristic mistakes than they are to intentional ones. However, stupid mistakes are easier to correct because once you learn the errors of your ways, you can consciously avoid making stupid mistakes of plagiarism. So, let's consider how to avoid stupid plagiaristic mistakes.

How to Avoid Plagiarism

Avoiding the first two items in the previous list seems like a no-brainer. Obviously, if you go out and borrow or buy someone else's work, you have intentionally plagiarized these works, and there is no lenience for you—a minimum of thirty years hard labor. Well, maybe that's a little drastic, but you should understand that the action of intentional plagiarism is seldom taken lightly, and in some schools it can result in suspension or expulsion. In the real world, getting caught in such an act could result in the loss of a job or at the very least the loss of trust in your work, probably forever.

Let us therefore concern ourselves with the remaining four items on the list, which do frequently occur among students and inexperienced writers as stupid mistakes. The first of these four items states: *Copying sentences, paragraphs, or whole pages from a textbook, Web site, or other written source without indicating the actual source of this material.* In truth, this one walks a thin line between a stupid mistake and an intentional one and may from time to time fall into either of these camps. However, in my nearly 25 years of teaching in colleges and universities, I have heard some very sincere students tell me they were unaware that lifting a few sentences or a paragraph here and there and dropping them into their own writing was plagiarism. I personally think some of the blame rests with certain elementary schoolteachers who insist that their students look up the definition of words and write out the full definition without citing the dictionary as the source or who encourage students to write topical papers using the encyclopedia as a source: students who dutifully copy the passages verbatim receive an A for their efforts.

But regardless of why many students believe this sort of plagiarism is acceptable, it simply is not. It is plagiarism—but with a simple fix. Never use someone else's written work without giving credit to that original author or authors. Now, how the material is cited does, in fact, change slightly when you are directly quoting an author's or authors' work. This brings us to the next item on my list: *Copying sentences, paragraphs, or whole pages from a textbook,*

Web site, or other written source without including proper quotation marks, page references, or indentation (in the case of longer excerpts)—even when proper citation of the actual source is offered.

The usual rule of thumb is when a quoted section is five lines or less, you encapsulate it between quotation marks ("quoted passage"). Following this quoted section, you cite, in text, the name of the author, the date of the publication, and the page reference where the original work appears. If you are quoting more than five lines of text, you should indent the passage on both sides—but without quotation marks; it's one or the other, not both—either indent or use quotation mark. Following the indented passage (typically on the next line and right justified), the citation is enclosed in brackets ([citation material]). Again, this citation should include the name of the author or authors, the date of the publication, and the page reference where the original passage appears.

The next item on my list is, *Paraphrasing sentences, paragraphs, or whole pages but failing to provide proper citation of the original source.* Apparently, many students believe that if they steal someone's ideas but not every word in the same order as the original author or authors set the material down, it is not plagiarism; this is a very wrong assessment. This one, however, is at least a bit more understandable as a simple stupid mistake. The fact of the matter is, if you take another author's idea(s), you need to reference that author. This is often done with what are hopefully familiar phrases, such as, "According to Joe Jones (2006) . . ." or "In a similar fashion, Marshal and Cates (2006) found. . . ." The material following these sorts of statements can be heavily paraphrased, almost unidentifiable with the original, but if the main points have actually been lifted from the original version, it is proper to cite these original authors. It is also a solid way to document your writing, especially if what you are saying, using the other author or author(s)' ideas and they are a little controversial.

The last entry on my list describes a very sloppy strategy that results in plagiarism. This element states: *False paraphrasing (changing one or two words) in sentences, paragraphs, or whole pages and failing to provide proper citation of the original source.* In this case, you take a statement such as the one offered by Maxfield and Babbie (2006, p. 217), which follows: "Field research encompasses two different methods of obtaining data: (1) making direct observation and (2) asking questions." In your paper, you decide to *falsely-paraphrase* the statement as follows: Field research involves two different ways to collect data: (1) making direct observation and (2) asking questions. While you certainly have changed a few words, it remains essentially what Maxfield and Babbie (2006) said in their original version. So, how do you avoid plagiarism? Simple—add the original authors as a citation as follows: According to Maxfield and Babbie (2006), field research involves two different ways to collect data: (1) making direct observation and (2) asking questions. Note that because it is not an exact quote—albeit a rather close paraphrasing—you are not required to place quotation marks around the statement or to include a page reference where the original was found. Failure to have cited Maxfield and Babbie, either as shown or with the citation enclosed in parentheses after the statement, would constitute plagiarism.

Now that you know what plagiarism is and some ways to avoid it, let us turn to some general issues regarding how to begin to write your research papers.

Identifying the Purpose of the Writing: Arranging the Noodles

When preparing to report information obtained from research, investigators should begin by considering the purpose of the study. If you want, as some sociological researchers do, to advance theory and conceptualization about certain patterns of behaviors, this is the goal you must aim for (see Burns, 1980; Glassner & Berg, 1980; Humphreys, 1975). A slightly different goal may be necessary if the purpose is to improve some particular component of the practice of a particular discipline, such as nursing (see Ipema, 1979; Jacobsen, 1979; Leininger, 1982; Peterson, 1985). Similarly, as seen in much of the literature in criminology, corrections, the justice community, and other political spheres, researchers may focus on policy issues (see Adler & Adler, 1983; Berg, 1987; Johnson et al., 1985; Michalowski, 1996; Skibinski & Koszuth, 1986; Tontodonato & Hagan, 1998).

In part, identification of the purpose goes hand in hand with understanding the audience. For effective written dissemination of research information, the character of the audience is as important to the writer as the character of the listening audience is to the speaker when presenting an oral presentation (Leedy & Ormond, 2005; Nachmias & Nachmias, 2000). If researchers are interested in reaching a selected audience, their reports must speak to issues and concerns relevant to that particular community. If, on the other hand, they want to reach a broader, more general audience, researchers must take care to address larger, more general concerns. A common mistake made by inexperienced researchers is coining terms to accommodate a given audience. One may "sociologize," for example, nursing issues, believing this will make them more understandable to sociologists. Conversely, one may "nursiologize"—to coin a phrase—sociological terms in order to make them more comprehensible to nurse researchers by using terms like *ethnonursing, transcultural nursing, participatory nursing action research,* and so forth. Both efforts are mistakes. Writing clearly and concisely and avoiding all unnecessary jargon from any particular social science discipline are the best tactics. In the remainder of this chapter, major components of standard social scientific reports are described.

Delineating A Supportive Structure: Visual Signals for the Reader

Generally speaking, written reports can be conceptually divided into several different segments, each of which contributes some element necessary for the reader to understand fully what the researchers say. In essence, these elements form the skeleton or supportive structure of the report. Supportive structure, as it is used here, refers to a number of major headings that give order to the research report. See Figure 12.1. The headings in a research report form a kind of outline of visual signals for the reader to follow. Headings in reports can be classified as occurring at different levels reflecting the general level of importance. These levels or heads are sometimes listed alphabetically (A, B, C, and D).

An A head generally appears entirely in capital letters. Frequently, this heading will be centered or flush left on the page and in bold type. In scholarly writing, the A head is reserved for announcing the major divisions of thought that appear in the written work or to designate major sections of the work.

Example:

THIS IS AN EXAMPLE OF AN A HEAD

The B head is centered on the page with the first letter of each word capitalized (articles and prepositions are lowercase). Given the flexibility of most word processors, this too is typically written in bold type. The B head signifies subdivisions of material related to the topic of the A head. It is important information, but not a major sectional division.

Example:

This Is an Example of a B Head

The C head is usually written flush left, and again, has the first letter of each word capitalized (articles and prepositions are lowercase), and is followed by a period. The C head is used to delineate subinformational categories of the

Figure 12.1 The Basic Scheme of the Traditional Research Report

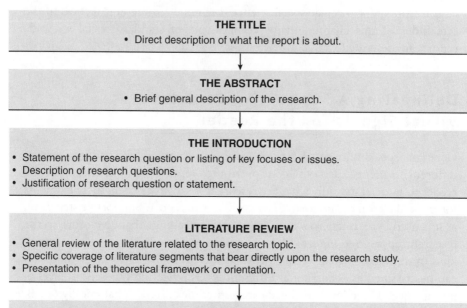

B head. These are important for categorizing or explaining information relevant to the major topical area indicated by the B head.

Example:

This Is an Example of a C Head.

The D level head is written indented from the left, with only the first letter of the first word capitalized. The heading is underlined and ends with a period (or occasionally with a colon). The D head is run into the paragraph, indented to line up with the other paragraph indentations on the page. Three spaces are generally left before the beginning of the first word of the paragraph. The D level head is used to label a specific definitional point or to enumerate a categorical listing with explanations. Again, this information is related to the broader information mentioned or described in a C level head.

Example:

This is an example of a D head.(:)   The paragraph would begin here.

Many of the sections are requisites of all research reports regardless of what specific label is used. The report typically consists of a series of A heads or sections that include:

1. *Title:*   usually appears on a *title page* (along with author information) as well as on the top of the *abstract* page (see later).
2. *Abstract:*   a brief description of the entire report.
3. *Introduction:*   basic research questions, key terms, and research focus.
4. *Literature review:*   a detailed examination of the extant research literature relevant to the report's topic.
5. *Methodology:*   a comprehensive description of how the researchers gathered data and analyzed these data.
6. *Findings or results:*   the presentation of information uncovered during the research process.
7. *Discussion and/or implications:*   an examination of these findings and consideration of how they may impinge on relevant groups, communities, or agencies.
8. *References, notes, and/or appendices:*   a section that contains the evidence that supports the research report.

Figure 12.1 illustrates the general scheme of a traditional research report. Let's consider each section in detail.

The Title

The title initially appears on the *title page*. It should be an A head placed at approximately the middle of the page and centered. Below the title should be the author's name and university affiliation information, also centered:

Example:

DRINKING AMONG COLLEGE STUDENTS ON AMERICAN CAMPUSES

By Dr. Bruce L. Berg
Department of Criminal Justice
California State University, Long Beach
Long Beach, CA 90840
(562) 985–1895

The title should give the reader a fairly good idea what the report is about. It should not be too cute or whimsical. Although that might be encouraged in English classes on creative writing, it doesn't tend to bode well for social science venues and audiences. The report title should also appear centered and at the top of the *abstract* page.

The Abstract

An abstract is a brief summary (50 to 200 words) of the most important (and interesting) research findings of a study. In addition, abstracts usually contain some mention of key methodological features of the study and relevant implications of the major findings.

Abstracts are always found in the beginning of a research report, but given their content, they cannot be created until after the report has been written. The major function of an abstract is to provide potential readers with sufficient information both to interest them and to help them determine whether to read the complete article. Often, researchers scan collections of abstracts (for example, journal indexes of abstracts) in order to identify potentially useful elements for their own literature reviews (to be considered presently). It is therefore critical that an abstract be both concise and precise.

As a broad guide to writing an abstract, regardless of the researchers' particular substantive interests, the following three key facets should be included:

1. A statement identifying the key focus or issue considered in the study.

    Example: This is the first study of drug trafficking in the United States to penetrate the echelons of the marijuana and cocaine business—[it concerns] the smugglers and their primary dealers.

2. The nature of the data analyzed in the study.

    Example: We spent six years observing and interviewing these traffickers and their associates in southwestern California and examining their typical career paths.

3. The major finding or result examined in the report.

   Example: We show how drug traffickers enter the business and rise to the top, how they become disenchanted because of the rising social and legal costs of upper-level drug trafficking, how and why they either voluntarily or involuntarily leave the business, and why so many end up returning to their deviant careers, or to other careers within the drug world.[1]

In some instances, you may want to include a fourth element that suggests the relevance of the research to a given agency, policy, or discipline:

4. Potential use or implication of the reported finding.

   Example: The findings of the current study outline the multiple conflicting forces that lure drug dealers and smugglers into and out of drug trafficking.[2]

These four elements should more or less suit virtually any research enterprise and may adequately produce an abstract consisting of as few as four sentences.

The Introduction

An introduction orients the reader to the study and the report. It should acquaint the reader with the basic research question or problem (Leedy, 2001). Introductions should be written in statement sentences that are clear and concise, and describe the type of writing that will follow (e.g., a descriptive report, an ethnographic narrative, a research proposal). Sometimes, introductions are referred to as *maps for the report*. Ideally, in addition to stating the research problem and placing it into theoretical and/or historical context, an introduction offers a sequential plan of presentation for the report. The reader is, thus, informed about what headings will be included and what each identified section will address.

It is additionally important to recognize that introductions can entice readers to continue reading, or turn them off so that they don't bother. The main attention-getting device, beyond the report title, is the opening sentence to an introduction (Meyer, 1991). A number of strategies are available to the writer. You might use a startling finding from the research, suggest some interesting problem from literature, or relate some relevant recent news event. Whatever you choose, it should be as interesting as possible. The introduction may be a distinct section complete with heading(s) or it may be combined with a literature review.

Literature Review

The basic intention of a literature review is to give a comprehensive review of previous works on the general and specific topics considered in the report. As Merriam (2001, p. 53) suggests, "The scope of the search is determined by how well defined the research problem is, as well as the researcher's prior familiarity with the topic." At least to some extent, the literature review foreshadows the researcher's own study. Chapter 2 has already elaborated on the procedures usually surrounding the development of a literature review (see the two-card method). During the writing stage of research, it is necessary to report on the state of the literature: its limitations and research directions.

For example, researchers may want to challenge previously accepted ideas or findings. It is important, therefore, that these competing conceptualizations be presented and errors or fallacies identified. In some situations, researchers might be attempting to replicate previous studies and improve on their use of theory or methods. In such cases, it is necessary to illustrate how these previous studies examined their subject matter.

To a large measure, the literature review may also serve as a kind of bibliographic index and guide for the reader, not only by listing other studies about a given subject but also by demonstrating where the current study fits into the scheme of things.

Literature reviews should certainly include reference to classic works related to the investigation and should also include any recent studies. Omission of some relevant recent study may leave researchers open to criticism for carelessness—particularly if omitted studies have more exhaustively examined the literature, identified or conducted research in similar areas, or pointed out theoretical and methodological issues the current study overlooks. The more thorough the literature review, the more solid the research report's foundation becomes.

It is important to remember that not all sources of information are considered equal or can be legitimately used in writing literature reviews. Moreover, there is a kind of generally accepted hierarchy of informational sources. As I see this hierarchy, there are certain pieces of information that are better accepted by the scientific community than others. This hierarchy is not a completely static or rigid rank ordering.

1. Scholarly empirical articles, dissertations, monographs, and the like (including electronic articles from referred online journals on the Internet)
2. Scholarly, nonempirical articles and essays (both referred and nonjuried articles and essays)
3. Textbooks

4. Trade journal articles
5. Certain nationally and internationally recognized newsmagazines (e.g., *Time, Newsweek, The Atlantic Monthly*)
6. Papers, reports, or other documents posted by individuals on various Internet Web sites
7. Certain nationally and internationally recognized newspapers (e.g., *The New York Times, The LA Times, The Washington Post, The Times* [of London])
8. Acceptable, lower order newspapers (e.g., *The Boston Globe, USA Today*)
9. Only when all other sources are unavailable, or when you want to add texture or detail, you should (sparingly) use a local newspaper
10. Written personal communications (letters, solicited comments)
11. Oral personal communications (face-to-face talks, telephone calls)

The elements listed in 1 through 3 offer the strongest documentary support in scholarly writing. Items listed as 4 through 7 offer moderately strong support to a document, and items 8 through 10 offer useful, perhaps colorful documentary sources of information. As one moves down the list, one should realize there is considerable loss of scientific confidence in the information obtained from these sources. These lower-order sources should be used only when noting some event or highlighting some already well-documented piece of information.

Like everything else, of course, too much of a good thing ruins the experience. Although certain types of research reports, such as a thesis or dissertation, expect lengthy (10–20 pages) literature reviews, reports and articles do not. Just as omitting a recent relevant article creates problems for a report, so too can an overdone literature review. The basic rule of thumb in writing literature reviews is to keep them long enough to cover the area but short enough to remain interesting.

Methodology

Inexperienced researchers often think the methodology section is the most difficult section to write. It need not be so. In fact, since methodology sections typically report what you did during the course of a research project, it may well be one of the easiest sections to produce. The central purpose of a methodological section is to explain to readers how the research was accomplished—in other words, what the data consist of and how data were collected, organized, and analyzed. It is actually quite interesting; yet, people who have little trouble describing intricate instructions for operating complicated medical equipment or repairing cars and electrical appliances pale at the thought of describing research methods.

The simplest, most straightforward way to write up the methodology section is to imagine explaining the process to a friend. Explaining the details about how the research was conducted is reasonably similar to telling a story. The points of detail most important to the researchers may vary from study to study, just as certain details in classic tales vary from storyteller to storyteller. Nonetheless, certain salient features of research methods tend to be present in most, if not all, methods sections. These features include considerations of subjects, data, setting, and analysis techniques.

Subjects   Methodology sections should include references to whom the subjects are, how they have been identified (selected), what they have been told about their participation, and what steps have been taken to protect them from harm. Ancillary concerns connected to discussions about the subjects may include how many are included, what determined their numbers, and how many refused to take part in the research and why (if it is known).

Data   In addition to identifying the nature of the data (e.g., interviews, focus groups, ethnographies, videotapes), researchers should explain to readers how data were collected. Details about data collection have several important purposes. First, they allow readers to decide how much credence to attach to the results. Second, they provide a means for readers to replicate a research study, should they desire to do so. This notion of *replication* is very important to establishing that your research endeavor is objective. If someone else can replicate your study, then the original premises and findings can be tested in the future.

Finally, data-collection sections frequently are among the most interesting aspects of a research report—particularly when the researchers include details about problems and how they were resolved. Some self-reflection and disclosure may be necessary to offer what the literature sometimes calls *subjective views of the researcher.* In addition to offering interesting and vivid experiences, these subjective offerings may allow future researchers a way around problems in their own research studies.

Setting   Descriptions of the setting can be important in reporting an ethnographic study or a door-to-door interviewing project. The reliability of the research data, for example, may depend on demonstrating that an appropriate setting for the study has been selected. In some instances, settings are intricately related to the data and the analytic strategies and may possibly contaminate the research. A failure on the part of researchers to consider these elements during the study may weaken or destroy their otherwise credible arguments.

Analysis Techniques   Even when data are to be analyzed through generally accepted conventional means, a discussion and justification of the analytic strategy should be offered. It is not good procedure to assume anything regarding a research report. Researchers should never assume that the readers will immediately understand what is meant by such vague terms as *standard content analysis techniques.* As suggested in Chapter 11, even so-called standard content analysis may have many possible analytic alternatives depending on which unit of analysis is selected and whether the approach is inductive or deductive.

Findings or Results

In quantitative research reports, the findings or results section commonly presents percentages and proportions of the data in the form of charts, tables, and graphs. Quantitative methodologists often use the two terms synonymously, although in fact, there is a slight distinction between them. *Findings* quite literally refer to what the data say, whereas *results* offer interpretations of the meaning of the data. In short, results offer an *analysis* of the data.

In the case of qualitative research reports, however, the findings or results section is not as easily explained. For example, in qualitative research reports, the analysis section often follows the methods section. Sometimes, however, the researchers forthrightly explain that data will be presented throughout their analysis in order to demonstrate and document various patterns and observations (see Berg, 1983, Bing, 1987; Dabney, 1993). Sections of qualitative reports are also often organized according to conceptual subheadings (often arising from the terms and vocabularies of the subjects).

When ethnographic research is reported, the findings are more accurately represented and labeled an *ethnographic narrative* followed by a separate *analysis* (Berg & Berg, 1988; Burns, 1980; Creswell, 2002). Of course, there may be occasions when weaving the ethnographic observations throughout the analysis seems an effective presentation strategy, creating a type of *content and narrative analysis* (Cabral, 1980; Manning & Cullum-Swan, 1994; Potter & Wetherell, 1992).

Reporting observations from a content analysis of interview data or other written documents may similarly be accomplished either by separately presenting the findings or by interweaving findings and analysis. What should be clear from the preceding presentation is that with regard to qualitative research reports, several options are available for writing about the findings (data) and results (interpretation of the data).

Discussion/Conclusion

The basic content of the discussion section will vary depending on whether the researchers have presented an analysis section or a findings section. In the former case, when an analysis section is included in a report, the discussion section frequently amounts to reiteration and elaboration of key points and suggestions about how the findings fit into the extant literature on the topical study area.

In the case of a separate findings section, the discussion section provides researchers with an opportunity to elaborate on presented observations. Frequently, in either case, after completing a research project, the social scientists realize they have gained both greater knowledge and insight into the phenomenon investigated. The discussion section provides a canvas on which the researchers may paint their insights. Occasionally, researchers gain Socratic wisdom; that is, they begin to realize what they—and the scientific community—still do not know about some substantive area. The discussion section allows the researchers to outline the areas requiring further research.

The discussion section also provides an opportunity to reflexively consider the research study and the research results. More and more these days, researchers are being acknowledged as active participants in the research process and not passive observers or mere scribes (Hertz, 1996). It becomes essential, therefore, to indicate the researcher's location of self within the constellations of gender, race, social class, and so forth (DeVault, 1995; Edwards, 1990; Williams & Heikes, 1993). Through reflexive personal accounts researchers should become more aware of how their own positions and interests affected their research. In turn, this should produce less distorted accounts of the social worlds about which they report.

References, Notes, and Appendices

Throughout the sections of a research report, references should document claims, statements, and allegations. Although a number of style texts recommend various ways of referencing material, there are chiefly two broad options: *notes* or *source references*. Superscript numerals can be placed in the text to correspond to notes, located either at the bottom of the page on which they appear (footnotes) or at the conclusion of the report (endnotes). The second broad option is source references, which appear immediately following the point in the text where a quote, paraphrase, or statement in need of documentation is made (the style used in this text). Source references are identified by the last name of a referenced author, the date of publication, and in the case of a direct quotation, the page(s) from which the quote has been taken.

In the social sciences, source references are more often used for documenting statements made in the text, and notes generally give further explanation to the text rather than cite source references. The following points concerning source references should be observed:

1. If the author's name appears in the text, only the date of the publication appears in parentheses.

   Example: According to Naples (1997) . . .

2. If the author's name is not used in the text, both the last name and the date of publication appear in parentheses.

   Example: The use of ethnographic narratives offers details on reflexive voice and anxiety (Michalowski, 1997).

3. When a reference has two or three authors, the last name of each author is included in text. For reference material with more than three authors, the first author is shown in text followed by "et al."

   Examples: Link and Cullen (1987) and Johnson et al. (1985) have examined various aspects of deviant behavior.

4. For institutional authorship, the agency that produced the document is considered to be the author.

   Example: Information on Index crimes suggests an increase (FBI Uniform Crime Report, 1985).

5. When several sources are offered to document one claim or statement, each complete citation is separated by a semicolon and presented in chronological order.

   Example: This has been suggested throughout the literature, especially by Beschner (1986); Cullen (1982); Glassner and Berg (1980); and Johnson et al. (1985).

6. When quoting directly, it is important to offer the page reference as well as the author's name and publication date in one of two forms.

   Example: Doerner (1983, p. 22) states, ". . ." or Doerner (1983: 22) states, ". . ."

During the past several years, the use of online journals, unpublished papers posted on the Web, online newspaper articles, and similar electronic documentary sources has necessitated a more uniform method for referencing these items. In the text, online items can be handled essentially as you would any other item. If there is an author, then the author's name is cited in the same manner as in the foregoing illustrations. If there is no specific author, but there is a sponsoring organization, then the organization is cited. For example, an article without an author found on the American Civil Liberties Union's Web site could cite *ACLU,* and any date indicated on the item. If no date is provided, then the convention should be to indicate *no date* in parentheses. *Example:* The use of such laws has been suggested to be both unjust and illegal (ACLU, no date).

References are listed alphabetically by the first author's last name, in a separate section entitled "References." A reference section must include all source references included in the report. As a matter of practice, the abbreviation "et al.," which is appropriate for citations in text, is unacceptable in a reference section. The first names of authors may be either indicated in full or by initial, unless you are writing for some particular publication that specifies a preference.

The better academic journals of each discipline differ somewhat in the format for writing up full citations in the reference section. These specifications are generally given in the first few pages of the journals and may change slightly from time to time. It is, thus, advisable to consult the particular journals associated with your discipline to ascertain the proper form for the reference citations. To get inexperienced researchers going, however, what follows is the format recommended for most social science journals and texts.

1. *Books:* Ribbens, J., & Edwards, R. (1998). *Feminist Dilemmas in Qualitative Research.* Thousand Oaks, CA: Sage.
2. *Periodicals:* Berg, B. L. (1986). Arbitrary arbitration: Diverting juveniles into the justice system. *Juvenile and Family Court Journal 37,* 31–42.
3. *Collections:* Peterson, B. H. (1985). A qualitative clinical account and analysis of a care situation. In M. M. Leininger (Ed.), *Qualitative Research Methods in Nursing,* 267–281. Orlando, FL: Grune & Stratton.

When writing up an online documentary item in the reference section, the format is again similar to that of standard references. References are fitted into the alphabetical listing by author's last name, or the initials of the organization. Even the layout of the reference listing of the online item parallels, in most respects, the layout of any standard reference listing. The major difference is that at the end of the reference entry, you include the Web site address. You accomplish this by writing *Available online at* and then the Web address.

Example: Despres, B. R. (August 1999). The da Vinci program: A narrative study of an alternative learning approach for life. *Educational Insights 5*(1). Available online at www.csci.edu.ubc.ca/publications/online/v05n01/despres.html

Presenting Research Material

The purpose of social research is to locate answers to social problems or questions. However, this is not enough: Once a possible solution is identified, it remains worthless until it has been presented to others who can use the findings. Social scientists have a professional responsibility to share with the scientific community (and the community at large) the information they uncover, even though it may be impossible for researchers to predict in advance what impact (if any) their research will have on society. To a large measure, how the research is used is a different ethical concern from whether it is used at all. How research is implemented is discussed in Chapter 2. This section concerns the dissemination of information obtained in research.

Disseminating the Research: Professional Meetings and Publications

There are at least two major outlets for social scientific research: professional association meetings and professional journals. Although the social science disciplines have less formal situations for verbally sharing research (for example, staff meetings, colloquia, training sessions, and so forth), these gatherings are often very small and for limited audiences, perhaps as few as four or five people. Professional meetings, however, have the potential of reaching far greater numbers of persons from many different facets of the same discipline (Byrne, 2001).

It is common, for example, for the American Sociological Association to have 2,000 or more people attend a conference. The American Society of Criminology has, at each of the past several years' meetings, recorded more than 1,000 people in attendance. Although nursing conferences are not quite as well attended, several hundred people do attend the annual gatherings of the American Association of Nursing. Professional meetings provide opportunities for researchers to present their own work, as well as to hear about the work of colleagues working in similar areas. Particularly for inexperienced researchers, such meetings can be very edifying—not only with regard to the content of the papers but also for building confidence and a sense of competence. Graduate students attending professional meetings and listening to established scholars present papers can often be heard to mumble, "I could have written that." Most professional association meetings now regularly include student sessions designed to allow student researchers to present their work in a less frightening and less intimidating forum than the main sessions but to present their work nevertheless.

The saying that academics need to publish or perish is still true today—only more so! The academic standards, for example, in nursing have risen to a level such that it is no longer sufficient for a person who wants to teach to hold a graduate degree in nursing. More and more nursing programs are requiring of potential teachers doctorates in nursing—and *publications.* Publishing articles both strengthens the social science disciplines and improves the chances of being hired in a vastly competitive academic market.

Getting published, however, is partly a political matter, partly a matter of skill and scholarship, and partly a matter of timing and luck. It is not, as some quantitative purists might have you think, a matter of having large aggregate data sets and sophisticated multivariate analysis (Cullen, 1989). Often, such orientations move so far from reality that the findings offer little of practical value and, even in statistical terms, have little practical validity.

Good research is simply that! It does not matter in terms of publishability whether the approach is quantitative or qualitative (Berg, 1989). However, new researchers should be aware that a kind of bias does exist in the world of publishing. This bias tends to favor quantitative research for publication. Thus, in some journals, you may find no qualitative empirical research published at all. Yet this does not automatically mean that all the studies the journal publishes are especially good. Neither the word *quantitative* nor the word *published* immediately translates into the term *high quality.*

The process of getting published is further complicated by the *blind referee system* that better journals rely on. This system involves having a manuscript reviewed by two to four scholars who have expertise in the subject of the paper and who do not know the author's identity. Based on their recommendations, the journal will either publish or reject the manuscript.

Pragmatically, this process can be very disheartening to inexperienced researchers, who probably have invested considerable effort in their research. It is important not to take personally a rejection of a manuscript by a journal. There are countless war stories about attempts to have some piece of research published. Many excellent scholars have experienced split decisions when two reviewers have disagreed, one indicating that the manuscript is the finest piece of work since Weber's *Economy and Society* and the other describing the manuscript as garbage.

Particularly when attempting to have qualitative research published, researchers can anticipate certain problems. It is fairly common, for example, to receive a letter of rejection for an ethnographic account or life history case study, and be told, in the letter, that the manuscript was not accepted because it failed to provide *quantified* results. In some cases this may have resulted because the journal sent your manuscript to a reviewer who does not understand qualitative research. In other cases, however, this may occur because the reviewer honestly felt your manuscript was not ready for publication. It is important not to always assume that the former explanation applies.

Inexperienced researchers should not become too discouraged about publishing their research. It is quite like any other game: To win, you need to know the rules, including the recognition that reviewers often have a variety of hidden reasons for rejecting a manuscript. For example, the reviewer may also be attempting to publish an article on the same subject and simply wants to kill off some of the competition. Of course, some pieces of research should not be published. As the old saying goes, "If seven people tell you you're drunk, perhaps you should lie down!" Yet you should not give up too quickly on a piece of research. Becoming familiar with the publication process from start to finish helps researchers gain perspective.

When a research project has been completed, the next step is to do some research in the library. Although experienced researchers often write their reports with a particular journal in mind, inexperienced researchers frequently do not. All journals in a given discipline are not directed toward the same audience. In fact, several social science journals are explicitly for quantitative research, whereas others are devoted to qualitative studies.

A perusal of the periodical stacks will sometimes reveal to inexperienced researchers several possible publication outlets. Researchers should carefully note which journals appear to publish which types of studies. Often, a declaration of a journal's purpose is included on the inside of the front cover or on the first few pages. Next, researchers should identify what particular writing style and format the journal requires. This information is typically listed under the headings, "Notice to Contributors" and "Submission and Preparation of Manuscripts." Writing up a manuscript in the correct form the first time around often saves considerable time and lamentation later.

Once the manuscript has been written, it is time to make a final assessment. Perhaps the hardest decision to make honestly is how good the manuscript really is. This critical concern is necessary for several reasons. First, it is always wise to send a manuscript to the best journal in which the researchers realistically believe they can be published. Underestimating may result in publication in a less prestigious journal than might have been afforded in a better journal. On the other hand, sending a manuscript of lesser weight to a high-powered journal simply increases the time it may take to get the article in print; there will be enough time lags as it is without such misjudgments. Although many journals indicate that manuscript review time varies from five to twelve weeks, researchers often wait eight or ten months merely to hear that their manuscript has been rejected.

A second reason for carefully choosing a journal to which to send your manuscript is the academic restriction against multiple submissions. Because it is considered unethical to submit article manuscripts to more than one journal at a time, these time lags can be a considerable problem. Choosing the wrong journal may literally mean missing an opportunity to have a timely subject published.

Although inexperienced researchers are often hesitant to call a journal to check on the status of a manuscript, they should not be. After patiently waiting a reasonable time (perhaps 12 to 15 weeks), it is not only acceptable but recommended to telephone the journal to check on the status of your manuscript. Journals are busy enterprises and like any other enterprise can make mistakes. Sometimes when researchers call they are informed that some error has been made and the manuscript has not been sent out for review. On other occasions, editors explain that they have been chasing after reviewers to make a decision. In yet other situations, editors may simply have no news about the manuscript. It is not likely, although inexperienced researchers may fear this, that a journal will suddenly reject a paper simply because the author called. In short, authors have nothing to lose and everything to gain by calling.

As the library research may indicate, and as Zurcher (1983, p. 204) explicitly states, "Some journals are more likely than others to publish papers reporting qualitative studies." Some of the journals that have traditionally published qualitative research and have continued to do so during recent years include *Journal of Contemporary Ethnography* (previously *Urban Life*), *Symbolic Interaction, Qualitative Sociology, Human Organization, Human Relations, Journal of Creative Inquiry, Journal of Social and Behavioral Sciences, Heart and Lung, Western Journal of Nursing, American Educational Research Journal, Journal of Popular Culture, Sociological Perspectives, Journal of Applied Behavioral Science, Signs, International Review of Sport Sociology, Journal of Voluntary Action, American Behavioral Scientist, Journal of Police Science and Administration, American Journal of Police, International Journal of Offender Therapy and Comparative Criminology, Journal of Marriage and the Family, Teaching Sociology, Criminal Justice Policy and Review, Nursing Research, Holistic Nursing Practice, Sociological Quarterly, Sociological Spectrum,* and to a slightly lesser extent during recent years, *Social Problems and Social Forces.*

There are a number of viable online electronic journals as well. While there are numerous sites on the Internet, I'll offer just a few here to get the inexperienced writer started: *The Qualitative Report* (www.nova.edu/ssss/QR/QR3–4/index.html), *Sociological Research Online* (www.socresonline.org.uk/socresonline/), *Educational Insights* (www.csci.educ.ubc.ca/publication/insights/online/), Nursing Standard Online (www.nursing-standard.co.uk/specialist/specialist.htm). As even these short and incomplete listings suggest, there are numerous outlets for publishing qualitative research.

A Word About the Content of Papers and Articles

Although it may go without saying that researchers must include in their reports accurate, truthful, and documented information, it may not be as obvious that it should be interesting as well. As Leedy (1985, p. 246) states, "There is no reason why a report should be dull—any more than there is a reason why a textbook should be dull. Both of them deal with the excitement of human thinking prompted by the fascination of facts in the world around us." I cannot count the number of times I have attended a professional conference and listened to a boring presentation. I can only assume that the pained expressions on the faces of others in the audience reflected opinions similar to my own.

When you listen to a quantitative, statistical, and perhaps convoluted report or wade through an article full of regression equations and path diagrams, you may reasonably expect a certain amount of dullness. But when you hear or read dull qualitative research reports, there is no reasonable excuse. Qualitative research reflects the real world. In its purest form, it reveals elements previously unknown or unnoticed by others. It can be as creative a contribution to human knowledge as the *Mona Lisa* is a contribution to art. There are no dull facts about social life, only dull ways of presenting them!

Write It, Rewrite It, Then Write It Again!

Experienced researchers realize that writing a research report is a multiple-level process. During those carefree high school days, many students could stay up late the night before a paper was due, writing the whole paper, and still receive a good grade. Unfortunately, in the so-called real world (which incidentally should include college) the submission of such a first draft is not likely to get the same results.

Becker (1986) has asserted that one possible explanation for "one-draft writing" is that teachers do not tell the students how the textbooks they read actually are written. Most students never have an opportunity actually to see either their teachers or professional writers or researchers at work and, thus, do not realize that more than one draft is necessary.

Most textbooks on writing have chapters on revising and recomposing (Walker, 1987), but students often think these chapters recommend merely editing for typographical and spelling errors. The notion of rewriting substantive portions of the report or adding interesting information learned after the first draft is complete may never occur to inexperienced researchers/writers.

Many inexperienced researchers/writers are simply unaware that virtually all effective writing goes through a series of revisions. Most research goes through many stages of development, versions of presentation, and editions before it ever reaches its intended audience.

For example, I was once asked to write a brief essay on politically correct behavior in criminology (Berg, 1991). After completing several drafts, I asked a few of my male colleagues to read it. They thought it was great. They told me it was hard hitting and shot from the hip. Next, I asked several female colleagues to read the essay. Both of these women describe themselves as *feminist criminologists*. They saw my essay through very different eyes than my male colleagues.

The first thing they asked me was what audience I wanted to reach. They explained that if my purpose was to reach a general audience, the essay as it was then written failed. Yes, it was hard hitting, but it was also too angry. If, on the other hand, I had a target audience of males upset with the way politically correct behavior was emerging in criminology, I was told, the piece might work. Four drafts later, my feminist colleagues agreed that the essay was ready for a general audience—although they both made it clear that they disagreed with my equalitarian position.

The important lesson here is not merely to have others read your drafts. It is important to *hear* what they have to say and to use this advice to improve the eventual final draft.

Certainly, there is no single all-purpose way to compose a research report. In fact, in the social sciences, researchers may want to write for several distinct audiences. In such cases, it may be necessary to write both multiple drafts and multiple drafts of different versions. For example, researchers may write at one level when the audience is their academic colleagues, for example, attending a conference. But this academic level of writing may be unacceptable if the audience is more diverse, as in the case of a report to a governmental funding agency that would be reviewed by professionals from several different backgrounds.

Agar (1986, p. 15) similarly suggests that ethnographies may be written up differently for different audiences, "In my own work the presentation of the same chunk of ethnographic material takes different forms depending on whether I write for clinicians, drug policymakers, survey sociologists, or cognitive anthropologists." When researchers write for their own disciplines, they write for a limited audience that is thoroughly familiar with the particular field of study and shares similar educational backgrounds. In contrast, when the audience consists of different kinds of readers, special limitations must be set on the form the written report should take.

Beyond the realities of different audiences requiring different types or levels of language, there is no single right way to say something. Often one way of saying something may be correct but uninteresting. Another way may be interesting but inexact. After three, or four, or more attempts, the authors may finally find an acceptable way to express themselves, but even that is not necessarily the only good way to phrase their ideas.

A fairly common problem all writers have occasionally is trouble getting started (Becker, 1986). Often, after having written a rather weak beginning, researchers suddenly find the words begin to flow with ease. When the writers reread the weak opening section, they will likely notice that they must rewrite, but if they do not bother to reread and rewrite the opening material, readers will probably not read beyond the poor beginning and get to those wonderful later sections.

Similarly, distance from their own writing frequently allows authors to see their presentations from a different perspective. Many researchers have experienced the phenomenon of reading a research paper they wrote several days earlier and then wondering, How on earth could I have written such drivel? On other occasions, many authors have reread something written a few days earlier and thought, I can hardly believe I actually said that—it's great! These self-reflective examinations of your own writing require some time between the actual penning of the words and the revisions. Usually several days is sufficient, although the actual time required may vary for different pieces of work.

Because of the advances in computer technology and software, it is now easy to rewrite, correct, and edit papers. Many word-processing programs now offer extensive spelling and thesaurus programs, further aiding researchers/writers in their quest to find and use just the right word. The advantages to using computers in both research itself and report writing simply cannot be overstated.

A Final Note

Throughout this book, qualitative techniques and analytic strategies, rather than quantitative ones, have been the focus. Although questionnaires and quantification procedures are probably the most extensively used techniques in the social sciences, they have tended to become inhuman and reductionistic. This criticism is not so much against the procedures, which certainly could enhance understanding in the social sciences, as it is against their indiscriminate application. As Coser (1975, p. 691) warned more than 30 years ago, "The fallacy of misplaced precision consists in believing that one can compensate for theoretical weakness by methodological strength." Application of sophisticated statistical procedures frequently seems akin to hunting rabbits with a cannon.

As suggested throughout this book, no single measurement class—quantitative or qualitative—is perfect. But neither is any data-collection procedure scientifically useless (Webb et al., 1981, 2004). Some may have been amused by Jelenko's (1980) description of the Wayne State rock (see Chapter 8), and others may have caught themselves smiling at the thought of Sawyer (1961, cited by Webb et al., 1981) sifting through the garbage of Wellesley, Massachusetts (see Chapter 8). Yet each of these studies suggests ways of accessing relevant and useful information. As a group, many of the nonreactive techniques described in this text are not as adequate in themselves as a well-constructed interview or ethnographic field study, but each strategy can be improved significantly through triangulation of methods.

The flexibility of the qualitative research approach permits exactly this combined use of innovative data-collection and data-analysis strategies. Conversely, many of the highly sophisticated quantitative data-manipulation strategies can become stilted because they require information in a limited specialized form and format. For better or worse, however, quantitative techniques are more quickly accomplished than qualitative ones, produce what is presumed by many social scientists to be more reliable conclusions, and offer what many public agencies consider truly reportable findings (percentages of variable occurrences).

That quantitative procedures remain predominant in the social sciences is not in itself a problem or a question. What must be questioned, however, is the preoccupation of so many quantitative social scientists with methods, often at the expense of both theory and substance. Qualitative strategies, on the other hand, are intricately intertwined with both the substance of the issues they explore and theories grounded in these substantive issues. If social science is to sort the noodles from the soup, it must do so in a substantively meaningful manner.

NOTES

1. The abstract shown is reprinted from *Social Problems 31*(2), December 1983, p. 195.
2. This last statement is my own creation and does not appear in the original abstract. It is included, of course, in order to demonstrate the use of an implications statement.

REFERENCES

Adler, P. A., & Adler, P. (1983). Shifts and oscillations in deviant careers: The case of upper level drug dealers and smugglers. *Social Problems 31*(2), 195–207.

Agar, M. H. (1986). *Speaking of Ethnography.* Beverly Hills, CA: Sage.

Becker, H. S. (1986). *Writing for Social Scientists.* Chicago: University of Chicago Press.

Berg, B. L. (1983). *Jewish identity: Subjective declarations or objective life styles.* Doctoral dissertation, Syracuse University.

Berg, B. L. (1987). The privatization of medical systems in correctional settings: The case of Florida. *International Journal of Offender Therapy and Comparative Criminology 31*(1), 21–30.

Berg, B. L. (1989). A response to Frank Cullen's "Having trouble getting published?" essay. *The Criminologist 14*(6), 7–9.

Berg, B. L. (1991). The progress of PC behavior in criminology. *International Journal of 35*(2), iii–vi.

Berg, B. L., & Berg, J. P. (1988). AIDS in prison: The social construction of a reality. *International Journal of Offender Therapy and Comparative Criminology 32*(1), 17–28.

Bing, R. L., III. (1987). *Plea bargaining: An analysis of the empirical evidence.* Doctoral dissertation, Florida State University, Tallahassee.

Burns, T. F. (1980). Getting rowdy with the boys. *Journal of Drug Issues 80*(1), 273–286.

Byrne, M. (2001). Disseminating and presenting qualitative research findings. *AORN Journal 74*(5), 731–733.

Cabral, S. L. (1980). Time-out: The recreational use of drugs by Portuguese-American immigrants in southeastern New England. *Journal of Drug Issues 80*(1), 287–300.

Coser, L. (1975). Presidential address: Two methods in search of a substance. *American Sociological Review 40*(6), 691–700.

Creswell, J. W. (2002). *Educational Research: Planning, Conducting, and Evaluating Quantitative and Qualitative Research.* Upper Saddle River, NJ: Prentice Hall.

Cullen, F. (1989). Having trouble getting published? *The Criminologist 14*(4), 1–4.

Dabney, D. A. (1993). *Impaired nursing: Nurses' attitudes and perceptions about drug use and drug theft.* Master's thesis, Indiana University of Pennsylvania, Indiana, PA.

DeVault, M. (1995). Ethnicity and expertise: Racial-ethnic knowledge in sociological research. *Gender and Society 9*, 612–631.

Edwards, R. (1990). Connecting method and epistemology: A white woman interviewing black women. *Women's Studies International Forum 13*, 477–490.

Glassner, B., & Berg, B. L. (1980). How Jews avoid alcohol problems. *American Sociological Review 45*(1), 647–664.

Hertz, R. (1996). Introduction: Ethics, reflexivity and voice. *Qualitative Sociology 19*, 3–9.

Humphreys, L. (1975). *Tearoom Trade: Impersonal Sex in Public Places* (Enl. ed.). Chicago: Aldine.

Ipema, O. K. (1979). Rape: The process of recovery. *Nursing Research 28*, 272–275.

Jacobsen, M. (1979). Qualitative data as a potential source of theory in nursing. *Image 4*, 10–14.

Jelenko, C., III. (1980). The rock syndrome: A newly discovered environmental hazard. *Journal of Irreproducible Results 26*, 14.

Johnson, B. D., Goldstein, P. J., Preble, E., Schmeidler, J., Lipton, D. S., Spunt, B., & Miller, T. (1985). *Taking Care of Business.* Lexington, MA: Lexington Books.

Leedy, P. D. (1985). *Practical Research.* NY: Macmillan.

Leedy, P. D. (2001). *Practical Research: Planning and Design* (7th ed.). Upper Saddle River, NJ: Prentice Hall.

Leedy, P., & Ormrod, J. E. (2005). *Practical Research: Planning and Design* (8th ed.). Upper Saddle River, NJ: Prentice Hall.

Leininger, M. M. (1982). Caring: A central focus for nursing and health care services. *Nursing and Health Care 1*(3), 135–143.

Manning, P., & Cullum-Swan, B. (1994). Narrative, content, and semiotic analysis. In N. K. Denzin & Y. S. Lincoln (Eds.), *Handbook of Qualitative Research*. Thousand Oaks, CA: Sage.

Maxfield, M. G., & Babbie, E. (2006). *Basics of Research Methods for Criminal Justice and Criminology*. Belmont, CA: Thompson/Wadsworth.

Merriam, S. B. (2001). *Qualitative Research and Case Study Applications in Education*. San Francisco: Jossey-Bass.

Meyer, M. (1991). *The Little, Brown Guide to Writing Research Papers*. New York: HarperCollins.

Michalowski, R. (1996). Ethnography and anxiety: Fieldwork and reflexivity in the vortex of U.S.–Cuban relations. *Qualitative Sociology 19*(1), 59–82.

Nachmias, C. F., and Nachmias, D. (2000). *Research Methods in the Social Sciences* (6th ed.). NY: Worth.

Peterson, B. H. (1985). A qualitative clinical account and analysis of a care situation. In M. Leininger (Ed.), *Qualitative Research Methods in Nursing*. Orlando, FL: Grune & Stratton.

Potter, J., & Wetherell, M. (1992). *Discourse and Social Psychology*. Thousand Oaks, CA: Sage.

Skibinski, G. J., & Koszuth, A. M. (1986). Getting tough with juvenile offenders: Ignoring the best interests of the child. *Juvenile and Family Court Journal 37*(5), 45–50.

Tontodonato, P., & Hagan, F. (1998). *The Language of Research in Criminal Justice: A Reader*. Boston: Allyn and Bacon.

Walker, M. (1987). *Writing Research Papers* (2nd ed.). New York: Norton.

Webb, E. J., Campbell, D. T., Schwartz, R. D., & Sechrest, L. (2004). *Unobtrusive Measures* (rev. ed.). Thousand Oaks, CA: Sage.

Webb, E. J., Campbell, D. T., Schwartz, R. D., Sechrest, L., & Grove, J. B. (1981). *Nonreactive Measures in the Social Sciences*. Boston: Houghton Mifflin.

Williams, C., & Heikes, E. (1993). The importance of researcher's gender in the in-depth interview: Evidence from two studies of male nurses. *Gender and Society 7*, 280–291.

Zurcher, L. A. (1983). *Social Roles*. Beverly Hills, CA: Sage.

Name Index

Subject Index